By gracious permission of
Her Majesty Queen Elizabeth,
the Queen Mother, Colonel-in-Chief

This portrait by Commander Denis Fildes, R.N., has been reproduced by kind permission of the Chairman and Members of the United Service Club.

HISTORY OF
THE MANCHESTER REGIMENT
1922–1948

FOREWORD

This foreword would not be complete without an expression of deep gratitude to our Colonel-in-Chief, Queen Elizabeth, The Queen Mother, for her gracious permission to include a reproduction of that beautiful painting of Her Majesty by Commander Denis Fildes which hangs in the main hall of the United Service Club. To the Chairman and Committee of that Club we offer our sincere thanks.

E. B. Costin

Major-General,
Colonel, The Manchester Regiment.

St. Mawes, Cornwall
May 7, 1953

CONTENTS

	Page
ILLUSTRATIONS	xi
MAPS	xv
AUTHOR'S PREFACE	xvii

Chapter

I.	FIRST BATTALION: 1922–1939	1
II.	THE FIRST BATTALION AND THE SINGAPORE CAMPAIGN	37
III.	THE FIRST BATTALION IN CAPTIVITY	79
IV.	FIRST BATTALION: JUNE 1942–JANUARY 1945	104
V.	THE ADVANCE INTO GERMANY: JANUARY–MAY 1945	211
VI.	SECOND BATTALION: MARCH 1924–SEPTEMBER 1939	255
VII.	THE SECOND BATTALION AND THE DUNKERQUE CAMPAIGN	304
VIII.	SECOND BATTALION: 1940–1944: KOHIMA AND IMPHAL	371
IX.	SECOND BATTALION IN THE BATTLE FOR MANDALAY	417
X.	D COMPANY, SECOND BATTALION: 1942–1945	464
XI.	*Part 1*: THE FIRST AND SECOND BATTALIONS FROM 1945 UNTIL AMALGAMATION IN 1948	497
	Part 2: REGIMENTAL AFFAIRS, 1922–1948	506

Appendix

I.	NUMBERS OF OFFICERS AND OTHER RANKS WHO WERE KILLED OR DIED DURING WORLD WAR II	526
II.	HONOURS AND AWARDS, WORLD WAR II	528
III.	SUCCESSION OF COLONELS SINCE 1922	533

CONTENTS

Appendix		Page
IV.	Succession of Commanding Officers since 1922	534
V.	The Colours	536
VI.	Regimental Marches	542
VII.	The Jesh Incident, March 1938	546
Index		551

ILLUSTRATIONS

QUEEN ELIZABETH THE QUEEN MOTHER, COLONEL-IN-CHIEF, THE MANCHESTER REGIMENT *Frontispiece*

Facing page

PATROL OF THE FIRST BATTALION NEAR IKRUIT ON THE SYRIAN FRONTIER	28
3-INCH MORTAR TEAM ON DONKEY PACK, PALESTINE, 1938	28
FIRST BATTALION, SINGAPORE, FEBRUARY 1940	44
THE FIRST BATTALION CARRYING OUT A DEFENCE EXERCISE, SINGAPORE ISLAND, OCTOBER 1941	48
LIEUTENANT-COLONEL E. B. HOLMES, M.C., DEMONSTRATING A NEW WEAPON TO A U.S. OBSERVER, SINGAPORE, OCTOBER 1941	48
SINGAPORE, OCTOBER 1941: THE FIRST BATTALION BUILDING AN ANTI-BOAT OBSTACLE, AND AT WORK ON BEACH DEFENCES	56
FIRST BATTALION OFFICERS, SHARSTED COURT, JUNE 1944	108
D COMPANY'S MORTARS IN ACTION AT S'HERTOGENBOSCH, OCTOBER 1944	180
POSITION COVERING VENLO ROAD, NOVEMBER 1944	192
GENERAL EISENHOWER WATCHING A DEMONSTRATION BY THE FIRST BATTALION IN HEYTHUIZEN CONVENT GROUNDS, NOVEMBER 1944	196
FIELD-MARSHAL MONTGOMERY DECORATING SERGEANT J. S. SULLIVAN OF FIRST BATTALION WITH THE M.M., DECEMBER 1944	200
B COMPANY GIVING COVERING FIRE FOR AN ATTACK NEAR GRIMBLEMONT DURING THE GERMAN ARDENNES COUNTER-ATTACK, JANUARY 1945	212
LIEUTENANT-COLONEL CROZIER IN HIS SCOUT CAR NEAR GOCH, FEBRUARY 1945	228
MACHINE-GUN CARRIERS OF 'A' COMPANY MOVING INTO ACTION FOR THE ATTACK ON WEEZE, MARCH 1945	228

ILLUSTRATIONS

Facing page

First Manchesters firing on the crossroads east of Rethem, April 13, 1945	244
Hmattaing post established by 12 platoon of C Company, Second Manchesters, November 1931	276
Regimental badge constructed by 'A' Company, at Gebeit, Red Sea hills, 1933	284
H.M. King George V, Colonel-in-Chief of The Manchester Regiment about to inspect the Guard of Honour under the command of Captain C. H. Keitley, m.b.e., Manchester, July 1934	292
The Officers, Second Battalion The Manchester Regiment on mobilization, Aldershot, September 7, 1939	300
The River Dendre, site of an action by D Company, May 1940	332
Kohima, showing Garrison Hill in the centre, Jail Hill in the right distance, and Treasury Hill in the left distance	396
An Air photograph of Kohima, showing the Aradura Spur in the background	396
Kohima. Trenches on D.I.S. ridge	412
An Air photograph of the road to Imphal soon after leaving Kohima	412
Men of B Company on the bank of the River Mu at Kabo Weir during the attack on Ye-U, January 1945	428
B Company on the march near Mount Popa, April 1945	428
One of D Company's guns in action during the attack on Ingyigon, August 26, 1944	476
Cpl. Mountain of D Company pointing out his defensive position to Maj.-General Festing, the Divisional Commander, near Hopin	492
H.M. King George V, Colonel-in-Chief of The Manchester Regiment, addressing the representative detachment of the Regiment in the grounds of Buckingham Palace, May 16, 1930	508
The Regimental Chapel, Manchester Cathedral, 1937	512

ILLUSTRATIONS

Facing page

COLONEL FRANCIS H. DORLING, D.S.O., COLONEL OF THE REGIMENT 1934–47   516

HER MAJESTY THE QUEEN, COLONEL-IN-CHIEF OF THE REGIMENT, ABOUT TO INSPECT THE PARADE, ALTRINCHAM, JUNE 1, 1948   520

HER MAJESTY TAKING THE SALUTE AT THE MARCH PAST, JUNE 1, 1948   524

HER MAJESTY INSPECTING THE OLD COMRADES   524

The illustrations facing pages 48, 56, 180, 192, 196, 200, 212, 244, 396, 412, 428, 476 and 492 are reproduced by courtesy of the Imperial War Museum.

MAPS

Number		Page
1.	Singapore island	40
2.	Singapore island: the British deployment	57
3.	Changi gaol	80
4.	The battle theatre in Normandy	122
5.	Cherbourg to the Seine	142
6.	Antwerp to Cologne	168
7.	From the Schelde junction canal to the Wilhelmina canal	172
8.	The approaches to s'Hertogenbosch	182
9.	The Maas from Maaseyck to Venlo	188
10.	From Antwerp to the Rhine	196
11.	The Ardennes	200
12.	The Reichswald Forest	215
13.	The Rhine from Wesel to Emmerich	232
14.	From Wesel to Bremen	238
15.	The crossings of the Aller	242
16.	Northern France and Belgium from Calais to Liége	314
17.	The battlefield on the Dyle	318
18.	The stand on the Dendre	334
19.	The stand on the Schelde	339
20.	The battlefield on the La Bassée canal	354
21.	The Kohima battlefield	395
22.	The north Burma theatre	419
23.	The Mandalay battle theatre	438
24.	The railway corridor	472
25.	The eastern approaches to the Irrawaddy	483

PREFACE

regiment were allotted, with all possible particularity; for whatever was achieved and endured by those brigades was achieved and endured by the machine-gun companies that served with them.

I hope that this review of the sources from which this history has been compiled will have made it clear how much the regiment owes to its own officers. My own personal debt remains to be discharged, and this is best done by acknowledging that, as far as I can understand, I am indebted to every officer in the regiment. For, from the day when Major H. R. C. Green, Colonel P. W. Buchan, Captain E. E. Henderson, and Major R. F. G. Burrows first extended the hand of friendship to me at Altrincham, no appeal for help has ever been unanswered, and those appeals have been sent out in every direction and to every quarter. It is simpler, therefore, to thank the officers of the regiment collectively than to close this preface with a list of names which would be identical with the official roll call. To this, however, I must add, that as the officers of the regiment seem to think that helpfulness and collaboration are just ordinary qualities, which call for no remark, it is highly incumbent upon anybody who benefits to make a proper acknowledgement.

A. C. BELL

Wrawby House
  Wivenhoe, Essex

CHAPTER I

1st BATTALION: 1922–1939

by MAJOR PEILE THOMPSON, M.B.E.

ON February 5, 1922, the 1st Battalion disembarked in Guernsey and on the same day A and B Companies under Lieutenant-Colonel W. K. Evans, C.M.G., D.S.O., sailed in s.s. *Courier* for Alderney and reached Fort Albert safely. Thus the battalion was divided between Guernsey and Alderney as follows:

Fort George, Guernsey...Battalion H.Q., C, and D Companies.
Fort Albert, Alderney...A and B Companies and the Vickers machine-gun platoon.

On February 9 the Guernsey detachment was inspected by Major-General Sir John Capper, K.B.E., K.C.V.O., Lieutenant-Governor and Commanding Troops Guernsey and Alderney District. On the same day the following letters were received congratulating the battalion on their service in Ireland.

G.O.C.
6th Division.
During my recent tour through the greater part of your divisional area, I was struck with the way both officers and men are cheerfully making the best of conditions which in many cases are far from comfortable and hardly to be expected except under active service conditions.

I fully appreciate the efforts made by the officers and non-commissioned officers for the comfort and well-being of their men, and their example to encourage by means of sport, which is so great a factor in the maintenance of health and discipline.

The physical condition, cleanliness and alertness of the rank and file were entirely satisfactory, as were also, generally speaking, the state of the barrack rooms and hutments, often under adverse conditions.

THE MANCHESTER REGIMENT

The condition of the horses was generally good and all credit is due to the exertions of the units to improve, in many cases, the only available and primitive accommodation.

I noticed a very great advance in the condition of the motor transport, which is undoubtedly due to the efforts that have been made to make the best of the last few months in order to have every available vehicle ready for more active work should it occur in the future.

The hospital and medical care of the troops was everything that could be desired, the proof of which is seen by the exemplary health record throughout the division.

It is a great satisfaction to me to be able to report that the old traditions of the Army are fully maintained in your division and the troops ready for any call that may be made upon them.

(*Signed*) C. F. N. MACREADY, General.
Commander-in-Chief, Forces.

November 18, 1921.

C.R. 6th Division.
No. 6581/A.

Hd. Qrs. 17th Inf. Bde.

It gives me great pleasure to convey to you for your information and transmission to all ranks in your brigade area the above remarks from the Commander-in-Chief, as a result of his recent tour through the 6th Divisional Area. In forwarding these remarks I wish to add my deep appreciation of the loyal support given to me by all ranks throughout the division and for the excellent work and the cheerful spirit in which the same has been carried out by all ranks, and which I feel certain will continue, and thus uphold the good name of the Army in Ireland.

(*Signed*) E. P. STRICKLAND, Lt.-General.
Cmdg. 6th Division.

Cork.
November 21, 1921.

No. 642/13.
November 25, 1921.

O.C. 1st Bn. Manchester Regiment.

Please convey to all ranks under your command the attached remarks of the Commander-in-Chief and the Divisional Commander.

I wish to take this opportunity of congratulating the units under my command on having earned the approbation of their Commanders, and of thanking all ranks for their good work they have done in maintaining this efficiency and high tradition of the Army.

     (*Signed*) H. W. HIGGINSON, Colonel Commandant.
Cork.   Cmdg. 17th Infantry Brigade.

            Headquarters,
            6th Division, Cork.
            December 20, 1921.

To: Lieut.-Colonel F. H. Dorling, D.S.O.,
  Cmdg. 1st Bn. The Manchester Regiment.

I send my hearty greetings to all ranks of the battalion on the seventh anniversary of a day that must stand out in their records as a very glorious one for them.

By their marked gallantry and dash they took Givenchy, which had been captured seven hours previously by the enemy, and by their determination and endurance held it in the face of great odds. But for the battalion on those two days, the line to the north and south must have been dominated by the enemy, and Bethune would have been at the mercy of the enemy's artillery.

At one time Givenchy remained the one point in that part of the British line that was held, and the full force of the enemy's attack fell on us.

I shall always look back with the greatest pride in the fact that I had the privilege and honour to command the battalion on that occasion.

     (*Signed*) E. P. STRICKLAND, Lieut.-General.
       Late Commanding 1st Battalion
         The Manchester Regiment.

         Irish Office,
         Old Queen Street, S.W.1.
         February 7, 1922.

My dear Commander-in-Chief,

 The Chief of Police has asked me to forward to you the attached letter expressing on behalf of the Royal Irish Constabulary and other police forces in Ireland, their high appreciation of the help given to them by the Army in Ireland throughout the recent disturbances.

In doing so, I should like to take this opportunity of thanking you for the assistance which you have invariably given to me during my tenure of office as Chief Secretary.

       Yours sincerely,
        (*Signed*) HAMAR GREENWOOD.

General The Right Honourable
   Sir Nevil Macready, G.C.M.G., K.C.B.,
      General Headquarters—Ireland,
         Parkgate, Dublin.

The Chief Secretary,
   Now that the demobilization of the R.I.C. has begun I have the honour to request that you will express to the Commander-in-Chief on behalf of this force their high appreciation of the help given to the police by the Army in Ireland throughout the recent disturbances. Besides the strong support of the armed forces of the Army, without the ready assistance always available all over Ireland in arming, equipping and training this personnel, in putting barracks in a state of defence and in supplying experienced officers for intelligence duties, etc., it would have been impossible for the R.I.C. to have reached its present high standard of efficiency.
   The R.I.C. fully realize the deep debt of gratitude they owe to the Commander-in-Chief, and the Army in Ireland, their comrades, *rebus in arduis*.
                    (*Signed*) H. H. TUDOR, Major-General.
                              Chief of Police, Ireland.
February 4, 1922.
Dublin Castle.

The battalion soon settled down to garrison life, but unfortunately this state of affairs was to be of very short duration, for on June 3 they once more embarked from Southampton en route for Ireland. During this period, however, a number of changes had taken place amongst the officers. Major C. Morley, Captains A. W. Cooper, F. V. Hollingworth, Lieutenants J. F. C. Dyer, F. Howarth, M.C., and 2nd Lieutenant R. Dobson had retired. Lieutenant T. L. G. Tod, R.F.A., who had accompanied the battalion to Guernsey, on account of the shortage of officers, had left to join 12 Brigade R.F.A., and 2nd Lieutenant E. M. Hickey and Lieutenant H. F. Whitmore had joined for duty.

On arrival in Ireland on June 4 the battalion moved to a tented camp at Enniskillen, where on June 8 two companies were ordered to occupy Belleek, which was on the boundary of the Free State and Northern Territory. As Belleek was supposed to be occupied by the Sinn Fein, the approach to it was carried out as an active operation. B and D Companies with one platoon from A and C Companies, with a section of 4.5 howitzers in support, all under command of Major A. E. O'Meara, formed the southern column operating round Lough Erne, whilst a column from the 1st Battalion the Lincolnshire Regiment formed the northern column. The southern column were carried for about sixteen miles in transport and bivouacked for the night near Long Island. At dawn on June 9 this column advanced to move round the south and west of Belleek. Orders had previously been given that no fire was to be opened unless fired upon, and if no fire was opened on the column it was to march back about two miles and cross Lough Erne by boat to the northern side, as the bridge at Belleek over the river was in Free State territory and therefore not to be crossed except if fired on.

However, fire was opened from the Free State territory on the northern column so the 4.5 howitzer section immediately opened fire on Belleek Fort. Republicans could be seen on the fort manning the walls, but the first shell from the howitzers scattered them, and after only slight opposition the fort was captured. The fort and village were occupied for twelve days when the column rejoined the rest of the battalion.

On August 17 the battalion moved to a tented musketry camp at Magilligan, and on September 14 moved once again to Dublin. Whilst in Dublin the following Officers joined the battalion: Lieutenants G. B. Champion, E. A. K. Robinson, and C. J. Walsh, from the Connaught Rangers; and 2nd Lieutenants D. B. Malaher and F. H. McCleary on first appointment. Later in the year Captain C. J. L. Shepperd and Lieutenant C. J. Walsh retired.

During their time in Dublin the battalion carried out their duties under great provocation, the republicans delighting in throwing bombs into the barracks. On December 16 the battalion was relieved of its duty and at 12 noon paraded for the last time at Arbour Hill and marched past the Commander-in-Chief, General Sir C. F. N. Macready, G.C.M.G., K.C.B., en route for the quay.

On December 18 it arrived back in Guernsey and was stationed as follows:

Fort George, Guernsey...Battalion Headquarters.
                                  Headquarter Wing.
                                  A and B Companies.
Fort Albert, Alderney...C and D Companies.
                                  Drums.

The stay of the battalion in Guernsey was most enjoyable. The island was too small for serious training but a good deal of musketry was carried out at Fort Homet.[1] This range was unique in that the firing points had to be carried down the beach and laid on the sand, so that shooting could only take place at low tide. The fort, which was built during the Napoleonic War, provided accommodation for one company.

The battalion rifle team, under the captaincy of Captain G. B. Champion, competed at Bisley and covered itself with glory. In the A.R.A. meeting, C.S.M. Cookson won the Roupell Cup, and the battalion team won the Roberts Cup, and in the N.R.A. meeting Captain G. B. Champion won the Queen Mary's Prize.

During this period a number of new officers joined the battalion: they were Lieutenant C. F. Webb from the Worcestershire Regiment, Captain C. S. Tuely from the Royal Irish Fusiliers, 2nd Lieutenant H. H. Ledward on first appointment, Major N. W. Humphreys, Captain A. W. U. Moore, and Lieutenants S. K. Pembroke, and C. H. Keitley. Major P. O'Brien retired.

The remainder of the battalion's stay in Guernsey and Alderney passed quickly and quietly. Sport of all kind was plentiful and all ranks took an active part in all the island's functions.

[1] When the Germans occupied Guernsey in 1940, the headland and the fort itself were made into a vast concrete bunker with some six to eight guns covering the beaches of Vazon Bay. The fort itself provided accommodation for the gun crews and technicians, until it was attacked by the R.A.F. Only the walls now remain.

SERVICE ON THE RHINE

On August 25 Lieutenant-Colonel F. H. Dorling, D.S.O., handed over command of the battalion to Lieutenant-Colonel and Brevet Colonel W. K. Evans, C.M.G., D.S.O.

Other changes in officers were: 2nd Lieutenant R. H. H. Stewart joined on first appointment, whilst Major C. D. Irwin retired.

On October 28 the battalion was relieved by the 2nd Battalion Duke of Cornwall's Light Infantry, and sailed for England, thence by Dover for the Rhine. They arrived at Gibraltar Barracks, Riehl, Cologne, on October 25, and became part of the 2nd Rhine Army Brigade. After four days settling in, the battalion was inspected by Colonel Commandant H. K. Bethell, C.B., C.M.G., C.V.O., D.S.O., Commanding 2nd Rhine Army Brigade.

2nd Lieutenant C. L. Archdale joined the battalion on first appointment.

On February 3, Lieutenant-Colonel and Brevet Colonel W. K. Evans, C.M.G., D.S.O., retired and was succeeded in command by Lieutenant-Colonel C. C. Stapledon.

The following officers also joined the battalion: Lieutenant G. F. Newsome, 2nd Lieutenants G. E. C. Rossall, W. A. Venour, and P. W. Buchan.

In May the battalion proceeded in groups for company training at Leidenhausen, at the conclusion of which a rifle team was again sent to Bisley. The results were even better than the year before. Captain G. B. Champion won the Army Rifle Championship, receiving the Watkin Cup and the A.R.A. Gold Medal, and also won the Roberts Cup, whilst the battalion team won the Britannia Trophy. Captain Champion and C.S.M. Cookson were selected for the Army team in the Methuen Cup.

In August the battalion took part in the Rhine Army small arms meeting, winning the Vickers Machine-Gun Competition, the Lewis and Hotchkiss Gun Match, Platoon Match, Young Soldiers Competition, Inter-Company Competition, Officers, W.O.s and Sergeants Match, and last, but certainly not least, the Rhine Army Championship Shield.

Later in the month the battalion marched to Nanderath for battalion training, which finished with the divisional manoeuvres in September, when they finally marched back to Cologne. The end of the year saw them once more on the move, this time to Konigstein where on December 4 they relieved a battalion of the French Army. Settling into their new station was quite a problem due to snow, so sleighs and G.S. wagons on runners were used to bring the baggage up from the station.

Konigstein provided a variety of sport and work. In March 1926 the battalion set to to enlarge the French 200-yard two-target range into a 500-yard-classification range, and so successfully was the work accomplished that in the Rhine Army small arms meeting, the battalion won the Young Soldiers Cup, the Officers, W.O.s and Sergeants Cup, the Revolver Cup, and the Rhine Army Championship for the second year running.

In September brigade training was carried out in Worsdorf-Limbach area, and at the end of that month the battalion took part in the divisional manoeuvres.

During this year 2nd Lieutenants H. D. Dook, W. J. Goldsmith, and R. A. Chauncey joined the battalion on first commission.

1927 was another great year of victories in the sporting world. In February the battalion won the Rhine Army Novices Team Boxing and followed this in April by winning the Rhine Army Team Boxing Championship. At Bisley, under Lieutenant D. B. Malaher, the battalion team won the Britannia Trophy, Sergeant A. Jones was third in the Army Rifle Championship, and Bandsman Smethurst won the Young Soldiers Class. Two officers and six other ranks qualified for the Army Hundred and two officers and four other ranks for the King's Medal.

In July the battalion Tug-of-War team won the Rhine Army Tug-of-War Championship. In August at the Rhine Army small arms meeting, Lieutenant C. L. Archdale won the Individual Rifle Championship, Lieutenant D. B.

and divisional training was carried out at Henham Park, Suffolk.

During the year 2nd Lieutenants P. Huth, G. A. Tod, N. B. Close-Brooks and N. C. Robertson Glasgow, joined the battalion on first commission, whilst Major F. S. Modera and Lieutenant R. A. Chauncey retired.

On March 6, 1931, Lieutenant-Colonel B. C. Freyberg, v.c., c.m.g., d.s.o., was promoted to Colonel and assumed the appointment of A.Q.M.G. Southern Command. Lieutenant-Colonel L. C. Bostock, o.b.e., m.c., was appointed to command.

The year passed quietly with various inspections and parades. One week was spent in Kent carrying out battalion training but brigade and divisional training took place in the garrison area. At Bisley Lieutenant C. L. Archdale tied with Lieutenant J. A. Barlow for the Army Championship, but was beaten in the shoot-off; the battalion team were runners-up in the Rhine Army Shield and Britannia Trophy.

A number of officers joined the battalion, Major N. Clowes, d.s.o., m.c., from the Australian Staff Corps, and 2nd Lieutenants B. A. P. Lambert, W. M. Clapham, G. A. Shepperd, W. E. Almond, and W. L. Ekin-Smyth, all on first appointment.

On October 20 the battalion left Shorncliffe for their new station in Gosport.

During 1932 the battalion carried out training with 9th Infantry Brigade on Salisbury Plain. On July 30 the battalion left Gosport to march to their training camp at the Bustard. The weather was bad and the path of the battalion lay across the main roads to the south coast, which were packed with Bank Holiday traffic. The nights were spent in bivouac areas at Botley, Romsey, and Porton. In spite of the difficulties the march was performed without a man falling out.

The same year Lieutenant C. L. Archdale won the Revolver Thirty Cup at Bisley and 2nd Lieutenant B. A. P. Lambert received his Army running colours.

The following officers joined on first appointment: 2nd

SUCCESSES AT BISLEY

Lieutenants W. M. Archdale, G. F. Doran, J. A. Hallmark, G. W. Ham, and R. V. Howell.

The year 1933 was to be the last year that the battalion was stationed in England, for the War Office had ordered that it would proceed to the West Indies early in 1934. In March Lieutenant-Colonel L. C. Bostock, O.B.E., M.C., retired and Lieutenant-Colonel B. G. Atkin, D.S.O., O.B.E., M.C., took over command.

The most outstanding event of this year was the success of the battalion rifle team at Bisley; it is doubtful if the achievements of this team have ever been bettered in the annals of the British Army. When the final results of the A.R.A. meeting were announced, the following successes were gained by the battalion: Army Rifle Championship at home, Watkin Cup, Roberts Cup, and Roupell Cup, all won by Lieutenant C. L. Archdale, who was also runner-up for the Army Hundred Cup; runner-up for the Army Rifle Championship at home and winner of the Army Hundred Cup, Colour-Sergeant A. Jones; Britannia Trophy and Rhine Army Shield both won by the battalion team. In addition, Lieutenant P. W. Buchan, Company Sergeant-Major F. H. R. Hand, Lance-Corporal G. E. Smethurst, and Private J. Clarkson were all within the first fifty for the Army Championship and qualified to shoot for the King's Medal.

Training this year was carried out at Codford Camp near Warminster, during which A Company carried out tests with the new experimental emergency ration. On the return to Gosport at the end of September the time was spent packing up until November 30, when practically the whole battalion proceeded on embarkation leave.

During this year the following officers joined: Captain G. L. Usher from the Worcestershire Regiment, and on first appointment, 2nd Lieutenants P. Thompson, J. B. R. Derham Reid, J. L. Fouracre, L. S. Dawson, E. C. C. Chichelle Plowden, J. P. Cochrane, and R. T. Benson. Lieutenant P. Huth retired from the Army.

On January 13, 1934, the 2nd Battalion arrived home from

Khartoum and, after a considerable interchange of officers and men, on January 23 the 1st Battalion embarked in the trooper *Dorsetshire*. The following officers embarked for service with the battalion in the West Indies: Lieutenant-Colonel B. G. Atkin, D.S.O., O.B.E., M.C.; Majors A. W. U. Moore and M. R. Davidson; Captains H. F. Whitmore, P. J. McKevitt, M.C., F. Brittorous, M.C., C. J. F. Abbott, M.C., J. A. Corley, M.C., M.M., H. S. Hoseason, J. H. Orgill, C. L. Usher, and T. A. Hibbard; Lieutenants C. L. Archdale, P. W. Buchan, W. J. Goldsmith, E. F. Woolsey, W. L. Ekin-Smyth, G. A. Tod, N. B. Close-Brooks; Lieutenant and Quartermaster F. M. Lewis; 2nd Lieutenants W. R. Clapham, B. A. P. Lambert, G. A. Shepperd, W. E. Almond, W. M. Archdale, J. A. Hallmark, G. W. Ham and R. V. Howell. (Lieutenant C. K. Mott was on leave and embarked later.)

The strength of other ranks embarked was: 8 warrant officers, 843 other ranks, and 50 families (69 children).

The only disadvantage of being stationed in the West Indies was that the battalion was to be split up between Bermuda and Jamaica. On February 3 the *Dorsetshire* arrived in Bermuda and the detachment comprising A and C Companies and the band, under command of Major A. W. U. Moore, disembarked and proceeded to Prospect. The following officers disembarked with this detachment: Major A. W. U. Moore (Commanding Detachment); Captains P. J. McKevitt, M.C., F. Brittorous, M.C., G. L. Usher and T. A. Hibbard; Lieutenant E. F. Woolsey; and 2nd Lieutenants B. A. P. Lambert, G. A. Shepperd, J. A. Hallmark, G. W. Ham, and R. V. Howell.

On February 8 the remainder of the battalion disembarked at Kingston, Jamaica, where they marched up to Up Park Camp to relieve the 1st Battalion the Northumberland Fusiliers. On arrival 33 other ranks, under Captain C. J. F. Abbott, M.C., proceeded to the hill station of Newcastle.

In May a letter had been received from the Lord Mayor of Manchester notifying the intention of the citizens of Manchester to present a set of silver drums to each of the regular battalions, and that it was hoped the Deputy Lord Mayor would be able to come out to Jamaica and present these drums. On October 9 Alderman W. Walker, Deputy Lord Mayor of Manchester, handed over the set of eleven silver drums to the battalion at a ceremony at which His Excellency the Officer Administering the Government and naval and civil officers were present. The drums were piled in front of the battalion. The battalion was formed up in line on the garrison cricket ground and received His Excellency with a royal salute. His Excellency then entered the cricket pavilion and was there introduced to Alderman Walker by the O.C. Troops, Brigadier J. A. D. Langhorne.

The battalion formed three sides of a square and the O.C. Troops and Alderman Walker moved forward to a position near the silver drums. Alderman Walker then addressed the battalion. He said that he felt very proud to have been the one selected to make this presentation on behalf of the Lord Mayor and the citizens of Manchester; that the committee who had originated the idea hoped that it would bind still further together the City of Manchester and the regiment which bore its name. He spoke also of the fine record of the regiment both in war and in peace, and said that it was a great thing for the battalion to have set out after the war to become the finest shooting battalion in the British Army. He also conveyed to the battalion the good wishes of the Lord Mayor and the citizens of Manchester.

Lieutenant-Colonel Atkin then replied on behalf of the battalion.

Eleven drummers, under the Drum Major, then moved from the rear of the battalion to a position in line facing the silver drums. Each drummer picked up his drum in turn and fell in in drum formation. The Drum Major then took post in front of them and marched back to the other drummers in rear. O.C. Troops and Alderman Walker returned to the pavilion and the battalion re-formed line.

The drums were then trooped in quick time from the left

flank. After countermarching a second time they took post in rear of the line. His Excellency then departed, the royal salute being given. The Commanding Officer then handed the battalion over to Major M. R. Davidson and joined Alderman Walker in front of the pavilion. The battalion then marched past the Commanding Officer and Alderman Walker. When No. 4 Company had given "Eyes Front" and was clear, the drums advanced towards the pavilion, countermarched, and took post in front of the battalion, which had wheeled round the side of the cricket ground. The battalion then continued its march out of the far gate of the cricket ground and returned to barracks.

On October 24 a guard of honour under command of Captain H. F. Whitmore was mounted at the Market Pier, Kingston, on the occasion of the arrival of the new Captain-General and Governor of Jamaica, Sir Edward Denham. This was the first time the silver drums were paraded since the presentation.

During this year Lieutenant W. J. Goldsmith died as a result of an accident, Captain C. J. F. Abbott, M.C., was invalided home, and Lieutenant W. J. Douglass joined from the depot.

On March 6, 1935, His Royal Highness the Duke of Gloucester arrived at Kingston on his official visit to Jamaica. A guard of honour of 100 other ranks, under command of Major M. R. Davidson, was mounted at Market Pier and a detachment of four officers and 100 other ranks, under command of Captain H. S. Hoseason, lined a portion of the streets. On March 7 His Royal Highness dined in the officers' mess and graciously presented the officers with a signed photograph of himself as a memento of the occasion. On March 16 the same guard of honour and detachment lined the streets on the occasion of His Royal Highness's departure from Jamaica. Four days later D/S Company provided a guard of honour during the short visit of Lord Galway, Governor-General Designate of New Zealand.

On May 6 His Excellency the Governor of Jamaica held

SERVICE IN JAMAICA

a review on the polo ground on the occasion of His Majesty's silver jubilee.

Garrison life in Jamaica was quite pleasant in spite of the heat of Kingston. Sports grounds were plentiful and inter-platoon competitions were instituted as often as possible. A polo ground existed in the barracks, and the officers' mess was able to produce quite a good team. Companies went up to the hill station of Newcastle for six weeks each year. The journey up was an adventure in itself, as the men were carried in local civilian transport to Gordonstown, and thence had a two-hours march up a mule track to get there. The camp was built on the side of a hill with the road from Kingston to Buff Bay running through the centre. The company lines were about 300 feet below the road, whilst the officers' mess was about the same distance above. Although there was little scope for games, apart from seven-a-side hockey on the main road, walks were plentiful and expeditions were made as far afield as the Blue Mountains. A training camp was instituted at the west end of the island, at Montpelier near Montego Bay, which proved very popular.

During the year Captain H. F. Whitmore died of heat exhaustion, Lieutenant G. A. Tod left for the depot, and Captain J. A. Corley, M.C., M.M., retired. Captain C. F. Webb, Lieutenant P. Thompson, and 2nd Lieutenant J. T. H. Gunning joined the battalion from the 2nd Battalion.

On June 5, 1934, at the Bermuda Command 41st annual rifle meeting at Warwick Camp the detachment gained a number of successes and in most events broke the existing record scores of previous years. The detachment also provided the guard of honour for the prorogation of the Bermuda parliament. On the occasion of His Majesty's silver jubilee the detachment took part in a searchlight tattoo, during which A and C Companies enacted Waterloo.

On September 26, 1935, with a hurricane warning flying, the Jamaica detachment was relieved by the 1st Battalion the Sherwood Foresters and marched to Malabres Wharf, His Excellency the Governor of Jamaica taking the salute en route. On arrival at the wharf they embarked on the *Dorsetshire* and sailed early on September 27. The first day at sea was most unpleasant as the troops were battened down due to the rough sea; but the second and third days were calm. The fourth day the hurricane swept round in a circle and the *Dorsetshire* had a bad time, being blown some fifty miles off her course. On October 1 she arrived in Hamilton Harbour, Bermuda, where the Jamaica detachment was disembarked and marched across the island to bathe. The same night the band and drums beat Retreat on the Bermudiana Water Front before His Excellency the Governor-General, Sir T. Astley Cubitt. On October 3, having embarked the Bermuda detachment, the whole battalion sailed for Southampton en route for Egypt.

At about 2 p.m. on October 13 the *Dorsetshire* dropped anchor in Southampton Water. Almost immediately the embarkation staff arrived on board and, due to the political situation in the Middle East, families were ordered to disembark the following morning. At 6 a.m. the following morning the *Dorsetshire* berthed at the New Dock, Southampton. Here two customs sheds had been taken over for a reunion and thanks to the excellent work put in by Major R. F. G. Burrows, commanding the regimental depot, and his staff the reunion was most successful. At about 9 a.m. the first special train from Manchester arrived, bringing friends and relatives to the party; this train, appropriately enough, was drawn by the new L.M.S. engine *The Manchester Regiment*. All troops were disembarked but, due to the short stay, were not allowed out of the docks. Lunch was served to everyone on shore, and a good time was had by all. At 2.30 p.m. the battalion fell in and marched back on board; at the final roll call not one man was missing. At 4 p.m., with the band playing " Auld Lang Syne ", the *Dorsetshire* sailed for Egypt.

The situation in the Middle East at this period was somewhat tense. Earlier in the year Mussolini, making as an excuse some border incident, had ordered the Italian army

THE MIDDLE EAST

to invade Abyssinia. The British and French governments had decided to apply sanctions in order to deprive Italy of certain essential war commodities. In reply the Duce had placed a large and well-equipped army in Cyrenaica, on the border of the western desert of Egypt, and threatened to invade the Nile valley should Britain and France carry out their threat. It was towards this turmoil that the *Dorsetshire* was slowly ploughing her way.

Whilst passing the coast of Spain one of the ship's propellers became fouled and it was decided to put into Gibraltar for inspection and repair. A route march was organized, but on entering the harbour the offending propeller became cleared and the ship was able to proceed on her way.

On October 23 Alexandria was reached and the harbour presented a formidable sight. In this harbour were concentrated practically the whole of the Mediterranean and Atlantic Fleets, whilst aground on the breakwater was the Italian liner *Orsona* on fire. It was said that she had been deliberately set on fire and that attempts had been made to sink her in the only deep-water entrance, in order to bottle up the British Fleet.

The battalion advance party under Captain R. H. H. Stewart, who had joined the unit at Southampton, was disembarked when the *Dorsetshire* sailed for Port Said, where the following morning the battalion disembarked and entrained for Moascar. Due to the situation the battalion found that the unit they were to have relieved was remaining and the only accommodation was a tented camp in the desert. On the first day the Brigade Commander of the Canal Brigade, Brigadier Sir Frederic Pile, Bt., addressed the whole battalion on the political situation. In spite of the rather uncomfortable conditions of the camp the battalion settled down quickly and a good liaison was soon established with the 1st Battalion the Royal Scots Fusiliers and 1st Battalion the Middlesex Regiment. The stay, however, was not for long, as on December 17 the first half of the battalion left for Mersa Matruh, followed the next day by the remainder,

Mersa Matruh was the chief town of the western desert of Egypt and lay on the coast about midway between Alexandria and the Italian border. The only method of getting to it by land was by rail to Fuka and thence by M.T. convoy to the town itself. The role of the battalion was to be the infantry unit with the mobile force which consisted of the 7th, 8th, and 11th Hussars, 6th Battalion the Royal Tank Corps, and later the 2nd Battalion Royal Tank Corps from England. In order to make the battalion mobile 19 (Lifting) Company, R.A.S.C., with 187 vehicles all told, was affiliated to it, and thus unknowingly was sown the seed of the modern Lorried Infantry Brigade with the Armoured Division.

The early part of 1936 was spent in digging slit trenches, sandbagging tents, and platoon and company training with 19 Company R.A.S.C. Several long-range patrols were carried out to give practice in using the improvised sun compass and mapping the desert, whilst others were used to bury petrol at night near the Italian border in case advanced landing grounds were required by the R.A.F.

On January 20 the battalion received the sad news of the death of His Majesty King George V, Colonel-in-Chief of the Regiment. The following cable was sent to Colonel F. H. Dorling, D.S.O., Colonel of the Regiment:

> Please convey Private Secretary deep sorrow felt by all ranks of the First Battalion at the death of their Colonel-in-Chief and expression of deepest sympathy to the Royal Family.
> Commanding Manchesters.

The following cable was received from Sandringham:

> Please convey my heartfelt thanks to all ranks for their message of sympathy in the sad loss of their Colonel-in-Chief.
> MARY.

On January 28 the British Forces in the western desert took part in a memorial service. The first attempt at this service had to be postponed owing to a sandstorm, but later in the day the sand cleared and an open-air service was held under arrangements made by 5 Division.

The undermentioned officers were also on parade: Lieutenant-Colonel N. Clowes, D.S.O., M.C., Major M. R. Davidson (second-in-command), Lieutenant W. E. Almond (A/Adjutant), Captain R. H. H. Stewart (No. 1 Company), Captain W. A. Venour (No. 2 Company), 2nd Lieutenant R. J. Griffiths (No. 3 Company), 2nd Lieutenant R. F. H. Griffiths (No. 4 Company).

The following N.C.O.s were selected for the colour party: Sgt. J. Flynn, Sgt. P. Perks, L/Sgt. V. Shield.

The colours were marched into church at the beginning of the service, and were received by the Commanding Officer, Lieutenant-Colonel N. Clowes, D.S.O., M.C., who handed each in turn to Captain R. Lloyd, the chaplain. The chaplain deposited the colours on the altar, and the service commenced. The Commanding Officer read the lesson, and subsequently unveiled the window, which had a background of green, and on it a gold fleur-de-lys, with beneath the numeral "LXIII".

The text of the sermon consisted of the words of St. Paul, "I am a citizen of no mean city".

At the conclusion of the service the chaplain handed back the colours to the Commanding Officer, who in turn returned them to the colour party. The colour party then left the church and the service concluded.

The Brigade Commander, after the service and on the brigade parade outside, presented Long Service and Good Conduct Medals to 3513665 C.S.M. Jones, A., and 3513067 Sgt. Metcalfe, C.

Earlier in the year the battalion had received notification that they would proceed to Malta during the forthcoming trooping season. Everyone was looking forward to a period of peace and quiet, but on November 12 these orders were cancelled and the new destination given was Palestine.

On November 20 the Port Said detachment returned to Moascar and on November 21 the Cyprus detachment returned. Before leaving Cyprus the entire detachment paraded before His Excellency the Governor and Com-

SERVICE IN PALESTINE

mander-in-Chief, Sir Herbert R. Palmer, K.C.M.G., C.B.E., who said:

> Major Pembroke, officers, non-commissioned officers, and men. I have come to bid you "God speed" on your departure from Cyprus. I would like at the same time to express my appreciation of your exemplary conduct while in Cyprus, of the friendliness you have shown to the people of the country, and the interest you have taken in your surroundings, and local events.
> Your conduct while in Cyprus has enhanced the reputation in Cyprus of the Manchester Regiment, to which you belong, and no detachment of any regiment that has ever been quartered in Cyprus has in greater degree earned the good wishes of us all.
> I wish you all and the Manchester Regiment on behalf of Cyprus all good wishes.

On December 29 the advance party left for Haifa in Palestine.

The change of orders for the battalion to move to Palestine instead of to Malta was due to the deterioration of conditions in Palestine and the necessity for having strong battalions in that country. It cannot be denied that the alteration in plans was the cause of some disappointment, particularly among the married personnel, as all families were ordered to proceed to Malta or England and were not allowed to accompany their husbands to Palestine. At the same time the decision was accepted very philosophically and, it may be said, with a certain air of anticipation and expectancy. Few of those serving with the battalion had experienced active service, and the prospect of soldiering under conditions which at least approximated to active service had its undeniable attractions.

The battalion arrived in Haifa on January 15, 1938, and proceeded at once to the area allotted to it, i.e., the Galilee and Acre administrative district. This area formed a rectangle some forty miles square, being bounded on the north by the Syrian and Lebanese frontiers and on the east by the Transjordan border. It should be noted that at this time and throughout its tour in Palestine, the battalion was acting in aid of the civil power, though later an increasing degree of responsibility was granted to the Commanding Officer. This was to culminate, shortly after the dispatch of the battalion from Palestine, in a system of military control throughout the country.

The police resources in the district were extremely meagre; the large towns such as Tiberias, Nazareth, Acre, and Safad, each had a small force which, as a rule, was fully occupied in endeavouring to preserve law and order in those towns, while the remainder of the police formed the garrisons of the numerous isolated posts located in the area.

The task of the battalion coupled with the size of the area, necessitated a wide dispersion, and at the outset it had Battalion Headquarters, H.Q., B, and D Companies at Tiberias, A Company at Acre, and C Company at Safad, with detachments each of one platoon at Mi'ilya and Saffuriya, found respectively from Acre and Tiberias. Many were the changes carried out in the ensuing nine months, but the foregoing was typical of the dispositions found necessary to compete with the task on hand.

The nature of the task necessitated a high degree of mobility, and in consequence, shortly after arrival, the necessary complement of vehicles was issued to make the battalion about 100 per cent mobile. The vehicles were for the most part 15-cwt. trucks, with a certain number of 30-cwt. lorries, supplemented where necessary with hired Jewish lorries.

Great difficulty was experienced at the outset in finding sufficient drivers to man all vehicles due to the sudden expansion. However, the difficulty was gradually overcome, although the list of accidents in the first two months was rather high.

The situation in Palestine was that most of the mischief was being carried out by a number of rebel gangs, consisting as a rule of a nucleus of so-called regular bandits, the remainder being volunteers or impressed local peasantry. In order to deal with these gangs the battalion, along with other battalions of the 16th Brigade, was ordered to form three mobile columns. Each column consisted of a Company Headquarters and three platoons with the necessary complement of signallers and stretcher-bearers to make it self-supporting. Both M.T. and donkey transport were provided the latter being used in country where M.T. could not operate. These donkeys were the cause of much trial and tribulation, particularly at the commencement, until the men became used to them. They fully proved their worth, however; in fact without them many of the operations carried out could never have taken place. The armament of the column was restricted to what could be carried on the available donkeys, but usually consisted of two Vickers guns, one Lewis gun, and one mortar, plus rifles. The 3-inch mortar was a new weapon to the battalion, but was to prove an invaluable ally on many occasions. In addition each column had with it a rodex lorry, this being a 30-cwt. lorry fitted with a special wireless set for calling direct for air support. With the aid of this set it was always possible to summon air support to assist in dealing with gangs and ambushes and such assistance was forthcoming in an incredibly short space of time, usually some fifteen to twenty minutes.

Air action usually took the form of low-flying bombing and machine-gun attacks, and very effective it proved, both in its material results and in its demoralizing effects. By means of a system of ground signals, co-operation between troops and aircraft was brought to a high state of efficiency.

During the first few months the energies of the battalion were largely directed towards the extermination of gangs operating in the area. The type of operation carried out was normally an encircling movement, the number of columns varying from three to eight, according to the size of the area to be surrounded. Due largely to the difficulty of obtaining reliable and up-to-date information—a very natural state of affairs in a land where the inhabitants, if not actively hostile to the government, were at least sympathetic towards the Arab cause—contact with the rebels was seldom achieved. On the rare occasions when contact was made, darkness usually intervened before any decisive result could be achieved, and with darkness the rebels were able almost invariably to slip through the net. The lack of tangible results was apt to be most discouraging, but the means adopted were at least effective in keeping gangs on the move and in preventing further depredations, and led eventually to the partial abandonment of large-scale gang activity. Columns operated more or less independently and the very nature of the operations demanded a high degree of initiative, resource and efficiency, not only on the part of the column commander, but from every officer, N.C.O., and man. Operations were usually ordered at short notice, and the speed at which columns were eventually able to turn out and move, was a tribute to the keenness and efficiency of all concerned.

The following is an account of an operation carried out by B Company in co-operation with A, C, and D Companies and a column from the Border Regiment:

On February 1 we were operating close to the North Frontier Road. We had received orders to proceed to occupy a village some three miles west of debussing point. We set off for this village at about 9.15 a.m. At 11 a.m., however, we saw aircraft circling over a wadi some two miles away to the south-west, and shortly afterwards we heard them bombing and firing machine-guns. We therefore abandoned our original objective and marched towards the sound of the firing. To reach our new objective, unfortunately, we had to cross first a spur and then a hill, the latter proving almost impassable with donkey transport. So difficult was the going that we did not reach the summit until 2 p.m. At this time all air activity had ceased; fresh instructions were asked by wireless and at about 2.30 p.m. we were ordered to proceed to occupy our original village. No sooner had these orders been received than air bombing recommenced, so we again marched towards the sound of the firing. At about 4 p.m., whilst negotiating a further spur, rifle fire broke out just in front of our advance guard (No. 7 Platoon). No. 15 Platoon of D Company was pushed up on the left of the advance guard and a wireless call sent for air assistance. Shortly afterwards we were really in action, and about ten minutes later the aircraft arrived on the scene.

The armed gang, which must have numbered about thirty,

PATROL OF THE FIRST BATTALION NEAR IKRUIT ON THE SYRIAN FRONTIER

3-INCH MORTAR TEAM ON DONKEY PACK, PALESTINE, 1938

retreated in front of us, but stood to fight on each successive ridge. Although we could never actually get to grips with them, fighting took place at times at ten yards range.

The country over which we were fighting was the most heartbreaking one could wish to meet, the whole area being a mass of huge rocks and high scrub; however, eventually we pushed them off the last ridge into a deep wadi. Unfortunately, by this time it was practically dark and they made good their escape. We managed, however, to account for three of them, killed, whose bodies were left behind, and we hope there were more whose bodies remained undiscovered.

Our casualties were nil, and considering the country and the nature of the fighting, we may be deemed exceedingly fortunate. Visibility at times, and in fact for most of the time, was nil, and this is well brought out by the fact that on the final ridge we were joined by a column of the Border Regiment on our right, of whose presence we had been completely unaware. Control was extraordinarily difficult and could only be maintained by Company Headquarters making personal contact with forward platoons on each successive ridge. The action covered the best part of two kilos, and lasted from 4 p.m., until dark, at about 6.15 p.m., when we occupied battle posts for the night. At this time the company had been almost continuously on the move over very difficult country since 9.15 a.m.

The next day provided more marching, but passed off without incident, and finally, at 7.15 p.m., we rejoined Battalion Headquarters, where the company got their first hot meal for forty hours.

In May it became clear that a great deal of illicit traffic in arms and ammunition was being carried out across the Lebanese and Syrian Transjordan frontiers, and with the object of curtailing this traffic the battalion was ordered to establish posts along these frontiers. Remembering that the total length of the frontier was some sixty miles, it is not surprising that these measures proved ineffective, the most that can be claimed being that it did tend to make smuggling a little more difficult. Later a substantial wire obstacle (Tegart's Wall) was erected along these frontiers and semi-permanent military and police posts were established. These measures, if not totally effective, certainly caused serious embarrassment to the rebel leaders in securing the necessary supply of arms and ammunition.

Another form of activity which fell to the battalion was the provision of escorts for police dogs, popularly known as beagling. These dogs were extremely efficient and well trained, and where any scent existed they could be trusted to follow it relentlessly. Escorts normally had a very strenuous time, as the runs would take them up hills and down wadis for hours on end, but seldom ended with a kill.

With the advent of the hot weather, it became necessary to evacuate Tiberias towards the end of May. Simultaneously a change in policy in dealing with rebel activities came into force. In view of the fact that gangs were dependent on villages for food and shelter, it was felt that the occupation of villages by detachments of troops and police might produce the most effective means of curtailing the activities of gangs. In addition it was decided to proceed with the construction of roads and tracks in order that the more troublesome districts might be made accessible to M.T. In pursuance of this policy a redistribution of the battalion was made, a fresh detachment being found at Sakhnin, the detachments at Mi'ilya and Acre being retained; the remainder of the battalion moved in to Old Trafford Camp, a tented camp some two miles north of Acre.

On August 16 the leading truck of the ration convoy to Sakhnin was blown up by a landmine; Lieutenant R. F. H. Griffiths was killed. The police dogs were quickly brought on the scene and followed the trail of the culpirt who had laid it to the village of Shaab. As a punishment it was decided to demolish certain of the houses in the village. On August 18 a party of Royal Engineers escorted by B Company (Tibcol) entered Shaab, and the following account of the operation was recorded by Major M. R. Davidson, who was in command of the battalion in the absence of Lieutenant-Colonel N. Clowes, who was on leave.

At 0730 hrs. on August 18, 1938, B Company proceeded to

Regiment, and the same day embarked on the trooper *Dilwara* at Haifa for Singapore. A number of wives had come out on this ship and there was a great reunion.

On the departure of the battalion the Commanding Officer received the following letter from Lieutenant-General R. H. Haining, C.B., D.S.O., General Officer Commanding British Forces, Palestine and Transjordan.

> I am writing you a letter to thank you, your officers, and also all your battalion for what they have done in Palestine. You have had some regrettable casualties, and you have had a strenuous time, coming on top of your experiences in the western desert, and roughing it in Egypt elsewhere.
> I hope you will have time in Singapore, in good new barracks, for a rest from chasing bandits, and a chance to settle for a while to some comfort.
> I saw a very good return of qualification of signallers the other day, and today am glad to see a very satisfactory inspection report for the year; so you go from Palestine with an enviable record of having done good work in the field, and in the training and organization of same.
> I hope you will turn over to your new role comfortably and easily.
> My best wishes always, and my sincere thanks to you all.
> Yours very sincerely,
> R. H. HAINING.

The following casualties were suffered and honours and awards granted during the tour of duty in Palestine:

Killed in action: 2nd Lieutenant R. F. H. Griffiths, R.S.M. J. Currie, L/Cpl. C. Heelan, Pte. W. Harper.
Accidentally killed: Pte. Penney.
Wounded in action: 2 officers, 9 other ranks.
Awarded the Military Cross: Lieutenant R. King-Clark.
Mentioned in General Orders for Gallantry: 8 officers, 28 other ranks.
Mentioned in General Orders for Devoted Service: 2 officers, 13 other ranks.

At the time the battalion embarked at Haifa the period now known as the " Munich crisis " was at its height. Due to the threat to apply sanctions to Italy during the Italian–Abyssinian War, Mussolini had allied himself with Hitler and had formed the Rome–Berlin Axis Treaty. Hitler taking advantage of the weak foreign policy of the British Government had first annexed Austria and then, against the code of ordinary decency, invaded Czecho-Slovakia and occupied Prague. The scene was therefore set for a second European War.

In consequence of the European situation, on arrival at Port Said, the troopship was held up and the battalion came under orders of the G.O.C. British Troops, Egypt. On September 28 the battalion received orders to disembark and proceed to Cairo and take over Abassia Barracks from the Royal Northumberland Fusiliers with C Company at Kasr-el-Nil Barracks. At once the battalion was deployed on guard, escorts, and garrison duties, and remained so until it was known that the meeting between Mr. Neville Chamberlain and Hitler at Berchtesgaden had provided a temporary lull in the crisis.

On October 1 the battalion received orders to re-embark at Suez on the *Dilwara*, and on August 4 the whole battalion, less six men who were still escorting a goods train in the western desert, went on board and sailed the same day for Singapore. The battalion finally reached Singapore on October 20 and proceeded to Tanglin Barracks.

On November 28 Major-General Dobbie, G.O.C. Malaya Command, inspected the battalion at a ceremonial parade, after which, he presented the silver bugles on behalf of the officers, men and families who had subscribed towards them.

It will be remembered that in 1937 the battalion had been reorganized as a machine-gun battalion and had by the time it left Egypt for Palestine carried out training as first-year machine-gunners. Due to the nature of the task it had to carry out in Palestine, very little time had been allowed for further training; consequently on arrival in Singapore the first task was to complete the training of the battalion. At this time there were only eight regular battalions of machine-gunners in the British Army, of which only two were allotted to the Far East, one to Singapore and one to Hong Kong.

In spite of all the assurance given by Hitler, the year 1939 was one of preparation and in the event of war the battalion was allotted some twelve miles on the east coast of the island to defend. This battle station was known as East Side.

On March 14, 1939, the battalion took part in a combined operations exercise in which they acted as enemy, landing by night from Tongkangs, against the island of Blakang Mati and the West Sector. On March 23 a liaison visit was made to H.M.S. *Manchester* by all ranks and their wives, during which the ship's company presented a photograph of H.M.S. *Manchester* to the battalion.

On March 25 an inter-services boxing competition was held between the Army and the Royal Navy; of the team of fifteen from the Army, seven were from the battalion.

On June 21 the battalion provided a guard of honour for Admiral Disoux, Commander-in-Chief of the French China Fleet. This was the first time that the new drill in threes was carried out in Malaya in public.

On June 30 Lieutenant-Colonel N. Clowes, D.S.O., M.C., handed over command of the battalion on appointment as Brigadier to the Military Mission in Cairo. Major M. R. Davidson assumed temporary command until the arrival on August 16 of Lieutenant-Colonel E. B. Holmes, M.C.

On July 28 Major-General Dobbie relinquished command of troops in Malaya and sailed for England. His appointment was assumed by Major-General L. V. Bond.

On August 3 the battalion commenced to pitch a tented camp for an Indian battalion which was part of a brigade group called Force Emu, which had been dispatched to Singapore under an emergency plan. This battalion on its arrival was 4/19 Hyderabads, and occupied this camp on the lower playing-fields of Tanglin Barracks until the outbreak of war.

On September 2 orders were received to put the mobilization plan into effect. On the following day news was received that once again Great Britain was at war with Germany.

CHAPTER II

THE 1st BATTALION AND THE SINGAPORE CAMPAIGN

WHEN war was declared in Europe the state of affairs in the Far East was uncertain but not serious. The Japanese were the only power in the east who could attack British possessions in western and south-western Pacific, and in September 1939 there were no strong indications that those who were in power in Japan intended to embark upon so great an adventure. Nevertheless, diplomatic relations between Great Britain and Japan were far from cordial. In 1931, the Japanese had expelled the Chinese from Manchuria and had there established a government, which, though nominally independent, was subordinated to Japanese interests; and the whole administration of the country fell under the influence of Japanese financiers and industrial magnates. The British government did not recognize the new authority in Manchuria, and had refused to reconsider their decision or to modify their policy. The American government followed the same course of conduct, saying that the Manchurian government had been forcibly established and that they would not recognize it.

The old cordial relations between Japan and England had thus been a thing of the past for eight years before war began, and the coolness that followed upon the Manchurian affair, during the years following, became something not far removed from downright antagonism; for the Japanese, not content with their conquest of Manchuria, embarked upon a plan of subordinating all China to their influence, and occupied the north-eastern provinces as far as the Yangtze and seized Canton.

The growing friction did not, however, constitute an outright threat to our positions in the Far East, and in September 1939 the balance of military power in the south-western Pacific was so well adjusted that, if the Japanese had then attempted to attack British possessions in the Far East, they would have been confronted with obstacles very difficult to be overcome.

The Japanese could probably have overrun the British settlement in Shanghai, and the colony of Hong Kong, in almost any circumstances, but for so long as the alliance between Great Britain and France continued firm, the Japanese general staff would not have found it an easy matter to do more than occupy these two British outposts. First (which perhaps was most important), the British Navy was only concerned with protecting commerce in the Atlantic, and for so long as the French navy assisted in this, it would always have been possible for the Admiralty to detach a fairly powerful force to the Far East, for the Germans had no battle fleet, and the French navy, being largely composed of cruisers and destroyers, was admirably adapted to trade defence. The Japanese would only have been justified in declaring war against England if a fair opportunity offered of conquering Malaya and Burma, and this was only feasible if they were assured of a crushing superiority of naval strength at the southern terminal of the very long sea-route over which their armies would have to be carried; they would not count upon this for so long as the Admiralty was in a position to detach strong forces to the Far East.

Furthermore, the French colony of Indo-China was on the flank of a Japanese advance into the south-western Pacific, and the Japanese general staff would assuredly not have attacked Malaya until their armies had previously attacked and seized the principal ports of Indo-China and had got control of its main arteries of communication. Even if it be granted that the French garrison in Indo-China would not have resisted a Japanese invasion successfully, it still remains true that it would have been a great overhead charge upon the Japanese army to establish full and undisputed control over a country that is spread over fifteen degrees of latitude and that this burden would sooner or later have sapped the strength of their striking force in Malaya and Burma.

All this did not, it is true, constitute a secure barrier against a Japanese attack upon our Far Eastern possessions, but at least it was a strong deterrent to an immediate Japanese advance into the south-western Pacific, and in the autumn of 1939 and the spring of the year following, our military policy was adjusted to what the state of Far East politics demanded. The British battalions that were then in Malaya were to remain there; the officers and men when fully trained would, however, be withdrawn to Europe and would be replaced by half-trained troops. For the rest, the beaches of the whole island were to be put into a state of defence and the units were strenuously trained.

Singapore was termed "the Fortress" although in fact it was only a flat island, surrounded by beaches suitable for landings, and divided from the mainland of Johore by a strip of water not much broader than the Thames at Putney; and it will here be proper to explain upon what principles it was to be defended.

The defences took in the east, south, and west coast of the island, where it was open to seaborne landings; but to the north, the defended line ran some forty miles inland, through the State of Johore so that any enemy who might attack down the Malayan Peninsula should be held before he was within artillery range of the naval base. This northern line took in the beaches of Mersing on the eastern coast of Johore, and ran thereafter along the River Sidili to Kota Tinggi. The defences were similar to the beach defences, but lacked the heavy artillery of the fixed defences.

The first ring of defences of Singapore Island was provided by the Royal Navy. An External Defence Officer R.N. was appointed to H.Q. Fixed Defences; this officer operated a number of small craft, whose duty it was to give early warning of the approach of a hostile fleet. In addition,

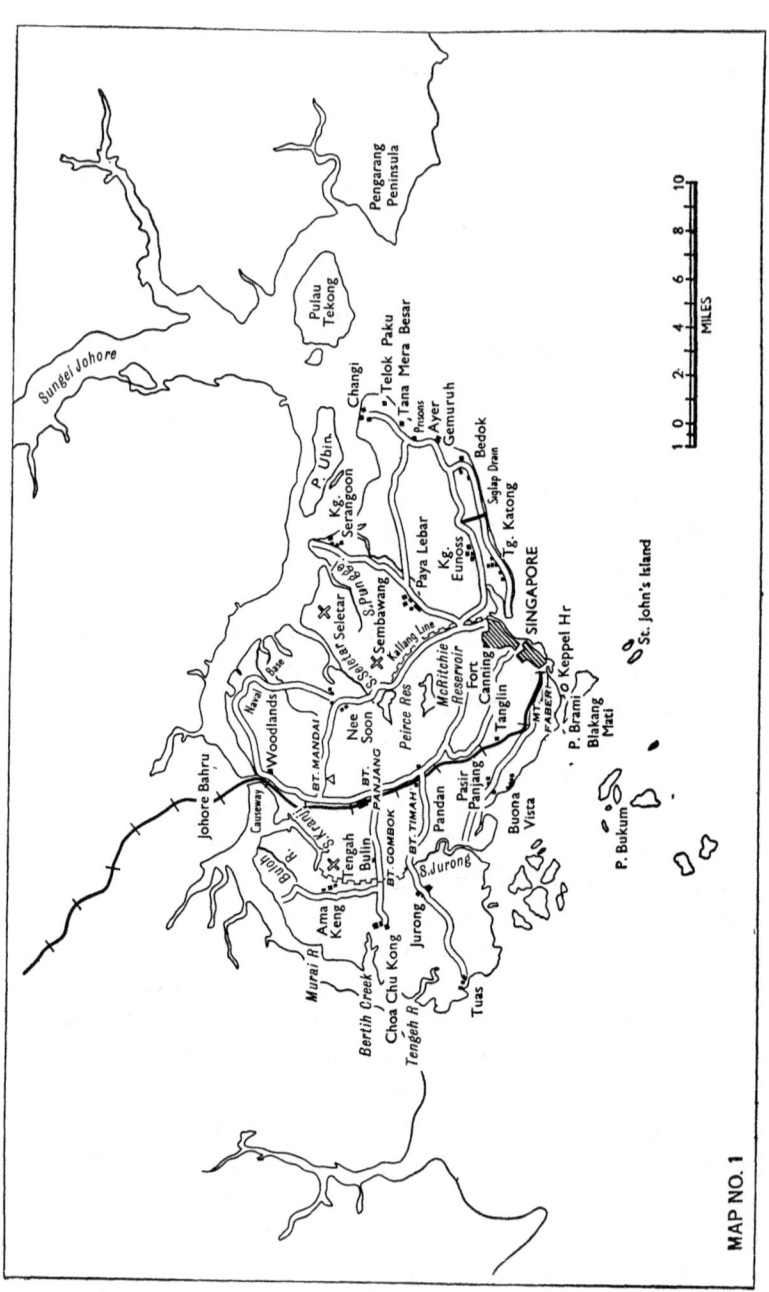

MAP NO. 1

THE DEFENCES

an inner ring of motor tonkans was established to communicate with the beach defences by means of pyrotechnic signals. These latter, however, proved impossible to operate, later, as the minefields when laid, impeded movement by night.

The second ring of defences consisted of the coastal defence batteries which were controlled by Commander Fixed Defences. These guns were divided into three categories: 15-inch guns capable of engaging a battleship at approximately fourteen miles; 9-inch guns for counter-bombardment against cruisers and smaller warships; and 6-inch guns for close defence. All these guns operated by night with the assistance of Coast Artillery searchlights. In addition the entrances to Keppel Harbour and the Straits of Johore at Changi were covered by boom defences and an illuminated area: the whole was defended by a number of Anti-Motor-Torpedo-Boat batteries.

The third ring was provided by the beach defences which were manned by the infantry and supported by static beach defence 18-pounder guns from the Mobile Coast Defence Regiment R.A. These 18-pounders were sighted in pairs on every beach where troops could land and were aided at night by beach defence searchlights. For the purpose of defence the island was divided into four sectors—East, Geylang, Town and West. A fifth sector took in the high ground of Pengarang in Johore, which dominated the entrance to the Straits of Johore. The 1st Battalion had been allotted East sector, which covered some nine miles of beaches from a large drain at Siglap to a point behind the boom at Changi. The sector was divided into four sub-sectors, each being manned by one company: A Company, Siglap sub-sector; B Company, Powder sub-sector; C Company, Ayer Gemuruh sub-sector; and D Company, Changi sub-sector. Each sub-sector was divided into two beaches, each being manned by one platoon with the third platoon of each company in close support.

The main defence on each beach was a series of pillboxes

designed to hold two medium machine-guns, an infantry Lyon light (a small searchlight with a beam of about 1,000 yards), with an earthbank in rear for an anti-tank rifle. One medium machine-gun had a wide arc to seaward; the other could fire partly to seaward, but its main role was a fixed-line shoot down the beach wire, which connected each pillbox. The crew of each pillbox was, therefore, one N.C.O., as fire controller, four machine-gun numbers, one Lyon light operator and one Lyon light engine operator, an anti-tank rifleman, and a telephone orderly. All communications were carried out by telephone from pillbox to Beach Headquarters, Beach Headquarters to Sub-Sector Headquarters, and Sub-Sector Headquarters to Sector Headquarters. In rear of each beach were support posts designed to cover the rear of each pillbox.

In addition to these forward defences, a line of Rear Defence Localities (R.D.L.s) was surveyed, into which reserves could be placed as soon as it became known where every penetration through the beach defences had been made.

As troops employed on Beach Defences might have to remain on the alert for some time, areas were earmarked behind each sub-sector for semi-deployment camps in which men could live by day and from which they had easy access to their beaches at night. Sector Headquarters was to be set up at the tenth milestone on the Changi Road.

The plan on mobilization was for all troops stationed in Malaya to concentrate on the island when Commander Malaya Infantry Brigade became Commander Beach Defences. In fact the two battalions from up-country had come down when war was declared, so that on September 3 there was on the island the whole peacetime garrison of Malaya, which was 1st Battalion The Loyal Regiment, 2nd Battalion The Gordon Highlanders, 1st Battalion The Manchester Regiment, 2/17 Dogras, and 1st Battalion The Malay Regiment. In addition reinforcements had arrived from India in the shape of Force Emu (12 Indian Infantry

Commanding Officer	Lieut.-Colonel E. B. Holmes, M.C.
Adjutant	Lieut. P. Thompson
R.S.M.	R.S.M. F. Hand

No. 1 Guard

Captain of the Guard	Lieut. J. A. Hallmark
Colour Officer	2nd Lieut. C. G. C. Holmyard
Lieutenant of the Guard	Lieut. J. T. H. Gunning

No. 2 Guard

Captain of the Guard	Major F. G. Brittorous, M.C.
2nd Lieutenant of the Guard	2nd Lieut. J. A. Gardner
Lieutenant of the Guard	Lieut. R. V. Howell

No. 3 Guard

Captain of the Guard	Major G. D. Cooper
2nd Lieutenant of the Guard	2nd Lieut. N. K. Evans
Lieutenant of the Guard	2nd Lieut. R. V. Edwards

No. 4 Guard

Captain of the Guard	Captain R. H. H. Stewart
2nd Lieutenant of the Guard	2nd Lieut. J. L. L. Perez
Lieutenant of the Guard	2nd Lieut. J. R. V. Brewster
Bandmaster	Bandmaster T. Grey, A.R.C.M.
Drum Major	P.S.M. F. Lewis

In the evening the sergeants' mess held their annual Ladysmith Ball, and on the following evening seventeen warrant officers and sergeants dined as guests of the officers in the officers' mess. The guest of honour during the two days was Mr. Bates Goodall, who had been a corporal with the 1st Battalion during the siege.

During the next two months Major Brittorous, M.C., Captains C. L. Archdale, N. B. Close Brooks, and Lieutenant J. A. Hallmark, together with a number of other ranks, left the battalion for the United Kingdom.

Digging and wiring R.D.L.s went on slowly all this time, but the system of defence was by no means complete in May

1940, when the utter overthrow of the French armies turned what had, up to then, been a distant and contingent menace into a danger of the first order. All the safeguards that had been enumerated in the first part of this chapter were gone, and the assumption no longer held good that if the Japanese did attack Singapore they would only be able to engage small carrier-borne air forces. For when France fell, the French colony in Indo-China was isolated and helpless; and there was nothing to prevent the Japanese from establishing themselves in such parts of it as they required, and so securing a chain of aerodromes and bases along their line of communications between Japan and Malaya. Soon after the Franco-German armistice was signed, news did indeed come through that the Japanese authorities were negotiating with the French governor of Indo-China. The official explanation that the Japanese were only anxious to secure safeguards that the northern parts of Indo-China should not be used to help and sustain the Chinese armies, in no way palliated the danger. The danger of invasion was henceforward stark and patent.

The first precautions consisted of measures for bringing the civil population under closer observation and control. As the Asiatic population of Malaya was in no sense a coherent society, but was more a collection of human beings who differed in language, religion, and customs, it was one into which an invader could easily infiltrate spies, agents, and informers. Great precautions were taken against rioting and civil commotions; guards were placed upon all vulnerable points, and an elaborate system was established for blocking all entries and exits from certain quarters of the town; while the police and civil authorities made house-to-house searches within the cordon. For the rest, the coastal fortifications and strong-posts were pressed on with. The garrison was put under five days notice for full deployment.

On July 1, 1940, a conference was held at Brigade Headquarters when the orders were given to commence clearing fields of fire and wiring the beaches in the following order of priority: (i) clearing and wiring along the beaches; (ii) wiring of support posts; (iii) erection of tactical wire (iv) wiring of R.D.L.s. The beach wire of two double apron fences was to be put up by R.E. contract. The following day a conference was held with the Field Engineer, East sector, when it was decided that the battalion should be responsible for clearing twenty feet behind the R.E. contractor's fence and in front of the fence to the sea. For this work, 400 coolies were allotted to the battalion. The Royal Engineers undertook the responsibility for all demolitions, the contractor's fence, and the thinning-out of forty feet back from the battalion clearing. On July 4, the first wire appeared in Changi, Ayer Gemuruh and Siglap sub-sectors.

In September 1940, it was learned that the Japanese government had made a political pact with Italy and Germany. If the bare words of the treaty were alone considered, it was an agreement that bound the signatories only to resist the spread of communism and Russian doctrines. Diplomats were, however, convinced that the treaty was, in effect, a military alliance. As it was useless to keep British troops in Shanghai any longer, the regiments there stationed were withdrawn to Singapore and the Malay Infantry Brigade was re-formed into two.

The order of battle for the regular troops on Singapore Island was now:

1st Malaya Infantry Brigade (Brigadier G. G. R. Williams)
1st Battalion The Loyal Regiment
2nd Battalion East Surrey Regiment (from Shanghai)
2/17 Dogras
1st Battalion The Malaya Regiment
2nd Malaya Infantry Brigade (Brigadier F. Keith Simmons, C.B.E., M.C.)
1st Battalion The Manchester Regiment
2nd Battalion The Gordon Highlanders
1st Battalion The Seaforth Highlanders

As 2/17 Dogras were no longer brigaded with the battalion their machine-gun platoon handed over their duties and approved armaments for Changi sub-sector to D Company. On September 7, C.S.M.s Reilly, Maloney, Flynn, and Sergeants O'Flynn and Little were granted emergency commissions with the regiment.

On October 2, further reinforcements arrived for the battalion. Twelve officers and 189 other ranks disembarked at Singapore, and were given an extensive course of training before being distributed to companies. On the same day Lieutenant R. V. Howell left the battalion for England.

On October 19, D Company carried out a demonstration, and manned their beach posts for the benefit of the Thailand Mission of Goodwill.

From this date to the end of the year various changes took place in the organization of the fortress and the battalion. In order to relieve Malayan Command of direct operational command of the island, Headquarters Singapore Fortress was formed, and Brigadier F. Keith Simmons was made General Officer Commanding. Brigadier F. H. Fraser, D.S.O., M.C., assumed command of 2nd Malayan Infantry Brigade. 1st Battalion The Seaforth Highlanders moved to Penang, and as on deployment the 2nd Battalion Gordon Highlanders manned the defences of Pengarang in Johore, it left East sector without any reserve. In order to remedy this, the battalion formed a rifle company known as R Company from its first reinforcements. This company consisted of a skeleton Company H.Q., with three platoons each of three sections armed with rifles, brens, and tommy-guns; in addition an extra M.M.G. platoon was formed to support this company. The duty of this company was a counter-attack role on any part of the sector where penetration might be made; each platoon was also trained in tank hunting. For this purpose it was made highly mobile with all the battalion transport; administrative transport was provided on deployment by eight hired Chinese lorries.

The last month of the year brought a slight improvement; for the Germans did not invade Great Britain, and General Sir Archibald Wavell's victories in North Africa announced

THE FIRST BATTALION CARRYING OUT A DEFENCE EXERCISE, SINGAPORE ISLAND, OCTOBER 1941

THE JAPANESE DANGER

to the whole world that the English still had the will and the power to strike quick and hard at their ring of enemies. Eastern people are quick to appreciate indications of strength and power, and the population of Singapore remained quiet. Nevertheless, the year 1941 came up dark and gloomy, for the Germans reinforced the Italians in North Africa, and regained most of the territories that General Wavell had so recently conquered. In addition the German army invaded and completely over-ran Jugoslavia and Greece, and captured the island of Crete with airborne troops. By thus establishing themselves in the Mediterranean, the enemy aggravated the isolation of all British troops outside Europe.

In the Far East, the Japanese pressed on with their plans for dominating the countries that bordered upon Malaya. After arbitrating upon a boundary dispute between France and Siam, and obliging both parties to accept their award, the Japanese government forced the French governor of Indo-China to grant them the right to establish military bases in the country. Henceforward the French authorities in Indo-China were quite subject to the Japanese, who moved considerable forces into the country during the summer.

The menace to our colonies in the southern Pacific was thus patent; and it soon became increasingly clear that the Japanese plan was very embracing, and that the government of Tokyo contemplated waging war against the United States and Great Britain, with the object of establishing their empire in Malaya, Borneo, and the Philippines.

During the remaining months of the year, the diplomats reported that tension was rising, and, as the political situation deteriorated, Japanese troop movements to Indo-China increased. The last chance of peace disappeared when Prince Konoye's government fell, for we know now that he honestly desired to find a middle way. He was succeeded by General Tojo, who was known to be the leader of the warlike party. (October 16, 1941.)

It was very much to the honour of the British soldiers in Singapore that the danger in which they stood in no way depressed them. No man there present was so weak in his understanding that he did not see what was coming. The rising tide of the war in Europe, its widening compass, the toll that German submarines were taking of British shipping, were making communications with England precarious and intermittent, and while driblets of reinforcements were from time to time arriving, Japanese forces were being assembled in enormous strength and were steadily approaching. No expert knowledge was needed to understand that the coming struggle would be fought out, not in the English homeland, where every cottage would be a place of succour, but in a jungle-covered island, inhabited by Asiatic people, whose sympathies were doubtful, and whose behaviour was incalculable. The danger was understood by all, and was by all accepted with an undaunted spirit.

In spite of the gathering war clouds, morale was extremely high, and in between the whirl of war preparation life in the garrison went on much the same as usual. Football, cricket, hockey, and boxing competitions, both command and unit, were held as often as circumstances would allow. This was fairly often, as most games in Malaya were played in the evening. In the boxing world the battalion soon, after its arrival, had made its presence felt in Malaya and remained champions in both team and individual championships right up to the capitulation. The Tolley Cup, open to teams from both forces and civilian clubs, was won on two occasions, and tied for the third time with the Singapore Police. The Command Open Team Championship was won two seasons in succession before the competition was abandoned owing to the war. The Army Boxing Team which defeated the Navy in the Lowther Grant Cup Competition in 1940 contained some eight or nine men from the battalion. It is interesting to note that a replica of the Tolley Cup is still with the battalion. The Australian Imperial Force salvaged it during the last days of Singapore and returned it to the battalion after the capitulation. It remained safely hidden during our captivity in the capable hands

The campaign that followed on the mainland is not relevant to this history, as the 1st Battalion was not engaged in it, and it will suffice to say that, after a series of battles, in which the British Army was at every point outnumbered and outgunned, General Percival ordered a withdrawal to the island of Singapore (January 27, 1942). His forces were then in the southern part of the peninsula between Pontian Kechil and Kota Tinggi.

The causeway across which all troops had to be withdrawn was covered by an outer bridgehead of two battalions, and an inner bridgehead of one battalion, and the general plan was that the various groups of the army should withdraw in succession to the neighbourhood of Johore Bahru, and that they should then be carried rapidly across into the island by motor transport. The last units of the mainland army came on to the island during the forenoon of January 31. The 18th Division (Major-General Beckwith Smith) had now arrived, together with the 44th Indian Brigade (a sister brigade to the 45th and as yet untrained), an Australian machine-gun battalion, and drafts to the number of about 2,000 for the Australian units. It will be proper, at this point, to review the island and its defences.

If the Army's plan of strongly fortifying the Johore mainland from Mersing on the east coast to a selected point on the western side had been executed; if a squadron of armoured ships and their auxiliaries had remained at the naval base; and if a garrison had been maintained of sufficient strength to man the fortified lines in Johore and the fortified points in Singapore island, then the island and the adjacent territory might properly have been called a fortress. The island to which General Percival withdrew what was left of the 3rd Corps and the Australian division, was, however, in no sense a fortress, and was merely a geographical feature of which some points had been fortified.

The two strongly fortified sectors were Changi, where the defences covered the sea approaches to the naval base, and the Keppel-Harbour–Mount-Faber sector, where the defences

SINGAPORE AND ITS DEFENCES

covered the sea approaches to the commercial harbour. There was a fire command in each of these sectors, and in each fire command there was a 15-inch gun battery, a 9·2-inch gun battery, and a number of 6-inch gun batteries. The garrison of the fixed defences was composed of the 7th Coast Regiment R.A., the 9th Coast Regiment R.A., the 16th Defence Regiment R.A., the 35th Fortress Company R.E., and the 41st Fortress Company R.E.

The anti-aircraft defences were sited in accordance with a War Office plan, which had been designed to cover the naval base, Keppel harbour, Seletar and Tengah aerodromes. The plan was not, however, due to be completed until 1942, and, if it had been completed, anti-aircraft defence would have been of a lower density than the anti-aircraft defence of London during the Battle of Britain. In January 1942, when the 3rd Corps crossed the Causeway the anti-aircraft defences of Singapore island were: 4 heavy anti-aircraft regiments, plus 1 battery; 2 light anti-aircraft regiments, less 1 battery; 1 searchlight regiment. The headquarters were at Fort Canning.

The beach defences upon which the battalion had been engaged since war began had been designed to meet a contingency rather different from the one that actually confronted the garrison in February 1942, viz. " to protect the islands of Blakang Mati, Pulau Brami, and the Pengerang area south of Johore against a seaborne attack."[1] When completed (the Manchesters had only been engaged on one sector) there were concrete pillboxes at 600-yard intervals along the beaches, and two switch-lines had been prepared to protect the centre of the island from landings on the east and west coasts: the eastern line ran between the civil airport of Kallang and the village of Paya Lebar; the western line ran along a ridge of rising ground between the upper waters of the Kranji and Jurong rivers.

As the whole system of defence had been designed to protect the naval base, there were no beach defences on the

[1] General Percival's dispatch, para. 434.

northern shore of the island, and it was only on December 23 that orders were given to construct them. By then, however, all points of military importance on Singapore island were being regularly, and often severely, bombed; and it was extremely difficult to obtain the labourers who were required.

The 44th Indian Brigade worked in the area and, notwithstanding the difficulties, accomplished a great deal. Sites for the forward defended localities and for reserves were selected. Artillery observation posts and gun positions were reconnoitred and selected. Localities of formation headquarters were fixed and communications arranged. Machine-gun positions were constructed. Oil obstacles and depth charges were placed in creeks. All available searchlights and Lyon lights were collected and were brought into use. Anti-tank obstacles were erected.

The air force was hardly contributing to the defences of the island; for it had been ordered to go to South Sumatra. The four main aerodromes in the island were being constantly bombed; and three of them, Tengah, Sembawang, and Seletar, were certain to be occupied by the enemy if the troops on the beaches made only a slight withdrawal. General Sir Archibald Wavell therefore agreed to the proposal of the Air Officer Commanding that only a force of eight Hurricanes and a few Buffaloes should remain on the island. The greater part of the air headquarters staff was sent to the Netherlands East Indies at the same time.

When it was determined to hold the island, the first point that fell to be decided was: What outlying points were to be held also? For there is a large cluster of small islands off the south-western coastline; an island in the Straits of Johore, called Pulau Ubin, lies opposite to the Changi sector; while the island of Tekong, and the Pengerang peninsula, at the mouth of the Johore river, are natural assembly points for an enemy who decides to attack the island from the east. With regard to the archipelago off the south-western coast, General Percival decided that Pulau Bukum, where there was a large oil store, was to be held, and that the island of

SINGAPORE, OCTOBER 1941
The First Battalion building an anti-boat obstacle, and at work on beach defences

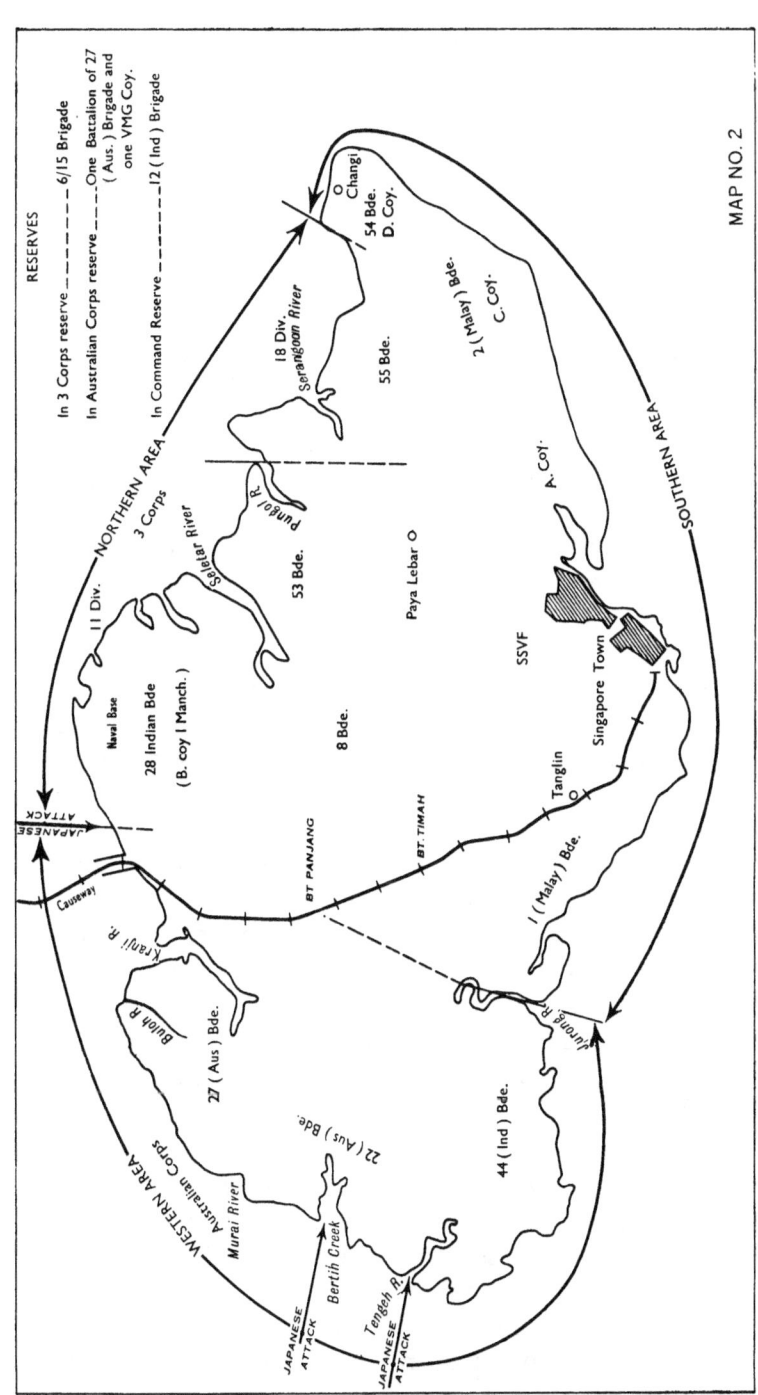

MAP NO. 2

Blakang Mati was essential to the fixed defences; but that the other islands could be made untenable by the fortress batteries, and that they need not be held. On the Johore side, an observation post was established on Pulau Ubin: the Pengerang peninsula, and the island of Tekong were garrisoned by the fixed defences and a unit from the Indian state forces. It remained to be decided how the formations and the units were to be stationed.

The 3rd Corps had suffered such losses during the fighting on the mainland and the retreat that it was reconstituted: what was left of the 11th Division was absorbed into the 9th, and the 18th Division was made part of the corps. The available troops were then thus distributed:

The 3rd Corps was allotted to the northern area, which ran from the western border of the Changi defences to a point a few hundred yards to the east of the Causeway. Paya Lebar village was inside this northern area, which was indented by three great creeks—the Serangoon, the Pungol and the Seletar. The area was one enormous rubber plantation, which was, however, traversed by several good roads: communications between the perimeter and the centre were not difficult.

The 18th Division was given the eastern sector of this northern area: Major-General Beckwith Smith placed the 54th Infantry Brigade (Brigadier Backhouse) on the right, and the 55th Brigade (Brigadier Massy Beresford) on the left.

The 11th Division was given the western sector. Major-General Key placed the 53rd British Infantry Brigade on the right and the 28th Indian Infantry Brigade (Brigadier Selby) on the left.

The 6/15th Brigade was in corps reserve.

The southern area was occupied by the 1st and 2nd Malay Brigades, the fixed defences, the Straits Settlements Volunteer Force and the fortress troops. The area took in Changi, Singapore, and all the shoreline between the two: it ended just beyond the Jurong river. The 1st Malay Brigade (Brigadier Williams) occupied the right (or western) sector.

GENERAL PERCIVAL'S PLAN

The Straits Settlements Volunteer Force occupied Singapore town. The 2nd Malaya Brigade (Brigadier Fraser), to which the 1st Battalion The Manchester Regiment was attached, occupied the left (or eastern) sector: the Pengerang peninsula and Tekong island were included in it.

The western area was ocupied by the Australian Corps and the 44th Brigade: it ran from the Causeway to the western shore of the Jurong river; Bukit Timah village was within the area. The shoreline of the western area is the lowest and most swampy in the island, and is indented by three large creeks—the Kranji, the Bertih, and the Tengeh —and by a great number of smaller ones. Major-General Gordon Bennett placed the 27th Australian Infantry Brigade (Brigadier Maxwell) on the right; the 22nd Australian Infantry Brigade (Brigadier Taylor) in the centre, and the 44th Indian Brigade (Brigadier Ballantyne) on the left. One battalion of the 27th Brigade and a machine-gun company were in area reserve.

The 12th Indian Infantry Brigade (Brigadier Paris) was in command reserve.

As everything that had previously been settled with regard to the defence of the base was put into the melting-pot when Johore was abandoned and when the command of the sea was lost, the principle upon which the island was to be defended had to be settled. Two alternatives offered: (*a*) to strive to prevent the enemy from landing; to hold him to his landing places if he did land, and to expel him from them by counter-attacks: or (*b*) to hold the coastline lightly; to accumulate as large a reserve as possible and to use it in a decisive action within the island. Whenever they are free to choose, professional soldiers invariably prefer the second alternative; but General Percival's choice was influenced by special circumstances. The island is covered by forest and rubber plantations which would very much assist an attacking force, in that they would enable it to conceal important movements and would restrict the use that could be made of the defenders' artillery. The military installations—the naval base, the aerodromes, depots, and ammunition dumps—were scattered all over the island; and it was almost certain that the enemy would capture some of them during a battle of manoeuvre. Finally, there was not room: Singapore island is only as large as the Isle of Wight; half of it would have to be abandoned to the enemy before the decisive engagement began; the remainder was not big enough to permit of the manoeuvres and movements of a decisive action. For these reasons, General Percival decided that the enemy must be met and fought to a standstill on the landing beaches or as near to them as possible, but he admits, "... It was not possible with the forces at our disposal, owing to the extent of the coastline, to build up a really strong coastal defence...."

The 1st Battalion's companies were in the 2nd Malay Brigade's sector and were in the positions that have been described in the beginning of this chapter. A Company was on the right, C Company was in the centre, and D Company was on the left at Changi. B Company had, however, been moved from Blakang Mati to the naval base, and was under the command of the 28th Brigade. The company's line of posts first took in the southern end of the Causeway; later the posts to the west of the Causeway were given to units from the Australian Corps. The company finally held nine beach posts on a front of 5,000 yards, and nine penetration posts. The beach posts were all single gun positions within 1,000 yards of the coast of Johore. They were very ingeniously disguised, and not one of them could be detected by a person standing twenty yards away from them.

Until the Japanese crossed the Straits of Johore (and they did not do so for a full week after the Causeway was blown), B Company was more in contact with the enemy than the other three. The front in which this company was stationed was, indeed, shelled and mortared by day and by night, and all movements had to be carried out during the dark hours. As the company was distributed over so many single gun posts, the feeding of them became very difficult. Hot meals did, however, reach every post during the nights that they

6/15th; the 22nd, which, at dawn on February 10, was in a forward position near Bulim was therefore ordered back to fill it. The brigade became very scattered during this retirement, and eventually re-assembled near Bukit Timah.

While the available formations were being distributed along the Kranji–Jurong line, the enemy attacked from the north and virtually turned the whole position. The new Japanese thrust was made along the main road between the Causeway and Singapore; and the 12th Brigade, which was at the right extreme of the Kranji–Jurong position, was driven out of Bukit Panjang village to a position well south of it. The 12th and 6/15th Brigades were now separated; General Percival therefore ordered three battalions to be detached from the 18th Division and to be concentrated near the racecourse. The commander of the western area now ordered a counter-attack to recover Bukit Panjang and Bukit Gombok, and, later, to re-establish the Kranji–Jurong switchline. The first part was successfully executed; but the enemy's progress elsewhere made it impossible even to attempt the remainder. For towards evening on the 10th, the enemy again pressed hard along the road; and as they put a large force of tanks into the struggle, they made a considerable advance towards Bukit Timah. After being held for some time by the 2/29th Australian Battalion the enemy captured the place. The whole of the western area, and a large part of the southern, was therefore turned, unless the Japanese could be expelled from the position to which they had advanced.

February 11. The three battalions that had been drawn from the 18th Division were formed into a special force, and under their commander (Lieutenant-Colonel Thomas) they attempted to recover Bukit Timah village; they failed and occupied a position to the south of it. Meanwhile, the Japanese, realizing the importance of their capture, advanced south-westwards from Bukit Timah and attacked the 6/15th Brigade on the Jurong river front from the rear. The forces on this part of the southern front were

DEFENCE OF THE RESERVOIRS

now withdrawn to a line that roughly followed the road between Bukit Timah village and Pasir Panjang on the southern coast.

The Causeway sector was still held; but the links connecting it to the positions in the south and centre were very weak; and Peirce reservoir was now exposed to an easterly thrust from the Japanese units in the centre of the island. Brigadier Massy Beresford was therefore put in charge of a special force of three battalions, a light tank squadron, a battery of artillery, and a detachment of mechanized cavalry (all drawn from the formations in the northern and southern areas) and was ordered to secure the pumping stations at the eastern ends of the two reservoirs and to make a good junction with Colonel Thomas's troops near Bukit Timah. The commander of the 11th Division was instructed to hold a line from the Seletar river to the Peirce reservoir.

The troops in the eastern and southern sectors were, for the time being, left in their positions; but arrangements were made for a big withdrawal if it became necessary. Colonel E. B. Holmes, M.C., the commanding officer of the 1st Battalion The Manchester Regiment, was ordered to form a perimeter defence with the following units, which were operating in his area:

1st Manchesters' H.Q. Company; 13th A.A.S.L. Battery (5th A.A. Regiment); 85th Anti-Tank Regiment (less four batteries); Anti-Tank Regiment (16th Defence Regiment R.A.); 41st Company R.E.; Carrier Platoon 2/17th Dogras; 22nd Company R.E.; 47th Mobile Workshop Company; H.Q. of the 2nd Malay Infantry Brigade.

By nightfall all these units were in the positions allotted to them.

In addition a special force called James Force was formed: its composition was five companies of the Federated Malay Straits Volunteer Force, one company of the 2nd Gordons, and B Company of the Manchesters.

The Japanese advance to Bukit Timah, in the very centre

of the island, was very grievous; for it was round that place that large stores of food, petrol and stores had been collected. Only fourteen days supplies of army food were stored in the part of the island that was still in our hands, and very little petrol remained. General Wavell, who visited Singapore on the 10th, no longer hoped that the island would be held.

February 12. At daybreak our troops were occupying a series of positions (it could hardly be called a line) from Pasir Panjang, on the south-west coast, past the McRitchie and Peirce reservoirs, and then to the source of the Seletar river. Beyond this line, however, the 22nd Australian Brigade was holding a very isolated position at Pandan. This point and Bukit Timah, in the centre, were the two hottest spots in the battlefield, and at dawn there was fierce, obstinate fighting at both places. At Pendan the Australians held the enemy for many hours, and did not withdraw until evening. At Bukit Timah, however, the enemy's tanks deeply penetrated our position and reached the northern suburbs of Singapore. Nevertheless our position was not broken, and Brigadier Massy Beresford's force re-formed a front on the line Mc-Ritchie reservoir–Adam road–Farrar road. Simultaneously, the Japanese guards very fiercely attacked our positions at Nee Soon village, near the head of the Seletar creek. Notwithstanding that the Japanese came on with the greatest stubbornness, and that they were supported by tanks, they were held by the 8th and 28th Brigades.

The line that was thus held was, however, in the last degree irregular, it followed no geographical feature or natural obstacle, nor was it adjusted to any network of roads and communications: it was, in fact, a mere registration of two days fighting.

> After visiting the front on the Bukit Timah road [writes General Percival], I formed the opinion that there was a very real danger that the enemy would break through on that front, into Singapore town. After consultation with the commander, northern area, I decided that the time had come to form a close perimeter defence round Singapore town itself.... Accordingly,

THE NEW PERIMETER

I instructed the commander, northern area, to withdraw the 11th Division, and the remainder of the 18th British Division from the beach defences, to select and occupy a position covering the water supply, and linking up, on the right, with the southern area north-east of the Kallang aerodrome. . . . I also instructed the commander, southern area, to make all preparations to withdraw from the Changi area and the beaches east of Kallang, as soon as he received orders to do so.[2]

The perimeter that was now to be occupied ran through the suburb that lies to the east of Kallang airport; thereafter it passed through a low-lying half-developed district until it reached the Woodleigh pumping station, then, turning west, it took in the McRitchie reservoir, and covered the western approaches to the town. The line ended on the coastline between Pasir Panjang and Buona Vista.

Up to this time, the companies of the Manchesters had held the positions that had been allotted to them, when general mobilization was ordered, and they had been unaffected by anything that had occurred in the western and northern parts of the island. The order to withdraw to the perimeter was an order to abandon positions that had been prepared with the greatest care, without firing a shot, and the men, who are no strategists, received it with mixed feelings. At three o'clock in the afternoon, at all events, Colonel Holmes received and transmitted an order that A, C, and D Companies were to withdraw, and were to occupy positions that should now be described with some particularity.

A Company was given positions in the Kallang line, which has already been referred to. The right of the company was to be at MacArthur bridge, which carries the Singapore–Changi road across the creeks on the northern side of the Kallang airport. The line then ran along the Wampoe creek (which is so tortuous that the line crossed it at several places), until it reached the municipal incinerator, in the north-east approaches to the town. The last, or northern, part of the line ran through very flat, rather blind country, where the

[2] Dispatch, para. 540.

town has not quite ended, and where the planted rubber estates are just beginning. The company's left-hand posts were near the main road between Singapore and Paya Lebar village.

C Company was allotted to a coastal sector to the west of the great Siglap drain.

D Company, which was farthest to the east at Changi, was to act as a rearguard to the withdrawal, and was to occupy a position where the Changi road crosses the road between Tampines and Tanah Merah Besar.

The battalion headquarters was moved to a house in the eastern part of the city (Dickson Street). It was a very crowded quarter, which was thronged with Chinese and Indians of the poorer sort.

As we have seen, B Company was attached to the force specially formed for the defence of the Changi area (James Force). Colonel James, who was in charge of the force, was ordered to occupy a line from the Siglap drain, through a large rubber estate to the Paya Lebar road.

The companies were all in their new positions by midnight. As the troops withdrew, Changi battery was blown up. Elsewhere, abandoned depots and installations were blazing and exploding. The men marched or drove through country that was illuminated by these tremendous conflagrations: every few moments a fresh explosion shook the ground on which they moved. The city round which they were assembling was itself blazing in several places, for the Japanese bombers were then in every sector of the sky. For the first time in this campaign of misfortunes, the men were depressed: neither the disasters on the mainland, nor the return of the 3rd Corps into the island, nor the steady advance of the Japanese, had ever shaken the men's conviction that these disasters were a rather painful preliminary to a brilliant victory. Now, at last, they doubted, and it is very much to their honour that they had not done so long before.

It was, unfortunately, unlikely that the Army would be able to make a protracted resistance. The last withdrawals

RESISTANCE CONTINUES

had left more food depots in the enemy's hands, and the food reserves now sufficed for about seven days only; petrol was almost exhausted, except for the reserves on Pulau Bukum; two water reservoirs (Pearl's Hill and Fort Canning) were empty or very low; in the town itself so many mains were broken by the shelling and the bombing that pressure was everywhere very low; 25-pounder, Bofors, and mortar ammunition was short.

The withdrawal was successfully executed, and at daybreak on February 13 the troops were in the new perimeter. The 1st Malay Brigade was in the Pasir Panjang area and was holding a position along the ridge: farther north, the commander of the western area organized an all-round, perimetric defence in the Tyersall Tanglis area, and brought all the units of the Australian forces into it. The 18th Division held the northern area, and covered the reservoirs with its three brigades in line (53rd right; 55th centre; 54th left). The 11th Division prolonged the line to the right of the 18th, and held positions between the reservoirs and Paya Lebar village: to the right of the 18th Division, the 2nd Malay Brigade held the eastern approaches to Singapore town.

During the day, the enemy pressed most heavily on the western side of our positions, and forced the Malay Brigade off a great part of the Pasir Panjang ridge: after dark the brigade was brought back into the Alexandra area, where they covered the main ordnance depot and the Alexandra magazine. The Alexandra hospital was outside the new line and this was most unfortunate for the sick and wounded who were left in it; for when the Japanese troops entered the hospital, later, they carefully and methodically butchered the inmates.

The severest fighting was thus on the western side; and the companies of the 1st Battalion were slightly redistributed in the line that was being occupied more or less calmly on the eastern side of the city.

A Company in the Kallang position, was strengthened by

three companies of the 9th Coast Regiment R.A., who had been turned into infantry after their batteries had been destroyed on the day previous. More reinforcements from a similar source (anti-tank gunners, A.A. searchlight infantry, sappers and miners) came in during the course of the day, and, as a consequence, the positions on the creek were strengthened and a force was formed for counter-attacking if the sector were penetrated.

C Company, between Tanjong Rhu and Siglap, was taken back from the beaches that they had occupied on the 12th, and put into a position along an east–west-going road about a quarter of a mile to the north of the town—their front still faced south. The company was in its new line by 20.00 hours: its duties were, however, different, for it was now to assist in any counter-attacks, that might be necessary if the sector were penetrated.

D Company, which on the previous day had been acting as a rearguard to the units that were withdrawing from Changi, was drawn into James Force, and was allotted a sector in the flat, marshy land to the north of the Perseverance estate. The front to be held was far longer than had been stated (2,000 yards instead of 1,000), and the ground was blind and difficult, as rubber plantations that were intersected with drains and ditches alternated with swampy watercress beds. When the position was with great difficulty occupied, B Company was to the right of it, and the troops of the 18th Division were to the left. It was the weakest part of the James Force line.

B Company, which was also in James Force, strengthened its position between the northern end of Siglap drain and Kampong Eunos. This sector was also very blind, and was most unsuitable to a machine-gun company.

As has been said, the Japanese thrusts were still from the north and the west, but indications were not lacking that the enemy would soon be pressing on this eastern sector also. The troops of the 18th Division (to the left of D Company) were under a spasmodic bombardment, and A Company, on

RESISTANCE ALMOST FINISHED

the creek, were under mortar fire during the night. The district where the battalion's headquarters were situated was shelled and bombed all day, and the crowding of that already over-crowded quarter, was made worse, for the 13th A.A.S.L. battery, and parties from the 2/17th Dogras and the 1st Mysore Regiment, moved in during the day.

During the afternoon, General Percival assembled a conference of general officers to discuss whether the positions that the troops then held could be enlarged by counter-attacks. The officers who were present unanimously answered that a counter-attack was out of the question. The commander of the naval forces now ordered every vessel under his command to leave Keppel harbour and to make for Java. Trained staff officers who were not immediately required, technicians and hospital nurses were evacuated. Colonel Holmes was ordered to send away any officers, N.C.O.s and old hands of the Manchesters who would be competent to form and train a new battalion. Two officers and twenty-eight men from the battalion left Singapore harbour at 1 a.m. on February 14 in H.M.S. *Dragonfly*. In addition, the last stock of petrol on Pulau Bukum was destroyed: the Rear-Admiral, Malaya, ordered this to be done, when General Percival informed him that the Army could no longer guarantee that the enemy would not occupy the whole island.

In the town itself all ordinary work was left undone; for the native labourers had simply sought places where they felt slightly safer from the shelling and the bombing, and they there remained. The docks were deserted; nothing was removed from the streets, which were blocked with the rubble of the bombed houses; water ran to waste from the broken mains and the burst pipes of the ruined buildings. The dead were not moved from the places where they had fallen, and this was a terrible affliction; for in that climate, putrefaction begins a few hours after death.

February 14. The enemy's severest thrusts were against the western and northern parts of the line; in the west they pressed back our troops on a line Alexandra–Gillman barracks–Keppel golf-course; but here the 5th Bedfordshires and Hertfordshires and a composite unit of the Royal Engineers made a desperate stand and held them. In the north and centre, the McRitchie reservoir was lost; but a large pumping station remained in our hands, and the Japanese did not, for the time being, stop the flow of water into the town.

In the eastern sector, which had been relatively quiet since the Japanese guards had been stopped at Nee Son village, the enemy began to move past our front, and to probe it; and B and D Companies of the Manchester battalion became engaged. They were the only companies who actually came to grips with the Japanese during the campaign, and it will not be improper to state what happened in their own words. Both companies, it will be remembered, were now in James Force, and were holding posts in the plantations and drainage courses between the Changi and Paya Lebar roads.

At about 16.30 hours [runs the narrative] Captain Gunning (B Company) sent Captain Mangnall up with the second-in-command F.M.S.V.F. to get in touch with the left flank V.M.G. positions and to contact the O.C. of B Company 2nd Dogras. Half an hour later, firing broke out in this area, and Mangnall ordered Lance-Corporal Brown to open fire on some fifteen Japanese who were riding down a path on bicycles, some 250 yards away. Some casualties were inflicted, the remainder dispersed into the rubber. As the enemy seemed to be trying to work round the right flank, Sergeant Evans and Sergeant Stranghair made a reconnaissance; they reported that the Japanese were moving east through the rubber, and they found nine enemy dead alongside nine Japanese bicycles.

Two posts under Lieutenant Branston, of which Corporal Fensome and Lance-Corporal Boyne were in charge, were in action at the same time and inflicted some casualties on the enemy, who were in the north of the Perseverance estate. The L.A. sections F.M.S.V.F. were now placed under this officer's command by Captain Gunning—a third section was sent to Captain Gardner on the right flank of B Company. Shortly uncovered his whole line, and that he must at once bring back his company to a position on the Paya Lebar road. A reconnaissance of the new position revealed that parties of Japanese were already on the line of retirement and, what was worse, that they were on it in some strength.

In the undergrowth, west of the road [runs the company's diary] and facing up towards our oncoming troops, the enemy established an L.A. which was shifted by a bayonet charge led with great dash by Lieutenant Sully. Sergeant Whitehead was unfortunately wounded. All available troops were so engaged when the Japanese opened up across the road with four M.G.s ... The personnel of the company were then in danger of being surrounded and cut off. The only way of getting the guns out, since they were on trucks, was to rush the company's vehicles (four 3-tonners and one 15-cwt.) and the anti-tank gun and truck straight through the enemy's position. This operation was successful....

While B and D Companies were thus being drawn back, C Company was ordered to withdraw all its south, or seaward-facing posts, and to take up a line that ran right through that part of the town that lies to the north and west of Kallang. H.Q. was set up at the pineapple factory on Grove Road. From this it would seem as though the breakthrough on the James Force line had been more serious than the battalion records show, and that a last line was now being formed in the eastern suburbs. The new position was occupied in the early afternoon. A Company were not affected by these movements and remained in their positions.

Soon after B and D Companies had reached the line to which they had withdrawn after the break-through during the forenoon, they were ordered to come still farther back to a position that ran right through the suburb of the city that lies to the east of Kallang. It would serve no useful purpose to describe this new position, for while the troops were moving into it the end came. Orders to cease fire and to lay down arms were even then being sent to all units, and by about 20.30 hours the orders became operative. The battalion assembled at the pineapple factory during the night, and received their first orders from their captors on the following morning.

The decision to surrender had, indeed, been taken some hours previously: for at a conference that General Percival assembled during the morning, the director of civil defences reported that the water supply was even more precarious than it had been on the day before, and that it would not last much longer. Food supplies sufficed for a few days only; ammunition was very short (with the exception of S.A.A.); and as the Alexandra magazine was then virtually in the front line, with fires raging all round it, no ammunition could be drawn from it. The government offices were being kept open by a skeleton staff, and the Governor's secretariat was still at work; but all offices, and most shops were closed and abandoned. The electric power plant was still working; but it was within the firing zone, and was likely to be demolished at any moment.

It was clearly no good remaining on the defensive as we were [writes General Percival]. As I viewed the situation, the alternatives were either (a) to counter-attack immediately to regain control of the reservoirs and military food depots and to drive back the enemy's artillery, with a view to reducing the damage to the water-supply system, or (b) to capitulate immediately. Formation commanders were unanimously of the opinion that, in the existing circumstances a counter-attack was impracticable.[4]

After the first preliminaries had been completed, General Percival and the leading officers of his staff met General Yamashita at the Ford factory near Bukit Timah village, and it was there agreed that the garrison—Army, Navy and Air Force—should unconditionally surrender, and that all firing and operations of attack and defence should cease at 20.30 hours.

The news that Singapore had surrendered reached

[4] Dispatch, para. 576.

England on the same day, for British time is several hours earlier than eastern time, and when the Prime Minister gave such explanations as he was able in the House of Commons, he suggested (without daring to state it outright) that the British Army in Malaya and the British garrison in Singapore had been sufficiently powerful to hold back the Japanese, and to avert the disaster. An inquiry was, however, refused on the excuse that as the Army and the garrison were all captured, the inquiry could not be exhaustive. The contention was sound; but it may be doubted whether the inquiry was refused because the government and the Prime Minister were so respectful of truth that an approximation to it would not satisfy them. The materials that were then available for an investigation would not have sufficed to trace the disaster from its origins to its conclusion; but they would have revealed that the plan for defending Malaya and Singapore was a bad one, in that it did not rest upon sound military principles. Over and above this, the inquiry that the government refused would have made it patent that General Percival was never given sufficient forces to execute even the bad plan that was imposed upon him; far less was he ever allotted an army that could have defended Singapore and Malaya against the force that the Japanese devoted to their conquest. No army can bring its operations to a successful issue if it is very much weaker than its opponent in men and guns; if it has no tanks at all (notwithstanding that its enemy is well provided with them); if its anti-tank artillery is quite insufficient; and if the air forces that were to have assisted its operations have been driven from the sky. This is what any inquiry would have exposed: who can be surprised that it was refused?

CHAPTER III

THE 1st BATTALION IN CAPTIVITY

It must first be explained that the 1st Battalion was very much dispersed during the years 1943, 1944, and 1945. The Japanese formed their prisoners into groups which were composed of men from many units. Parties of Manchester men were put into more than one group, and as more information has survived about some parties than about others it is not possible to follow the fortunes of each with equal particularity. For the sake of clearness it will be as well to make a brief enumeration of the parties that have, thus far, been traced.

(1) The party that was sent to Changi camp immediately after the fall of Singapore. The bulk of the battalion was included in this group, and the parties that were subsequently separated were, for the most part, detachments from it.

(2) The party that was removed from Changi and sent to Kampong Tanjong (July 1942).

(3) The advanced Thailand party under Lieutenant Stevenson, which was removed from Changi and sent to Thailand (June 1942).

(4) The main Thailand party, which was sent up country from Changi in October 1942.

(5) The party that was sent to Thailand from Changi in April 1943.

(6) The party that was sent to Japan from Singapore (April 1943).

(7) The party that was sent to Formosa from Singapore (June 1944).

As would be expected, we have most information about the first of these groups, for, whilst the Manchesters were included in it, they were still a battalion. It is, indeed, possible to trace the fortunes of this group from the very beginning.

During the last hours of the siege, when the Manchester companies were taking up the positions in which they were to make their last stand, groups of demoralized men were from time to time wandering along the roads, and, as they passed, they advised the Manchester men to lay down their arms and to give in. The men answered that they would not do so, as they had plenty of ammunition left and they intended to use it. Notwithstanding the desperate position in which they stood, the men were cheerful until the very end, and when they marched away into captivity they were still in good heart. Colonel Holmes, who led them, put a photograph of the King on his back, where the men following him might see it, and the men sang as they marched. All felt, without being lectured, that it was now their duty to display no sorrow or depression, and none failed in his duty.

A large part of the garrison was sent to Changi camp, and

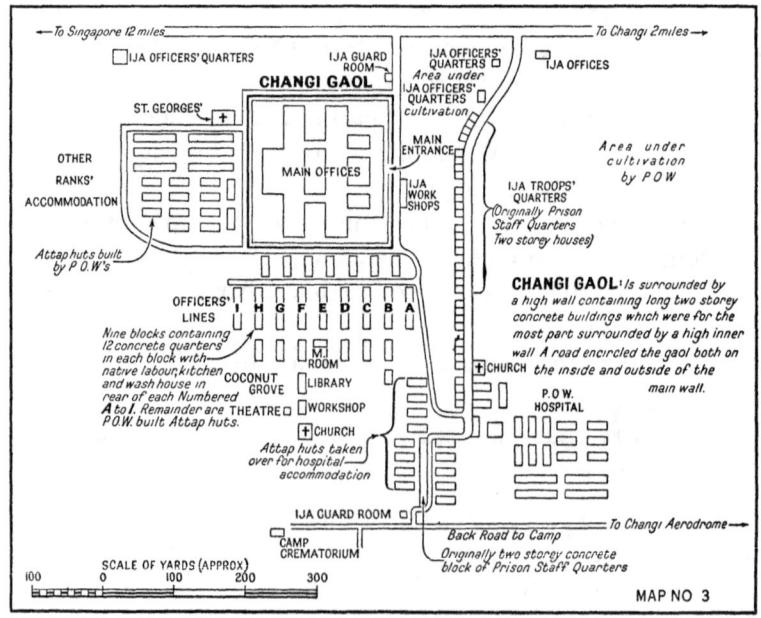

the divisional and brigade staffs continued to exercise their authority in administrative matters. The quarters allotted were far too small; for the block where the Manchesters were lodged was built to accommodate 100 persons. Actually 800-odd men were put into it, and there was the same degree of crowding elsewhere. The water supplies had been broken by bombing, and by the demolitions that were carried out when the area was abandoned; as a consequence sanitation had to be extemporized. Also the Japanese did not make themselves responsible for feeding their prisoners for some weeks after capture. The command headquarters staff, therefore, allotted accommodation to each unit as equitably as was possible, and all available food supplies were put into a general pool, and were then distributed by the R.A.S.C. staff. The R.E. units then set to work to secure water supplies for the camp, and successfully accomplished it. After a few weeks, each block had an assured supply of water, and there were no more bucket-and-pail queues numbering thousands of men. The water was only allowed to be used at certain hours, but it was a great contribution to the health of the prisoners that water should be obtainable, for meals were, thenceforward, better cooked and more regularly served. A tolerably hygienic sanitary system, called the borehole, was devised, and as flies are in the East, as elsewhere, great carriers of disease and poison, cigarette prizes were distributed to the best fly-hunters in the block. After a month, the improvement in the camp was quite remarkable, and there was nothing then in it that was positively dangerous to health. On the other hand, the very best that the camp had to offer would, by ordinary standards, be judged great hardship, for the officers and men were still living in a malarial tropical island, and were far more crowded than the inhabitants of the poorest Asiatic slum.

Moreover, it was soon apparent that the Japanese did not intend to issue enough food to their prisoners, and this made a new difficulty. A central fund was raised for buying food from outside, and great trouble was taken to learn the elements of Asiatic cooking in order that the rice which the Japanese did certainly issue should be prepared as palatably, and in as many ways, as possible. So much ingenuity was exercised that a variety of rice dishes were discovered, or invented, and a fairly eatable rice bread was prepared with yeast that was manufactured in the camp. In addition to all this, vegetable gardens were started, and a small but steady supply of potatoes, Chinese radishes, kong kang, spinach, and onions was assured. This is, moreover, not surprising, for English artisans, workmen, and labourers are as skilled gardeners as any people in Europe.

A new duty, the care of the sick, was, however, soon imposed upon the British staff. When Singapore fell, the sick and the wounded were scattered all over the town, in public and private hospitals; they were then all transferred to Changi, and a hospital, called Roberts hospital, was set up in what had previously been the R.A. barracks. As the Japanese practice was to supply as little as possible for the living and healthy, and practically nothing for the sick or the dying, this introduced a new hardship and a new difficulty. To Englishmen it was inconceivable that sick men should be without beds if beds were available, and practically every barrack bed was withdrawn to the hospital. Extra beds were, it is true, improvised out of pieces of old timber, string, and sacking; but many men slept on concrete or on the hard ground.

The crowding was, however, alleviated as time went by, for when the Japanese settled down to administer Singapore, they embarked upon an embracing programme of airfield construction, and even upon rebuilding. Working parties were then required daily, and were sent away from Changi camp. This considerably reduced the numbers in the concentration area, but the men engaged on working parties were not too well off. Some were, it is true, lodged in hutted camps, but large numbers were herded into native huts, which were very dirty, and the hours of work made it impossible for the men to improve matters as they had done at

Changi. The greater hardship was, however, that while they were in these working parties, the men were less in contact with their own officers than they were at Changi, and were more immediately subordinated to Japanese N.C.O.s and sergeants. A more particular account of these creatures and of their habits, will be given later.

One of the greatest achievements of the British staff at Changi was the establishing of what was called Changi University. Even in the old days of voluntary enlistment, the British Army drew in men with an extraordinary range of accomplishments, and in a modern British Army every class of the population is represented. Competent teachers of law, literature, mathematics, and engineering, were collected, and classes were given in these and even in other more recondite subjects. In addition, the Army education authorities organized regular daily classes for Army certificates of education. Attendance was voluntary, but high.

By the spring of 1942 life was as tolerable as it could be made in the circumstances, and the Japanese introduced a novelty which was turned to the benefit of the sick. Officers were allowed sixpence a day amenity pay, N.C.O.s fourpence, and men twopence-halfpenny. Later, officers were allowed a sum that approximated to their ordinary pay. A small proportion was actually paid to them, the remainder was banked—the recipients never knew where. In accordance with their custom, the Japanese stopped the amenity pay of sick men as soon as they went sick, and these additional allowances to those who were still in good health, enabled them to redress the cruel practice of the captors. A hospital fund, to which the officers contributed by a regular deposit from their allowance, was instituted, and the sick men in Roberts hospital received a small weekly allowance of cigarettes and comfort money. It was greatly appreciated, for the hot weather, the insufficient food (it was never enough in spite of everything that the cooks and the messing staffs could do), and the malaria-laden air of a tropical island, were by now making a heavy sick roll, and between two and three thousand men were being tended in the Roberts hospital.

Up to the summer of 1942 it can be said that although the Japanese treatment of their prisoners had fallen far below the standard that they had followed during their war against the Russians, at least they had not flagrantly disregarded the Geneva Convention. In August 1942, however, the Japanese authorities advisedly and deliberately defied it for, in that month, all officers and men were ordered to sign a form in which they undertook not to escape, nor to help another to escape, either directly or indirectly, and to acknowledge that any man who contravened any particular of this promise deserved the death sentence. It would be a waste of time to prove by quotation from books upon international law, that this order violated established practice. What is more important is that it disregarded an immemorial rule of military honour, for it has always been recognized, by Asiatics as well as by Europeans, that it is the plain duty of a prisoner of war to escape from captivity if he can. When this order was circulated, General Percival had been sent away to Japan, and Colonel Holmes was in charge of all British and Australian prisoners of war. Colonel Holmes and his staff made the strongest representations to the Japanese authorities, and the men, to whom the implications of the order were explained, refused to sign. The Japanese then ordered that everybody in Changi camp, the sick included, should move to Selarang barracks—a building which, in peace-time, had accommodated a single battalion.

The scenes on the road to Selarang [says the regimental *Gazette*] defy description. Thousands of troops making their way there, laden with all their belongings, and, in many cases, with the belongings of sick or weaker comrades who could not manage to carry them. . . . By the evening of the same day all troops were confined in the new area. Seven double-tier barrack blocks and a barrack square 250 by 150 yards, were allotted for the accommodation of 14,000 men. The peace-time allocation raining on the men's kit. That the men did not stand up when he came through; that, although it was a holiday, men were still sleeping; and that clothes were hung behind their beds. He was told that the men were sleeping because the I.J.A. had been working them all night, from 8.30 p.m. to between 2 and 3 a.m.; that the men hung their clothes up to dry because they had to work in the sea and mud, getting them soaked and filthy; that most of the men had only one pair of shorts; and that unless they hung them up to dry, they would put them on wet when they went to work again. He stated that the men should be taken out on holidays to do games and physical training, but when asked for ground on which to do it, the question was shelved. I was instructed that the cookhouse area should be levelled off; but when I asked for permission to use the transport vehicles, and where I should get the filling from, the answer was—" Ask Mr. Hosoe." The visit was really quite helpful.

Mr. Hosoe, to whom Major Hyde was so often directed, was an officer in charge of the administrative side of the Japanese engineer corps. He was a person of some authority; for he was surrounded by a large clerical staff; and Major Hyde never saw in him any trace of brutality or savagery; when interviewed, at all events, he was always polite and affable. But when Major Hyde, on the instructions of the Japanese inspecting officer, laid all these matters before Mr. Hosoe he was given, in reply, a long lecture about how visiting officers should be received. At the very end, because Major Hyde stuck to his point, notwithstanding Mr. Hosoe's endeavour to deflect him from it, a concession was granted that lorries and handcarts could be used to draw soil and rubble for the cookhouse area. This, however, was brought to nothing by the Japanese three-star private in charge of the handcarts, who said that he took his orders from Mr. Fukishima and not from Mr. Hosoe, and refused to release them. Major Hyde thus winds up the episode: " As a consequence, practically no work was done."

This was merely ridiculous; but, in some cases, this sub-division of authority, jealousy and fear of displeasing some distant higher authority was serious. Early in October there

DIPHTHERIA

was a nasty outbreak of diphtheria in the camp and Major Hyde made the following entry in his diary:

Had a long session with the Japanese guards in the morning over the diphtheria epidemic, and over sending them to hospital. They said they could only send away very sick men: little sick men must remain in camp. Tried to get more accommodation and permission for the men to sleep outside and on the beaches. When the commander (a two-year private soldier) saw what I wanted, he replied, ". . . cannot understand, wait till tomorrow. Ask officer." There is no senior Nippon N.C.O. or officer living in this camp who can take a decision in an emergency.

It is needless to add that when Major Hyde renewed his representations on the following day, he was given another evasive, postponing answer.

The explanation is, probably, that the privileges of high rank in an Asiatic army are very high, and that it is risky to draw a senior officer's attention to anything that may be unpleasant to him. If this is so, the prisoners at Kampong Tanjong were exceptionally ill placed, for Captain Fukishima, who was in charge of it, was not the kind of man who would risk anything. As far as those who were most in contact with him could judge, he had been at great pains to secure himself a safe job, and he was determined not to lose it. An officer in his post must, however, have been in no very easy position, for the higher Japanese officers seem to have been very much feared. A flying visit from any one of them was a serious matter.

But, although high rank was treated with unbounded deference, authority, as such, appears to have been weak and vacillating on all major issues. The records from Kampong Tanjong testify to a maladministration and inefficiency that is surprising in such a purposeful people as the Japanese. In small matters of daily routine the N.C.O.s seem to have been utterly without method. Working parties who had received orders from one N.C.O. were given new orders by another, which the first N.C.O. countermanded. Even nominal returns were filled in wrong for lack of the most elementary discrimination. What, however, is most unexpected, is that the reclamation work at which the whole camp was engaged, was very ill done. Those who have visited the great ports and harbours of Japan would expect that Japanese civil engineering would always be well performed. This, however, is what Major Hyde records about the sea wall on the Kalang river.

Another very high tide. A great amount of the work done has been damaged by these tides. The piles which were driven 20 feet into the mud have moved sideways owing to the weight of the reclaimed soil on the land side. The piles have also taken a general list to sea, their tops being, in places, 9 feet out of the original alignment.

There are many other entries of the same kind—whether the sea wall was ever satisfactorily completed does not appear. The last entry on the subject is "*November 13, 1942*: Sea wall completely collapsed." The records of this camp end at about this date.

The Japanese high command was presumably already feeling the burden of maintaining armies that were so deployed as theirs, for even at this time (late autumn, 1942) the Japanese detachment in the Pacific island of Guadalcanal was brought to a standstill because its supplies were spasmodic and precarious. The Japanese army commanders in Burma must also have foreseen that it might some day be difficult to hold so distant a conquest unless their supply lines were improved. In order, therefore, to make timely provision against a British counter-attack, the Japanese authorities embarked upon the immense project of building a railway right across Thailand and southern Burma, and so connecting Moulmein to Bangkok. A glance at the map will show what labour and skill were required to bring the undertaking to a successful issue: for many hundreds of miles of track followed the valley of the Kwab Noi; thereafter it scaled the mountains on the Burma–Thailand frontier at the Three Pagoda Pass, and joined the Moulmein–Tavoy railway at Thanbazayat.

CHOLERA

The first railway party was sent away early (June 1942); twenty Manchester men were in it, under Lieutenant Stevenson, and we have but little information about them.[1] The big transfer occurred in October 1942, when the Japanese authorities ordered that all fit men in Changi should be moved to Thailand. The first echelon, which was a composite group from the Manchesters, the Loyals, the Gordons, and the Argyll and Sutherland Highlanders, left Changi on October 27.[2] The Japanese officers assured everybody that it would be a change for the better—they would live in better air, they would be less crowded, and they would enjoy better food.

This group was sent to Chungkai, on the Kwab Noi river. They reached it after a journey in which they suffered severely, for they were herded into trucks by day and by night in such numbers that nobody could lie down, and no arrangements whatever were made to allow the men to answer the calls of nature. The staging camp at Ban Pong was so flooded that the water was up to the sleeping platforms. All this was, moreover, a preliminary, or an introduction to what was coming.

The first echelon worked on the Chungkai section of the line until January 1943, when they were moved up the line to Bankau, where they did not remain for long, for in May they were ordered to march to Tarkanun. Each camp was worse than the one before, and it was here that cholera cases were first reported.

After working at Tarkanun for several more months, the party was moved still farther up the line to Kan Krai. The mixed group which had left Singapore in October was 650 strong—it now numbered about 180. The party was still working at Kan Krai when the railway was completed; the Japanese then ordered that everybody should return to Changkai—only thirty-seven officers and men of the original party were then surviving.

Another party, called F and H groups, was moved out of

[1] Party number 3, see *ante*, p. 79. [2] Party number 4, see *ante*, p. 79.

Singapore in April, 1943; and a detachment of 320 Manchester men under Major Hyde was part of it.[3] The officers of the party had been assured that they and their men would be moved by rail, for their destination was farther up the line, near the Three Pagoda Pass. Actually, the party was marched for 192 miles through staging camps that were unfit for animals, and, what was worse, through a district where cholera was raging. The men were exhausted, and their strength was terribly reduced when they were at the end of their march, when Major Hyde made the following entry in his diary:

All men were very tired. Spent day cleaning up the camp area. Rations shocking, 15 oz. of rice, practically nothing else. Troops were wet and cold. Camp in terrible condition. Japanese officer arrived 6.0 p.m. Only officers' hut has roof. Hours of work 08.30 hours to 19.00 hours. This means reveille at 05.30 hours. Breakfast in darkness. Return to camp after dark. No lights, no cooking utensils available except our twelve containers and a few Jap. rice cookers. Feeding in relays, every meal in darkness.

On the day following Major Hyde made the sinister entry, "Private Champion down with cholera." On May 30 when the party had completed their first month at San Krie, the entry ran thus:

Rogation Sunday: 24 deaths during 24 hours. Diarrhoea and dysentry rife, almost no treatment available. Two more saline injections arrived for cholera patients. Isolation hospital full. 105 patients, some probably acute dysentry. Cooking utensils insufficient to keep patients supplied with hot water. Ultimatum to Jap. guard, 3 days holiday to clean camp. Men lying in ordinary hospital trying to keep warm with bits of sacking.

Thereafter, the entries became worse and worse, and on the following Sunday Major Hyde made this record:

General post takes place. Camp deaths stand at 128 out of 1,600 approximately. Australian camp 47 deaths. New Australia camp 84 out of 2,000. British camp north 64 out of 600, all within a fortnight to three weeks.

[3] Party number 5, see *ante*, p. 79.

BUSHIDO IN PRACTICE

It was not until late in September that there was any relaxation, so that these entries are a mere introduction or a preliminary to the dreadful record. Three hundred and twenty Manchester men were in F and H forces when they left Singapore, and 223 of them never returned.

A considerable number of prisoners appear to have been left in Singapore after the drafts had been sent up-country to the Thailand railway, and a Borneo draft was formed out of this residue in April 1943.[4] It was about 1,500 strong and thirty-two Manchester men were included in it. This group never reached Borneo, and after a call at Formosa, they were dispatched to Japan. Their transport ship that carried them was bombed and sunk, and the Japanese, who were as cowardly as they were cruel, abandoned ship and made no attempt to save the prisoners. A Japanese destroyer did, however, pick up as many men as were still alive after four hours in the water, and it would appear as though most of the Manchester men were saved. They were eventually placed in a camp on Honshu island, where they were joined by another party of Manchesters about whom we know very little. The prisoners at Honshu were employed in mines and quarries, and it does certainly appear as though the Japanese authorities in Japan were men of a better class than the Japanese authorities abroad, for of the fifty-seven Manchesters who were imprisoned at Honshu, only four died in captivity.

The railway was completed in October 1943, and prisoners were then moved back to their base camps. Some of the Manchester men were returned to Chungkai. Major Hyde, with what was left of F and H forces, was back in Changi (Singapore) by December. Soon after the Thailand prisoners were thus returned to Changi another alteration was made in it. For the Japanese authorities decided to station their own troops in the Selarang section of Changi; they cleared Changi jail, and put our prisoners into it. It was rare that the Japanese did anything indulgent or good-natured, and

[4] Party number 6, see *ante*, p. 79.

the prisoners in Selarang were very much surprised that their captors allowed them to take away all the small aids to comfort that they had accumulated at Selarang (electric light fittings, etc.).

Chungkai, where the great base camp was established is in Thailand, on the middle part of the Kwab Noi valley. Matters were much improved at this place, after the prisoners returned from the railway camps; but the diseases that had been contracted during the earlier months, beriberi, malaria, and starvation, continued to take their toll, and, in the words of the regimental *Gazette*, the camp cemetery, which was planned for 160 graves in 1942, now contained nearly 1,400.

The alleviations in Chungkai did not, unfortunately, continue until the war was over for the Japanese drew 10,000 prisoners out of the camp during May and June 1944 and dispatched them to Japan. A party of about 1,300 men left Siam on June 6, and sixty-three Manchesters were included in it.[5] This group went to Min (Borneo), thence to Manila, and thence to Formosa. The captors treated these men as they had treated their prisoners in the railway camps, and the list of those who died in the suffocating holds of the *Hofoku Maru* is very high. Although the men were reduced to the lowest possible state by starvation, dirt, and exposure, their spirit was still unbroken, and when the doctors reported that four sick men could only be saved by a blood transfusion, four Manchester men at once offered the blood of their emaciated bodies, and insisted that it should be given.

The *Hofoku Maru* was machine-gunned by Allied planes, and then bombed and sunk when she was two days out of Manila. The Japanese officers and men abandoned their ship when the machine-gun bullets began to hit her, and when she was bombed and sunk the prisoners were alone. As many men as could got out of the prisoners' holds (a large number remained in them for the ship sank in two minutes) took to the water, were picked up by a Japanese destroyer,

[5] Party number 7, see *ante*, p. 79.

and were carried to Formosa. The officers of the destroyer were no better than the officers of the *Hofoku Maru*, for they refused to give any medical attention to the survivors and, what was worse, they refused to give drink to the wounded.

Of the 1,287 officers and men who were embarked in the *Hofoku Maru*, only 243 reached Formosa. They were virtually naked, and after being issued with a rice sack per man, they were sent to the prison camp at Takau. A relatively small number of prisoners had been at this place for some time past. Lieutenant Nagayama was the Japanese commandant, and Major T. W. Moor, R.A., was the senior British officer. We do not know much about this camp; and what we do know is bad. Nearly 75 per cent of the prisoners suffered from malaria; and beriberi made ravages. Lieutenant Nagayama refused, obstinately, to stir a hand on behalf of the prisoners; and the Japanese doctors who visited the camp from time to time merely looked at the dying, suffering men and went away again. For eighteen whole months a diet that would have alleviated the beriberi was refused.

There appear to have been some Manchester men at the camp before the survivors from the *Hofoku Maru* arrived, and of one of them—Private Joinson—we know this. In April 1943, he attempted to escape in company with an American soldier of the U.S. Marine Corps: both were captured, and were condemned to death after being subjected to severe torture. Then, by Lieutenant Nagayama's orders, they were paraded before the camp, where all present were stirred by admiration for Private Joinson, who seemed as unconcerned as though he were on an ordinary parade at home, notwithstanding that his whole body was racked with pain, and that he had only a few more minutes to live.

After these withdrawals were completed a large number of men were still left in the Thailand camps, and they suffered considerably during the Allied air attacks on the railway.

In February 1945 there was a general withdrawal to a

large, consolidated, prisoners' camp at Kanburi, and it was here that the prisoners received the news of their liberation. We have not much information about the state under which the prisoners lived at Kanburi, for we have no exact figures of the numbers that were evacuated to it, nor of the sick lists, nor of the death-roll. What we do know is that as defeat approached the Japanese, so their treatment of their prisoners improved. "All base camps were improved," says the regimental *Gazette*, "and generally smartened up. Working conditions were much easier, and food moderately good." Thenceforward, only petty vexations were inflicted.

Some officers cannot endorse the statement that food deliveries were improved; for they say that the Japanese were no longer able to issue an adequate ration to their prisoners. They add, moreover, that this positively worried the Japanese as the clouds of retribution were then gathering fast.

By this time, however, the lot of the prisoners was slightly better, in that Red Cross parcels were, at last, being delivered. One parcel was delivered to every ten men, on Sundays: it was not much, but it was appreciated. And on this point one must remember that Red Cross comforts first began to be delivered at the end of 1944: it was an alleviation that the Japanese only allowed when they were anxious about the future.

It will probably be best to say no more than this about the barbarous treatment that our prisoners endured, for it has already been exposed in several places. Mr. John Coast has displayed every relevant circumstance in his book, *The Railroad of Death*; in a special number entitled "Malaya, Thailand, and Burma", the regimental *Gazette* gives an accurate and extremely restrained account of the whole business. Though copies are not easily obtainable, the trials of these Japanese officers who were brought before an Allied court have been printed and circulated, and can be consulted. It will, therefore, serve no useful purpose to re-inspect facts that have already been so thoroughly ventilated; and it

Major Hyde testifies to Captain Wakabayashi's consistent endeavours to improve matters, and Mr. John Coast frequently refers to another Japanese officer who was never anything but humane and forbearing.

In bare justice, attention must also be drawn to one more point. In December 1943, when the fortunes of the Japanese armies were still high, and when their victories were still unchecked, the Japanese military police ordered Lieutenant-Colonel Dillon of the R.A.S.C. to report on the state of the prisoners in the Thailand camps. Colonel Dillon did what was asked of him, and exposed the abominations of those places in a sober and extremely dignified paper. What were the preoccupations of the Japanese military police when they demanded that report, and what happened to it after they received it? Nobody can now trace its course through the complicated and tortuous channels of the Japanese military administration, and nobody can say what were its consequences in a service where authority was so divided and subdivided. Some of the prisoners who survived the Thailand camps believe that the alleviations which they subsequently enjoyed at Chungkai and Kanburi, were largely due to the representations that some Japanese authorities made to Tokyo; others are sceptical and maintain that no Japanese officer, high or low, was willing to lose favour with the hierarchy by making a stand on behalf of the prisoners, and that the report that Colonel Dillon was asked to prepare was, by those who received it, used as a face-saving expedient, or a safeguard against subsequent inquiries. It is natural that men who suffered so much should be of that opinion; still, if all circumstances are dispassionately considered, it is only fair to assume that Colonel Dillon's report was called for in good faith by a group of Japanese officers who thought that their service had befouled itself, and who wished for a reform.

Finally, what happened to Major Buchan provokes reflection as it supplies evidence of the hidden decencies that lie concealed in the heart of a Japanese officer of the worst sort.

MAJOR BUCHAN'S TREATMENT

The affair began at Chungkai, where men from the Manchester battalion were working on the railway with parties from the Gordons and the Loyals. Lieutenant Kiriama, of the Japanese engineer corps, was superintending the work, and he, being anxious to acquire a reputation for zeal and energy, struck the men freely, and slapped their faces whenever he felt inclined.

After suffering this for some time Major Buchan and his officers decided to order that all work should stop when the next case was reported to them, and, as this occurred soon after, the order was given and the men obeyed it. Lieutenant Kiriama then selected Lieutenant Sully for punishment, made him hold a shovel over his head, and ordered him to remain in that posture before all his men. On seeing this, Major Buchan ordered Lieutenant Sully to put down his shovel and to come to lunch. Soon afterwards, Lieutenant Kiriama appeared, and Major Buchan told him that it was improper that an officer should suffer indignity before his men. Lieutenant Kiriama repeated his order; Lieutenant Sully refused to obey it, and all the men, including the men from the Gordons and the Loyals refused to work. Major Buchan and Lieutenant Sully were now put into the guardroom, where they were made to stand to attention for an hour. They were then brought before the Japanese camp commandant.

Lieutenant Kiriama opened with an angry tirade, to which Major Buchan replied that he had been placed in charge of the working parties, and that he would not allow an officer to be misused before his men. After listening impassively to both sides the Japanese camp commandant gave judgment. He opened with a long lecture on the enormity of the offence that had been committed; sabotaging the work of the Imperial Japanese army, and for so long as the lecture continued, things looked ill for the offenders. At the very end, however, the admonition took a sudden and unexpected turn. Major Buchan and Lieutenant Sully had never committed the offence before, and the camp commandant had therefore decided to dismiss them without punishment. If this had stood alone, it would have been a heavy blow to Kiriama's pride: actually the blow was doubled, for he was reprimanded in private.

Soon afterwards, one of the interpreters warned Major Buchan that Kiriama was seeking vengeance, and told him, that, if he were ever in real danger he would do well to look Kiriama in the face, and then to repeat some Japanese words which the interpreter made Major Buchan learn by heart.

A few weeks later Major Buchan and his men were moved up the line to a camp where Kiriama was in sole charge. At this place the rations were even worse than they had been at Chungkai; the listless and exhausted men were quite unable to accomplish the tasks allotted to them; the programme of work fell behind schedule; and Kiriama's credit with his superiors was in jeopardy. He therefore ordered the work to be continued after the hour at which work normally stopped; Major Buchan refused to transmit the order and the men supported him. Major Buchan and Lieutenant Moir Byers of the Gordons were brought before Kiriama, who at once recognized Major Buchan. Both officers were taken to the parade ground and were there beaten and ill-used for a whole half-hour, as a preliminary to what was to follow. The men stood staunchly by their officers and were not in the least intimidated by the savage exhibition on the parade ground; they were indeed with difficulty restrained from attempting to rescue their officers by force, and contrived to let Kiriama know that not a stroke of work would be done if Major Buchan were executed. Two lieutenant-colonels added their warnings, but Kiriama was inflexible, and answered that Major Buchan and Lieutenant Moir Byers were to die; this, indeed, was what he intended at that moment.

When the beating that preceded the execution was over, Major Buchan and Lieutenant Moir Byers were ordered to kneel down, and Kiriama and his sergeant-major drew their swords. The two English officers now prepared for death; and before Major Buchan kneeled on the ground to receive the swordstroke, he warned Kiriama that he would increase his difficulties a thousandfold if he executed his purpose; for one thing was quite certain, that the men would not work again if their officers were put to death for attempting to protect them. Then, at the very end, Major Buchan repeated the words that the interpreter had taught him: their meaning is, "*I appeal to your better feelings*". Kiriama was thunderstruck; several times he repeated the words himself, as though he expected that Major Buchan would add to them. Major Buchan said nothing and awaited the outcome which was that the death penalty was cancelled and that a further course of ill-usage was substituted for it.

A Japanese officer to whom Japanese rules of conduct are familiar would probably understand Kiriama's behaviour and motives without difficulty: to Englishmen both are quite unexplainable. Kiriama was a savage ruffian, but he sacrificed the vengeance that he had sought for so long when the words, "I appeal to your better feelings," were addressed to him. Would the same appeal to a European ruffian of the same quality as Kiriama have been as effective?

CHAPTER IV

1st BATTALION
JUNE 1942—JANUARY 1945

THE first attempt to reconstitute the 1st Battalion was made a few days before Singapore fell, when Colonel Holmes was ordered to send away a party of officers and men who would serve as a nucleus for the new reconstituted battalion. During the night of February 13/14 a specialist party twenty-six strong, from the Manchesters, a similar party from the 2nd Battalion The East Surrey Regiment, and three men from the R.A.O.C. embarked in H.M.S. *Dragonfly*, a small river gunboat, which sailed during the dark hours. When daylight came up, the *Dragonfly* was still at no great distance from Singapore and she was soon recognized by the Japanese planes which were then reconnoitring the approaches to the harbour. Nine planes attacked the *Dragonfly* soon afterwards, and as the first stick of bombs hit her in the mess deck she sank at once. Most of the crew and the parties on board perished; but four men contrived to reach Sumatra, after enduring great trials and sufferings.

No members of the old 1st Battalion were thus incorporated into the new one which was formed in June 1942, by a War Office Order that the 6th Battalion was to be reconstituted into the 1st. When this order was issued the 6th Battalion was at Withernsea, ten miles east of Hull; Lieutenant-Colonel J. H. Orgill was the commanding officer and Major H. B. D. Crozier was the second-in-command. The battalion was an ordinary infantry battalion with a normal strength of about 800.

In August 1942, Lieutenant-Colonel Orgill was ordered to take up a staff appointment in South-Eastern command, and Lieutenant-Colonel H. S. Hoseason relieved him. At about the same time the battalion was ordered to be reconstituted

ALLOTTED TO THE 53RD DIVISION

as a divisional support battalion. These battalions, which were then being formed, were concerned principally with light A.A. defences and their numerical strength was considerably lower than that of ordinary infantry battalions (580–600). The battalion was now moved to Gandale Camp, near Catterick; from there to Chilston Park, Kent; and from there to Hildenborough, four miles from Tonbridge. The battalion was now placed under the command of the 53rd Division and was thus constituted:

A Company (Major T. A. Hibbard) was the Divisional Support Company.

B Company (Major H. B. D. Crozier) was attached to the 158 Brigade.

D Company (Captain C. B. Walker) was attached to the 160 Brigade.

H.Q. Company (Captain A. I. F. Simpson) and C Company (Captain J. P. Pardoe) were to provide officers and men for A, B, and D Companies, and were to act as holding companies.

The battalion was re-equipped at Hildenborough and was training in its new duties during the remainder of the year.

The year 1942 was not a particularly cheerful one: the Germans were triumphant throughout Europe, and it was then difficult to conceive that sufficient forces would ever be collected to make them loose their hold, far less expel them. For the United States, who alone were able to assemble the military strength that might in the end turn the tide of war in our favour, were, at the time, unable to check the Japanese conquests in the south-western Pacific; it was, indeed, during the first half of the year that Burma was overrun, and that the Japanese completed their immense deployment in the islands of the eastern archipelago. In Russia the German armies advanced all through the summer, captured the industrial district of the Donetz basin and even reached the Maikop oilfields in the foothills of the Caucasus. In North Africa, General Rommel drove our army before him and was with great difficulty brought to a stand at Alamein, the last defence line of the Nile delta. Far-sighted persons, and persons who were privileged to inspect state papers upon the conduct of the war, were still reasonably confident that not even this succession of victories would suffice to protect Germany and Japan against the overwhelming pressure that England, the United States, and Russia would eventually exert. For military officers in high positions, with the documents and maps of the War Office and Cabinet war rooms before them, could see that the Japanese armies in the East and the German armies in Russia were very much over-deployed. They were, in consequence, morally certain that the board would soon be set for a great counter-offensive; and that when launched it would have surprising consequences.

Officers and men who were doing military exercises in the very heart of the English countryside, and who got their news from the morning and evening broadcasts (if they had time to listen to them) or from the daily papers (if they had time to read them), had no such alleviations, and were only able to protect themselves against the depressing effect of bad news by ignoring it, or by persuading themselves that bad news was good. Now although it has to be admitted that the English practise this artifice more adroitly than any nation in the world, and that this is very much to their credit, as their skill in it is a by-product of their courage and firmness in danger, it nevertheless remains true that the English can distinguish good news from bad, and that they are thankful enough when they are relieved of the duty of pretending that things are going well when, in point of fact, they are going badly. During the last months of the year 1942 the first indications of final victory were, at last, declaring themselves, and the effect upon the men was so remarkable that it was noted in the battalion diary. Late in October the British 8th Army attacked and utterly defeated the Germans and Italians at Alamein; for the remainder of the year the news from that quarter was of a German retreat that was often

BETTER NEWS AT LAST

equivalent to a rout. In the first week of November an Anglo-American army landed in North Africa and established itself firmly in Algeria. These were the first British victories since Field-Marshal Wavell's campaign in North Africa two years before. Two years is a long time to wait for good news, and it is very much to the honour of the British Army that the two-years wait had never depressed them.

The exercises upon which the 53rd Division was engaged were, moreover, becoming more and more indicative of the task that the Army would sooner or later undertake, and were stimulating evidence that a return to the continent of Europe was not a vain hope (as the faint-hearted had asserted), but a project that was being methodically perfected. Exercise Thetford was "to train formations in a rapid advance and a subsequent withdrawal across water obstacles". Exercise Canute 3 was to practise "moving the unit to a port of embarkation, crossing an imaginary sea, and landing as part of a follow-up division".

In February 1943, the battalion was moved to Sheerness, and it was from this place that the officers and men took part in a severe endurance test called Exercise Spartan, which lasted for thirteen days. During the first months of the year, the indications that the German fortunes were on the wane became stronger; for a Russian counter-offensive which had been started during the first winter months culminated in the great victory of Stalingrad, where a German army of a quarter of a million men was virtually annihilated; and in the relief of Leningrad, which had been practically encircled for many months. In North Africa the 8th Army were still reaping the harvest of their great victory at Alamein and had reached Medenine in Tunisia.

In May the battalion was moved from Sheerness to Chilston Park camp, and its constitution was once again drastically changed. The battalion's equipment and tactical training had been much altered by the order which converted it from an infantry to a divisional support formation, but at least the old framework of a battalion—A, B, C, D, and a

Headquarters company—had been retained. The establishment of a divisional support battalion was now changed, and the old companies were in large measure replaced by a new formation called a group. The consequences of this are most easily appreciated if they are set out in a diagram.

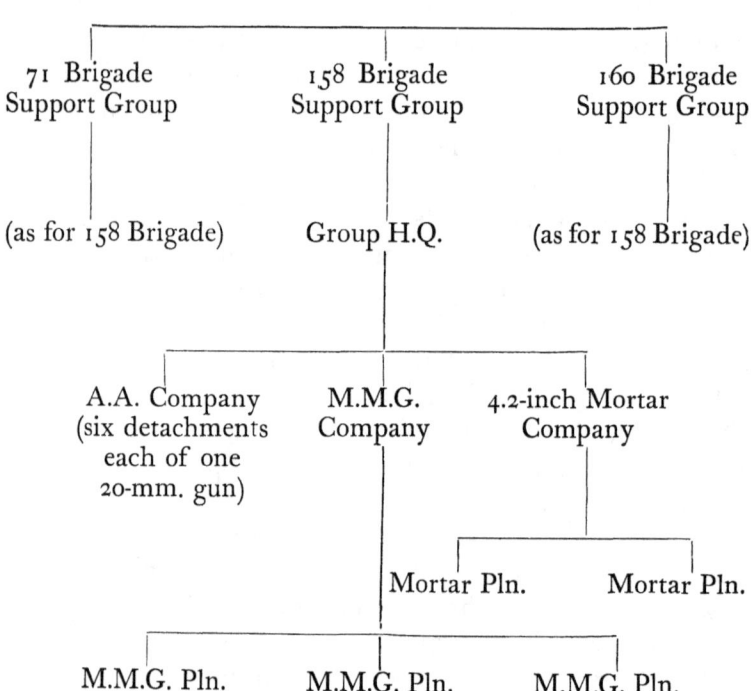

The immediate consequence was that what may be called the corporate life of the battalion, which has always exerted so strong an influence over British units, almost ceased; for the support groups were much separated from the headquarters group, and, when they were doing their training and their field exercises, they were more under the supervision and control of their Brigade Commander than of their own commanding officer.

During the summer and autumn of the year 1943,

degree that is rarely possible in war, when officers whom the men know well are so suddenly and so often replaced by newcomers. Even the changes in organization had been productive of one good consequence, that the officers had been given a more comprehensive training in tactics than they would have received if the battalion had, all the while, remained a machine-gun unit. Above all, the fighting spirit of the battalion was high. The officers and men were well aware that the task of fighting and beating the very flower of the German army was likely to be far harder than anything that had hitherto been accomplished by the British army; but nobody doubted that it would be successfully performed. Nothing now remained to be done but to receive and to execute the order to embark.

The battalion's order of battle was:

Commanding Officer: Lieut.-Colonel C. H. P. Harington, M.C.
Second-in Command: Major H. B. D. Crozier
Adjutant: Captain L. Marsh
Intelligence Officer: Captain J. Paynter
Signals Officer: Captain S. C. M. Dobbs
Quartermaster: Captain C. T. A. Basham
Technical Adjutant: Lieutenant J. Thorpe
Officer Commanding A Company: Major G. L. Northcote
Second-in-Command A Company: Captain C. A. Simpson
Officer Commanding B Company: Major E. F. Woolsey
Second-in-Command B Company: Captain G. R. Abbs
Officer Commanding C Company: Major G. A. Tod
Second-in-Command C Company: Captain D. C. L. Nolda
Officer Commanding D Company: Major C. B. Walker
Second-in-Command D Company: Captain J. P. Pardoe
Officer Commanding H.Q. Company: Captain N. J. Clapham

* * * * *

The order to embark was received on June 14, and the battalion moved off in the following order. The advance party, under Major Crozier, left for the marshalling area at Woodford on the 15th. A Company entrained at Sittingbourne on the following day and went to the marshalling

THE BATTALION LANDS IN NORMANDY

area with the 71st Brigade. On June 18 the remainder of the battalion followed; before they left, the following message from the Colonel of the Regiment was read out to them: " We at home, will follow the fortunes of the battalion with interest. The honour of the Regiment is in your hands; we know that you will not fail ".

The battalion moved through Maidstone, Lewisham, and London, and reached Woodford (Essex) at about 11.00 hours. It was a lovely summer night, and as the long column passed through the sleeping countryside a succession of flying bombs passed overhead. " The bombs followed us all that dark drive," says the regimental *Gazette*, " and when we arrived in London, just after dawn, some of them dropped far too close to be pleasant."[1]

The officers and men remained at Woodford for two rather trying days. "There was a vast amount of sand in that camp, and this, combined with the strong winds meant, of course, that you slept in sand, had sand for every meal, and found it very hard to keep the weapons free of it".[2] There was general relief when the battalion was moved to the West India docks and was embarked in s.s. *Samneva*. B Company were carried in s.s. *John A. Sutter*, an American liberty ship which carried 2 Canadian Corps H.Q.

The *Samneva* left her berth just before midnight, and steamed down the river to Sheerness, where she anchored in the early morning. For five days, which the officers considered very trying, the *Samneva* remained at anchor; but at 21.00 hours on the 25th the Captain weighed and took his place in a large convoy. At dusk on the 26th, the *Samneva* was off Arromanches, and on the day following disembarkation began. When the battalion moved to its first point of concentration, just south of Bayeux, thirty-five officers and 699 N.C.O.s and men had been put ashore. This, however, was not effected without misadventure. For the commanding officer, and the battalion headquarters which should have

[1] *Manchester Regiment Gazette*, Vol. XII, No. 1, p. 41.
[2] Ibid., p. 42.

been one of the first parties to land, was, in point of fact, the last. They were transferred from the ship to a large self-propelled raft, called a "Rhino", and as the propelling machinery broke down the raft and its complement drifted about; when the officers and men were, at last, rescued they had been without food or drink for thirty-six hours.

The battalion was under the command of the 53rd (Welsh) Division (Major-General R. I. Ross, D.S.O., M.C.), whose composition was:

71 Infantry Brigade:
    1st East Lancashire Regiment
    1st Oxfordshire and Buckinghamshire Light Infantry
    1st Highland Light Infantry
158 Infantry Brigade:
    4th Royal Welch Fusiliers
    6th Royal Welch Fusiliers
    7th Royal Welch Fusiliers
160 Infantry Brigade:
    4th Welch Regiment
    1/5 Welch Regiment
    2nd Monmouthshire Regiment
Divisional Artillery:
    81 Field Regiment
    83 Field Regiment
    133 Field Regiment
    71 Anti-Tank Regiment
    116 Light A.A. Regiment
Divisional Engineers:
    285 Field Park Company
    244 Field Company
    282 Field Company
    555 Field Company
Reconnaissance and M.G.:
    53 Recce Regiment
    1st Battalion The Manchester Regiment

The 53rd Division was under the command of 12 Corps (Major-General Niel Ritchie, C.B., D.S.O., M.C.), whose other formations were the 59th and 43rd Divisions.

* * * * *

BATTLE TACTICS REVIEWED

It is necessary, at this point, to make a brief digression upon the changes that had taken place in the conduct of operations since the British armies had operated in France and Flanders, thirty years previously. The digression is the more necessary in that anybody who studies the campaign upon which the battalion was about to be engaged can hardly fail to be bewildered that such changes should have occurred in so short a time. In the war that nearly all Englishmen are familiar with (1914–1918) immense armies confronted one another for years on end without being able to expel their opponents from the hastily prepared trenches that they held; and it was only after four years of continuous battering that the German armies made an advance of strategic significance, and that the British, French, and American armies did the same, though with greater effect.

The campaign in Holland and northern Germany, on the other hand, is a struggle in which field fortifications far stronger than any that could have been prepared twenty-five years previously are repeatedly breached and carried; in which villages that have been turned into fortresses are cleared on a first assault; and in which positions prepared with all the elaborations that are possible in a mechanical age are overrun by the attacking side. The least curious can hardly fail to inquire, " What is the explanation of this revolution in military science? " Unless an explanation is attempted the narrative that follows would be very difficult to understand.

It should be made clear, at the outset, that although the fluctuations that occurred between 1914 and 1940 in the relative power of attack and defence was exceptional, it was so only by its speed. A detailed examination of the whole subject would certainly prove that fluctuations have been continuous although their pace has been slower. At the beginning of the eighteenth century, for instance, fortified lines were so strong that Marlborough never dared to assault them directly, and always passed them by subterfuge and manœuvre. A hundred years later Napoleon's advice to his generals was, "*Si vous voulez être battus retranchez vous*". These two facts are, in themselves, evidence of a change whose successive stages have not been closely examined: but if the examination were made it would almost certainly show a steady increase in the efficiency of small-arms fire which culminated in the extraordinary power of the machine-gun in the war of 1914. General Daun's confidence in defensive tactics, Contade's surprise at the effects of the British rifle-fire at Minden, the unshaken defence of the British squares at Waterloo, the murderous losses that the Prussian infantry with their needle guns inflicted upon the Austrians, the failure of the Federal armies to break into the Confederate positions in the Wilderness, are, probably, writings on the wall, which the leaders of military opinion in Europe ignored or did not appreciate. For it must be added in bare justice, that in the year 1914 all military experts in Europe misread the signs; the German, the French, the Italian, and the British armies were all trained for a war of manœuvre, when a war of manœuvre was no longer possible.

If, however, the contrast between the two wars is to be even briefly explained, we must, first, be clear on one point: Why did the deadlock of the 1914 war occur? Why was offensive power so completely eclipsed? The question has been examined in a voluminous literature and it is, by good fortune, unnecessary to review the whole of it; for Sir James Edmonds's survey is authoritative: no professional soldier has ever disputed it. After preparing for a war on the Napoleonic model—a war of strategical moves, marches and counter-marches—the general staffs of all countries were suddenly involved in siege warfare, and they did not grasp the implications of it. Siege warfare, as it was then understood, was that a breach was made in a fortified perimeter, and that the attacking troops were poured into it from trenches that had been prepared in the approaches: Badajos and Ciudad Rodrigo are classic examples. Now the bare breaching of a fortified position was as possible in 1914, as it was a hundred years previously. "Great masses of men will go through anything", wrote Colonel Henderson in his *Science of War*, and this was soon proved to be true. For even when our artillery was inadequate and our supply of munitions was insufficient, our troops frequently overran the German fortified line.[3] In this there was nothing new, although the proper size of the breach, and the best method of making it, were difficult questions. What was new, was that in siege warfare as it had up to then been practised, the defending side was cooped up within the walls of a fortified town, or inside a circle enclosed by a ring of forts; whereas in the new state of warfare the defending side fought with the roads and railways of half a continent behind them. The consequence was that a bare breaching of the German lines in France could not, in itself, be as decisive as a breach in the perimeter of a fortress; for it did not deprive the defending side of its power of manœuvre, nor did it sever the defenders' communications with their reserves. This was, of course, grasped at once by professional soldiers; and in all plans for an attack upon the German positions provision was made for a rapid advance through the breach towards the German communications centres beyond. It was this second part of the programme that proved impossible or nearly impossible to execute. Every expedient was tried but the explanation of the final failures was virtually the same as the explanation of the initial ones.

Once this set piece was over (the break-in) [writes Sir James Edmonds], there came unforeseen delays. Command of the operations became slow and difficult, and the assistance of the infantry by the artillery was hampered by the breakdown of the telephone system. The vulnerability of our means of communication and our method of intercommunication in the face of modern artillery, and the difficulty, under conditions of siege warfare, of getting reinforcements to the required positions, at the proper time, up trenches already congested, exceeded all expectation and calculations. The enemy thus gained time to bring up reinforcements, and to construct a retrenchment (to use the old word of trench warfare) behind the breach. Thus

---

[3] See General Gough, *Fifth Army*, pp. 108 et seq.

equilibrium was very quickly restored, mere repetition of first effort only brought repetition of failure, and, for the moment, all hope of further progress vanished except after renewed preparations and an entirely fresh attack.[4]

This held good to the very end, and nobody should imagine that the great advances that were made in 1918, first by the German armies against Amiens, and secondly by the Franco-British armies along the whole battle front, are testimonials that the initial difficulties had been overcome. The great advance beyond the German positions was possible only because the German reserves were exhausted.

From now onwards (summer 1918) [writes Colonel Fuller], attack followed attack but all were of short duration and there was no pursuit, because advancing troops could not be supplied. In all these battles, the same difficulty confronted the Allies, which, earlier in the year, confronted the Germans, namely, the maintenance of battle energy by supply and reinforcements.[5]

The operations that are about to be described were brought to a successful issue because this standing difficulty of maintaining the initial momentum of an assault was overcome: it was overcome by mechanization which ensured that (1) simultaneously with the initial breaching, all obstacles between the attacking troops and their objectives—mines, wire, anti-tank obstacles—were removed or made passable, and (2) that a sufficient number of reinforcing troops were carried through the breach on to the enemy's communications beyond. The long deadlock of the 1914 war continued because heavily laden troops were expected to march over ground where an unencumbered man would only walk painfully and slowly: in 1944 they were carried in tracked vehicles.

Military historians will some day describe how the difficulties of mechanizing an army were examined and overcome, and will show which difficulties were foreseen and dealt with in peace, and which others were overcome by the

[4] *Military Operations, France and Belgium*, 1915, pp. 151, 152.
[5] *Future Warfare*, p. 76.

MODERN PRACTICE

improvisations, trials, and errors of war. Such a long inquiry would, however, be quite out of place in this history. Nevertheless the mere statement that mechanization prevented the deadlock of the 1914 war from being repeated in the next one is not, in itself, a sufficient introduction to the narrative which follows. The introduction will, however, be tolerably complete if a model, or standard attack of a modern battalion is described with some particularity.

In the first place, it must be understood that assaults on the model of the battle of the Somme are no longer undertaken. An attack on a wide front is now a number of simultaneous or successive attacks at a number of selected points in the enemy's front. As a consequence, artillery is now used differently: the barrage that fell upon whole miles of the enemy's front is a thing of the past; it has been replaced by heavy concentrations upon relatively small areas, which aerial photographs have shown to be key points in the enemy's defence line. Secondly, as each assault is directed against a relatively narrow front, all forward moves, all operations against mines, wire, and anti-tank ditches are made under cover of smoke screens. These smoke screens are laid by the artillery with great precision; and it can be said without exaggeration that, let the wind blow from where it will, an enemy position can always be blinded.

Under the cover of this smoke screen, the first breaching operations are carried out by throwing or laying explosive tubes or ropes (bangalore torpedoes and vipers) across the enemy's minefield and wire-belt. The narrow channel that is thus made is enlarged by flail tanks which explode mines without damage to themselves; the anti-tank ditch is then filled in by fascine-carrying or bridging tanks, which make a passage over which the gun tanks can pass later. During these breaching operations the gun tanks are moved up to supplement the artillery bombardment, by engaging such targets as were not included in the original fire plan. Every point from which the defenders can resist the attack is thus under fire when the assaulting infantry is brought forward in carriers which are sufficiently armoured to protect the infantrymen inside them against anything except an unexploded mine or a direct hit. The assaulting infantry are then put down as near as possible to the channels that have been made in the belts of mines and wire and they establish a bridgehead on the far side of the anti-tank ditch. At this point a number of new positions in the enemy's defence line will probably have manifested themselves, and enemy tanks will have come into action to resist the advance; subsequent operations are therefore carried out, as circumstances require, by the tanks and the forward infantry of the attacking troops.

In some cases, generally when the preliminary operations have gone well and good communications have been maintained between the forward infantry and the guns farther back, the artillery assists in reducing the newly discovered targets. More usually, however, the artillery adheres to the prearranged plan, and the guns are lifted on to selected targets farther back when the assaulting infantry and the tanks move forward from the bridgehead. Mortar-fire is, however, very much employed during the last phases of an assault.

When a position is carried, by these methods, the breach cannot be repaired by erecting a new position a mile or two miles back, for the way into the enemy's rear is wide open, and the tanks and the infantry reserves are free to pour through it.

As no two points in a fortified system are exactly similar, fire plans, tank approaches, the demolition of obstacles, minefield clearances, in fact, every detail of an assault, is specially planned whenever an attack on an enemy position is ordered. Nevertheless, the principles that have just been reviewed are always as strictly adhered to as the available number of guns, tanks, flame throwers, and armoured vehicles allows. The foregoing is, however, a description of a model attack—an assault in which every mechanical aid is available —and it should not be imagined that every advance that is described in the following pages was thus executed. The

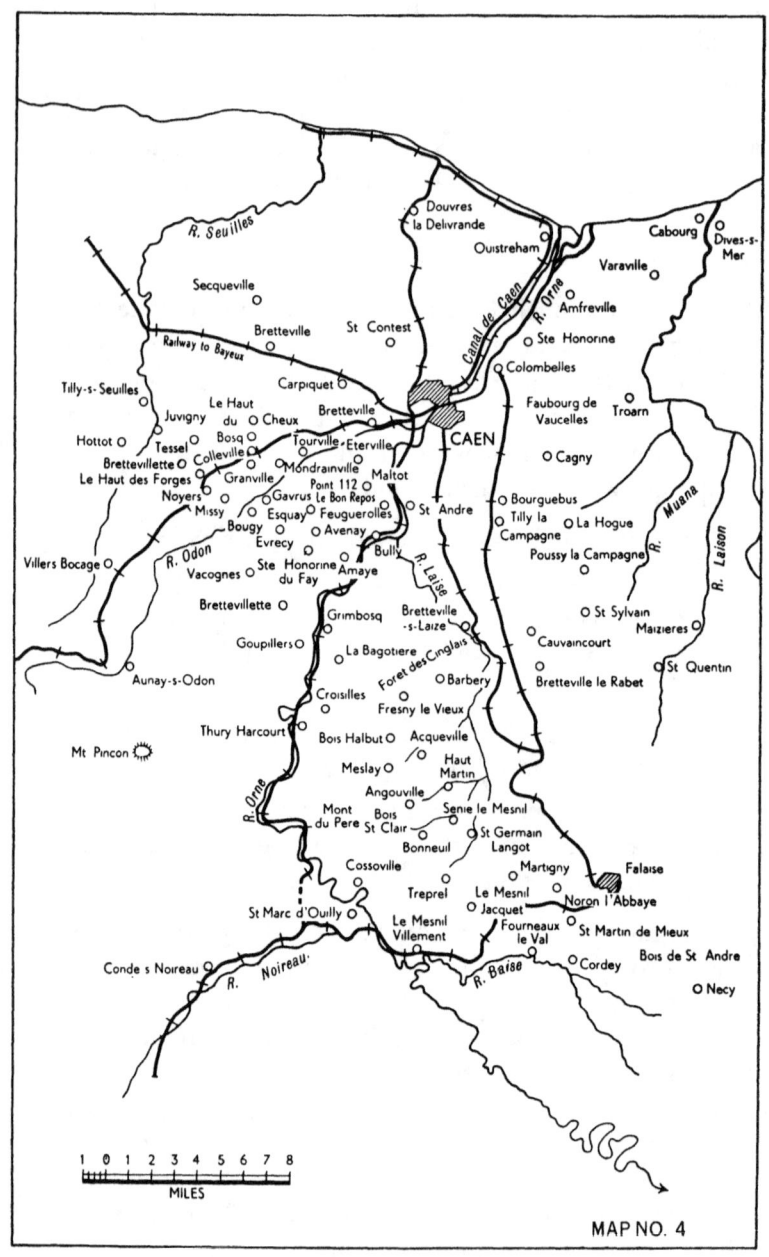

with multi-barrelled mortars called "moaning minnies", and this was the battalion's baptism of fire in France. Life in the forward zone was unpleasant and risky: the whole battalion was in slit trenches; the slightest movement brought down fire; and visiting platoons was, in consequence, extremely difficult; indeed experience soon proved that these visits of inspection could only be made when the Germans were attending to another area. The extraordinary nature of the fighting on which the battalion was about to be engaged and the hazards attendant upon it are illustrated by the following incidents, which occurred soon after the battalion moved into the forward area. B Company was ordered to reconnoitre towards Bretteville and Le Mesnil, and on reaching the zone that was occupied by the forward infantry, the company commander came upon an officer who was telephoning hard and anxiously from the bottom of a trench. Realizing at once that something serious was afoot, Major Woolsey waited until the telephoning was over, and then learned that German tanks were attacking and that they had just overrun the very ground that B Company had been ordered to reconnoitre.

It was, moreover, a source of continual speculation among the officers and men that in the fields where D Company was posted there was a sound, undamaged British tank. The only thing that was missing was the crew, whose battledresses were neatly folded inside the tank; their unit knew nothing about them, except that all signals and messages from the tank had ceased at a certain hour and on a certain day.

In order to retaliate against German shelling the mortar company made its first experiments in what was known as "nomad" shoots. The company commander placed one, or more platoons after dark in a chosen position in the forward area, and opened up on German posts that had been located during daylight; after subjecting the target to a heavy fire, the platoon or platoons moved off to a new position and repeated the performance. The device was excellent in itself; it was harassing and troublesome to the enemy, and it made it appear that our mortars were more numerous than was actually the case. Nevertheless, the exact manner in which these shoots were best conducted raised a difficult question. The mortars were generally fired from a zone that was held by infantry, and although the Germans needed time to locate the mortar positions they usually did so, with the consequence that the retaliatory fire which followed was borne by the infantry; for the mortars and their crews were then gone. Was it, then, proper that a unit which had been designed and equipped to support infantry should thus be instrumental in causing them additional losses, and, which was almost worse, in making the infantryman resentful and distrustful of all machine-gun and mortar units? These nomad shoots were, however, so useful that it was impossible to forgo them because one of their consequences was bad. Major Crozier hoped that a way out would be found by firing the mortars from points in the no-man's-land that lay between the infantry positions, for the front was not continuous; but the officers of the mortar companies deemed this to be impossible, as every square yard of the no-man's-land was patrolled after dark, and a mortar platoon would be quite helpless if it were attacked by a German patrol. The question was never settled in a hard and fast way: but the alliance between the battalion and the infantry was so good that it became possible to consider each case on its merits and to avoid the ill consequences. Moreover, the work of the wireless signallers reached so high a standard that, on one occasion, fire was put down forty-five seconds after it was asked for.

At a conference that was held at 12 Corps headquarters, soon after landing, the commanding officers were told that the 43rd and 59th Divisions would be employed in an operation that was shortly to be undertaken; but that the corps would not immediately be employed in a forward movement, and that the 53rd Division was for the time being to hold its positions against any attack that the Germans might launch against them.

* * * * *

THE ALLIED PLAN

It will now be proper to make a brief survey of the operations that had preceded the landing of the 53rd Division and to explain the plan to which it was about to contribute.

As designed by General Eisenhower and his staff, the invasion of France was to open by landing five divisions on the beaches between Ouistreham and Varreville. After the British and American forces had established a continuous bridgehead along this section of the Normandy coast, they were to capture Caen, Bayeux, Isigny, and Carentan, and were then to isolate Cherbourg by pressing on to the western side of the Cotentin peninsula. When a firm front had been set up against an attack from the south, an army corps was to move north against Cherbourg and was to carry it. While Cherbourg was being reduced, the Anglo-American armies were to move south and south-east, and were to establish themselves between the Loire and the Seine and thence along the line of the Seine. During this advance towards central France an additional army (the 3rd U.S.) was to follow the southerly movement along the Cotentin peninsula, turn west into Brittany, and capture all the ports in that part of France as far as Nantes.

Three months after the Allies had first landed, it was hoped that a force of between thirty-five and forty divisions would be holding a line from Le Havre to Orleans and would be ready to carry Paris; behind them, the army that had overrun Brittany would hold the line of the Loire to the coast at Nantes. The part allotted to the British Army in those operations was that it should be on the left wing of the American advance and that after carrying Caen, it should clear the line of the Seine below Paris.

It was not expected that these operations would be decisive: but it was at least hoped that the German armies in France would be roughly handled, and that they would lose heavily in men, guns and equipment while they were resisting the Allied advance to the Loire and Seine.[7] After

[7] Report by the Supreme Commander to the Combined Chiefs of Staff on the operations of the Allied Expeditionary Force, p. 9. (Hereafter this document will be referred to as R.S.C.)

carrying Paris the Allied armies were to advance northward to the valley of the Somme and along the Marne towards the German frontier. General Eisenhower hoped that he would be able to reduce the fighting strength of the German armies still further during this second advance: but he did not expect that the German forces would be crushed and brought to surrender until large parts of Germany were invaded and the Ruhr occupied.

When 12 Corps was ready to operate, a large part of this project had been carried out, almost as designed; but one section of it had proved to be impossible of execution for the time being, and this had considerably modified the whole plan.

The continuous bridgehead had been formed within the period of time allowed for; the 9th U.S. Division had reached the western coast of the Cotentin, and three U.S. Army Corps—the VIII, XIX, and V—were facing south between the crossings of the Douve and Caumont. To the north of them the VII U.S. Army Corps was advancing towards Cherbourg. Three army corps were now deployed on the British front. The 30th Corps (7th Armoured Division, 49th Infantry Division, 50th Infantry Division) held the right of the line, between the valley of the Aure and a position to the east of Tilly-sur-Seuilles which was in their hands. To the left of the 30th Corps, 8th Corps (Guards Armoured Division, 11th Armoured Division, 15th Infantry Division, 31st Tank Brigade) held a rather shorter line of about three and a half miles, near the southern side of the railroad between Caen and Bayeux; east of the 8th Corps was the 1st Corps (3rd British Infantry Division, 3rd Canadian Infantry Division, 51st Infantry Division, 33rd Armoured Brigade, 4th Armoured Brigade, 80th and 76th A.A. Brigades) which held the northern approaches to Caen and the left extreme of the British Army's position at the mouth of the Orne. It had not therefore been possible to carry Caen within the time appointed, and this greatly influenced the operations that were subsequently undertaken.

OPERATIONS AGAINST CAEN

While the 12 Corps was concentrating and was preparing to take its place in the forward area, Field-Marshal Montgomery made a great exertion with the forces that were then in line in order to assist the American operation against Cherbourg and also for a purpose that will be explained later. After five days of severe fighting the British positions to the west of Caen were pushed forward and the following points were firmly held: On the right, the 49th Division (30 Corps) held Juvigny, Tessel, Bretteville, and Rauray: the village of Bretteville was, however, still in German hands. On the left of the 30th Corps, the 8th Corps debouched from the country to the north of Cheux, crossed the railway between Caen and Villers Bocage, secured all the crossings of the Odon between Gavrus and Fontaie, and carried all the woodlands and spinneys on the southern bank round Baron. The Divisions of the 1st Corps still held their positions to the north of Caen: but at the eastern end of the British line, the 51st Division captured Sainte-Honorine, on the right bank of the lower Orne.

While the British Army was thus pressing back the German forces on the western side of Caen, the VII U.S. Corps captured Cherbourg (June 27). General Eisenhower attached great importance to the capture of this place, as it was of the highest moment that the Allies should hold a regular harbour, with wharves, basins, and unloading equipment, at the earliest possible date. When Cherbourg was carried, however, it was found that the German garrison had so thoroughly destroyed the port equipment, and that they had so carefully blocked the wharves and quays with sunken ships and every other kind of obstacle, that the harbour was not going to be usable for a considerable time. The rapidly expanding armies in northern France were thus still supplied through the extemporized harbours at the beaches, and as the capacity of the artificial moles and wharves had been reduced by a spell of very bad weather, it was an open question whether it would be possible to assemble and maintain an army that would be of sufficient strength to expel the

Germans from western France. The manner in which the German High Command distributed and employed its forces was, however, giving General Eisenhower extremely good indications of the course that he should himself pursue.

When the Allies first landed in France, the 7th German army was immediately available to oppose the invasion; for its zone of operation was Normandy and Brittany: the 15th German army, which was holding the Pas de Calais, was available as a reinforcement as soon as the Allied intentions were ascertained. The 7th army was composed of nine infantry and one panzer division: the 15th army group was stronger: the two together formed Army Group B and were commanded by Field-Marshal Rommel. Over and above these forces, the 1st and 19th German armies (Group G, General Blaskowitz) were stationed along the Biscay coast and the Riviera, and could be called upon to reinforce the northern groups if the commander-in-chief, Field-Marshal von Rundstedt, thought it necessary. Finally, Panzer Group West, under General Schweppenberg, although a training and administrative command, was composed of formations that were available for operations in the field.[8] It was believed that about sixty divisions, of which ten were of the panzer type, were thus available for operations in France; and that thirty-six infantry and six panzer divisions were stationed in the coastal area between Holland and Lorient. Of these forces, however, twenty-four divisions were of the coastal defence type, which could not be used in moving warfare; and seven were under training. This left a fully equipped fighting force of seventeen infantry and ten panzer divisions.[8] This was not enough to roll back the tide of the Allied invasion if it really gained a good impetus; but if it had been used to the best advantage, to strike quick and hard at the British and American divisions while their flow of supplies and reinforcements was below what had been

[8] See R.S.C., p. 23; and Montgomery, *From Normandy to the Baltic*, p. 17 and Map 3.

THE GERMANS MISLED

allowed for, the German army might have compelled the Allies to withdraw from France.[9]

The German generals did not, however, use their forces as wisely as would have been expected from such great students of the art of war as they have always been supposed to be. First General Rommel, who commanded in Normandy, was far too confident that the British and American forces would be unable to penetrate the beach defences and coastal fortifications, and did not make proper arrangements for a defence in depth or for assembling a strong mobile force for attacking the Allied bridgeheads while they were still so shallow that the divisions holding them had no room for retreat. Secondly, the enemy high command was quite deceived by our pretence that we intended to land another army in the Pas de Calais. If the enemy intelligence staffs had made even a rough estimate of the naval forces, commercial tonnage, and specialized equipment that had been expended in establishing the artificial harbours at the beachheads, and if, in addition, they had calculated at what rate men, guns, vehicles, and ammunition were being landed, then surely it would have been evident that not even the British and American armies, navies, merchant fleets, and factories would suffice to maintain two exertions of such magnitude. The enemy staff did not, however, draw the inferences that were proper to be drawn from the facts available, and were for weeks misled by our simulations. As a consequence, every gap or breach that we made in the German positions was hastily plugged by forces drawn from the local reserves of the 7th German army, and by such formations as General Blaskowitz could release from the Biscay and southern zones; but the 15th army was left alone in the Pas de Calais waiting for a second wave of invasion that never arrived.

This policy was certainly not the best that could have been devised; but it had at least made one section of the Allied plan impossible of fulfilment. From the beginning

[9] See R.S.C., p. 35.

General Rommel treated Caen as the principal bastion of his line of resistance, and there stationed all his armour and his best infantry divisions. When the divisions of 8 and 30 Corps were attacking the western and south-western approaches to Caen, the enemy's line between the mouth of the Odon and the western coast of the Cotentin was made up of fifteen divisions, or of groups of formations that were being used as divisions, and the distribution was peculiar in that the whole strength of the line was in its eastern part (where six panzer and two infantry divisions were deployed); and that nothing but infantry was facing the four army corps of the 1st U.S. Army. In detail the German deployment was this:

Opposite 1 British Corps:
    346 Infantry Division.
    21 Panzer Division.
    12 S.S. Panzer Division.

Opposite 8 British Corps:
    1 S.S. Panzer Division.
    9 S.S. Panzer Division.
    Part of 2 S.S. Panzer Division.

Opposite 30 British Corps:
    Part of 2 S.S. Panzer Division.
    Panzer Lehr Division.
    Part of 2 Infantry Division.

Opposite U.S. V Corps:
    Part of 2 Infantry Division.
    3 Parachute Division.
    Formations from 352, 353 Infantry Divisions.
    30 Mobile Brigade.

Opposite U.S. XIX Corps:
    Formations from 352 Infantry Division.
    Formations from 266 and 275 Infantry Divisions.
    17 S.S. P.G. and 6 Parachute Regiment.

Opposite U.S. VII and VIII Corps:
    Formations from 255 Infantry Division.
    353 Infantry Division.
    Remnants from 91, 77, and 243 Infantry Divisions.

west of the Canal de Caen. On the extreme left the 43rd Division, which had been put under the command of 8 Corps, supported the Canadian division's left by thrusting along the left bank of the Odon towards Verson and Bretteville. At first light on July 8 the attacking troops went forward, and by the afternoon of the following day troops from the divisions on the right and left wings met in the streets of Caen, and all that part of the ruined town that lies to the north and north-west of the Orne was in our hands. The Germans, who had resisted every inch of our advance with the greatest courage were, however, neither beaten nor broken, and they still held the Faubourg de Vaucelles on the southern bank.

During the attack on Caen the 53rd Division was not ordered to leave its positions to the north of the road between Caen and Villers Bocage; and the mortar company (D) of the battalion was, perhaps, more engaged than the others. The targets allotted to it were mostly enemy positions round the little village of Bretteville; but on July 6 the company was directed to bring Noyers under fire, where the enemy were known to be concentrated. This was the most important target that had been allotted to the company since it landed, and there is a note of pride in the entry in the battalion diary. "Mortar fire brought to bear within a maximum of ten minutes from time asked for by the infantry. Numerous buildings hit." Nevertheless, these days of watching and waiting in a defensive position were not altogether to the battalion's liking. "Things are developing into the routine of static positions," wrote Major Crozier, "and I hope it doesn't last long." Cheux, where the battalion headquarters was established, was shelled every day; and the little village, which had never been impressive or beautiful was half rubble: two of the battalion's vehicles were hit, and in the extreme forward area A Company suffered most, for one of its gun positions was hit on the 6th.

In addition, German snipers paid great attention to the battalion's positions: "It is incredible," says the regimental

ADVANCE TO THE ODON

Gazette, "what effect a single determined Boche will have on the troops in the neighbourhood when he is up a tree, well provided with food and ammunition, and ready to die for the Fatherland. They were very difficult to find, and were mostly young fanatics who stayed where they were and sniped until they were found and killed."[11]

During these operations the U.S. army captured La Haye du Puits and Saint-Jean de Daye in the Cotentin peninsula. General Bradley's forces were thus still some way from the starting point for the break-out operation which was to sever the German line; and there were disturbing indications that the assault on Caen, severe and successful as it had been, had not altogether fulfilled its purpose of holding all the German armour in the British sector.

The 2nd Panzer Division appeared in the Saint-Eny district on July 5; and when Caen was finally carried, and the intelligence division at army headquarters was able to review the state of the enemy's forces, it appeared that 1 S.S., 22 S.S., Lehr, and 21 Panzer Divisions had been withdrawn and put into reserve. This might well have been a preliminary to moving them west against General Bradley; and Field-Marshal Montgomery decided that he could best prevent it by pressing hard against the enemy position to the west of Caen.

The purpose of the whole operation was to enlarge the bridgehead over the Orne, and to gain ground towards the Odon. The part that the battalion played can be appreciated by following the fortunes of the brigades with which the companies operated. A Company and a platoon of C Company were attached to 71 Brigade, B Company to 158 Brigade, and their contributions will be most easily appreciated if they are dealt with in that order.

The headquarters of 71 Brigade was to the south of Cheux, in the woods round the little hamlet of Le Haut du Bosq (July 15), and the task assigned to it was to press the enemy out of his positions on the main road between Noyers and

[11] *Manchester Regiment Gazette*, Vol. XII, No. 1, p. 43.

Mondrainville and to reach the heights that overlooked the Odon valley. The enemy held Gavrus when the operation was planned: but on the day before it started a patrol by the 2nd Monmouths (160 Brigade) discovered that the Germans had abandoned the place itself, but that they still held the rising ground to the east of it.

At three in the morning (July 16) the attacking units left their positions and made for a large wood just south of the *grande route*. They reached it and fought their way forward, foot by foot, until they had reached the central part. Here the enemy counter-attacked, and drove them back to the north-west corner of the wood. The enemy, says the brigade diary, were very determined, and their positions were well concealed. At full daylight some of the woods and spinneys that were to be carried were in our hands, but the line that we were to occupy was by no means cleared. All that morning men fought, hand to hand in the woodlands, and neither side got any particular advantage; but in the early afternoon reinforcements from the Oxford and Buckinghamshires arrived; they attacked with fixed bayonets and at last the positions that had been so bitterly contested were in our hands. The brigade line ran along the crest of the heights that overlook the Odon valley between Bougy and Gavrus (19.00 hours July 16). On their right troops from the 59th Division had cleared Le Haut des Forges, and the 1st East Lancashires were in contact with them round Missy. What contribution did A Company make to this desperate fighting? We know only that they assisted in it; nothing else is to be found in the written records.

As has been explained, B Company were attached to 158 Brigade, whose headquarters were established at Mouen in the early hours of July 15; the brigade was placed under the orders of the 15th Division for the operation that was about to be undertaken. The starting point was the bridgehead position between Gavrus and Baron, which had been held against the German counter-attack of July 1, and the villages of Evrecy and Esquay were the places that were to be cap-

THE ADVANCE IS CHECKED

tured. The attacking troops started off at 23.30 hours on July 16, but, as the brigade diary laconically puts it, " owing to thick fog the operation did not succeed and the battalions were forced to withdraw."

On the following day the attack was launched for the second time, with the intention of carrying Evrecy; when Evrecy was secured the brigade was to move along the bed of the little stream that runs past the two villages and enter Orne at Bully. The enemy seems to have known that an attack was coming; for the troops were heavily shelled and mortared when they were on the starting line. Nevertheless they moved off at the appointed time, and completed the first part of their advance through some open tillage fields, on the reverse side of a summit, known as Hill 112, which subsequently earned a very bad reputation. This part of the operation went well, for at 22.00 hours the forward battalions reported more prisoners than they could manage. Soon afterwards, however, the advancing troops passed the hill summit and were in full view of the Germans. The enemy now opened from Evrecy and from a number of well-concealed positions in front of the village; the attack was stopped, and by midnight the battalions were back at their starting points after suffering losses; for the war diary specifically states that the brigade was " too weak to attack again."

B Company supported this ill-starred operation from the right flank and suffered severely; for the Germans located the machine-gun positions and mortared them heavily; the three platoon commanders were lost on that day.

Strangely enough, Evrecy was entered, for a short time, by a troop of 17-pounders which reached the village by the main road, almost without opposition. It did not, however, take the Germans long to ascertain that the unit was alone and unsupported; they then turned on the troop and utterly destroyed it.

By good fortune the regimental *Gazette* has recorded another detail of this day's desperate fighting.

On July 17 Lieutenant Brown was working with 4 R.W.F. in a consolidation role in an attack on Evreux. They were heavily shelled on the start line for the attack and sustained many casualties. Next day, they ran into some M.M.G. fire on the crest of Hill 113, and the attack was driven back. Lieutenant Brown, in his carrier . . . with his two operators . . . got over the crest of this hill and into some cover, where he could overlook the enemy positions. Here he stayed all night under heavy fire, and next morning was able to pass back valuable information. At 10.30 hours he was ordered to withdraw, which he did, unfortunately dislocating his knee while taking some quick evasive action.[12]

160 Brigade relieved the troops in the forward area during the night of July 17, and by daybreak on the 18th the three battalions were holding a position between the eastern side of Gavrus and the northern edge of Esquay village. The 4th Welch were, however, slightly drawn back towards Baron. From this position a patrol was pushed right into Esquay on the following day; but all was quiet until the afternoon of July 21, when the 5th Welch were severely attacked. The point of contention was a place called Le Bon Repos—a point where the sideroad between Esquay and the Orne valley crosses the *grande route* between Caen and Evrecy. A cluster of French poplars surrounds the crossroads, and a few yards to the north another track joins the road that goes towards the Orne. The local German commander was evidently very anxious to secure this ganglion of roads and lanes; for after battering it with mortars, the Germans came on at company strength. The first attack was held by artillery and mortar fire; but it was renewed at 18.00 hours with four tanks assisting. Heavy machine-gun fire was directed against the German infantrymen, who, however, were now so close to the British position that artillery fire could not be used against them. The struggle raged until 23.00 hours when three enemy tanks got right into the posts that the Welshmen had held so stubbornly, and by midnight the crossroads were in the enemy's hands; four of our anti-tank guns were lost:

[12] *Manchester Regiment Gazette*, Vol. XII, No. 1, p. 44.

THE CANADIANS ADVANCE

three officers and 116 N.C.O.s and men were killed or missing. D Company was certainly responsible for the heavy mortar fire that brought the first attack to a standstill; as for the machine-gunners who contributed so valiantly to the second struggle between 22.00 hours and midnight, it would appear that every available company of the battalion was engaged, for the record reads: "All companies fired in support of 160 Brigade p.m. July 21. In neighbourhood of 80,000 rounds fired." [13]

At the western end of the British line Noireau was surrounded but not quite carried, and in the centre troops from the 43rd Division captured Maltot, which the Germans had held when it was first assaulted. The greatest advances were, however, made to the east of the Orne, where the Canadian Corps, 1 Corps and 8 Corps attacked in the flat intersected land between the lower Orne and the lower Muance, cleared the Faubourg de Vaucelles, and established our line from Saint-Andre to Bourguebus, Cagny, and thence to the outskirts of Troarn (where the woodlands of the Muance valley assisted the enemy's defence and brought our advance to a standstill), Maltot, in the Orne valley; and by the 50th Division (30 Corps) which carried Hottot at the western end of the line.

On July 12, however, 12 and 2 Canadian Corps became operational and the 8th Corps was moved into reserve for the time being.

When the army was regrouped, the 53rd Division with which the Manchesters were operating still held the part of the line that had originally been allotted to it. The axis of the divisional front ran south-west towards Missy and Haut des Forges: the 15th Division was on its left, with a front facing towards Gavrus and Bougy; the 43rd Division was on

---

[13] The Battalion Sitrep for midnight July 20 gives the following company positions: A Company in the woods between Mondrainville and Tourville. On the left bank of the Odon, near the bridge between Mondrainville and Baron; B Company was at Les Vilaines on the reverse slope of Hill 113; C Company in the woods near Tourville; D Company in some open ground near Mondrainville.

the extreme left with its front towards Eterville. The 59th Division (which, for the time being, was under 30 Corps) prolonged the 53rd Division's line to the right.

The battalion headquarters was moved from Cheux to Coleville, and it was from here that the commanding officer directed it during the operation upon which it was about to be engaged.

The main purpose of these operations was not, however, to gain ground, but to hold the enemy's armour in the eastern part of the Anglo-American battle front, and in this they succeeded. The indications disappeared that the Germans contemplated transferring armoured divisions to the American front, and one was actually brought back from the Caumont area to stem the Canadians' advance on the eastern side of the Orne. Profiting by this the Americans had captured Saint-Lo, and had reached the high ground to the east and west of it.

> By July 18 [writes General Eisenhower] the first and second armies had taken up the positions from which the break-through operation could be started. We had now the requisite room to manoeuvre and our divisions in the field had been built up to fifteen U.S. (including three armoured) and fifteen British and Canadian (including four armoured), against which the enemy had twenty-seven, eight of which were armoured. On account of the losses that we had inflicted, however, the actual strength of the enemy was no more than the equivalent of six panzer or panzer grenadier divisions and ten full-strength infantry divisions.[14]

Field-Marshal Montgomery writes: "We were now on the threshold of great events."[15]

Owing to the foul weather that had impeded our operations from the beginning, the great thrust was delayed for several days, during which the 1st Canadian Army took the

---
[14] R.S.C., p. 44.
[15] *From Normandy to the Baltic*, p. 79.

THE BATTLEFIELD IS TRANSFORMED

field. The British 1st Corps and the Canadian 2nd Corps were placed under its command.[16]

On the part of the front where the battalion was posted the crossroads round Le Bon Repos remained an inflamed point of the battle line. The mortar company and every available machine-gun platoon were now ranging upon it. On the night of July 24 the 4th Welch raided the place in strength under cover of a fire in which every machine-gun that could be brought to bear was fired, and the officers and men were much gratified to learn from one of the prisoners that he and his mates had not dared to put their heads above their trenches for so long as the machine-gun fire was continued.

* * * * *

Meanwhile the great American thrust was successfully delivered (July 25–31). The German formations to the west of the Vire were utterly defeated and broken; those to the east of it were forced out of their positions with severe losses, or were compelled to retire because the western side of their line was melting away. By July 31 the U.S. troops had captured Granville and Avranches, and the German high command were endeavouring to wheel back their line with the area Tessy-sur-Vire–Caumont as a pivot. The whole battlefield was in fact transformed.

Field-Marshal Montgomery now manoeuvred to occupy the area which the Germans proposed to use as a hinge for their withdrawal: 8 Corps on the extreme right of the British line was to sweep down to Le Beny Bocage, and was thereafter to operate towards Vire and Tinchebray; 30 Corps was to operate towards Villers Bocage and Aunay-sur-Odon; 12 Corps, which was to act as the left-hand pivot, was to advance towards the Orne as far as was necessary for the purpose. It

---

[16] The major formations of the Anglo-American armies were:

1st U.S. Army: V, VII, XIX Corps
3rd U.S. Army: VIII, XII, XX Corps } General Bradley's Army Group.

2nd British Army: 12 and 18 Corps
1st Canadian Army: 1 (British) Corps, 2 Canadian Corps } F.-M. Montgomery's 21st Army Group.

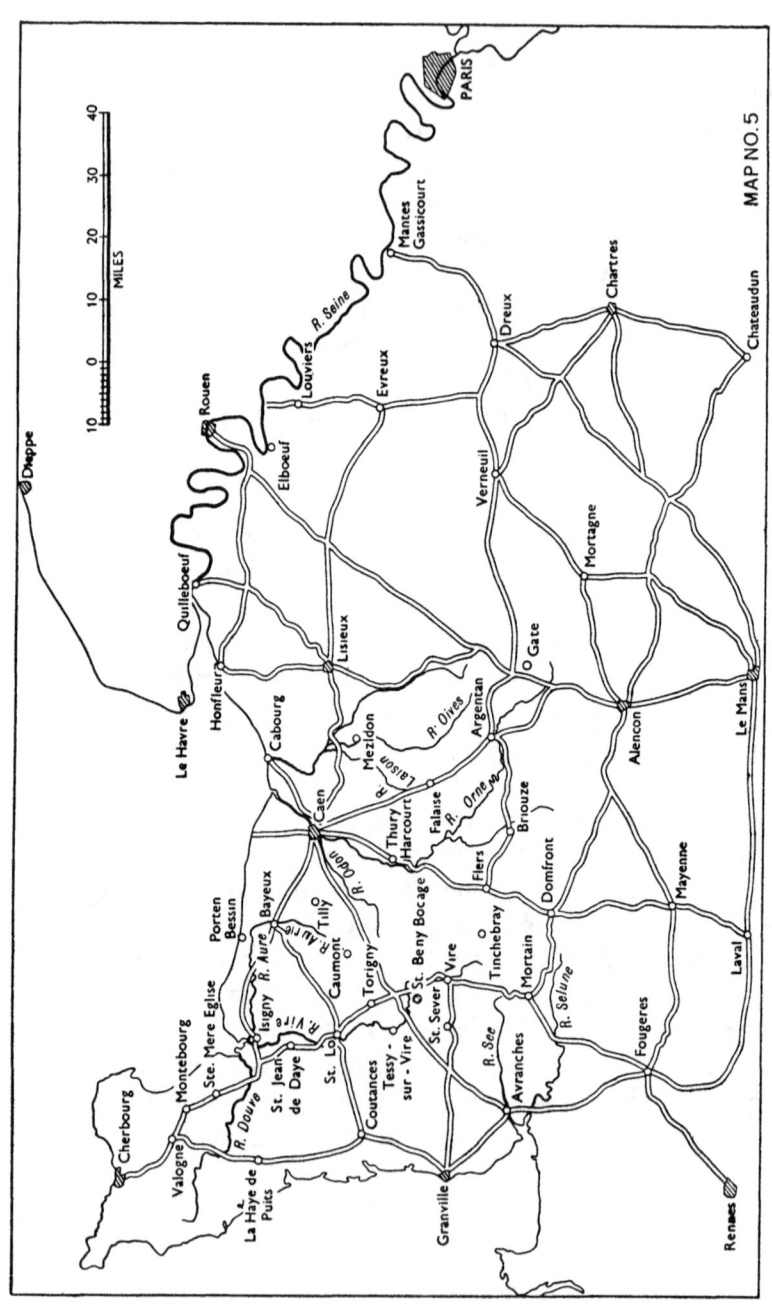

The operations in which the battalion was engaged during the next three weeks will best be understood if the great manœuvres of which they were a part are first explained.

August 4 to 7. The American forces on the extreme right wing advanced so rapidly that it was soon patent that the Germans could not resist at all in central Brittany. Rennes was occupied on August 4, Mayenne and Laval were overrun on August 6, and the 5th U.S. Infantry Division then reached the line of the Loire, between Nantes and Angers. Seeing therefore, that no organized resistance was to be expected from this quarter, General Eisenhower changed his original plan: and instead of directing the whole of the 3rd U.S. Army towards the west (as was first intended) he ordered the VIII Corps to reduce the ports of Brittany, while the other two Corps of the 3rd Army (XV and XII) were to occupy Le Mans and then operate northward towards Argentan.[18] On August 7 Le Mans was, in effect, occupied by the XV U.S. Corps and the great turning movement was at once begun.

This, however, was complementary to what Field-Marshal Montgomery had decided before it was certain that the German left had so completely collapsed: to advance his right wing towards the Orne and to assault Falaise from the north with the 1st Canadian Army.

The Canadian army moved forward on August 7 after a heavy aerial bombardment of the German positions in front of them. The German troops resisted the assault with the utmost courage and tenacity: but the Canadians reached a line between the Forêt de Cinglais and Poussy-la-Campagne on the following day. As they did so, 43 Division on the right wing cleared the Mont Pinçon summit, but 59 Division's advance against the river line at Thury Harcourt was very stiffly resisted and little progress was made.

Meanwhile, however, the Germans committed their army to a manœuvre that proved fatal to them. On August 7 they opened a counter-attack from the Mortain area with 2 Panzer, 1 and 2 S.S., 116 Panzer, 10 S.S., 84 and 363 Divisions.

[18] R.S.C., p. 53.

THE GERMANS COUNTER-ATTACK

The purpose of the thrust was to recapture Avranches and so to sever the communications of the U.S. formations that were advancing against Le Mans. The 15th (British) Division was, for the moment, driven out of Esthy; and the attacking Germans also secured a footing in the zone that was occupied by the 11th Armoured Division. The main weight of the counter-attack fell, however, on the troops of General Bradley's VII (U.S.) Corps; and, according to General Eisenhower, the American intelligence staff had been collecting indications that something of the kind was impending for several days, and were ready for it. Mortain was yielded on the first day, but the American divisions that were then moving south between Mortain and Avranches were called into the new battle zone, and, in Field-Marshal Montgomery's words, "The result of the battle was never, for a moment, in doubt."[19] In this the German generals were in full agreement with ours: not one of them believed that the manœuvre could succeed: most of them were convinced that it would be the introduction to a great disaster, but they were compelled to execute it, because Hitler ordered it. A man who, when he was a soldier, had never been thought fit for a higher rank than that of a corporal was thus overriding the most experienced generals in Europe, and they were obliged to submit to him. This was, moreover, happening in a country where the soldier's profession has always been held in the highest honour.

August 8 to 12. The northerly movements of the XV (U.S.) Corps was fairly started on August 9: detachments were left at Le Mans and Beaumont to secure the crossings of the Sarthe. East of the Orne the Canadians with the Polish armoured division operating on their left reached Bretteville le Rabet, Cauvaincourt, and Saint-Sylvain (August 9). On this part of the front the German resistance was still extraordinarily stiff and well conducted, and the clean break-through that Field-Marshal Montgomery had hoped for proved impossible. Nevertheless, the Canadians and the

---

[19] *From Normandy to the Baltic,* p. 97.

Poles fought on without relaxation or respite; by August 11 they reached Saint-Quentin and Mouzieres, in the valley of the Laison. This tributary of the River Dives flows from right across the front of the Canadian and Polish advance between steep, deeply wooded banks, and the Germans had, as far as they were able, turned it into a fortified anti-tank ditch. Once again the Canadians were halted, but they never slackened their pressure.

From the allied landings in June [writes General Eisenhower], until that day the enemy resistance in that sector had exacted more Allied bloodshed for the ground yielded than in any other part of the campaign. Without the great sacrifices made here by the Anglo-Canadian armies, first for Caen, and then for Falaise, the spectacular advances made elsewhere by the Allied forces could never have come about.[20]

At the other end of the British line the German resistance was as determined and as skilful as it was before Falaise, and 59 Division's advance towards the Orne was slow and bitterly contested. Nevertheless, the division secured a crossing below Thury Harcourt on August 11 and pushed patrols into Croisilles on the eastern bank.

Notwithstanding the great stand that the Germans were thus making, matters were going ill with them. Up to the present very few details about the German counter-attack from Mortain have been revealed, but we know that a thrust from Barentan was brought to a standstill during August 9 and 10; that a conference was held at General Bradley's headquarters on August 10; that it was then decided that the German manœuvre could not possibly succeed; and that the last details of the encircling movement were then brought out.[21] The northerly movement of the XV Corps, which was begun on August 9 was, indeed, pressed with all possible vigour and on August 12 the American advanced formations were in the outskirts of Argentan. As the Germans still had a great mass of troops in the country between Mortain, Dom-

---

[20] R.S.C., p. 56.
[21] R.S.C., p. 54.

GERMAN RESISTANCE WEAKENS

front Flers, and Tinchebray, a large part of their army was not in great danger. It was indeed during the course of this day, that the Anglo-American intelligence began to receive indications that the Germans were beginning a general withdrawal. The indications were, for the moment, strongest in the Mortain zone, where the Americans reported a general easterly movement.

August 13 to 20. The American turning movement went forward without intermission: on the 13th their troops passed Argentan and reached Gace. Nevertheless, the Germans still held some positions between Argentan and Briouze, which they held with the utmost desperation in order to safeguard the withdrawal of the formations round Mortain.

The German troops were for the first time losing their cohesion: eleven different formations were identified round Argentan: and even in those parts of the battle zone where the German defence had been most stubborn, the Allies began to master it. On August 14 the Canadians broke through the German defences on the Laison and approached Falaise from the north-east. On the 16th they had virtually encircled Falaise; and although the U.S. forces moving north from Argentan did not meet the Canadians and the Poles until some days later, the date August 16 can nevertheless be called the day when the great struggle was decided. In the eastern part of the British battle line the German resistance was also crumbling; for the bitterly contested passage of the Orne at Thury Harcourt was in our hands; and, as will be shown later when the movements of the battalion are examined, German resistance between the Odon and the Orne was by then virtually over. Inside the pocket the German formations were disintegrating and were streaming eastwards.[22] The German position was, however, without remedy, for by this time formations from the U.S. 3rd Army had pressed eastwards as far as Breux. We can now return to

[22] Field-Marshal Montgomery: *From Normandy to the Baltic*, p. 104.

the battalion and can examine the part they played in the great manœuvres that have been described in this preamble.

* * * * *

The big movements of 59 and 43 Divisions towards Mont Pinçon and Thury Harcourt and of the Canadian Army towards Falaise were separated by the valleys of the Orne and the Odon during the first part of the Canadian advance, and by the valleys of the Orne, the Odon, and the Laise during the second part. The 53rd Division and its three brigades were operating as a link between the east and west wings of the British Army through this country between the valleys; and although the tasks performed were less striking than those done in other parts of the battle zone, it was nevertheless of the highest importance that they should be scrupulously executed; for it depended upon 53 Division that the German formations upon its front were never allowed to use the line of the Orne as a sally port for operations against the rear communications of the advancing Canadians.

The country between the three rivers differs materially from the very flat country to the east of it between the Orne and the Dives. Of the three rivers that most influence its features, two—the Odon and the Laise—rise in the Mont-Pinçon–Mont-du-Pere line of hills; the third river—the Orne—has cut a steep gorge through them. The land between the three valleys thus slopes downwards towards the north; the river streams run through fairly steep natural embankments, and the woods and spinneys that are so common in all parts of the country become larger and more numerous as the ground rises. The slopes of the Mont Pinçon and the Mont-du-Pere are covered with large woods; and there is a belt of forest between Grimbosq on the Orne and Bretteville on the Laise. The country is traversed by four *grande routes* which converge on Caen; but the principal communications of the district, and those upon which all troops operating within it have to depend, are the countless small side roads between

THE NEW BATTLEFIELD

the *grandes routes* and the even smaller tracks and lanes between the sideroads, which are mostly flanked by high hedges and are rather indifferently drained into ill-cleared ditches at the foot of the hedges and farm walls. Villages and hamlets are scattered in great profusion over the countryside which has always supported a fairly dense population. The villages are generally mere clusters of houses round a village church, and as the small flower gardens and well-kept road frontages of an English village are unknown in France they look stark and forbidding to English eyes.

Just before the movements that have just been described began, the brigades of the division were re-constituted as it was found inconvenient to maintain a brigade that was formed from the battalions of one regiment. When re-organized the brigades were thus composed:

71 Brigade
    4th Royal Welch Fusiliers.
    1st Oxfordshire and Buckinghamshire Light Infantry.
    1st Highland Light Infantry.

158 Brigade
    7th Royal Welch Fusiliers.
    1st East Lancashire Regiment.
    1/5th Welch Regiment.

160 Brigade
    6th Royal Welch Fusiliers.
    4th Welch Regiment.
    2nd Monmouthshire.

As has been explained the patrols from the three brigades detected an enemy withdrawal between the Orne and the Odon on August 4. In the evening of that day General Ross congratulated the division on discovering the movement so quickly, and another message was transmitted from the corps commander that the enemy were to be followed rather than closely pursued. On the following day the advance that was now beginning was being made through a battle-swept area of indescribable desolation. Villages were mere heaps of rubble, hardly a house or a barn in the open country was untouched; the inhabitants had abandoned a country where no man could live and work, and only the unburied dead remained. It seemed strange, moreover, to walk unmolested over such places as Hill 112 or Le Bon Repos, where for weeks on end no human being had dared show himself for an instant.[23] The valley near Esquay which was popularly known as "the Valley of the Dead" was everywhere covered with craters, and the trees were so stripped of their bark and foliage that it seemed as though the whole country were in the grip of a bitter winter. "It didn't seem possible for the Germans to have survived at all," wrote Major Walker in his diary, "But their dug-outs were very strong. Most of them were roofed over with logs, several layers thick, laid criss-cross, and all sawn to length and then turfed over. A real sappers' job."

On the day after the order to follow the enemy was given the battalion headquarters was moved from the Chateau de Tourville to a farmhouse just on the outskirts of Avenay, and the three brigades were then holding the following positions:

71 Brigade was on the right bank of the Odon between Gavrus and Evrecy and Esquay; A Company of the battalion was attached to them and the company headquarters was in the fields outside Evrecy.

160 Brigade was on the left bank of the Orne between high ground to the south of Evrecy and Amaye, with the 4th Welch pushed forward to the heights that overlook a sharp bend in the river below Grimbosq. C Company was operating with them.[24]

158 Brigade with B Company under command was watching the large bend in the Orne between Maltot and Feuguerolles.[25] D Company (Mortars) was near battalion headquarters at Avenay.

---

[23] The signpost at Le Bon Repos was found to be riddled with M.G. bullets (MK. 82) which the battalion had fired. The C.O. took away the signpost, but it was unfortunately lost subsequently.

[24] This is nowhere explicitly stated but C Company H.Q. was near Amaye, in the Brigade Area (see battalion war diary, August 6).

[25] B Company's position is left blank in the battalion diary: the company was presumably operating with 158 Brigade.

A GREAT LOSS

In the early morning of August 5 the 2nd Monmouths reconnoitred the bridge to the east of Amaye, and ascertained that the enemy were on the opposite bank; but that they were not in any great strength; in the eastern part of the divisional front formations from 59 Division, moving towards Odon, began to press into 71 Brigade's area: Brigade headquarters was therefore moved eastwards to the hamlet of Les Mains. 160 Brigade conformed and made a left step towards Maizet.

On the day following (August 6) 176 Brigade of 59 Division secured the crossings of the Orne at Grimbosq, and stationed two battalions on the eastern bank. Further up, its advance was slow and bitterly contested. It was on this day, also, that the battalion suffered a grievous loss, for Major Northcote, the commanding officer of A Company was killed when his jeep ran over a mine near Sainte-Honorine-du-Fay. Major Northcote had served with the battalion since the beginning of the war, and he was by everybody much respected and beloved. He was, indeed, an officer whose exceptional qualities had excited the deep and lasting affection of which the British soldier is sometimes capable. He is remembered as a gentleman who was *sans peur et sans reproche*, and to this day his photograph is shown to recruits who are drafted to A Company, by N.C.O.s who joined the regiment after his death.

The 12 Corps commander now decided to press on hard from the Grimbosq bridgehead, and by so doing, to compromise the German position at Thury. He therefore ordered 158 Brigade to leave its position between Maltot and Feuguerolles, to concentrate round Sainte-Honorine-du-Fay, and to take over the bridgehead from 59 Brigade; 53 Brigade was then to pass through the bridgehead and advance against Falaise on a two-brigade front. The first part of this movement was completed on the following day (August 7), when the Canadians launched their assault upon the German positions east of the Orne.

158 Brigade was not, temporarily, under the command of

59 Division and B Company went with them into the bridgehead. The battalion headquarters was ordered back to the Chateau de Tourville. The roads in the areas that had been recently captured were extremely bad, and there were practically no lateral routes; it was therefore deemed best to keep battalion headquarters out of the devastated zone, until it was decided where the main crossing would be made. 160 Brigade continued to patrol its section of the Orne.

More orders for the advance upon Falaise were circulated on August 8. 71 Brigade was to advance, by bounds, on a two-battalion front towards the villages of Treprel and Saint-Germain-Langout from the bridgehead at Thury Harcourt. The 249th anti-tank battery and A and D Companies of the battalion were attached to the brigade, with Major Crozier in command of the two companies. All that day and the day following, therefore, the brigade waited for news that 59 Division had captured the bridgehead at Thury, and no news came. Farther north, at Grimbosq the newly won bridgehead was continually attacked, and it was only on the 9th that 176 Brigade was relieved. The battalion headquarters was moved forward to Sainte-Honorine-du-Fay.

This plan for a converging advance upon Falaise from Grimbosq and Thury was, however, made impossible by the desperate resistance that the Germans opposed to 59 Division's attack against Thury; for 177 Brigade, to whom the task of securing the bridgehead was given, could not reach it. The mortar company was engaged in this bitter fighting and Major Crozier, who was waiting at Sainte-Honorine-du-Fay for the order to advance, made the following entry in his diary: " 177 Brigade of 59 Division are stuck west of Thury Harcourt. Had a bad night trying to get through to them and find out if they wanted help. Sent two mortar platoons to support 177 Brigade, who are now under 53 Division." When the order was received that A and D Companies were to operate with 71 Brigade, it was no easy matter to recover the two detached platoons. " Hell of a party trying to get the boys back," adds Major Crozier. " I had to borrow an village of Bonneuil, which stands upon a side road that connects Falaise to the Orne valley round Clecy. A deep belt of woods lies to the north of Bonneuil and the road along which the Welch Fusiliers advanced passed through it. Two platoons of the mortar company were operating with the Welch battalion. What followed is illustrative of the uncertainties that now prevailed about the enemy's position and movements. The 4th Royal Welch Fusiliers, with a platoon from the battalion accompanying them, reached some high ground which they had been ordered to secure, and to use as a starting point for their final attack on Bonneuil; and they do not appear to have been resisted at any point (22.00 hours August 13). Every available company of the battalion was certainly engaged in the engagements of the day; for that unboastful, but very accurate statement, the sitrep, records, "M.M.G. and mortar companies engaged in support operations this time." In order to make it certain that the last objective near Bonneuil should be carried, as quickly as possible, a company from the Oxford and Buckinghamshires was sent forward to support the Welshmen, and before they even reached them they were cut off and surrounded by German parties from the village of Angouville and the forests near it (dawn August 14). The Welshmen went straight on to the positions they had been told to seize, and held them by the evening. In their rear the Oxford and Buckinghamshires and two companies of the Royal Welch Fusiliers were virtually beleaguered all day by parties of Germans who strove to force them out of their positions, though quite unsuccessfully, as the besieged and isolated companies flung back every attack and knocked out several tanks and fighting vehicles. The explanation of these sudden appearances of the enemy, from points and areas where they had not been located, was that very large numbers of Germans were at this time retreating eastwards. The main current of men and vehicles was thus flowing along the larger roads into Falaise. A considerable number of subsidiary currents were, however, running through the sideroads to the north and

THE END OF THE BATTLE

south of the main routes, and one of them was flowing across the battalions of 71 Brigade. There was, however, no real danger from these bands of flying Germans: a company from the 2nd Monmouths was sent forward by 160 Brigade which was now reaching this part of the battle zone and it easily cleared the route between brigade headquarters (near Bois Halbut), the beleaguered companies midway, and the forward companies near Bonneuil: the brigade diary justly sums up these confusions and surprises: "The enemy's strength in this area was almost spent."

As has been said, platoons from the battalion were engaged in all this day's fighting: details of how and where they were employed are, unfortunately, not available. By evening (August 14), therefore, 71 Brigade was distributed in what may be called packets of companies between the high ground just to the east of Bonneuil, the forest of Sainte-Clair, and the village of Haut Martin, just north of it. The day's advance was completed by 160 Brigade, which had crossed the Orne during the 13th, and after making a preliminary concentration to the north of the Forêt de Grimbosq had moved south and carried the villages of Bonneuil and Treprel. This last capture was of the highest importance; for in consequence the *grande route* between Falaise and Conde-sur-Noireau was now commanded (p.m. August 15).

* * * * *

The great battle was now practically decided; for the Canadians and the Poles had by then made breaches in the last German defence line to the north of Falaise; and the Americans were past Argentan. On the day following (August 16), 158 Brigade reached Noron-L'Abbaye on the outskirts of Falaise; a few hours later the 12 Corps commander warned all the formations under his orders that the battle was practically over, and that all commanding officers were to prepare for the pursuit that would soon begin.

When this instruction was circulated the three brigades

were lining the road between Falaise and Le-Mesnil-Jacquet: 71 Brigade was on the right, with a company thrown out to the eastwards to watch the point where the road forks into two; 160 Brigade was spread out between Le Mesnil and Noron-L'Abbaye; 158 Brigade were around Noron itself. The battalion headquarters was then at Acqueville: the tactical headquarters was near Saint-Germain-Langot; A and B Companies were close to it; C Company was on the high ground near Treprel, at the back of 71 Brigade's area; D Company was on the southern edge of a belt of woodland to the north of Noron L'Abbaye.

The order to prepare to pursue the enemy eastwards proved a little premature; for it appeared that the northern end of the road between Falaise and Argentan had still to be cleared, and that there were still enemy parties in the little valley of the Baise to the west of the main road. Falaise stands in a semicircular cup of hills which are the offshoots of spurs of a north-west- and south-west-going ridge to the south of the town. The river Baise flows through a gorge in the hills and joins the Orne at Le-Mesnil-Villement.

Late on the evening of August 16, 71 Brigade was ordered to press forward two battalions and to secure the line of the Baise between Furneaux-le-Val and Cordey.

The 1st Highland Light Infantry and the 4th Royal Welch Fusiliers started off in the early afternoon of the 18th, and A Company went with them. The first part of the advance was not much opposed; but as the two battalions climbed the ridge that overlooked the river they were stiffly resisted. They fought their way up the slopes, with A Company firing in support, and were on their last objective at eight o'clock in the evening. The brigade commander was then ordered to make a night advance eastwards, and to occupy a wooded spur that commanded the Falaise road about four miles south of the town. The Highlanders were directed on to a crossroad farther north. The tactical headquarters of the battalion was now on the slopes below the main road in

AFTER THE BATTLE

the Bois-de-Saint-Andre, and the commanding officer ordered A, C, and D Companies to support the movement.

German prisoners were now pouring in in such numbers that defeat and disaster must have been universally admitted in the German Army. Nevertheless, small parties of officers and men were still valiantly resisting at isolated points, in order that they might assist their comrades to get away. The battalion helped to overcome one of these last desperate stands at the little village of Pierrefitte where a handful of brave Germans repelled the first attack of the Oxford and Buckinghamshires, and were only overwhelmed by a second attack in which D Company put down 400 bombs.

As far as the battalion was concerned this was the end of the battle; for the orders that were now given to prepare to pursue were not cancelled. The battalion headquarters were set up at Necy, and the overhauling of vehicles and equipment was at once taken in hand. The men had suffered more than the vehicles; for B Company was just a little over half strength although its transport was up to establishment.

The state of the battlefield; its ruined towns and smouldering villages, the roads blocked for miles with abandoned equipment, amongst which the bodies of men and the carcases of dead horses were putrefying in the sun and rain, has been so often described that it would serve no useful purpose to repeat the description. The purely professional records of the victory are, in any case, more impressive than these catalogues of broken vehicles and of tanks deserted by their crews, for they are the memorials of men who had won a resounding victory, who grasped the greatness of their achievement, and who were too proud to insert one boastful word into their records.

A joint P.W. cage was established [runs 71 Brigade diary] to deal with P.W.s from 71 and 160 Brigades, and the armour and recce, and during the day some 400 or so assorted P.W.s passed through. An extraordinary variety of identifications including 1 S.S. Pz., 2 Pz., 12 S.S. Pz., and 102 S.S. heavy tank battalion, together with odds and ends from supply troops, labour organizations and so on, as well as the usual and expected infantry divisions was received and somehow dealt with. If evidence were wanted of the disintegration of the German army it was here. More prisoners came in from battalions and the Recce Regiment, and again they were a motley collection, some in civilian clothes and many without papers or weapons (Russians used as labour troops) and among them a few unpleasant Nazi types from 9 S.S. Pz. and 10 S.S. Pz., with a warrant officer and N.C.O.s from 21 Pz. division. . . . The signs were unmistakable: we had overtaken a routed army.

The next entry runs: " The day was spent in bathing and resting . . . not a gun was heard."

The battalion had, in fact, been suddenly transferred from savage fighting to deep peace; all the officers and men were assembled for a church parade in a single small field, and the church service was read in a calm that was reminiscent of an English village green. Yet a single bomb would have obliterated the whole battalion, and if an air attack by one plane had been even possible it would have been madness to have gathered the men together in such a place.

The disaster was far more terrible than any that had overtaken the German army during the course of the war. For at Stalingrad the resistance of von Paulus's army had cast a lustre upon the German arms, and North Africa was lost more because the Italians were cowardly and treacherous than because the German troops and their leaders failed in their duty. In the battles of Normandy there were no similar mitigations: at one blow fortifications had been breached whose strength had been proclaimed for years by the German trumpet-blowers on the broadcast, and by the German publicity agents in the press: thereafter the flower of the German army had fought the British and American forces for ten weeks on end, and were flying from them in rout and confusion as a consequence. The brave resistance that the German soldiers had made in many parts of the battlefield was no counterpoise to the stupendous disaster that had overtaken the Germans; for these were incidents

THE PURSUIT BEGINS

which historians and students of war will collect long afterwards: whereas the victory was announced daily in figures of prisoners taken and of material and equipment collected which staggered the imagination. And just as there was no possible means of disguising the disaster, so there was no means of suppressing the implications that were proper to be drawn from it: and as the broken remnant of the German army swarmed eastwards, the German soldiers learned that the French, whom they had so recently overthrown and conquered, had risen against them in open defiance.

* * * * *

The first general order for the pursuit of the shattered Germans was issued on August 26, when the major purpose of the operation was stated to be " to destroy all enemy in the Pas de Calais and Flanders and to capture Antwerp." In order to effect this the 21st Army Group was to advance to the lower Seine and to secure crossings at Pont-de-l'Arche, Les Andelys, Louviers, and Vernon. The 1st Canadian Army was to take the lower crossings, and was to act as a flank guard to the 2nd Army by clearing the Germans out of their pockets on the right bank between Pont-de-l'Arche and the sea; by reducing Le Havre and Dieppe; and by operating towards Saint-Omer and Bruges. The 2nd Army was to operate towards Arras, Amiens and Saint-Pol, "with all speed and quite irrespective of the progress of the armies on the flanks"; 12 Corps was to be on the left and 30 Corps on the right; the armoured divisions were to lead the advance; the infantry divisions were to clear out any centres of resistance that the armoured formations decided to pass.

The pursuit that was thus planned was executed as it was conceived and will, on that account alone, rank as one of the marvels of military history. The history of the pursuit is indeed a list of points seized, or of towns captured according to programme or slightly in advance of it. Between August 23 and 25, 12 and 30 Corps were up to the line of the Seine; and the Canadian Army reached the river in the Elbeuf bend. By August 27 the Canadians were across the Seine. By the night of August 28, 43 Division (30 Corps) had established a deep bridgehead at Vernon and 11 Armoured Division began to pass through it. By August 29, 15(S) Division (12 Corps) was across the Seine at Louviers and the armoured formations were passing through it by nightfall.

The advance through northern France was, therefore, begun on August 28 and 29 and it was executed with such relentlessness and fury that Brussels was entered on September 3 and Antwerp on the day following. At no point were the German generals able to organize a concerted resistance; for the British armoured columns advancing deeper and deeper into occupied France tore such rents in the network of communications that, in the words of the 2nd Army's historian, " command and control were almost negligible."[28]

The 53rd Division moved up to the Seine on August 27, but it was not until midday on the 30th that the battalion crossed the river at Louviers. By the evening the battalion headquarters was at Lyon-la-Forêt on the northern side. The subsequent race through northern France was chiefly remembered by the cordial welcome that was everywhere given to us, and by the mean and despicable acts of vengeance that the French and Belgians were taking upon those of their countrymen whom they were pleased to call *collaborateurs*. At one place, the Maquis cut the throats of some A.A. gun crews who had surrendered in all good faith, and a young French girl danced upon the dead bodies as the British troops arrived. At Lyons women with shaved heads were first seen: later on, at Brussels a crowd of unfortunate creatures were publicly exhibited in cages that were ordinarily used for wild beasts. These displays excited great contempt, for the British Army cared for none of these things, and it seemed to the English fighting man to be particularly despicable that the French who had run before the

---

[28] See 2nd Army Account of Operations, Vol. 1, pp. 194 *et seq*.

Germans in battle should inflict these cruelties upon defenceless people.

Such incidents as did occur served as reminders of the tremendous victory that had just been won. On September 2, B Company harboured at the village of Arguyle; as the whole battalion had been on the move for two days and nights the men were extremely tired, and they slept heavily. When they awoke they found that they were surrounded on all sides by German soldiers who wished to surrender. On the same day, harbour parties which had crossed the Somme behind the armour found that they were surrounded by Germans; the armour had just passed through them, and when Major Crozier and Lieutenant Pring were examining one end of a village for billets the Germans were in the other. There was no fight left in these men, for a few moments later the divisional catering officer captured twenty prisoners.

A few days later B Company were ordered to clear a flying-bomb site. The officers and men approached the wood where the installation was situated with great curiosity, and were astounded to find that the bomb site was just a camouflaged ramp of timber, with a few huts near by. The construction was indeed so simple that not a square yard of concrete was anywhere visible.

> In each town [says the regimental *Gazette*] we met cheering crowds and we were deluged with flowers. Whenever we stopped, the girls leapt on to the vehicles and kissed the occupants, and their parents produced the odd bottle that had been kept for the occasion. Monralet, Arras, Bethune, Armentieres, and so into Belgium where the welcome was, if anything, more terrific.... We harboured near Menin, of last war fame, and, from there, moved straight up to Antwerp—158 Brigade with C Company leading ... In Antwerp, battalion H.Q. took over Fort No. 2, just outside the city, and companies went into action in the town and dock areas.[29]

---

[29] The actual distribution of the battalion was: two mortar platoons at the Sportspalast, overlooking Merxem. Captain J. Waddington's platoon of A Company in a factory also overlooking Merxem. The enemy could be seen here and the result of a short burst could be observed. A platoon from C Company in a block of flats west of the dock area in support of a company of 1st East Lancashires. (Lieutenant Coulston's notes.)

Everybody was under the exhilaration of victory.

As soon as the battalion headquarters was set up in Antwerp, the regimental flag was hoisted over the fort, on which Major Crozier remarked that it was good for morale, although dangerous, as the Germans who were shelling the town from the northern side of the Albert Canal, could hardly fail to notice it. The underground storehouses and magazines of the fort extended for nearly thirty acres and were packed with German equipment, which the Belgians were very anxious to pilfer. They would, indeed, have emptied the place but for Major Crozier's timely precautions. Life in Antwerp was a peculiar alternation between war and peace.

For the first time since we left England [runs the regimental *Gazette*], we saw attractive females beautifully turned out; shops full of things to buy, hotels and pubs doing a roaring trade, tramcars and, in fact, what seemed to be normal life in a large city. Then, to show how wrong we were, a shell would burst and demolish a shop; a crowd would collect for a short time and then life would go back to normal again.[30]

Service in the dock area provided a succession of the same strange contrasts.

There were two mortar platoons in action in the desolate dock area, defending an important sluice gate, the key to the port, with a platoon of the Welch Regiment and Lieutenant Dobson's platoon of machine-guns. This was war; mortar crews in slits, O.P.s up on the gates; tubes dug in—all the familiar props, and yet, ten minutes away in a jeep, and one was back in the gaiety, lights and temptations of a Continental city.... And so it went on, odd and sudden things happening by day, and a general meeting every evening at the American bar of the Century Hotel, where we discussed the day's events over a very large choice of drinks.[30]

On September 14 Lieutenant-Colonel Harington left the battalion to take up a staff appointment at division; Major Crozier took command until his successor arrived. By this time preparations for another advance were well advanced.

---

[30] *Manchester Regiment Gazette*, Vol. XII, No. 1, p. 47.

operations.[33] A week later a large number of formations, whose presence was not even vaguely indicated on September 14, were known to be present.

The plan for advancing to Arnhem was in effect a plan for the conquest of central Holland. Airborne forces were to seize the crossings over the water obstacles that traversed the main line of advance from Eindhoven to the River Maas. "This," in the words of the 2nd Army's historian, " would form a carpet for the swiftly moving columns which were to break out from the Escaut bridgehead, join up with the airborne forces holding the area Grave–Nijmegen–Arnhem and then place themselves north, over the lower Rhine."[33] In order to effect this:

The 1st British Airborne Division and the Polish Parachute Brigade were to capture the bridges over the Rhine, at Arnhem, and to dominate the surrounding country.

82 U.S. Airborne Division was to capture the crossings of the rivers Maas and Waal at Grave and Nijmegen.

101 U.S. Airborne Division was to capture and dominate all obstacles on the line of 30 Corps, advance on the road Hechtel, Eindhoven, Veghel, Uden, Grave.

30 Corps was to advance with all possible speed and secure the area Nunspeet–Arnhem. The order of march was to be: the Guards Armoured Division, 43 Division, 50 Division.

8 Corps was to secure the right flank of 30 Corps by operating towards Weert, Soerendonk, and the Maas.

12 Corps was to secure the left flank of 30 Corps by operating towards Rethy, Arendonck, and Turnhout.

53 Division, with which the battalion was operating, was to contribute to 12 Corps operations by bridging the Schelde canal to the north of Lommel and at a point five miles west of it; operating towards the Eindhoven–Turnhout road and capturing the villages of Eersel, Duisel, Reusel, pressing on thereafter towards Tilburg through Hilvarenbeek, Diessen, and Esbeek; setting up a strong protective patrol between

[33] Ibid., p. 225.

Tilburg (whose capture was desirable but not essential) and Turnhout; bridging the Wilhelmina canal opposite Oirschott and Naastenbest.

On September 17 the operation was begun; for on that day the 1st British Airborne Division was put down at Arnhem, but little or no news was thereafter received from it.

82 U.S. Airborne Division was put down in the Nijmegen–Grave area and seized Grave bridge. The bridge at Nijmegen was, however, still held by the enemy.

101 U.S. Airborne Division was put down at Son between Eindhoven and Saint-Oedenrode, and captured the bridge at Veghel.

The Guards Armoured Division advanced as far as Valkenswaard and carried it.[34]

* * * * *

When the operation was thus fairly started, 53 Division, with which we are henceforward particularly concerned, was round Lommel, where the battalion headquarters was established.

The divisional orders were that 158 Brigade was to establish the bridge over the canal opposite Lommel; and that 160 and 171 Brigades were to pass through it and advance towards the Eindhoven road. A, C, and D Companies were all deployed in the fields and spinneys on both sides of the road that runs north from Lommel.

The country was divided into countless small tillage fields which were bounded by hedges that were just high enough to obstruct the view. A fair number of marshy fields formed unexpected and quite difficult obstacles to troops that had been obliged to leave the road; canals and small watercourses increased the obstacles. Fields of cultivated saplings were very numerous, and they served as admirable lurking places for small bodies of enemy troops. The country is, in fact,

[34] See Field-Marshal Montgomery: *Normandy to the Baltic*, p. 139.

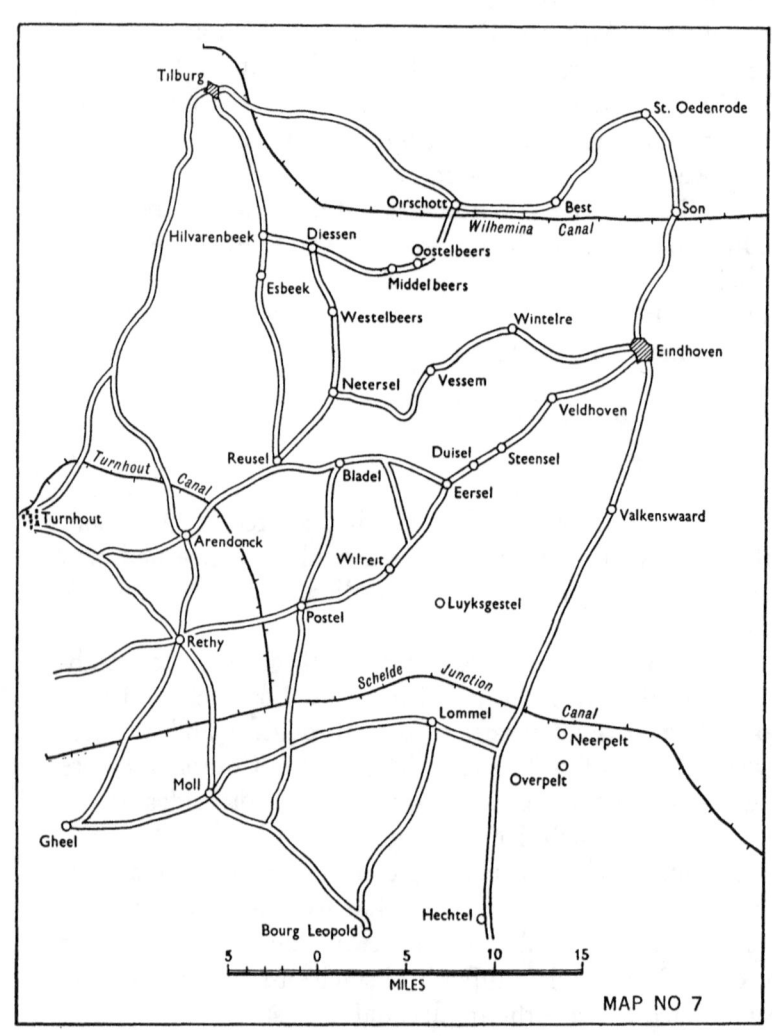

MAP NO 7

THE FIRST ADVANCE

as blind as a countryside can be; for not a knoll or hummock commands the monotonous expanse of fields and hedges. An officer who fought over it remembers the fighting as a succession of advances and of unaccountable checks, as the enemy's chief point of resistance was always, or nearly always, out of sight, small parties of Germans with a few automatic weapons could and often did check the advance of a whole division by preventing bridging operations for hours on end.

In the evening of September 17 the 1st East Lancashires and the 7th Royal Welch Fusiliers opened the attack, with A Company supporting them, and before dark the bridge site was cleared. At first light on the 18th the 1/5th Welch passed into the bridgehead and enlarged it under heavy covering fire from D Company's mortars; after this all companies stood down and waited for orders to cross the canal. In the early afternoon 160 Brigade crossed the canal with B and D Companies and turned westwards. By evening they had passed Lyksgestel and were in Wilreit; they had also established the second bridge that was provided for in the corps plan. 71 Brigade, to which A Company was attached, crossed the Lommel bridge during the afternoon of the 18th and struck north-eastwards towards Eindhoven. By the evening of September 18 the opening moves in the corps plan were all completed; small bombs were dropped on the tactical headquarters of the battalion during the night, but they did little damage.[35]

The second part of the advance—that is the thrust towards the villages on the Eindhoven–Turnhout road—was, however, not so easily accomplished; for new formations were being located, and the enemy's resistance became stiffer every hour. In fact, the division was now engaged in three days of confused and desperate fighting which is practically impossible to describe in detail. The total results are, however, tolerably clear; for by the evening of September 22, 71 Brigade was between Wintelre and Middelbeers, with A

---

[35] Lieutenant Coulston's notes.

Company attached to it; 158 Brigade with two platoons from D Company was facing westwards and was fighting for Westelbeers and Netersel; 160 Brigade with B Company and two platoons from D Company was facing west round Postel. The 7th Armoured Division had been moved eastward and was holding the canal behind them. The battalion headquarters was at Veldhoven and Lieutenant-Colonel P. H. Earle, Royal Northumberland Fusiliers, was now in command. Every mile of the intervening land of fields, spinneys, and villages had been desperately fought for; and the enemy showed no signs of yielding; they appeared, indeed, to have been reinforced round Middelbeers and Postel. Even while the succession of struggles for fields, crossroads, villages, and spinneys was still fairly recent, the recollections of the officers were vague and misty, and this is always proof that at the time they exerted themselves to the utmost and that they were very exhausted when the fighting at last died down. "Steensel, Veldhoven, Netersel, Bladel, Casteren, Reusel, are a few of the places those taking part will remember," says the regimental *Gazette*. "The Boche was in great strength in this area, he was fighting fiercely and he knew the country over which he was fighting, with the result that the next few days were extremely unpleasant."

It was in this fierce fighting that Sergeant Bardsley of A Company distinguished himself by his courage and endurance. The brigade with which he was operating (158) had just carried Oostelbeers; but the Germans counter-attacked, and Sergeant Bardsley was wounded by shrapnel, and one of his guns was disabled by mortar-fire. The infantry who were hard pressed by the counter-attack called for help, and although Sergeant Bardsley was suffering grievously (his face was much lacerated) he brought two new guns into position and controlled their fire. While doing so, he was struck down by new wounds in the hands and shoulder.

The situation was usually vague [continues the regimental *Gazette*], and one never quite knew when and where to expect the Boche. Major Woolsey had the pleasure of shooting at a

BAD NEWS FROM ARNHEM

German staff car, which appeared rather suddenly down a road one day, and one of B Company's platoons had a grand direct shoot near Arendonck at forty Boche, at a range of 500 yards. Studying ground from a church tower, officers were surprised to see a German soldier appear below them, who, presumably did not know that we had taken the place. That same tower at Netersel had three shells put through it ten minutes after Captain de Gaye had moved his mortar O.P. down.

And so it went on—information always vague—plenty of villages waiting to be liberated, and the one good thing about it all was that the hens were laying quite well. . . . Ten cigarettes would produce anything up to fifty eggs and we made the most of it.[36]

* * * * *

Although the battle was confused and baffling to those who were fighting in the forward area, its features were clear enough to those who were following its course on the operational maps at army headquarters. About three miles to the west of Arnhem, and on the northern side of the Rhine, the British Airborne Division was surrounded on all sides by formations from the 2nd S.S. Panzer Corps. The signals that had been received from the commander of this unfortunate division left little doubt that its position was desperate; for on September 19 he had stated that food and ammunition were very short, and since then he had received none, as the R.A.F. had dropped the additional supplies in the wrong place and the Germans had captured them.

South of the Rhine the Polish Parachute Division was in a better posture; for it had been in contact with the 43rd Division since the day previous. The operation had, however, been successful in this respect, that a corridor between Nijmegen and the approaches to Turnhout, and between Nijmegen and Weert was fairly securely held. As a consequence the crossings of the Waal and the Maas were in our hands. On the other hand, the corridor was, as it were, walled up on both sides by a large number of German

---
[36] *Manchester Regiment Gazette,* Vol. XII, No. 2, pp. 83 *et seq.*

formations whose presence had not been suspected when the operation had been planned. They had certainly been hastily collected; but their presence and the fine fighting spirit that they had displayed (they had cut the corridor between Uden and Veghel on September 21 and the Guards had only reopened it after bitter fighting) was striking evidence that the Germans were neither as beaten nor as demoralized as General Montgomery had imagined when he planned the operations.

It had, however, been decided during September 22 that Arnhem could not be captured and the 1st Airborne Division was to be extricated and withdrawn by 43 Division. The operations that were undertaken after this date were, therefore, undertaken for the purpose of strengthening and enlarging the corridor while the Airborne Division on the other side of the Rhine was evacuated.

* * * * *

For the next three days, therefore, the battalion and the brigades to which it was attached continued to batter at the villages on the Eindhoven road; but very few details have survived. This much, however, is clear.

On September 23 A Company was fighting round Middelbeers with the Highland Light Infantry (71 Brigade); the fighting was stiff and bitter; for at one time the Germans overran number 3 platoon during a counter-attack. B Company was in the woods round Postel doing harassing shoots on the orders of 160 Brigade. C Company (158 Brigade) was on the Eindhoven road round Duizel. D Company was drawn back towards the Maas–Schelde canal.

Some progress was nevertheless made on this day and the day following; for, by the afternoon of September 24, D Company was fighting round Vessem, a good six miles to the north of where it had been reported on the previous day. On the other parts of the divisional front the fighting blazed round the same contested points.

THE ARNHEM DISASTER

On September 25 Lieutenant-Colonel Earle visited the companies in the forward area and gave orders that the battalion headquarters should be moved westward to Steensel. At the beginning of the day the brigade areas were reported as: 71 Brigade, Wintelre and Middelbeers; 158 Brigade between Westelbeers and Bladel; 160 Brigade between Reusel and Arendonck, where they joined hands with the troops of 15 Division who had captured Turnhout the previous day. They do not appear to have altered their positions greatly during the course of the day; Reusel which was still in the enemy's hands was stiffly held against attacks by 160 Brigade, and an enemy attack at Netersel was held by the 1/5th Welch and C Company. Reusel was, however, captured by the 4th Welch after the 6th Royal Welch Fusiliers had attacked it unsuccessfully three times.

The battle was, however, now drawing to a close; the corridor had again been cut and was again opened; and during the dark hours the broken remnants of the 1st Airborne Division were brought across the lower Rhine at Renkum. It was a fragment only; for of the 10,000 men who were put down only 2,800 were brought out; and the 4th Dorsets who were put across the river as bridgehead troops were virtually obliterated; for only twenty of them ever returned to the south bank. When the disaster was finally liquidated the corridor between Nijmegen and the Belgian frontier was nevertheless firmly held.

The disaster at Arnhem has been excused and belittled by saying that it was only part of an operation which was 90 per cent successful. The contention does not, however, stand a minute's investigation. In the 2nd Army's account of operations the major purpose of operation Market Garden is quite candidly stated "It was to finish the war in 1944" (Vol. 1, p. 247). The major purpose was thus in no sense effected, and it is quite absurd to say that nine-tenths of it was achieved because our armies secured a good starting point for their operations in the coming year.

*　*　*　*　*

Soon after the battle for the corridor was ended, Field-Marshal Montgomery informed General Eisenhower that the 21st Army Group would not be able to advance farther north for the time being, and that the immediate pressing tasks were to clear the Schelde, to put the port of Antwerp into working order, and to force the Germans out of their positions on the western bank of the Meuse between Maaseyek and Venlo.[36a] When this message was sent the supplies of all the Allied armies in France, Belgium, and Holland were still being carried from the improvised harbour on the Normandy beaches, and the time was approaching when this single supply line would prove insufficient, notwithstanding the exertions, improvisations, and ingenuities of the supply services. The shortage of vehicles can, indeed, be judged by this one incident. When the technical adjutant was sent to Corps headquarters to collect replacements, he was passed farther and farther back, and only obtained them when he reached Bayeux in Normandy. An improvement was, however, in sight, for the Canadian Army had cleared the whole northern coast of France, and Rouen, Le Havre, Dieppe, Boulogne, Calais, Nieuport, and Ostend were in our hands; also Terneuzen was captured and the clearing of the Schelde had begun. In the west the Americans had captured Brest. Nevertheless the Germans had so methodically and carefully destroyed the harbour equipment at each of these places, that a great deal of work remained to be done before they could be used as regular harbours for supply.

With regard to the second task of clearing the western bank of the Maas, Field-Marshal Montgomery intended that it should be done by 8 and 30 Corps, and that the 1st Canadian Army and 12 Corps should be responsible for the northern and western sides of the Nijmegen corridor.

A large regrouping of the forces was thus ordered during the last days of September and early October, and 53 Division was moved into the area between the Rhine and the Waal—which was then called the island—as a consequence.

[36a] See Map No. 9, p. 188.

THE BRITISH ARMY REGROUPED

The operations that Field-Marshal Montgomery thought most likely to advance the end in view were that the Canadian Army was to press hard towards Rosendaal and Bergen-op-Zoom with its right flank, and to clear Beveland and Walcheren with its left. Simultaneously the 2nd Army was to make a strong thrust on the axis s'Hertogenbosch–Breda.

"I intended," writes the Field-Marshal, "not only to clear up the Antwerp situation with all possible speed, but also to push the enemy back across the Maas in order to establish a firm and economical flank along the river. I hoped that, as the 2nd Army's operations developed, the enemy opposite the Canadian Army would weaken in face of the threat to the main escape routes to the north.[40]

* * * * *

The new plan "Required a complete regrouping of divisions and command responsibilities, and involved turning face from east to west."[41] 30 Corps was therefore made responsible for all country north of the Maas, and 12 Corps, to which was allotted the duty of making the principal exertion, was moved to the south of it: the 15 (S) and 51 (H) Divisions were placed under corps command, whose composition then was:

> 53 (W) Division.
> 51 (H) Division.
> 15 (S) Division.
> 7 Armoured Division.
> 33 Armoured Brigade.
> 6 Guards Tank Brigade.
> 4 Armoured Brigade.

Rather before midnight on October 18 the battalion moved out of the Nijmegen bridgehead: headquarters was

---

[40] *From Normandy to the Baltic*, p. 150.
[41] *2nd Army Operations*, p. 254.

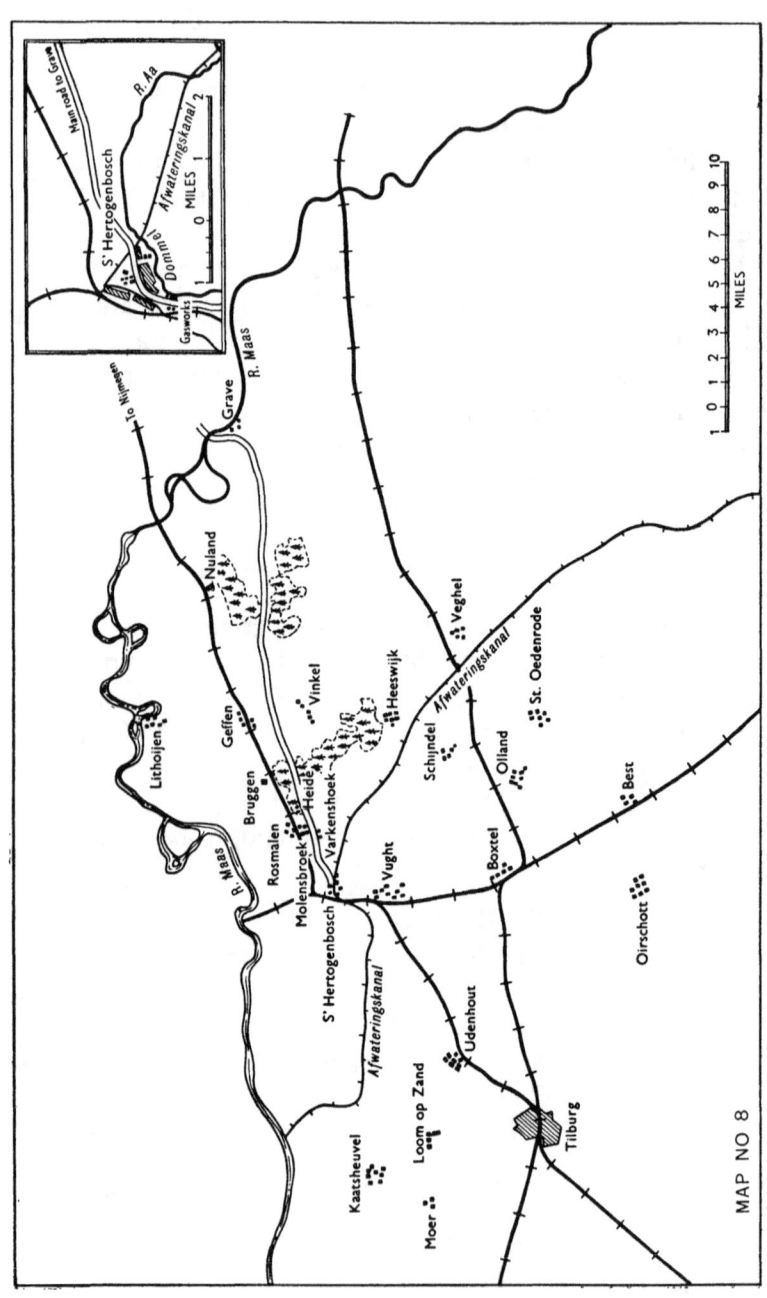

THE NEXT ADVANCE

at Grave during the preparations, which should now be briefly described.

When 12 Corps was redeployed and redistributed, the 53rd Division's front ran from the Maas near Lithoijen to the little hamlet of Vinkel, which lies a little to the south of the main road between Grave and s'Hertogenbosch. The 7th Armoured Division and a battalion from 15 (S) Division prolonged the front through the outskirts of Heeswijk (which the enemy still held) and Veghel. South of the Afwaterings canal 51 (H) Division and a brigade from 15 (S) Division held a front that covered Saint-Oedenrode and met the Wilhelmina canal near Best. As far as could be ascertained the enemy command had allotted the country between s'Hertogenbosch and Tilburg to 88 Corps, whose headquarters was near Zaltbommel: 712 Infantry Division was north of the Afwaterings canal, facing 53 and 7 Armoured Divisions, 59 and 245 Infantry Divisions prolonged the enemy's front through Schinjndel, Olland, and Oirschott. In the impending operation 53 and 7 Armoured Divisions were to clear the country to the north of the Zuidwillemsvaart and to capture s'Hertogenbosch; 51 (H) and 15 (S) Divisions were to clear the triangle Vught–Best–Veghel and were then to operate westwards against Tilburg and Kaatsheuvel. After s'Hertogenbosch was cleared, 7 Armoured Division was to join the pursuing forces and would act on their right wing.

The divisional plan was that 160 and 71 Brigades should open the advance towards s'Hertogenbosch with 160 on the right and 71 on the left. When these two brigades had cleared the woods that lie between the railway and the main road between Grave and s'Hertogenbosch, 158 Brigade was to pass through them and assault the town. The battalion headquarters was set up at Oss; B and C Companies were attached to 160 Brigade; A Company to 71; D Company was kept back and was to be used as circumstances demanded.

The attack opened at 06.30 hours on October 22 with a flame-throwing attack upon the village of Nuland. Later on in the day, when Nuland was occupied, the battalion was deeply impressed at the destruction that had been wrought by the flame-throwing tanks—not an object in the village had escaped the flames; the whole place was little but a heap of cinders and charcoal. By noon, the leading brigades were past Geffen and were up to the eastern edge of the woods in front of them. Thereafter the enemy's resistance became very stiff, and Major Crozier, who was put in charge of all the forward companies, noted in his diary, "There was a bad hold-up at 14.00 hours." Nevertheless, towards evening the 1st East Lancashires reached the little hamlet of Bruggen which stands on the northern edge of the woods about two and a half miles beyond Geffen. The enemy had abandoned it and it was blazing. On the left, 7 Armoured Division forced their way through the woods and reached Middelrode. The divisional commander then drew back his leading troops as he did not want to engage them in heavy street fighting after dark.

Further to the left, 51 (H) Division advanced towards Schijndel during the night of October 22/23. The enemy were not able to resist so stiffly on this part of the front, and by noon (October 23) Schijndel was carried. The Germans were, indeed, fighting at a great disadvantage and were hardly using artillery at all against the Armoured and 51 Divisions.

At 06.30 hours on the 23rd, 160 and 71 Brigades renewed their attacks and towards nightfall they had debouched from the woods and were in the villages of Molenbroek and Varkenshoek, two miles east of s'Hertogenbosch. The fighting on this part of the front was very bitter; but, farther south, 51 (H) Division made a good advance. It was now decided that 158 Brigade should make the final assault upon 'sHertogenbosch on the following day.

The 158th Brigade moved off at 02.30 hours on the 24th and at 08.30 hours the leading battalions were in the eastern outskirts of the town. Colonel Earle now went to the brigade headquarters for a conference, at which it was decided that the whole of D Company should support the final attack upon the town, and that C Company should guard the right flank. Major Walker therefore moved the mortars up and deployed them just west of Molenbroek early in the afternoon. It was from behind the continuous fire of the mortar company that the 1/5th Welch reached the centre of the town, and the 2nd Monmouths reached Herven and Orten on the right flank. One detail of this long covering shoot has survived, and it is valuable, as it indicates the skill and tactical acumen with which these shoots were conducted. Lieutenant Weaver's platoon so overpowered a small enemy detachment that they captured a regimental sergeant-major.[42]

The Germans had, however, by no means yielded. In the woods round Heide small parties of men still fought desperately on while in s'Hertogenbosch itself the Germans destroyed the bridge in the centre of the town and clung obstinately to the western side of it. By good fortune a smaller bridge in the north-eastern part of the town was captured undamaged, and this enabled the 7th Royal Welch Fusiliers to cross the waterway that runs through the town in an east-to-west direction, and to clear the southern side. By nightfall the town was practically in our hands, but the Germans still held its western approaches and formed a strong defensive position along the leg of the Afwaterings canal that runs north-east and south-west, through the south-western approaches to the city. The 158th Brigade faced the Germans from the eastern side of the canal: the 1/5th Welch were in the northern, the 7th Royal Welch Fusiliers were in the central, and the 1st East Lancashires were in the southern part of the line. The Germans were still fighting bravely from any group of houses that they could cling to; and they actually flung back the 1/5th Welch from a bridge that they had captured, and recovered it.

It was now decided that 158 Brigade should secure a crossing on the Afwaterings canal on the day following; and that 71 Brigade should pass through it and operate westwards between the railway and the Afwaterings canal. The

[42] Lieutenant Coulston's notes.

machine-gun companies were not to be used in the first part of the advance; but the mortar company was ordered to keep a group of factories in the western part of the town under continuous fire.

The 1/5th Welch did, certainly, make a small bridgehead on the western side of the canal during the forenoon of the 26th, and the 7th Royal Welch Fusiliers were passed into it. At the southern end of the line, the East Lancashires also established a bridgehead; and by nightfall the whole of 158 Brigade was on the western side; 71 Brigade was not, however, sent into the bridgehead. The position of such Germans as still clung to the outskirts of s'Hertogenbosch was now fast becoming untenable; for on this day (October 26) 51 (H) Division carried the town of Vught, and secured all the passages of the stream that runs past it. The Armoured Division reached Udenhout.

The Germans attacked 158 Brigade's bridgehead during the morning of the 27th, and C Company assisted in repelling the attack. This was the enemy's last stroke in this area; and after making a slight advance they withdrew to the north-west. The 53rd Division's contribution to the battle was now made, for during the course of the day orders were that the division was not to advance beyond the canal; and that 71 Brigade, which was to have been passed through the bridgehead, was to hold a front between Vught and Helvoirt.

The reason for the change of plan was that the 51st and the Armoured Divisions were making such advances on the south and south-western sides of s'Hertogenbosch that a westerly advance by 53 Division was no longer needed. During the night of October 27, troops of 15 (S) Division occupied Tilburg, and by then the Armoured Division was farther back between Udenhout and Helvoirt. A pivoting movement brought the Armoured and 51 Divisions to a line between Geertruidenberg and s'Hertogenbosch, and by November 1, the battle was over save only for the clearing of the country between Afwaterings canal and the river Maas, which was left to 51 Division. The capture of s'Hertogen-

THE BURGHERS' HOSPITALITY

bosch was well reported in the British press and this very much encouraged the men of 53 Division, for although the pressmen had not deliberately exalted the prowess of one division at the expense of another, it did nevertheless appear to many that publicity had not been fairly distributed. The explanation was probably that the war correspondents had inclined to congregate at places where the Guards Armoured Division was operating, and that other places in the battle zone were not so much visited. The struggle for s'Hertogenbosch was peculiarly satisfactory to the battalion in that every company had been engaged in the assault. A Company had been fully employed during the preliminary bombardment; C Company had accompanied the infantry as they advanced along the road and railway, and had acted as their flank guard; B Company assisted the final advance into s'Hertogenbosch by engaging positions that the tanks reported. "It is often said that a machine-gun battalion is only useful in a defensive role," says the *Gazette*, "but this operation showed very clearly how we can work in an attack, and it was, from our point of view, an admirable demonstration and very much appreciated by the division." As usual D Company had been employed throughout; every brigade commander had asked for as much mortar fire as could possibly be supplied whenever an advance was being planned or executed; and the company were privileged to see by proof positive that their weapons and their management of them were good. "During the day" [October 24], runs the battalion diary, "members of D Company visited the areas which had been engaged by their 4.2-inch mortars and found conclusive evidence of the accuracy and effectiveness of their fire. In one case four dead Germans were found in a slit trench which had received a direct hit from a 4.2-inch mortar bomb."

A description how s'Hertogenbosch was carried would be incomplete unless it placed the generous spirit of its citizens on record. A year later, 53 Division was made the guest of the battered town, and for the three days that the British

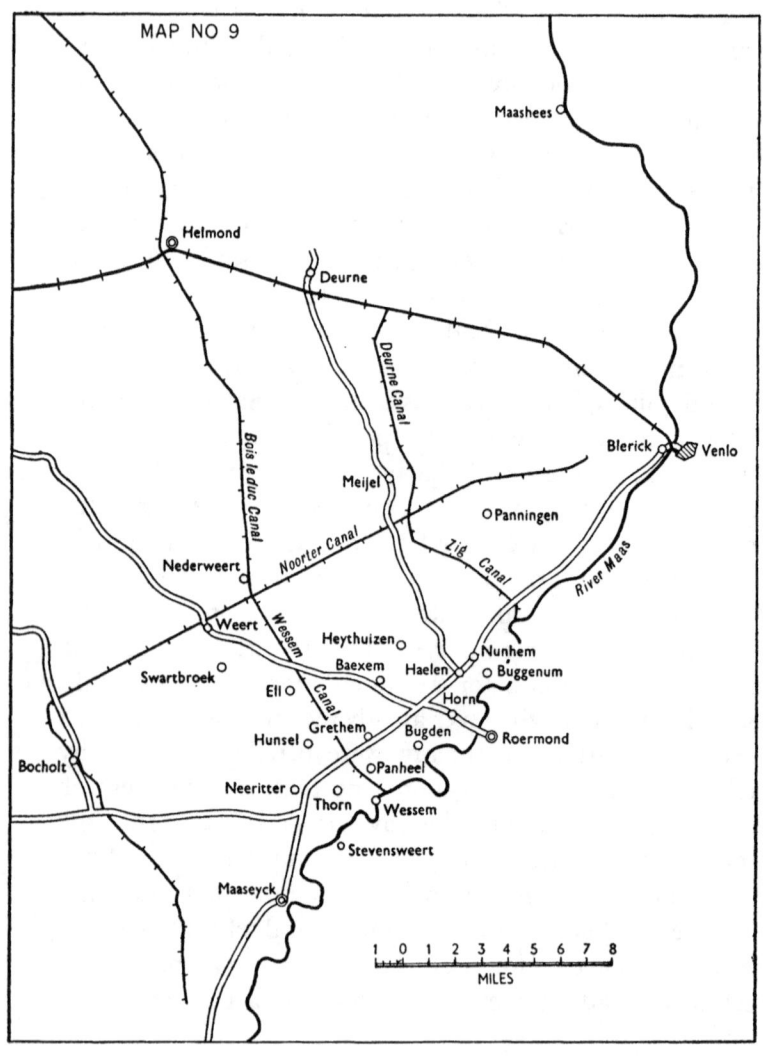

allotted to 53 Division was to force the Wessem canal, to push on to the Zig canal, and then to form a defensive front along the Maas between Buggenum and Wessem. The 51st Division, operating on its left, was to cross the Noorer canal at Nederweert; while the 7th Armoured Division on the right was to seize the locks at Panheel.

The ground on the eastern side of the Wessem canal, which the enemy was holding, is higher than that on the western in consequence of which the brigades of 53 Division were drawn back to form a defence in depth, and, in the words of the 158 Brigade diary, "There was little observation of the canal line itself." In the original dispositions 158 Brigade was posted round Weert; 71 Brigade was at the south end between Thern and Neeritter; 160 Brigade was drawn right back round Bocholt, and was ordered to counter-attack if the Germans attempted to cross the canal in force. The enemy's strength was believed to be one battalion between the railway crossing and Wessem. The plan finally decided upon was that 160 Brigade should move to a concentration area near Hunsel, force a crossing opposite Grathem, and that 158 Brigade should be passed through it and operate towards Beegden and Horn.

As the operation started (November 14) a message came through that 7 Armoured Division had captured the locks at Panheel, and that 51 Division had crossed without difficulty at Nederweert. The 4th Welch and the 2nd Monmouths now went forward and began to force the canal. At half past nine the 4th Welch were across, but the 2nd Monmouths were stiffly opposed and one of their companies was pressed back. Some time after midnight, however, the setback was remedied and the Monmouths signalled that the third battalion (6th Royal Welch Fusiliers) could then cross. By daylight the bridgehead was established and 158 Brigade prepared to pass through. There was some delay in completing the Class 9 bridge on which the brigade was to cross; but in the early afternoon all was ready and the 1/5th Welch went over. They were followed by the East Lancashires and before

POSITION COVERING VENLO ROAD, NOVEMBER 1944

THE WESSEM CANAL

nightfall Baexem was carried. On the day following, the advance was pressed as far as Haelen and Nunhem (November 15). The enemy had, in fact, resisted less stiffly than had been expected. The 71st Brigade crossed during the afternoon of the 16th and by nightfall were " in positions facing the Meuse."[46] The patrols reported that the Germans had established a line of defensive positions across the Roermond bend, and that, although the defences were not strongly manned at the moment, a considerable body of troops was stationed slightly behind them. By November 22 there were no enemy west of the Meuse in the Roermond area. " Enemy opposition opposite Roermond had been light," writes the 2nd Army's historian; " his object was to delay us as cheaply as possible."[47]

By good fortune a concise but quite circumstantial account of how the battalion was employed during the crossing of the Wessem canal has been entered in the battalion diary. During the first part the whole battalion was engaged in supporting 160 Brigade; the mortar and the machine-gun companies kept enemy positions and likely lines of communication continuously under fire. When 160 Brigade had successfully forced the crossings the companies were again attached to their brigades and advanced with them. The mortar company was heavily employed during the last part of the operation when 71 Brigade cleared up the Roermond bend. One of the last of the enemy's strong points in this area was a brickworks which the Germans defended to the last. The Oxford and Buckinghamshires succeeded in carrying it on the 22nd and the mortar company was pounding it till the very last moment.

On November 26 the battalion headquarters was established in the convent of Franciscan sisters at Heythuizen; even in a photograph the building and the gardens round it look so calm, so well tended, and so tidy that it is almost impossible to associate them with the operations of war. The

[46] Brigade diary, November 16.
[47] Vol. I, p. 270.

countryside is here one of the flattest and most monotonous in western Europe; the autumn rains had turned the fields into great lakes of mud, and the roads which served as causeways across them were in so bad a state that heavy vehicles could only be used on the big thoroughfares.

On November 30 General Eisenhower inspected battalion headquarters and saw a demonstration of machine-guns and 4.2-inch mortars going into action.[48]

Everybody thought that active campaigning was finished for the year and that it would not be restarted until the following spring, and affairs were then in this posture:

30 Corps and 84 U.S. Division of the 9th American Army had carried Geilenkirchen and had cleared the enemy out of a small salient between Hatterath and Puffendorff. The new line of positions was, however, so waterlogged that wheeled vehicles could not reach the forward areas, and it was impossible to continue operations in that area.[49]

12 and 8 Corps had completed their operation against Venloo and had cleared Blerick. D Company was temporarily attached to 15 (S) Division and assisted in the clearing of Blerick; it was subjected to heavy counter-battery fire during the operation.[50] The Canadian Army had cleared the country on the southern side of the Schelde and had also crossed to Walcheren island and had carried Flushing. On the mainland they held Breda, Bergen-op-Zoom, and Rosendaal.

These gains had, moreover, been used to the full; for a convoy had been safely brought into Antwerp on November 28, and the port was being used as a supply base. This very much raised the striking power of the northern group of Allied armies.

The 9th U.S. Army was attempting to make a breach in

---

[48] The demonstration was given by platoons commanded by Lieutenant John Weaver and Captain de Gaye.

[49] It seems that General Eisenhower never intended to go into winter quarters in the old style. See *Account of 2nd Army's Operations*, Vol. I, p. 297.

[50] Lieutenant Coulston's notes.

WINTER BILLETS

the Siegfried line round Aachen and Duren, and had been fought to a standstill.

The 1st U.S. Army was preparing to attack the dams between Heimbach and Duren: for General Bradley considered that no substantial advance could be made in his sector of the front until this was done, as these dams control the flood waters of the river Roer.

The 3rd U.S. Army had captured Metz and was advancing up the valley of the Moselle.

The 6th U.S. Army was well established in Alsace-Lorraine.

The 7th U.S. Army had captured Strassburg and was pointing towards Karlsruhe.

When the operation against Roermond was completed 53 Division was put into corps reserve.

The battalion was, however, still engaging known enemy positions across the river. A Company was at Kessenich—a sort of garrison overlooking a bend in the Meuse—and was sending out patrols; B Company was at Helen with a platoon in Buggenem; C Company was at Neer; D Company was in Buggenem and near Maasbree.[51]

A winter training programme for all units and formations was approved and circulated: the following entries in Major Crozier's diary are fairly descriptive of what was then anticipated:

There is no subject more likely to start a civil war in the Army than accommodation. I have been struggling all day to get decent winter billets for the battalion and have come up against dozens of others doing the same (December 6). We are starting next week on a full-blown winter training programme complete with cadres and a regimental training school. They have started a divisional school in Louvain, so it looks as though we were all set for the winter. (December 8.) Everything very quiet and static. (December 9.)

A few days later Lieutenant-Colonel Earle was pronounced to be too unwell to take up an appointment to the

[51] Lieutenant Coulston's notes.

14th Army in Burma, and Major Crozier was given command of the battalion. He was certainly very familiar with the officers and men; for he had been the second-in-command since the battalion was re-formed in June 1942. On the very day after Lieutenant-Colonel Crozier had made his first visit to all the companies as commanding officer,

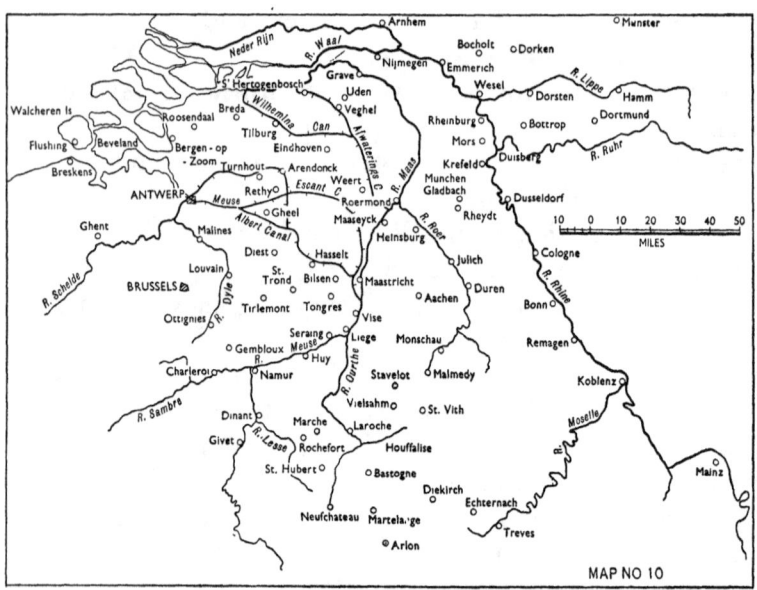

the battalion was ordered right back to the suburbs of Antwerp. Headquarters was at Litith; A Company was at Contich; C Company was near by; D Company was at Wavre Notre Dame; B Company was away from the battalion under the command of 15 Division. (December 18.) As Lieutenant-Colonel Crozier put it: "Hopeless business getting round the battalion: it is split up all over Belgium."

Although the officers and men of the battalion did not learn it until a couple of days later, the German high command had made a last bid for victory by launching an attack in the Ardennes: and 53 Division had been moved to the

GENERAL EISENHOWER WATCHING A DEMONSTRATION BY THE FIRST BATTALION IN HEYTHUIZEN CONVENT GROUNDS, NOVEMBER 1944

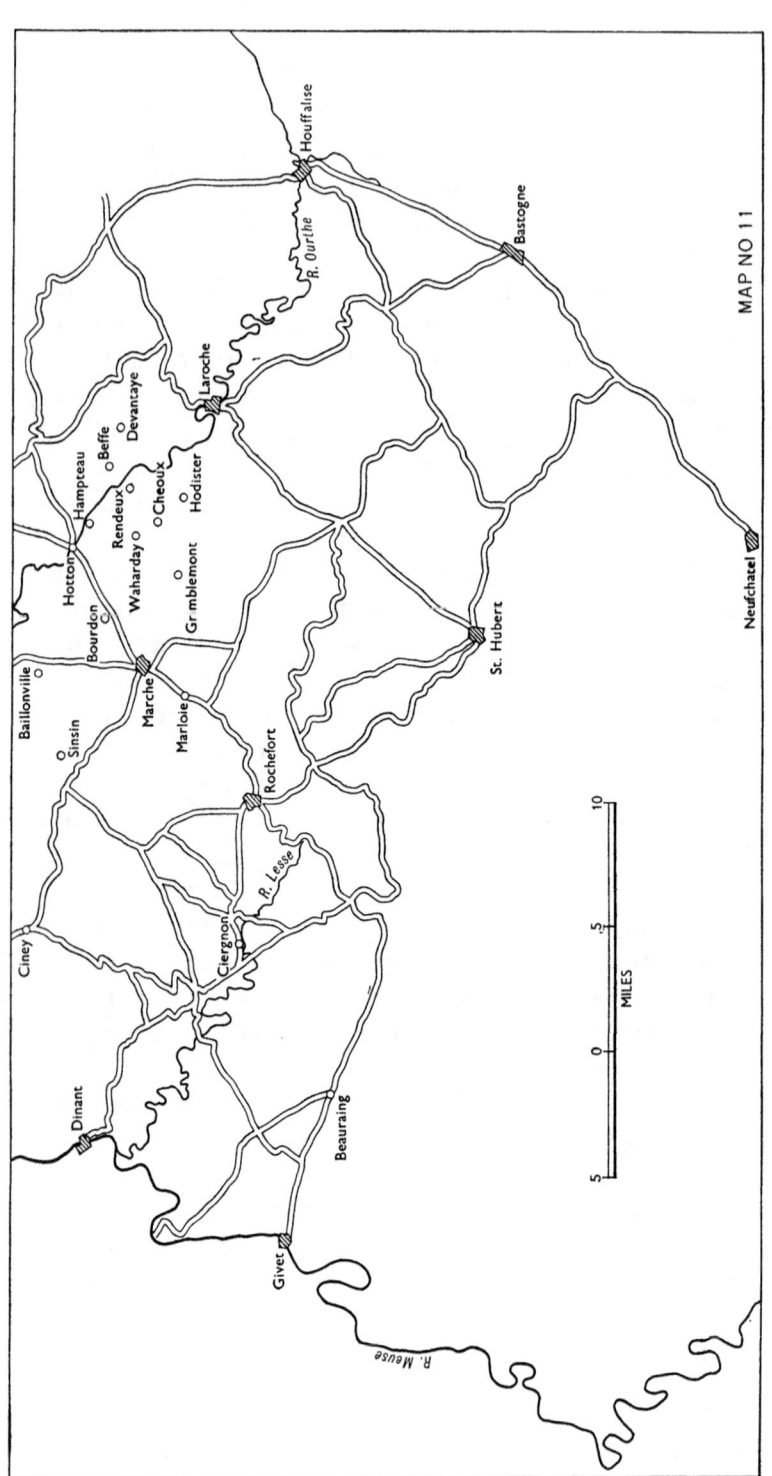

MAP NO 11

FIELD-MARSHAL MONTGOMERY DECORATING SERGEANT J. S. SULLIVAN OF
FIRST BATTALION WITH THE M.M., DECEMBER 1944

THE OLD BATTLEFIELD

Armoured Brigade and 61 Reconnaissance Regiment, which had also been placed under command, were forward, round Gembloux. The headquarters of the battalion was at Duysbourg, near the north-eastern edge of the forest Soignies: A Company was near headquarters; B Company was in the open country near the little hamlet of Vrebos; C Company was in the Lasne valley near Tombeek; D Company was near Genappe.[53a] The chances and the hazards of war had thus thrown the battalion into the country where the 2nd battalion had fought in the opening engagements of the war in western Europe, three and a half years previously. The next few days were spent in preparing battle positions. "Very strong positions they were too," adds the regimental *Gazette*. "The ground was as hard as iron and covered with snow, and digging was extremely difficult; the weather, though cold, was brilliantly sunny and the work was carried out in double quick time."[54]

It would appear as though reports of the German thrust were not too numerous the week that followed upon the redeployment of 30 Corps; but the general inference was that the magnificent resistance of the Americans in Bastogne was impeding the German advance. On December 23, at all events, 43 Reconnaissance Regiment sent patrols across the Meuse and they reported that Marche, Rochefort, and Ciergnon were not then occupied. "This was surprising," writes the 2nd Army's historian, "as there was little between him and the river. Twenty-four hours had elapsed with no appearance of the enemy on the almost open road to Liège." At battalion headquarters it was determined that the enemy should not be permitted to interfere with the time-honoured customs of the British Army and on Christmas Eve "the Technical Adjutant visited the other ranks' leave hotel in Brussels to make arrangements for the Christmas decorations."[55]

[53a] See Map No. 17, p. 318.
[54] By a truly extraordinary chance A Company's positions were dug on the battlefield of Waterloo.
[55] Battalion diary, December 24.

By Christmas Day, however, the posture of affairs in the battle area and the enemy's intentions were tolerably clear. Five panzer and five infantry divisions were drawn out between Rochefort in the west and Malmèdy in the east: most of them were facing north to resist the growing pressure from the 1st United States Army. Between Rochefort and Diekirch there were two panzer, two panzer grenadier, six infantry, and one parachute divisions. Bastogne was still held by the United States Airborne Division.

The main thrust was, therefore, down the valley of the Lesse towards Dinant. Armoured units had been located west of Rochefort on December 23, but they were reconnaissance forces only; for the main mass of the enemy's thrust divisions (116 Panzer, 9 Panzer, 2 Panzer, and Panzer Lehr) were between Marche and Saint-Hubert.[56]

When the general state of affairs was thus clearly delineated, Field-Marshal Montgomery decided to make the VII U.S. Corps into a mass of manoeuvre and to assemble it round Marche. In order to relieve it of every duty save that of striking hard at the enemy salient, Field-Marshal Montgomery also decided, although only after some consideration, to put 30 Corps across the Meuse, and to deploy it between Givet and Hotton on the right of the VII U.S. Corps. The attack against the northern side of the salient was to begin on January 3 and was to be directed up the valley of the Ourthe towards Houffalise.[57]

It would not be relevant to the purpose of this history to review the complicated orders that were issued to give effect to the Field-Marshal's plan, and it will suffice to say that as a consequence of the first series of orders 30 Corps was moved up to the Maas between Givet and Huy, and that it was then redeployed on the easternside of the Maas between Givet and Hotton. When the corps was thus brought up on the right of the VII U.S. Corps its composition was: Guards Armoured Division; 6 Airborne Division (recently

---

[56] See *Account of 2nd Army's Operations*, Vol. 1, p. 304 and Map 12.
[57] *From Normandy to the Baltic*, p. 178.

flown out from England); 53 Division; 29 Armoured Brigade; 33 Armoured Brigade; 34 Tank Brigade.

Two divisions were deployed forward: 53 Division on the left, 6 Airborne Division on the right; 53 Division was strengthened by 33 Armoured Brigade; 6 Airborne Division by 29 Armoured Division and 34 Tank Brigade.

The battalion accompanied 53 Division. A and D Companies, which were then attached to 71 Brigade, moved off first and spent Christmas Day in the ice-bound country between Namur and Givet. The remainder of the battalion followed at the end of the year. When the counter-attack was about to begin, the division was holding a front between Marche and Hotton. A and D Companies were near Marche with 71 Brigade; B and C were round Hotton with 158 Brigade. Battalion headquarters was at the village of Sinsin. The move from the Dyle had been very difficult for the country was in the grip of a bitter winter; roads, fields, towns, villages, and dwelling places were all covered by a carpet of frozen snow. " The weather conditions are foul," wrote Lieutenant-Colonel Crozier on December 28. " Everything covered with a two-inch layer of ice, making roads almost impassable, and a thick fog with visibility down to four or five yards. D Company coming back a distance of sixty miles had only four vehicles in after seven hours. After twelve hours they still had over twenty vehicles missing.

The trouble was that the tank brigade (33rd) was moving with the divisional column and that the tanks with no ice studs on their tracks simply could not hold the road and caused road block after road block. On December 30 the battalion moved only fifty miles in twelve hours. Nevertheless the battalion drivers lost not a single vehicle, and although the men had been issued with no special winter clothing save only a few extra pairs of socks, and were compelled to tie straw and sacking round their legs and feet to protect themselves against frost-bite, not a single soldier in the battalion fell out from exhaustion in that ice-bound country. Nor should it be forgotten that a whole army staggered, slithered, or crawled into its new positions under the same conditions of difficulty and hardship and was ready to perform what was demanded of it at the time appointed.[58]

When 30 Corps was deployed in the country to the east of the Meuse, indications were already appearing that the power behind the German thrust was declining, and that the worst danger was past. German tanks and armoured vehicles had certainly pressed down the valley of the Lesse during Christmas week, and some had been engaged within three miles of the Meuse. The mass of assaulting troops had nevertheless not been able to go beyond Rochefort. Nor was evidence lacking that brave, skilful, and resolute though the German Commander-in-Chief had been, he had yet attempted something that was beyond the strength of the German army: for while the VII U.S. Corps was assembling, it had become engaged with some advanced enemy units round Celles; and when the American troops entered the village they found in it six self-propelled guns, which the Germans had not been able to withdraw because their supply of petrol was exhausted and could not be renewed. Also, the 3rd U.S. Army, whose redeployment was not as difficult and as laborious as that of the Anglo-American forces on the northern side of the salient, had begun to press the German forces between Saint-Hubert and Diekirch and had relieved Bastogne.

* * * * *

The division was deployed in front of the main road between Marche and Hotton with the divisional headquarters at Baillonville. The 71st Brigade was on the right in the southern approaches to Marche. On their left was 158 Brigade with the 2nd Monmouths under command in the

---

[58] The American troops, who were given a first-class issue of winter clothing, suffered far more severely from frostbite than ours. The explanation is that a frequent change of socks (upon which Colonel Crozier insisted) is a better safeguard than fur-lined boots which are not changed.

extreme left of the line near Hotton. The last orders given were that the enemy was to be expelled from the country between Marche, Hotton, and the little village of Reckname near Laroche. The ground in front of the division rises to a north-east- and south-west-going ridge about 1,200 feet high. Beyond the ridge a small crossroad runs through the villages of Cheoux, Waharday, and Rendeux; beyond the crossroad, the ground rises again to a rounded summit about 1,400 feet high. The country is everywhere covered with pine woods, and a man who is passing through the woods can rarely see more than ten yards ahead of him, as the lower branches of the trees droop down to the ground. An officer who was about to engage in the battle wrote in his diary that the country was beautiful beyond description; for the grey skies that had accompanied the heavy snowfall had disappeared, and the snow-covered hills and villages were resplendent in a glittering sunlight. The advance was timed to begin on January 4, and on the day before, news came in that the VII U.S. Corps on the left had reached Beffe, Devantave and Malempre.

At 08.00 hours on January 4 the division moved forward; as the advance began the skies clouded over and snow again began to fall. The 1st East Lancashires and the 1/5th Welch started the attack, and at 10.15 hours they had made such progress on the rising ground ahead of them that the 2nd Monmouths who were held back during the opening part of the advance were ordered to go forward. Soon afterwards 71 Brigade started their attack against a rounded summit to the south of Marche. The 160th Brigade, which was in reserve, was moved up to Hotton and Hampteau.

Throughout the day progress was irregular: the enemy's infantry and armour did not put up much opposition; but mines were extremely troublesome and they held back the 1st Highland Light Infantry in 71 Brigade's sector. Late in the afternoon 158 Brigade renewed their advance with the 7th Royal Welch Fusiliers on the right and the 1/5th Welch on the left, and again the mines broke up the attack; for the

Royal Welch Fusiliers were held up by them, while the 1/5th Welch made good progress. At the close of the day the Oxford and Buckinghamshires were on the high ground to the south of Marche: the 1st Highland Light Infantry were on their left towards Grimblemont, which the enemy still held, the 1st East Lancashires and the 7th Royal Welch Fusiliers were between Grimblemont and Cheoux. The 1/5th Welch were in some thick woods to the north of Cheoux; the 2nd Monmouths were just outside Rendeux. The snow had fallen all day and towards evening a hard frost set in. There was thus but little communication between company and company, and none at all between battalion and battalion: each group knew roughly where the enemy were standing in the snow-covered woods ahead of them, and that was all. Communications with divisional headquarters appear, however, to have been very well maintained, for the exact position of every forward company was duly noted at nightfall. During the day the divisional commander reported that his front was little but a thin red line and asked that 53 Reconnaissance Regiment should be sent to him, and this was done.

The attack was restarted at full daylight on the next day (January 5). The frost, following upon the heavy fall of snow, had formed a surface of hard slippery snow upon which the men reeled and staggered. The 2nd Monmouths, on the extreme left, renewed their attack on Rendeux; but the Germans fought them to a standstill outside the village. In the centre the 7th Royal Welch Fusiliers pushed on to the very edge of Grimblemont: on their left the 1/5th Welch made a slight advance; but the woods and the steep slope on their sector made all movement very difficult. Towards evening the enemy launched a counter-attack, which transformed the battlefront. The Germans would appear to have assembled on or near the sideroad that passes through Cheoux: when ready, they came on at a strength of about 400 and were supported by a well-directed fire from tanks that were hidden in the woods. The blow fell heaviest upon front that had been held when the German armies started their onslaught. Field-Marshal Montgomery now, " Undertook the withdrawal of all British troops from the Ardennes with the greatest possible speed, in order to regroup for the battle of the Rhineland."[60] The 53rd Division's move to Eindhoven was part of this withdrawal and regrouping.

[60] *From Normandy to the Baltic*, p. 180.

CHAPTER V

THE ADVANCE INTO GERMANY
January—May 1945

WHEN the German onslaught was thus brought to nothing General Eisenhower was free to mature and perfect his plans for defeating the German armies. He had always been persuaded, and nothing that had subsequently occurred had made him deviate from his original opinion, that the German forces would be unable to resist the Allies when the Ruhr was isolated; for this great industrial area was the heart and lungs of armed Germany. As to the best way of isolating the Ruhr he writes thus:

> Since we could not attack the Ruhr frontally, we must by-pass it, and the most favourable terrain lay to the north of it. I was equally certain that this main effort to the north should be accompanied by a secondary effort, as strong as our means permitted, after the main, northern thrust had been provided for, from the Mainz Karlsruhe area in the direction of Kassel.

In other words, two large forces were to debouch into northern and north-western Germany and were to sever the communications between the Ruhr and the central and eastern parts of the country. The preliminaries to this final manoeuvre were, however, arduous and difficult, for General Eisenhower was persuaded that the last decisive thrust could only be attempted after all the German forces to the west of the Rhine had been defeated and their defences overwhelmed.[1] If this was to be accomplished, it was essential that operations should be continued during the winter months, no matter what the difficulties might be, in order that the Germans should be given no opportunity of collecting and training reserves.

The northern thrust, which was to be the major one, was

[1] See R.S.C., p. 109 et seq.

entrusted to Field-Marshal Montgomery, who was left in command of the 9th U.S. Army after the American forces that had been placed under his orders during the Ardennes battle had been withdrawn. He had thus three armies under his control: the 2nd British, 1st Canadian, and 9th American. The territory which was to be cleared before the British and American armies could line up along the Rhine is in the shape of an inverted V, of which the two long sides are the courses of the Maas and Rhine. The two riverbeds are close together at the northern end, or apex of the triangle, and are about fifty-eight miles apart at its southern end. Nijmegen stands at the apex, Maastricht and Cologne at each end of the base. The central and southern part of the country between the two rivers is largely an industrial area, for Krefeld, Munchen–Gladbach, and Rheydt are all inside it. The northern part is agricultural, a country of woods, tillage fields, and small market towns. The area is, however, sub-divided by a third river, the Roer, which joins the Maas at Roermond and forms another inverted V with the towns of Roermond, Maastricht, and Julich at its northern, south-western, and south-eastern corners. The country between Julich and Roermond is so flat that the River Roer here often flows in three or more parallel courses; the district can, indeed, be flooded by manipulating the dams in the upper reaches. Field-Marshal Montgomery decided that this country between the Maas and the Roer ought to be cleared before the greater operation of advancing to the Rhine was undertaken.[1a]

The 21st Corps was ordered to take the task in hand, and was allotted 7 Armoured Division, 43 Division, 52 (L) Division, 8 Guards Tank Brigade, and 8 Armoured Brigade. The Germans had constructed three east- and west-going lines of field fortifications in the area: the first passed by Linnich, Wurm, Tripsrath, Waldenrath, Breberen, Havert, and Susteren; the two others were parallel to the first and were sometimes one and sometimes nearly three miles from

[1a] See Map No. 10, p. 196.

B COMPANY GIVING COVERING FIRE FOR AN ATTACK NEAR GRIMBLEMONT DURING THE GERMAN ARDENNES COUNTER-ATTACK, JANUARY 1945

THE ADVANCE AGAINST HEINSBERG

one another. The defences of the Siegfried line ran north and south through the eastern part of the area, near the towns of Dremmen, Uetterath, and Wurm; Heinsberg, which was an outpost of the Siegfried line, was strongly fortified. Two German divisions, the 183rd and the 176th, held the district, but no tactical reserve was available.[2]

* * * * *

On January 16 the 7th Armoured Division debouched from Susteren and began the operation, in weather so foul that it was doubtful whether the state of the roads and countryside would not bring everything to a standstill. Nevertheless, the endeavour was persisted in, and by January 26 the Germans had abandoned the whole area: they were evidently unable to put up a stiff resistance, for they withdrew from the Heinsberg defences after we had delivered the preliminary attacks against them. Everything (save the weather) was ready for the advance to the Rhine, and the weather was a formidable obstacle; for, in that part of Europe, the days in January are very cold, and the cold is aggravated by bitter winds and slashing rainstorms. The muddy roads and the even muddier fields freeze hard at night, and the rain by day, being just (but only just) above freezing point, covers the frozen sludge with a film of water.

When the Roer triangle was cleared, preparations for the advance from the Maas were well forward, although some of the formations that were to be employed were still in their training areas. The fronts allotted to each group were these:

The Canadian Army, reinforced by 30 Corps, was to hold the Maas front between Nijmegen and the sea, and was to attack in a south-easterly direction from the Nijmegen bridgehead.

The 2nd Army was to hold the Maas to the south of the Canadians and was to support their advance.

[2] See George Blake, *Mountain and Flood*, Chap. XI, for an admirable account of the operation in the Roer-Maas triangle.

The 9th U.S. Army was to advance towards the Rhine from a front between Julich and Roermond.

If the operation was brought to a successful issue the sector of the Rhine which each group was to hold was: the Canadian Army from Rees to Nijmegen; the 2nd Army from Rees to Mors; the 9th U.S. Army, from Mors to Dusseldorf.

The Canadian Army's advance, with which we are henceforward more particularly concerned, was to be made in three successive bounds, or, as the operation orders styled them, *phases*: (1) to the line Gennep–Asperden–Cleve; (2) to the line Weeze–Udem–Calcar, with the crossings at Emmerich so well secured that the Germans would not be able to debouch on to our communications by that way; and (3) to the line Geldern–Xanten. This advance was to be made by 30 Corps, which was composed of: 15 (S) Division; 51 (H) Division; 53 (W) Division; 2 Canadian Division; 3 Canadian Division.

The task allotted to 53 Division was to clear the northern part of the Reichswald forest with 15 (S) Division operating on its left towards Kranenburg and Emmerich, and with 51, 43, and Guards Armoured Division on the right. A brief description must now be given of the Reichswald forest if the difficult duty that was thus placed upon the division is to be appreciated. The forest, which is about nine miles long and five miles wide, covers a large part of the country between Cleve and Gennep; there is a wide corridor in the forest at Groesbeek; but on the north-west side of it the preserved woodlands continue to the suburbs of Nijmegen. This second section is, however, on the Dutch side of the frontier and is not called the Reichswald, although it is part of the same natural feature—a large zone of pine woods in the flat land between the Rhine and the Maas.

The German engineers had constructed the northern end of the Siegfried line in the Reichswald. The fortifications covered a ridge of high ground at the northern end of the forest and ran north-east and north until they reached the

THE REICHSWALD

Alter Rhein at the village of Wardhausen. They consisted of a continuous line of trenches, which was bastioned by strong points wherever a suitable site could be found; in front of the trench lines an anti-tank ditch ran by Kranenburg and Mehr and joined the Alter Rhein near Keeken.

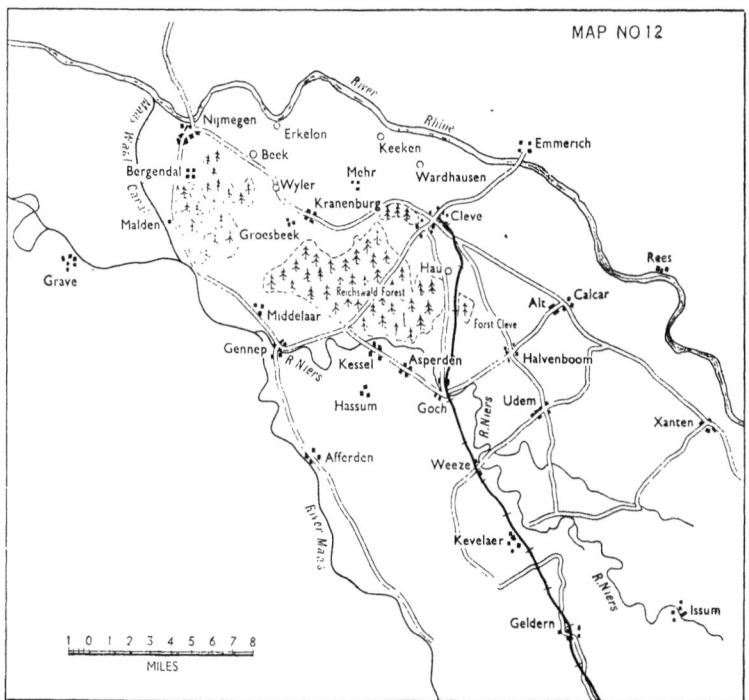

From the southern edge of the Reichswald, defences of the same pattern—trench lines, strong points and an anti-tank ditch—ran south-eastwards towards Goch and then due south. This review of the main course of the Siegfried defence line is, however, rather misleading, for it was no longer a line but a belt of fortified perimeters. "The striking feature of recent work," runs the division's intelligence report, " is that instead of simply elaborating and strengthening the defence lines it apparently transforms their character. The principle appears to be no longer that of a defence line, but of a defence net. The whole area is, in fact, being split up into a series of self-contained boxes enclosed by trenches, and, in some cases, by anti-tank ditches and river lines." In addition to this, all towns within the Siegfried belt were strongly fortified: Cleve, Goch, Weeze, Kevelaer, Udem, and Calcar were defended by an elaborate network of trench lines, strongpoints and anti-tank ditches. To the east of the Siegfried line was a second series of fortified positions called the Hochwald lay-back. Its northern end rested on the Rhine at Rees, and from this place it ran south to Geldern. Like the front line, this secondary line was made up of trenches and strongpoints; but it had this peculiarity, that the main anti-tank ditch was in the middle of the trench system.

This fortified belt was not very strongly occupied. The 84th Infantry Division, with 2 Parachute Regiment and Battle Group Katzman under command, held a sector between Erkelon on the Rhine and Middelaar near the southwestern tip of the Reichswald. The sector was nearly ten miles long and one engineer battalion was the only divisional reserve that our intelligence branch had been able to locate. On this general question, what reserves could the local commander count upon, the intelligence branch thought it probable that one additional division would be brought into the Hochwald lay-back after our first assault was delivered. We had, therefore, this great advantage that the battle would open with five divisions attacking one.[3] But even after due allowance was made for this great superiority in men and guns, a dispassionate balance sheet of advantages and difficulties left a formidable list of entries on the difficult side, not the least of which was that General von Rundstedt had thoroughly penetrated our intentions. One of the orders of the day which this dauntless old soldier issued, just before the battle opened, began thus:

Soldiers of the Western Front. The enemy is massing for a major offensive against the Rhine and the Ruhr. He will employ all his available strength to break into the western

[3] See Appendix Z, 158 Brigade War Diary for January 1945.

not continue the attack, as the road between Groesbeek and the forest was by then (noon February 8) unusable. Nevertheless, at the end of the second day's fighting the two forward brigades had mastered the curving ridge of high ground that runs across the northern part of the Reichswald forest. The 160th Brigade were on the central part of the ridge; 71 Brigade were to the westward of them and 158 Brigade were making ready to pass through and renew the onslaught. This ridge was in a sense the key to the Reichswald defences, as the enemy had emplaced the strongpoints of their fortifications along it; and it was of ill omen to them that 15 Division, operating on the left of 53 Division, seized and cleared the highest point of the ditch, which is called the Matterhorn, during the course of the day.

February 10. The machine-gun companies and the mortar company did not go forward with the infantry during their first advance into the forest, and remained in their deployment positions waiting for a summons from the forward area; 13 and 15 platoons of D Company were asked for by 160 Brigade during the early hours of February 10; and D Company's headquarters was established at Frasselt. The roads behind the division were now so bad that all maintenance vehicles were compelled to use the supply roads of 15 Division. A conference was held at divisional headquarters during the forenoon, and it was then decided that the machine-gun companies would not be wanted for the time being; nevertheless B and C Companies were summoned forward into 160 Brigade's area during the afternoon, and were warned that they would have to carry their guns and equipment. The order was inevitable in the circumstances, no doubt, but it was very severe; for even on the well-laid roads of England, a machine-gun and its equipment is a heavy burden. A gun and its tripod weigh ninety pounds, and the gun is an awkward load, whose weight can never be distributed; a box of only 250 rounds of ammunition weighs eighteen pounds. These loads had to be carried for miles through the slush of the forest, and, although the exertion was very great, not a man fell out. The first entry into the Reichswald made a deep impression on the officers and men, for the spreading branches of the great fir trees shut out the light; and the gloom, the wet, and the sludge made the place sinister and forbidding. The men knew, moreover, that the road behind them, from Groesbeek to the forest was not merely unusable for the time being: it had disappeared and had to be completely rebuilt. The road was, indeed, completely destroyed; for a Churchill tank which had tried to use it, was so sunk in the mud that only its turret was visible.

February 11. Few, if any, reinforcements were reaching the enemy, who were still endeavouring to hold our advance in the Reichswald with a miscellany of units belonging to 84 Division, and with three forward battalions. When, therefore, the advance was begun at 08.00 hours, it made good progress. The troops of 160 Brigade crossed the Cleve road during the forenoon and pressed on to the eastern part of the forest: on their right the East Lancashires (158 Brigade) established themselves about three-quarters of a mile from the eastern edge of the forest; 71 Brigade were farther inside the forest on the right rear of 158 Brigade. B, C, and D Companies were now all in the forest and were following the leading battalions. D Company was in action when 160 Brigade crossed the Cleve road, but the machine-gun companies were still being used to hold all captured ground against a possible counter-attack.

February 12. During the evening of the previous day, reinforcements had at last reached the enemy; for during the course of the day's fighting it was ascertained that formations from the 15th Panzer Grenadier and the 15th Panzer Divisions were in the forward areas. When, therefore, the advance was resumed at first light our troops found that they were more stiffly resisted than they had been since the battle began. During the forenoon leading battalions of 160 Brigade certainly reached the corner of the forest that abuts the Cleve–Goch road, near the village of Hau; but they were here brought to a standstill by the desperate opposition of the enemy in front of them. B Company's guns were brought into action, and were ordered to cover certain targets with indirect fire; but nothing that was done availed to break the enemy's resistance; and at the end of the day the brigade was on the edge of the forest, certainly, but it was still unable to debouch into the open country beyond the Cleve–Goch road. To the south of 160 Brigade, 158 Brigade were resisted equally fiercely: they were fought to a standstill when they advanced to conform to 160 Brigade's forward movement. Soon afterwards a counter-attack fell heavily upon the East Lancashires and they were compelled to give ground. C Company was severely engaged during this part of the fighting; and, indeed, whenever the Germans counter-attacked, or seemed likely to do so, the calls for machine-gun fire were sharp and insistent. To the south of 158 Brigade, the Oxford and Buckinghamshires and the Highland Light Infantry advanced towards the south-eastern edge of the forest, but they were still well within the forest belt at the end of the day. The ground in the forest itself was now so churned that it was becoming doubtful whether the necessary food, water, and ammunition would be carried across it to the battalion in the front line. Lieutenant-Colonel Crozier set out to visit the forward platoons; and after he had reached the Gennep road with great difficulty and very slowly, his jeep sank down to its axles and he could go no farther.

The battalion diary informs those who study it that at ten o'clock that night the technical adjutant reported, that "the battalion maintenance train had successfully delivered supplies to the forward companies." It was no mean achievement.

February 13. The information that was collected during the previous day's fighting showed that the enemy were reorganizing their front; for the 84th Division which had up to then been the formation responsible for the defence of the forest was now put under the orders of the 116th Panzer Division. From this it was to be inferred that the new batta-

THE SOUTHERN SIDE OF THE FOREST

lions that had just been identified were not isolated units taken from another part of the theatre; 130 Brigade of the 45th Division was put at one hour's notice, and was sent into the forest in the rear of 71 Brigade.

It was, indeed, 71 Brigade which started the day's attack, with the Highland Light Infantry on the right and the 4th Royal Welch Fusiliers on the left. D Company was moved forward to the brigade area, and was in action during the last part of the attack. It would seem as though the brigade commander decided to press forward in an easterly direction, along the narrow-gauge railway that traverses the southern part of the forest; for in the early part of the afternoon the leading battalions debouched into the open country on the eastern side of the forest belt.

The 158th Brigade also attacked in a southerly direction, across the axis of 71's advance, and they emerged into open ground during the afternoon. C Company, who were supporting the advance, suffered severely: Captain Gunnell, the second-in-command was among the casualties. The river Niers runs along the southern edge of the Reichswald; and a sideroad from Cleve crosses the river at a little distance from the forest boundary. When the leading battalions of the brigade came out of the woods, the 7th Royal Welch Fusiliers pressed forward to seize the bridge; but the Germans, who were still fighting for every millimetre of ground, rallied and drove them back. At the end of the day, therefore, the division was at last clear of the forest. The 160th Brigade were still on the eastern side near Hau; 71 were astride of the single-track railway; and 158 were facing the Niers. It will be proper at this point to make a brief review of the other parts of the battlefield.

* * * * *

The greatest advance had been made on the left, where the Canadians had reached the left bank of the Rhine opposite Emmerich. On their right the troops of 15 Division were in Cleve and were clearing it. On their right 43 Division were pressing down upon Bedburg. The positions held by 53 Division have already been described. On their right 51 Division had captured Gennep and Kassel. Field-Marshal Montgomery considered that "the first phase of the operation was completed."[8] Nevertheless, the chances of pressing the operation to a decisive finish must still have appeared uncertain. The Rhine was in flood, and the Canadians were moving in boats from one island village to another; the Nijmegen–Cleve road upon which 43, 15, and 53 Divisions so largely depended, was under water between Wyler and Kranenburg, and only D.U.K.W.s could use it; the Reichswald was almost impassable, and the state of the troops on its eastern and south-eastern edges may be judged by an urgent signal that the 4th Welch (160 Brigade) sent out during the forenoon of the 13th: "Require water, would appreciate any assistance available."

It can hardly be doubted that our troops would have been driven into the mud and water in their rear if the enemy had been able to strike them hard while their communications and supplies were so precarious; but, against this, it must be remembered that the advance between the Rhine and the Maas had been ordered because it was assumed that the Germans would not be able to assemble a mass of manœuvre in that area, and that the assumption was correct.

What, however, was of most prejudice to our operations was that the 9th U.S. Army which was to advance from the Roer to the Rhine was still unable to move. The lower Roer had overflowed its banks, and it was quite impossible to start a great operation across the miles of flooded meadows that lay on the American front. "Operation Veritable had to continue alone."[9]

February 14 *and* 15 were spent patrolling. Progress on the right was, however, continued; for there 52 Division was thrown in on the extreme right of 30 Corps, and it reached

[8] *From Normandy to the Baltic,* p. 191.
[9] *From Normandy to the Baltic,* p. 192.

GOCH CAPTURED

Afferden on the Maas. On February 16, 71 Brigade made a move forward to some high ground that overlooks the village of Asperden. It was not, however, until the following day that orders for the next move forward were received. The 43rd Division on the left was almost held up; the 53rd were therefore ordered to clear everything up to the Cleve–Goch railway.

February 17. The 160th Brigade moved out at 08.00 hours and to their surprise they were not resisted. A small quadrilateral woodland, called Staatforst Cleve lies to the east of the Cleve–Goch railway, and the brigade consolidated on its western edge during the afternoon. It was decided that no machine-gun support was required for this advance; two mortar platoons were, however, engaged.

On the right, 71 Brigade attacked southwards to clear the ground between the river Niers and the main road, with the Oxford and Buckinghamshires on the right and the Highland Light Infantry on the left; they were stiffly resisted but they reached their objectives. The 158th Brigade did not participate in the day's advance and remained in their positions at the south-eastern side of the Reichswald. The intention at this time was to press on most vigorously along the two river lines and to leave the Germans in the Cleve–Goch–Calcar area in a pocket.

February 18–20. The decisive moves in this part of the battle theatre were indeed made by 15 Division and the Canadians. Realizing that Goch was now the buttress of the German positions between the Rhine and the Maas, General Horrocks, the commander of 30 Corps, deployed 15 Division to the north of the town and ordered them to attack along the right bank of the river Niers. The division moved off at 15.00 hours on the 18th, and by nightfall had got well into the northern suburbs. The British troops pressed on during the night, captured the German commander, Colonel Matussek, during the street fighting, crossed the bend of the river that flows through the town, and during the 20th made themselves masters of the place. Simultaneously, the

Canadians in the north forced the Germans back from the Goch–Calcar road and got astride of it between the village of Alt and the Havenboom crossroads. The German positions were now untenable, and the enemy commanders had no option but to retire to the second line of fortified positions, which our intelligence officers called the "Hochwald lay-back."[10]

* * * * *

The 53rd Division was granted a breathing space during these days. "Our troops' activity had been on a reduced scale," runs the divisional intelligence summary. "A day of minor attacks and readjustments," wrote the commanding officer on the 18th, and on the 20th, "For once very little news; the whole front seems to have slowed down." Nevertheless, the battalion was in no rest billet. Lieutenant-Colonel Crozier established the battalion headquarters to the west of Goch, assembled B, C and D Companies near by and called up A Company from Groesbeek: by one of the chances of war this company had not been in action since the advance against the Reichswald had begun. The dreadful toll that the waterlogged forest and the weather had taken of our equipment is well illustrated by this further entry in the commanding officer's diary: "The battalion furiously overhauling everything and getting ready for the next push. L.A.D. busy hauling carriers out of the forest today. They recovered six. We are now only seventeen vehicles down."

February 23 and 24. The orders for the next operation, which was styled Operation Leek, were not long delayed. The 8th Armoured Brigade was put under command of 53 Division, which was deployed to the south of Goch across the Goch–Weeze railway line. The advance was to be made southwards against the town of Weeze, which was fortified and was held by two or three battalions of the 7 Parachute Division. The advance was to be begun by 160 Brigade, to

[10] See 53 Division Intelligence Summary, February 18, 19, 20.

SERGEANT LEESON

be continued by 71 (which was to capture Weeze), and was then to be exploited by 158, which was to clear the woodlands in the country to the south of the town. The 15th Division was to operate on the left of the division; 52 Division was to protect its right flank.[11]

The 51st Division lay to the south-west of Goch, facing the enemy who held a position to the north of Weeze but were under orders to hold their area only. As the Germans were holding the south-western approaches to Goch, a counter-attack against the right and rear of the advance was highly probable, and Lieutenant-Colonel Crozier concentrated the whole battalion and a company of the King's Royal Rifle Corps on the right bank of the river Niers, to the north of Goch. From this position, the battalion received requests for D.F. fire from the brigades to the south and to the east, during the operation that can now be briefly described. The battalion had never been employed in this way before, and the operation was, in Colonel Crozier's words, "The most complicated battle we have fought yet."

The 15th Division moved off on the 23rd and at 06.00 hours on the 24th 160 Brigade started the advance of the 53rd Division. The enemy resisted far more stiffly than had been expected, and at the end of the day 71 Brigade, which was passed through 160 when they were brought to a standstill, just managed to capture the village of Holst. Platoons from B Company supported this attack, and came under heavy fire from 88-mm. guns, nevertheless the company got their guns into position for the action on the following day.

February 25–26. The Oxford and Buckinghamshires and the Highland Light Infantry moved out of Holst at first light; but they were stopped soon afterwards opposite an anti-tank ditch which the Germans held strongly. It was during this day's fighting that Sergeant Leeson of A Company distinguished himself by an act of extraordinary valour. After the two battalions had drawn back from the anti-tank ditch, Sergeant Leeson saw several wounded in

[11] See George Blake *Mountain and Flood.* Chap. XII.

front of his position. He left his gun pit, and, not once but several times, traversed the shell-swept zone before him, and brought the wounded in.

The 51st Division now moved forward and captured a small village on the right flank of 71 Brigade.[12] This, in the commanding officer's words, eased our right flank position a lot. The 71st Brigade was now ordered to take over the whole divisional front: 160 Brigade was concentrated at Goch and 158 to the north of it.

February 27-28. The original plan for capturing Weeze by successive bounds in a southerly direction was now altered; and it was decided: that 160 Brigade should relieve 8 Infantry Brigade (15 Division) which was holding a position to the north of Weeze on the eastern side of the Niers, and should then pass on into the bend of the river which flows by the eastern side of the town; that 158 Brigade should then pass through 160 Brigade and attack Weeze from the east; and that, while this was being done, 71 Brigade should advance down the eastern side of the river and carry the anti-tank ditch.

The 2nd East Yorkshires of 8 Infantry Brigade were holding the bridge where the road between Udem and Weeze crosses a little tributary of the Niers. Relieving them, which fell to the 6th Royal Welch Fusiliers, proved extremely difficult, as the whole of the country round the bridge could be observed from the enemy's posts in Weeze. The relief was done under incessant shelling and mortaring; but it was completed by about midday. The 7th Royal Welch Fusiliers at once passed through the bridgehead and attacked the enemy in the bend of the river. They were accompanied by Major Woolsey, for the brigadier of 158 gave orders that a safety officer from the machine-gun battalion should accompany the forward infantry and report their advance to battalion headquarters. The attack was carried out during the dark hours, and flame throwers were much used. All through the

---

[12] On the night of February 25, the battalion put down a concentrated fire on Obernelsum in support of an attack by 51 (H) Division.

Division was relieved by the 52nd. The 7th Manchesters relieved the battalion which was then moved to Holt, a small village between Venloo and Goldern.

The rest was well earned and was almost over due. On March 2, Lieutenant-Colonel Crozier entered in his diary, "The division is almost dead beat." The high-ranking officers very handsomely acknowledged what the division had achieved. Field-Marshal Montgomery, whose practice has always been to be so sparing of compliments that those who received them shall be certain that they are well earned, expressed his high appreciation of the division's performance; General Crerar did the same; and when the division was taken from 30 Corps command, General Horrocks thus ended his letter of goodbye: "Humbly, I would like to say well done to every individual man for the courage and endurance you have put forth."

It is, of course, inevitable that the documentary records of a campaign should be inadequate memorials of fortitude and valour; for when these things are represented in words only a desiccated image of them remains. There is, nevertheless, in the battalion records a document, which is as illustrative of the labour and the sufferings that all men who were engaged in that battle endured, as the repeated references to the cold, the wet, the mud, and the failing supplies of food and water. The document is the photograph of a landscape which is carpeted in such deep snow that only a bare outline of the roads, the hedges and the fields is visible; behind the snow-covered fields there is an enormous tract of dark forest. It is a country from which even the beasts are withdrawn until the land again emerges from beneath its icy covering; where the hardiest peasant can do no work, and remains by his fireside. Yet this was the prospect before the men of 53 Division when they moved from their positions on the morning of February 8, and this was the country where they fought and died and lay wounded.

* * * * *

THE NEXT OBSTACLE, THE RHINE

The operation of clearing the Rhine and securing a deployment area for an advance into the plains of northern Germany was, indeed, virtually completed when the division was withdrawn from the battle theatre: for on March 3 our troops met the Americans round Geldern; on March 8 the Canadians carried Xanten; and two days later the last German formation had retired across the Rhine. What was, perhaps of even greater prejudice to the German armies was that the Rhine was now not only reached, but crossed. For, on March 7 the 1st U.S. Army captured the Remagen bridge in a usable condition, and so opened a gateway to the supply lines of all the German armies between Bonn and Emmerich.

When the British and American Armies had thus reached the Rhine, Field-Marshal Montgomery intended to cross the Rhine with two corps (12 and 30) between Emmerich and Wesel; to secure a more or less continuous bridgehead in the flat land between the Rhine and the Ijssel; to break out of the bridgehead towards Bocholt and Dorsten; and, thereafter, to sweep into northern Germany along such axes of advance as circumstances indicated to be the most suitable. The 9th U.S. Army was to secure a bridgehead from the point where the Ruhr and the Rhine join, to Bottrop and Dorsten; having done this, the Americans were to operate towards Hamm and Münster.

In the British sector 30 Corps was to be on the left with an assault front from Emmerich to Mormter. The 12th Corps front was to run from Mormter to Wesel. The boundary between the British and American armies ran near the line of the Dorsten–Rhine canal, although the canal itself was in the American sector. The Allied superiority in men and guns was now very great. The whole line of the Rhine between Krefeld and Emmerich was held by the 1st German Parachute Army; only four divisions were facing the 9th U.S. Army between Essen and Cologne; while between Essen and Emmerich there were seven divisions with a reserve force of doubtful composition called the 47th Panzer Corps near

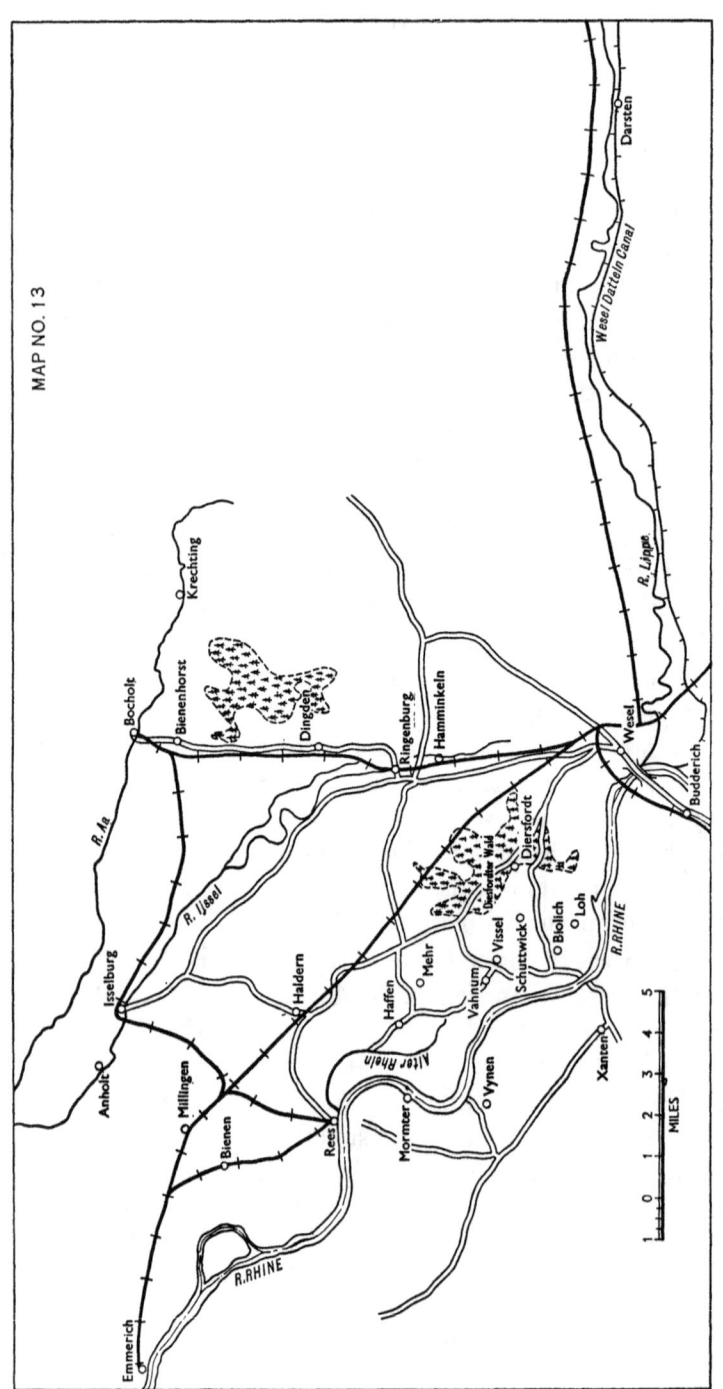

REGROUPING FOR THE CROSSING

Emmerich.[13] The 21st Army Group and 9th U.S. Army combined were thus overwhelmingly stronger than any forces that the enemy could deploy against them; for 12 Corps, with which we are more immediately concerned, was alone composed of 7 Armoured Division, 15 (S) Division, 52 (L) Division, 53 (W) Division, 4 Armoured Brigade, 34 Armoured Brigade, 1 Commando Brigade, and 115 Infantry Division. In addition, it was arranged that the XVIII U.S. Airborne Corps, which was composed of the 6th British and 17th U.S. Airborne Divisions should assist in the operation.

Assembling and redeploying these great forces was, however, an arduous and a difficult operation; for when the country between the Rhine and the Maas was cleared, the formations that were required for forcing the Rhine were very scattered, and collecting the enormous quantities of ammunition and engineers' stores that were needed for the prolonged bombardments that were anticipated, and for the bridging operations that were the first essentials for executing the plan successfully, was a task of the first order.[14]

In detail, the plan was that 3 Canadian Division was to hold the left sector of the bridgehead, and was to capture Emmerich if its capture was deemed necessary; 15 Division (30 Corps) was to cross near Rees, and was to capture Rees and Haldern; 43 Division was then to enter the bridgehead and occupy its left sector.

On the right of 12 Corps sector, the 1st Commando Brigade was to cross near Wesel and capture it. Simultaneously 155 Division was to cross between Vynen and Xanten, and was to establish a bridgehead between Haffen and Schuttwick. Ten hours after these crossings had been made, the two divisions of the airborne corps were to be dropped in the country just beyond the bridgeheads of the 1st Commando Brigade and 51 (H) Division.

The 53 (W) and 7 Armoured Divisions were then to enter the 51 (H) Division bridgehead and were to operate towards

---

[13] *From Normandy to the Baltic*, p. 201.
[14] See *Account of 2nd Army's Operations*, Vol. II, p. 345.

Bocholt and Dorken. In order to do this, at the time required, 53 Division was to concentrate round Kevelaer.

The division moved to its assembly area on March 23; and the battalion accompanied it. The short rest at Mollem had been very much enjoyed and had been spent in a manner characteristic of the Belgian inhabitants and of the British visitors.

We had a glorious football match against the locals [runs the regimental *Gazette*], at which Tommy Woolsey replied in perfect French, but in a pretty foul accent to the Mayor's long address of welcome, and he was presented with a large bouquet of flowers. I think we won the match all right, but the *entente cordiale* was the thing and that was tremendous. What little we understood of the Mayor's speech was pretty flattering.

* * * * *

An army that is fighting against Germany cannot fail to be stirred when it crosses the Rhine; for although that great river is not the political frontier of Germany it has been more consecrated in poetry, legend, and tradition than any natural feature in Europe.

The order to cross was received on March 25, but the actual time of crossing was changed by a later order, with the consequence that the division did not cross until the afternoon of the 26th. By nightfall, however, the three brigades and divisional headquarters were in the bridgehead. Their first assembly area was between Vissel and Bislich. The battalion crossed during the first part of the afternoon; the headquarters was set up on the left of the bridgehead between Vissel and Vahnum. It will be proper, at this point, to make a brief review of the battle in which the division was now engaged.

The crossings began at 21.00 hours on March 23, when the leading battalions of 51 Division went across at Rees; and by midnight on the following day the division had established a solid bridgehead between Bienen, on the left, and the marshes of the Alter Rhein to the south-east of Wesel.

An hour after 51 Division went across, the 1st Commando Brigade crossed the Rhine below Wesel, and by first light on the 24th the whole brigade was in what was left of the town. The bombardments that it had suffered had turned it into an expanse of ruins.[15]

At 02.00 hours on the 24th, the 44th Brigade of 51 Division crossed, and by midnight the division had established a bridgehead which ran through Haffen and Mehr and along the south-western edge of the Diesfordter Wald to Schuttwick and Loh.

At 10.00 hours on the 24th the troops of the U.S. Airborne Division began to land in the open country to the north-east of the Diesfordter Wald; by midnight they had carried Hamminkeln, had cleared the northern and southern edges of the forest, and had joined hands with the forward battalions between Schuttwick and Loh.

Throughout these operations the Germans had resisted bravely where they could, and at places their artillery was well directed and difficult to deal with. Nevertheless they were overwhelmed and stunned by the weight and the precision of the blow that had fallen; and at no point was the surge across the Rhine brought to a standstill. The great national river had proved no obstacle to the invaders of the Reich.

It would be superfluous to review the operations of the next two days in detail, and it must here suffice to say that the first rush was not checked; in fact it gained momentum, for by the evening of the 26th, when the 53 Division was across, the whole "bridgehead of the 2nd Army front became a continuous line."[16] The line was naturally extremely irregular, and ran from Bienen on the left through Milligen, Haldern, and Hamminkeln. The indented and fluctuating line of the bridgehead did not, however, represent the extent of the victory, for the Ijssel, which, in these parts, runs parallel

---

[15] See the striking photograph in *Account of 2nd Army's Operations*, Vol. II, p. 351.
[16] *Account of 2nd Army's Operations*, Vol. II, p. 355.

to the Rhine and makes a broad water obstacle with its dikes and polders, had been reached at several points, and the crossing at Ringenberg was in our hands.

Field-Marshal Montgomery was satisfied that the victory was decisive: "Except in areas that were held by the parachute divisions," he writes, "German resistance had disintegrated."[17]

As soon as 53 Division was in the bridgehead, General Ross assembled an operation group at his headquarters, and issued orders for an advance on Bocholt through Ringenberg. Lieutenant-Colonel Crozier circulated the order to the battalion during the evening of March 26. The battalion had now reverted to its regular organization: A Company was under command of 71 Brigade, B Company was with 160, C Company with 158. Platoons from D Company were to be attached to the forward brigades as circumstances demanded.

It should be firmly held in mind, therefore, that when 53 Division advanced against Bocholt it was breaking down one of the last centres of organized resistance, and that it was subsequently pursuing a beaten enemy or overrunning German territory so fast that such German troops as had survived the disaster were deprived of all rallying points.

Bocholt was, however, captured by a regular operation in which three brigades were deployed. The main road between Bocholt and Wesel and the railway line that runs alongside of it, divide the southern approaches to the town into two parts; to the east of the road and railway the land is deeply wooded; to the west of them the country is open farm land. The villages of Ringenberg, Dingden, and Bienenhorst stand on the main road.

March 27. The 4th Armoured Brigade led the advance, advanced through Ringenberg and occupied a position just beyond it. The 160th Brigade passed through them and by midnight the crossroads and bridge in the middle of the village of Dingden were in the hands of the 6th Royal Welch

[17] *From Normandy to the Baltic*, p. 207.

Fusiliers. The 158th Brigade advanced on the left of the road and railway and secured the line of the crossroad that runs into Dingden from the west. It does not appear that any of the battalion's companies were in action on this day; the battalion headquarters was established in a Hamilcar glider near Hamminkeln, and B Company, which was the farthest forward, was south of Ringenberg at nightfall.

March 28. The river Aa runs through the town of Bocholt and makes a corridor of open land along the northern side of the woods that lie to the east of the main road. The 53rd Recce Regiment approached the stream of the Aa during the course of the day; they were met by spandau and mortar fire, and it was not until after nightfall that the patrols were able to ascertain that the bridge at the village of Krechtung was blown.

The resistance along the Aa thus showed that Bocholt could not be carried by a wide turning movement, and the advance on either side of the main road was continued. The 4th Armoured Brigade with the 4th Royal Welch Fusiliers under command, fought their way through the woods and secured the sideroad that runs along the northern edge of the wooded area and enters the main road at Bienenhorst: 160 and 158 Brigades made an equal advance along the railway and to the west of it; and by nightfall the leading battalions of the three brigades were in the southern approaches to Bocholt, B, C and D Companies were all engaged in this day's fighting; for the Germans were fighting far more stubbornly than had been expected: road blocks on the main and sideroads repeatedly held up the advance, and wherever the Germans could challenge our advance through the woods they did so.

March 29. At first light the 2nd Monmouth and the 5th Royal Welch Fusiliers (160 Brigade) moved forward and entered the southern part of the town. They were stiffly opposed by small arms and mortar fire, which covered each road block, but towards noon they reached the river line. B and D Companies were severely engaged during this first

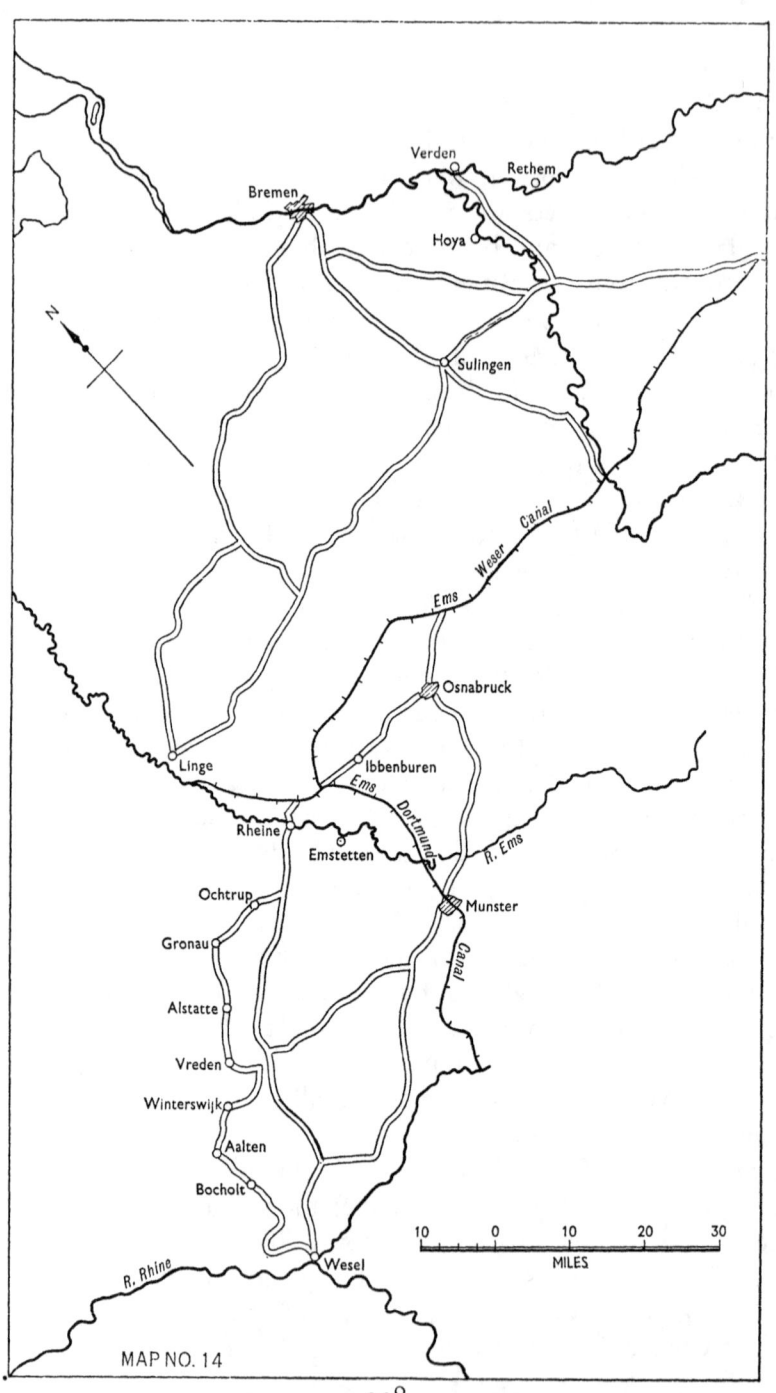

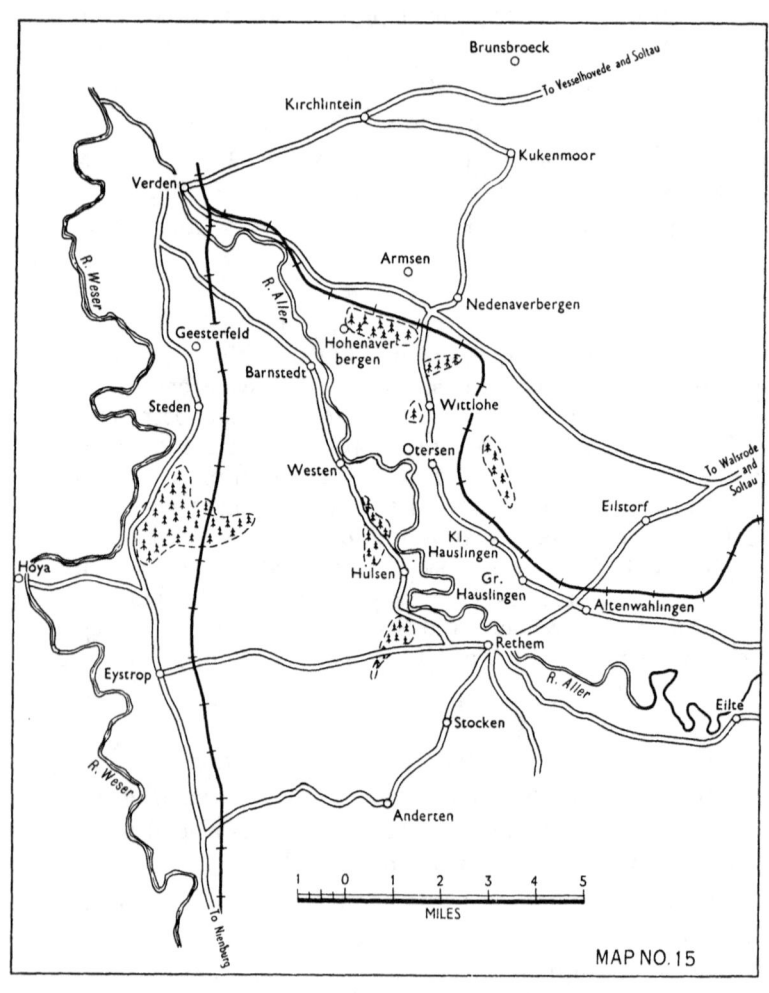

THE STAND ON THE ALLER

The enemy could make no stand in the great moors to the south of Sulingen, but as the Weser was approached it seemed as though the Germans were going to try to hold the river line. The division and the battalion headquarters were established to the west of Hoya on April 9, and news came in soon afterwards that 16 Brigade, which was then temporarily under the command of 7 Armoured Division had secured the crossing at Hoya; but that a bridge had still to be built as the town bridge had been blown.

Towards midnight 158 Brigade went over the newly constructed bridge behind a covering fire from B, C, and D Companies, and the leading battalions (1/5th Welch and 7th Royal Welch Fusiliers) pressed forward towards Rethem. During the forenoon, however, the 1/5th Welch which were then leading, were brought to a standstill by a well-placed enemy force about three miles to the west of Rethem. The advancing troops were, moreover, soon impressed by the skill and cunning with which the Germans were prolonging the hopeless struggle. The country between the Weser and the Aller is covered with woods and spinneys, which the infantry had not been able to clear, as every unit in the army was virtually under orders to advance at all possible speed. Parties of Germans were in consequence lurking in the woods and were closely watching our movement along the road. These men allowed all the provost's road signs to be put up without showing themselves, and then ambushed small parties and single officers as they passed along the divisional axis.

During the first action at Rethem, the Germans took prisoners, but Private Parry of the 1/5th Welch, who was among those who were cut off, feigned to be dead, remained motionless while a German N.C.O. looked at him, and got back to our lines.[19] He then reported that the enemy had shot their prisoners in cold blood, and Captain Brian de Grineau of the *Illustrated London News*, reproduced pictorially and in all good faith what Private Parry told him by

---

[19] His own account of the inspection was that he was savagely kicked, which might conceivably be true.

word of mouth. On the left of the picture is a large double roofed barn, and at the foot of it some British soldiers are standing with their backs to the barn wall. The inscription above these men reads "Defiant Welshmen being mown in sweeps of gun." In the centre of the picture, a burly man with a gun at the hip position is called "S.S. executioner with captured Bren gun." On the right a German officer is "kicking bodies for signs." The other objects in the picture are a burning house, a group of German soldiers who are herding the British prisoners towards the barn, and another group of German soldiers who are coming round a street corner to watch the butchery or to lend a hand. The title of the picture is "Lest we forget. The massacre of the Welsh prisoners at Rethem: an episode which shocked the world, drawn by our war artist, Captain de Grineau, at the scene of the murders." [20]

Not a particle of this was true, for when our troops did finally get into Rethem, it was found that the Germans had sent their wounded prisoners to hospital, and had scrupulously observed the laws of war.

* * * * *

The river bed of the Aller, upon which the Germans had decided to make a stand is extremely twisted: its average direction is north-west but the large bends and loops in which it flows deviate very much from this, and if anybody were to travel by boat from Celle to Verden (where the Aller joins the Weser) he would often be steering due north or due south. The left bank is sharper and better defined than the right; for there is a broad ribbon of flat, marshy land on the northern and eastern side of the river between Otersen and Verden. The land between the Weser and the Aller rivers is fairly open, although woods and spinneys often reduce the view. Rethem is the principal crossing place in the lower reaches of the river; it is here that the main road

[20] *Illustrated London News*, April 21, 1945.

FIRST MANCHESTERS FIRING ON THE CROSSROADS EAST OF RETHEM,
APRIL 13, 1945

THE ALLER IS CROSSED

to Hamburg is carried across the river; but between Rethem and Verden there is a secondary crossing at Westen. It was in this flat, sleepy country that a few handfuls of brave Germans decided to make a last desperate stand.

The line of the Weser appeared, however, to have been completely abandoned; for the 2nd Monmouths (160 Brigade) occupied Nienburg without difficulty; and the 4th Welch turned north from Eystrop and seized Steden. Divisional headquarters was, therefore, moved up to Eystrop.

April 11. When the first advance against Rethem was stopped, 71 Brigade was moving up from Lemforde. A, C, and D Companies were, however, all available when the 1/5 Welch made a second attack (early a.m. April 11) and they kept the enemy's positions under continuous fire. Once again, however, the attack failed. To the north and south of this kernel of enemy resistance our troops made good progress for the 6th Royal Welch Fusiliers carried Stocken and Anderten, and the 7th Royal Welch Fusiliers captured Hulsen during the course of the day.

During the afternoon the 2nd Monmouths came up from Nienburg on the Weser (where they had been relieved by the 7th Armoured Division), and they attacked the uncovered enemy position to the west of Rethem from the south under a strong covering fire from A, C, and D Companies. The Monmouths advanced over flat open country, and the enemy met them with a heavy fire from spandaus, bazookas, infantry and railway guns, and the attack failed.

Shortly after this third failure, however, an important piece of news came in: the 4th Welch (160 Brigade) patrolling downstream with two platoons of B Company, had crossed the Aller at Westen without being resisted. It was now decided that 160 Brigade should relieve 158 at all points that they were holding between the Weser and the Aller; that 158 Brigade should cross at Westen; and that 71 should pass through 158 and capture the crossroads to the East of Rethem and the high ground round them.

In point of fact the Germans evacuated Rethem during

the night of April 11–12, but this was not known at the time.

April 12. General Ross gave orders that the entire 1st Manchesters should support the new operation; and the commanding officer, after examining the ground, decided that the battalion would be best employed if it remained on the west bank of the river and supported the advance from a flank. As the country to the south of Westen is open and can be swept by machine-gun fire, B and C Companies were ordered to support 71 Brigade; A and D were attached to 158, as it was thought that the mortars would be most effectively used against the German positions in the woodlands to the north and north-east of Westen. B and C were, therefore, stationed on the eastern edge of a strip of woodland to the south of Westen; from this position the guns commanded the road along the east bank, between Otersen and Alten Wahlingen, and all the intervening country.

The plan was duly executed, and at 02.30 hours the 1st East Lancashires and the 7th Royal Welch Fusiliers crossed at Westen. They were met by small-arms fire which was never strong enough to stop them, and the villages of Wittlohe and Otersen were captured by daylight. These places were of great importance to the operation, as they are astride the Verden road, and so long as they were in our hands German reinforcements from the north (if there were any) would be stopped. A bridge across the river was completed by about noon: but 71 Brigade were not then able to go over. Meanwhile, however, news came in that the Germans had abandoned Rethem and were concentrating somewhere to the east. The 2nd Monmouths occupied the town in the early afternoon and found that the German resistance had cost them dear. The place itself was shattered by the bombardments that it had suffered, and the dead still littered the streets.

Late in the day the Oxford and Buckinghamshires and the 1st Highland Light Infantry came up to Westen and crossed the river; after reaching Otersen, they turned south and made ready to attack the villages of Gross and Klein Hauslingen. Meanwhile the 4th Welch (temporarily under command of 158 Brigade) moved north and occupied Barnstedt and Geestefeld on the western bank.

April 13. At first light the 1st Oxford and Buckinghamshires moved out against Gross Hauslingen, and as they debouched from Otersen and advanced southwards, the wisdom of Lieutenant-Colonel Crozier's arrangements was very much confirmed: for the Germans moved southwards also, across the open country between the road and the river which was swept by the machine-guns of B and C Companies. The gun positions had been well chosen and the fire was very destructive. Gross Hauslingen was carried, but snipers infested the whole area and the place was not properly cleared until late in the day. The 4th Royal Welch Fusiliers, therefore, passed through the Oxford and Buckinghamshires and captured the crossroads to the east of Rethem and the village of Alten Wahlingen which lies a little beyond the crossroads. The Germans resisted this further advance with extraordinary tenacity and courage, and the 4th Royal Welch Fusiliers only just contrived to get three companies into Alten Wahlingen by nightfall.

*   *   *   *   *

As the purpose of the whole operation was to open a road along which the 7th Armoured Division could operate against Soltau, and as the enemy's resistance on the Rethem–Walsrode road was proving to be so exceptionally stiff, it was decided that 158 Brigade should advance northwards against Verden to see whether a route could be opened by that way. The commanding officer decided to support this advance to the north as he had supported the advance to the south, viz., from the left bank. He therefore stationed A and D Companies on either side of Barnstedt; their guns and mortars commanded a considerable length of the Verden road, but a wood covered a stretch of the road to the north of Otersen. As the two companies were emplacing their guns, one of the platoon commanders, Lieutenant Murray Smith, detected parties of Germans on the other side of the river; they were digging trenches, and what was truly surprising, their backs were turned towards Barnstedt, as the trenches appeared to be facing north and east. These Germans suffered severely before they got away.

The 7th Royal Welch Fusiliers led the advance and reached this very part of the road. They were then attacked from a large wood that lay to the north of them, and this was part of a general concerted counter-attack; for, at the same moment, a recce squadron was attacked from the woods to the east of Otersen, and a large number of its vehicles were made unusable. All troops in Westen were now formed into a local defence force, and the 2nd Monmouths were called up from Rethem. Two platoons of A Company were brought back and added to the defence fire.

April 14. The German counter-attack was, however, by no means over, for at daybreak it was continued in 71 Brigade's area, round the crossroads and Alten Wahlingen. Here a company of the 4th Royal Welch Fusiliers was overrun; two companies of the 1st Highland Light Infantry were very hard pressed, and two companies of the Oxford and Buckinghamshires were called up. The brigade held its positions, but only after very stiff fighting.

The 158th Brigade continued its advance to the north, and once again the battalion was able to assist the infantry materially. The brigade had not got clear of the wooded area during the day previous; and as the leading battalions moved off, A and D Companies received a message that the Germans were resisting stiffly from a wood to the west of the road. D Company was therefore ordered to mortar the enemy's positions in the wood, and A Company were directed to keep their guns ranged on the open ground at the northern edge of it. This arrangement worked admirably; the heavy and well-directed mortar fire drove the Germans out of the wood, and as they left it, our machine-guns opened up on them and took a heavy toll. A German and men were unable to keep awake if they sat down for two minutes.

* * * * *

On April 22 the advance into Germany began again, and the battalion headquarters was moved north to Ludingen: on the day following it was at Scheesel on the main road to Hamburg. The end was now very near; for the Russians were in Berlin, and on this day General Eisenhower ordered the following order of the day to be read aloud to all ranks.

The battle of the Ruhr has ended with complete success following hard upon the complete destruction of German forces west of the Rhine. Twenty-first Army Group thrust powerfully across the Rhine with 9 U.S. Army under command. Simultaneously, rapid drives across the Rhine from the Remagen bridgehead by the 12 and 6 Army Groups provided the southern arm of a great enveloping movement which completely encircled the entire German Army Group B and two corps of Army Group H. The booty is immense and is still being counted: the enemy's total losses in killed and wounded will never be known. The rapidity and determination with which this brilliant action was executed tore asunder the divisions of Field-Marshal Model and has enabled all army groups to continue without pause their drive eastwards into the heart of Germany.

There is, indeed, not much more to be said. The advance to the Elbe was delayed for a few days, because 53 Division was ordered to assist 52 Division to capture Bremen, which still held out. As a consequence 160 and 71 Brigades were engaged for several days in the country between the autobahn and the Hamburg–Rothenburg road. On April 26, however, Bremen fell and the battalion, less A and B Companies, was ordered to move on Hamburg with 158 Brigade. On April 28 battalion headquarters were at Brackel; and here the battalion waited for three days; for the 11th Armoured Division was under orders to cross the Elbe and to push on towards Lubeck, and the bridge across the river had to be left clear for them. On May 2 the battalion crossed the Elbe and moved along roads that were so blocked

THE END

with traffic that the rate of advance was less than two miles an hour.

The last days of the battalion's war service are best described in the commanding officer's own words:

May 3. After a fantastic day of negotiations with high-ranking German officers, Hamburg formally surrendered at 18.00 hours. We are not moving in tonight but are going in at first light tomorrow. The battalion is to do the job of putting piquets round the town tomorrow. Battalion H.Q. move to Bergdorf.

May 4. Today we entered Hamburg and occupied the town. All resistance has ceased and the whole northern German army group, including Denmark, has surrendered. The battalion has the fantastic job of putting piquets all round the city—a city about one and half times the size of Glasgow. We have to disarm the German army, enforce the curfew, house and sort out thousands of released Allied prisoners of war of all nationalities, and displaced persons without homes. Quite the worst job I've had so far, and much worse than any battle.

May 5. The battalion gathered in over 3,000 prisoners alone today. In addition we have had over 2,500 Russians, Poles, French, and a large number of slave workers to sort out. The Germans are proving quite amenable to discipline and there have been no incidents.

Lieutenant-Colonel Crozier was now stricken down with influenza, but he wrote on May 7 that he was getting better; that the battalion had dealt with 15,000 prisoners since they had entered the town; that V.E. day would be celebrated shortly and that, "We must try to do something about it." When V.E. day did at last arrive the commanding officer wrote this:

We held our V.E. day today. Well, the war in Europe is over, just eleven months since the start of the Normandy campaign. It will go down in history as one of the model campaigns of all time. I don't feel like celebrating. I can't help thinking of the awful sights I have seen in Germany and all over Europe, and of the colossal task now in front of us. It will take a lifetime to get back to normal.

The entry is as representative of what the men whom Lieutenant-Colonel Crozier had led were then thinking as anything that has been put to paper. A wild cry for vengeance against the beaten enemy was then rising from every corner of Europe: the fighting man cared for none of these things, and was thinking only about the normal life which he had left with such misgivings and which he so longed to resume.

CHAPTER VI

2ND BATTALION
MARCH 1924—SEPTEMBER 1939

by BRIGADIER T. B. L. CHURCHILL, C.B.E., M.C.
and LIEUTENANT-COMMANDER A. C. BELL

VOLUME II of the Regimental History, when it closed, left the 2nd Battalion in Jubbulpore, India, where on March 24, 1924, it had completed the celebrations to mark the hundredth anniversary of its raising. Five days later the battalion provided a Guard of Honour at the Circuit House for the Viceroy, the Earl of Reading, and attended a garrison ceremonial parade in his honour.

Owing to the heat of the plains, it was customary to form a detachment in some convenient hill-station to which those in the battalion who were convalescent from illness, and the young band-boys, could be dispatched in order to avoid the full rigours of an Indian summer. The battalion used Chaubattia for this purpose, and the hill-party was duly dispatched in March with a small administrative staff under Captain M. R. Davidson. This detachment remained in being until October, though the personnel was changed over from time to time.

Another detachment was formed this year at Fort Graham in Gnatong, Sikkim, a post which had originally been established as a result of the Sikkim Expedition in 1888. This post was 12,300 feet above sea level and was situated at the foot of the Jalap La Pass into Tibet, some seventy miles by road from Darjeeling. It was the highest post in the world occupied by British troops, and the kit men wore on detachment quarterguard included balaclava caps, snow-goggles, thick lined greatcoats, warm gloves, blue serge trousers, khaki puttees, and boots. Shortly after the battalion's detachment was withdrawn the post ceased to be occupied by a European garrison, and an Indian police detachment was established instead.

Company and battalion training was carried out at Nimkhera Camp, some seven miles from Jubbulpore. Usually two companies at a time occupied the camp site for three weeks, and the training season commenced in October when the weather was cooler. Companies marched out to the camp, and the routine consisted of field exercises during the day with organized games after tea. A battalion platoon league was instituted which was played off successively, and at the end of camp inter-company sports were held. The battalion went into camp in December, and brigade training followed shortly afterwards. Signal classification of the battalion signal platoon was carried out during brigade training.

On October 10 communal disturbances broke out in the city and a platoon, under Lieutenant F. C. Egan, had to be dispatched to Kotwali in hired motor-buses the same afternoon. It was employed in piqueting the streets, and the following day a company, under Major J. S. Harper, M.C., proceeded on the same duty, but fortunately the riots subsided and the troops were recalled to barracks.

In November the Governor of the Central Provinces, Sir Frank Sly, held a durbar in Jubbulpore, and the battalion provided a Guard of Honour; and on January 1, 1925, the usual Proclamation Parade was held. By this time the battalion's stay in Jubbulpore was drawing to a close and during January detachments of the 1st Battalion the Hampshire Regiment arrived to relieve the Manchesters, whose next station was to be Rangoon and Port Blair, in the Andaman Islands. The main body of the battalion left Jubbulpore by train on February 12.

During the year 1924, Major C. D. Irwin, M.C., retired on retired pay, and Major G. P. Wymer, D.C.M., reverted to the half-pay list on account of ill health. Captain G. C. Dailey, M.C., resigned in September, and Lieutenant S. E. Hollins died in Jubbulpore hospital two days after the regiment marched out.

During the move to Rangoon the three detachments of the regiment were most hospitably received by the 2nd Battalion the Border Regiment at Barrackpore, where the Manchesters detrained after a thirty-six-hour journey. On the ship from Calcutta to Rangoon the battalion had the honour of travelling with T.R.H. the Prince and Princess Arthur of Connaught, who took a keen interest in the men's comfort, and on their last night on board conducted in turn the regimental band for three or four pieces.

In Burma, the battalion was stationed in Rangoon, with a company detachment at Port Blair, the Government of India's penal settlement in the Andaman Islands. In Rangoon, the barracks were on the edge of the town, and consisted of tall wooden edifices built on high piles so that there was no ground floor, but, instead, a space open on all four sides, with a concrete floor. These barracks were known as Sale Barracks, situated at the top of Sule Pagoda Road and not far from the great Shwe Dagon Pagoda, the holiest Buddhist shrine in Burma, whose golden pinnacle dominates the flat countryside for many miles around.

In March 1925, Major-General H. C. Tytler, C.B., C.M.G., C.I.E., D.S.O., the General Officer Commanding the Burma Independent District made his first inspection of the battalion. He himself had been gazetted to the regiment in 1886, and served with the 2nd Battalion at Agra until transferred to the Indian Staff Corps in 1887.

A few days later, the battalion trooped the Colour in the presence of Sir Spencer Harcourt Butler, the Governor of Burma, and before a huge crowd of British officials and of Burmese, on the occasion of the anniversary of the raising of the regiment; and it continued to keep this custom throughout its stay in Burma.

The battalion consisted of four rifle companies and Headquarters Wing, the latter comprising, besides administrative personnel, the Machine-Gun Group, the Signal Group and the Band and Drums. During its stay in Rangoon companies went into camp for three weeks at a time at a site on the Prome Road, some ten miles north of Rangoon, while the Machine-Gun Group used a camp at Okkyin where the groups of the other battalions in Burma also were concentrated annually. It was customary to turn over 25 per cent of the Machine-Gun and Signal Groups annually before April 1, in order to build up a reserve of trained signallers and machine-gunners in the battalion. The battalion's annual camp was held at Syriam on the opposite side of the Irrawaddy to Rangoon and took place in January or February, being followed by brigade training, which usually lasted for four or five days.

At this time the standard which a soldier was required to attain to qualify for proficiency pay (sixpence a day) was that he must be in possession of a second-class certificate of education, he must be a second-class rifle shot or a second-class Lewis gunner, or a first-class revolver shot, or a qualified machine-gunner or a signaller; and in addition he must be considered by his company commander to be in all respects an efficient soldier. A further necessary qualification reflects the threat to health and efficiency which resulted from a garrison situated on the edge of a seething waterfront town: the soldier was required to have been free from venereal disease for six months, judged from the date of his discharge from hospital.

The men of the battalion, as was to be expected of a city regiment, enjoyed the amenities of Rangoon and took full advantage of the shops, cafés, cinemas, and the bathing facilities in the many lakes near Rangoon; and the excellent racecourse was a constant draw every Saturday. The Burman was a keen gambler and loved racing, and the meetings provided close and well-handicapped races, mostly for the Burma-bred ponies, standing just over twelve hands and capable of carrying surprisingly heavy weights. On the other hand, the disadvantages of the station were its hot damp climate, the prolonged rainy season accompanied by many insect pests, and the prevalence of dengue fever, which took a heavy toll in the battalion in its first year in Rangoon. In addition, training suffered by the absence of any ground within reach of barracks where company schemes or field firing could be carried out.

A feature of the battalion's stay in Rangoon was the visits of H.M.S. *Effingham*, the flagship of the Naval Commander-in-Chief of the East Indies Squadron. When this ship came up the Rangoon River, competitions in football and boxing were arranged and parties of men were taken over the ship.

In December 1926, Field-Marshal Sir William Birdwood, the Commander-in-Chief in India, inspected the battalion, and later Lieutenant-Colonel J. R. Heelis, M.C., who had succeeded to the command of the battalion from Lieutenant-Colonel W. B. Eddowes on March 5, 1925, received a letter from General the Hon. Sir Herbert Lawrence, Colonel of the Regiment, which read:

I feel sure that it will be interesting and satisfactory to you and your battalion to know that I have just received a private letter from the Field-Marshal Commander-in-Chief in India, referring to his visit to Rangoon when he saw the 2nd Battalion. He speaks in the highest terms of all that he saw and adds that the battalion has the best of reputations. I congratulate you and your command and wish you all good fortune in 1927.

The battalion continued to do well, for at the beginning of 1927 it won both the Burma Sports Championship and the District Rifle Meeting which were held in Maymyo and to which the battalion had sent teams.

During the three years that the battalion was in Rangoon it found the company detachments at Port Blair on Ross Island in the Andaman Islands group. The Penal Settlement of Port Blair was situated in South Andaman, which is one of the islands in the Andaman group in the Bay of Bengal. It consists of several small islands, Ross, Chatham and Viper and a large part of the mainland, called Aberdeen, on which the gaol was situated.

Ross was the most important island, and on it were built Government House, the church, the clubs, and the barracks. A company of an Indian Army battalion was also stationed at Port Blair and besides the Penal Settlement there was also a small European community. The troops were stationed there for internal security reasons as there were many thousands of convicts, either in gaol or working on the islands, over 90 per cent of whom were murderers.

Port Blair was a very popular station both with officers and other ranks, who were glad to leave the steaming heat of Rangoon for a few months.

There was no lack of occupation in Port Blair. There was sailing and snipe shooting for the officers, and excellent bathing and fishing for all. Ross was too small for playing grounds, but on Aberdeen there was a golf course, cricket, hockey, and football grounds, all on a large maidan constructed by convict labour upon a swamp. A free ferry for troops plied between Ross and Aberdeen, whenever required.

The cost of living was very low, as all labourers and servants were convicts, and their wages were controlled by the Chief Commissioner.

The only disadvantage was that there were no newspapers, and the population had to be content with a small news-sheet, printed on the island and reporting local news. The mail came about once a fortnight with the result that the detachment tended to become very out of touch with the world.

There is a note in the battalion *Digest of Service* dated July 1927: "The Brigade Commander, Colonel-Commandant R. E. Solly-Flood, C.M.G., D.S.O., gave a lecture on Mechanization." This is an indication of how military thought was already examining the problems which this new factor presented, for the next ten years were to see the disappearance of the mule and the horse from the establishments of the infantry.

In December 1927, the battalion provided a Guard of

the battalion in Maymyo at the end of their company's tour of duty in Mandalay.

Major-General F. E. Coningham, C.B., C.S.I., C.M.G., D.S.O., succeeded Sir Henry Tytler as General Officer Commanding Burma Independent District, and he inspected the battalion in May 1928. In November the regiment held its own Rifle Meeting on the Maymyo ranges, and the companies, two at a time, then went to Wetwin camp for a fortnight's company training.

The Viceroy of India, Lord Irwin, visited Burma in November 1928, and a strong Guard of Honour with additional personnel to provide day and night guards was dispatched to Mandalay under the command of Major E. L. Musson, D.S.O., M.C. After the Viceroy's departure a letter of appreciation was received by the Commanding Officer from "Viceroy's Camp, Mandalay", in which the Military Secretary conveyed more than ordinary praise:

> His Excellency has told me to confirm in writing what he said to you last night, that the Guard of Honour formed by your battalion at Government House on the day of his arrival here was quite the best he has seen for some time. Not only was the physique of the men excellent, but their turn-out was exceptionally good, and it was quite obvious that every man had taken a very great deal of trouble so as to ensure that his appearance on the Guard of Honour should not only do honour to the Viceroy but also be a credit to his regiment.
>
> His Excellency also wishes me to thank you for the Guard which was mounted over Government House all the time he has been here. The turn-out and smartness of the sentries has been very good indeed.

In June the news reached the battalion that in the Army Rifle Association non-central matches fired in 1928, Lieutenant and Quartermaster F. Snow, D.C.M., had won the Revolver Cup.

On July 1, 1929, the battalion was reorganized into three Rifle Companies, one Machine-Gun Company and Headquarters Wing, and the Indian Platoon was transferred from Headquarters Wing to D/M.G. Company. The main result of this reorganization was that the armament of the battalion, which ever since the end of the war in 1919 had included only four machine-guns in the Machine-Gun Group (later termed the Machine-Gun Platoon) was now increased to eight machine-guns in one company consisting of two platoons (one mule pack and one draught) of four guns each.

On October 8, 1929, the battalion held a farewell parade for its retiring Commanding Officer, Lieutenant-Colonel J. R. Heelis, M.C., and formed hollow square to hear his farewell address. On this occasion Major E. B. Costin, D.S.O., commanded the battalion, Lieutenant J. M. T. F. Churchill carried the King's Colour, and his brother, 2nd Lieutenant T. B. L. Churchill, carried the Regimental Colour.[1] Major E. L. Musson, D.S.O., M.C., was appointed to command from November 5, 1929, and on November 26 he left Maymyo with the main body of the battalion on change of station for Trimulgherry, Secunderabad, Deccan, travelling by way of Rangoon and Madras. The battalion arrived in Trimulgherry on December 4.

During its stay in Maymyo the battalion was unlucky to lose two of its junior officers; 2nd Lieutenant A. H. Thompson died as a result of an accident on a motor-bicycle in February 1928, and 2nd Lieutenant Lloyd Trevor died from enteric fever in September 1929, which he contracted while on leave in the jungle, shooting elephant. He had recently served as aide-de-camp to General F. E. Coningham, the District Commander, and he was a popular and promising officer.

On April 1, 1929, Captain C. H. Keitley, M.B.E., succeeded Captain S. K. Pembroke as adjutant, and on April 10 Captain and Brevet-Major E. B. Costin, D.S.O., the West Yorkshire Regiment, who had been promoted Major and posted to the Manchester Regiment, joined the battalion; 2nd Lieutenants C. H. R. Hyde, V. A. Chiodetti, and C. K. Mott joined on first posting while the battalion was in Maymyo, and Captain

[1] A film was made of this parade and was presented to Lieutenant-Colonel Heelis, who presented it to the Regimental Museum in 1950 where it is now preserved.

G. F. Newsom and Major J. F. Macartney, M.C., left the battalion on retirement. Captain C. D. Moorhead passed the entrance examination for the Staff College and was allotted a vacancy in the course that began in 1930.

In Secunderabad the battalion was to find a very different type of station from Maymyo. Apart from the fact that the lush green Burmese countryside was exchanged for a dry and dusty plain with rocky outcrops, the new station contained the biggest garrison in Southern India, with two British infantry battalions, a brigade of Indian infantry, a brigade of Indian cavalry, as well as a British cavalry regiment; and in addition there was a horse battery and a field brigade of artillery, while in Hyderabad, the seat of the Nizam, there was an additional garrison of Indian State Forces comprising infantry and cavalry as well as other arms. Here in Secunderabad there was the typical atmosphere of an Army garrison town with a strong and healthy feeling of rivalry as between units and a high professional standard in training and military efficiency.

The battalion was quartered in Gough Barracks, Trimulgherry, which was an old well-laid-out barrack site, with large and cool barrack rooms, good institutes and excellent sports grounds and amenities. The nearest neighbours were the 2nd Battalion the Suffolk Regiment, who were stationed in Meadows Barracks, about one and a half miles distant and with whom a close sporting rivalry sprang up and lasted for the duration of the battalion's tour of duty in Secunderabad. The two battalions were old friends, having been stationed together on the Curragh in Ireland in 1914 and having fought side by side at Le Cateau on August 26, 1914.

In the middle of December the Viceroy, Lord Irwin, paid a visit to Hyderabad State, and the battalion was once more required to find a Guard of Honour for him, as well as day and night guards, at Faluknuma Palace where he was staying with the Nizam of Hyderabad. Major C. S. Tuely commanded the Guard of Honour, and he, Captain H. R. C. Green, who commanded the Officers' Guard stationed in the "inner ring", and his subaltern were sent for by Lord Irwin shortly before his departure and thanked for the part the regiment had played in his visit. Recalling that it was almost exactly a year since the battalion had furnished guards for him at Mandalay, he presented a silver cigarette box to the officers' mess to mark the two occasions.

This year brigade training was carried out from barracks and included a three-days exercise in which the men had to sleep in bivouacs at night. Flights were also arranged for selected officers and N.C.O.s in aircraft of the R.A.F.

The Hill Party left for Wellington in the Nilgiri Hills in March, sixty-seven men and their families proceeding thither in the first instance under two officers.

At sport the battalion found a very high standard to compete with due to the keen competition existing in so large a garrison station, but it nevertheless won the Deccan District Boxing Competition in 1930 and was runner-up in the Southern Command Championship. In the Army Rifle Association Non-Central Revolver Competition Lieutenant and Quartermaster Snow was once more the winner.

Field-Marshal Lord Birdwood paid his final visit to the battalion in August before leaving India, and in October Brigadier H. R. Headlam, C.B., C.M.G., D.S.O., the Brigade Commander of the 12th (Secunderabad) Infantry Brigade, to which formation the battalion belonged, paid a farewell visit, as did Lieutenant-General B. Burnett-Hitchcock, C.B., D.S.O., the Commander of Deccan District, and both issued Valedictory Orders.

There are two records in the battalion's *Digest of Service* which illuminate the type of transport in the battalion at this time and the conditions under which the men served: there is a record that the Brigade Commander inspected the mules on the strength of the battalion—a reminder that the platoon automatic weapon, the 1914–18 Lewis gun, was still carried by mule-pack, as were the machine-guns in the Machine-Gun Company; and it is also recorded that an order was published that in future boot-boys would be abolished in the battalion, and barbers would not be allowed to enter barrack-rooms.

The battalion went into camp at Mianpur in December, an excellent site thirteen miles west of Secunderabad, which provided a good manœuvre area; but the brigade camp in January was held at Ghatkesar, situated fifteen miles from barracks and entirely devoid of shade and with little water. However, the men marched back fit and bronzed. At this time too the new Commander-in-Chief in India, Field-Marshal Sir Philip Chetwode, inspected the battalion at work. On April 4, 1931, the Colour was trooped before a large garrison audience and on May 18 the Commanding Officer and the adjutant departed to the hills to inspect the Hill Detachment. The battalion settled down to routine work in an unusually hot summer, and musketry instruction was in full swing.

At 6.15 a.m. on Saturday, May 23, the acting adjutant, Lieutenant T. B. L. Churchill, was riding on to the parade ground to dress the markers prior to the battalion parade, when he was surprised to see the brigade staff-car arriving at the Orderly Room at that early hour. A staff officer was the bearer of orders for the battalion to mobilize with the 12th (Secunderabad) Infantry Brigade for service in Burma. Major Tuely, the acting Commanding Officer, decided to continue with the parade; but at its conclusion he announced to the assembled officers that the battalion was to mobilize forthwith, and this was the preface to the feverish activity which any soldier well knows is the accompaniment to a mobilization. Telegrams recalling officers from leave and courses were sent out and mobilization equipment was issued to companies. Although the battalion's mobilization scheme legislated for a mobilization in "Z + 89 days", the operation was in fact completed in a fortnight. A Depot Company was formed in Secunderabad, and the first company to proceed on service, C Company, under Major K. S. Torrance, M.C., left Secunderabad for Burma by train on June 6. The rest of the battalion followed on the 7th and 8th, D/M.G.

Company having had a difficult task to be ready in time since it was caught in the throes of reorganizing from a two-platoon (one pack, one draught) basis to a three-platoon (all pack) organization.

The reason why these orders were so suddenly received was that the inhabitants of a large part of the Irrawaddy valley were in open rebellion. Rebellion in Burma is not unknown, but the history of Burma under the British crown has, on the whole, not been an unhappy one. The native aristocracy certainly lost some of the status that they enjoyed under pure native rule, but the great commercial enterprises of the European colonists and settlers enriched the whole country, and some part of the wealth that was acquired by the rising trade increased the revenues of the upper and middle classes of the population. An overwhelming proportion of the people are, however, peasants, who live in villages that are clustered together in the great alluvial valleys, and to them the benefits of British rule were not so patent. Under the *pax Britannica* they enjoyed regular, moderate taxation, which was a great improvement upon the capricious levies that Eastern princes impose upon their subjects; but in the year 1930, all the evils of native rule were forgotten, and among the peasants the government of the old native princes was talked of in a legendary way, as a period of great splendour. Also, it is doubtful whether the peasant farmers were easier or more comfortable under British rule than they were before it, for they lived by selling the produce of land that had been so subdivided that farms were little more than plots. Populations who live thus are, of necessity, poor, and this had been the structure of Burmese village society for countless generations.

In the year 1930 a number of influences were disturbing both the upper and the lower strata of the Burmese people. First, which was the real starting point of all the subsequent trouble, the price of paddy was falling. As paddy is the principal crop, nine-tenths of the rural population were distressed and anxious, for small peasants simply cannot accumulate reserve stocks, and only a few exceptionally favoured farmers can accumulate reserves of money. The disturbance was, moreover, not purely economic, for many Indian settlers in the country had acquired land, and they (either because their methods of cultivation were more scientific, or because they had funds upon which they could draw) were actually underselling the Burmese in the falling market. The Indian settlers in the country aggravated the distress by lending money, at cruel rates of interest, to the impoverished villagers. In the towns the pressure of Indian competition was also felt by small tradesmen and native shopkeepers. It was a further disturbing influence that the separation of India from England was being canvassed throughout the East, and that the reports of the commissions that were preparing the way for the new order in India were read and studied in the Burmese towns. Distorted versions of all this reached the peasant population, who interpreted what they heard as an indication that the British Empire was at last crumbling. Political influences were thus operating amongst a population that was severely harassed by distress and low prices.

The people who were thus disturbed have many engaging qualities. In ordinary times they are cheerful, friendly and obliging. British officers serving in the country testify, almost without exception to the hospitality and good nature of the villagers. These good points are, however, offset by great weaknesses. The mass of the population, though nominally Buddhist, have never understood (far less digested) the mild, philosophic doctrines of their religion, and are saturated in superstition. In addition they are excitable, and when excited, quarrelsome and vindictive. Feuds, murder for injuries, and murder for revenge, are so well sanctioned by custom that the police hardly ever attempt to bring the authors of them to justice. Finally—and although this cannot be called a vice, it was one of the starting points of the trouble that followed—the Burman, whether rich or poor, is proud of his race, and responsive to appeals that are made

THE REBELS AND THEIR LEADER

upon a racial note. A society thus constituted and thus disturbed is good material for a political enterprise, and as Eastern people have been nurseries of bold adventurers, it is not altogether surprising that a Burman called Saya San kindled rebellion in the distant villages and made himself the leader of it. Those who had watched the man, and who knew the details of his life, believe that he hoped to become King of Burma. He was certainly endowed with great abilities, for when he raised the flag of rebellion in the Tharawaddy district (seventy-five miles north of Rangoon) he was at the head of a considerable force, which he had raised in secret by persuading the village headmen to support and assist him, and by setting up a network of chairmen and assistant chairmen, who supplied all rebel gangs with food, collected and transmitted news of the British forces, and kept all informers under observation.[1a] His levies were then equipped with such arms as had been collected (mostly breech-loading guns called Shomis, and fighting dahs), and with magic handkerchiefs and charms for deflecting rifle bullets from their point of aim. By December 1930, considerable areas in the Tharawaddy district were virtually under the control of the native rebels.[2]

Special troop trains conveyed the battalion across India in a four-day journey in the height of the hot weather to Calcutta. The temperature was over 110° in the shade. At Calcutta the troops embarked for the sea journey to Rangoon, and on arrival dispersed by companies by train to their dispositions which were as follows: Battalion H.Q., H.Q. Wing, D/M.G. Company, and C Company (less two platoons), Mandalay; B Company, Meiktila; A Company, Shwebo; two platoons C Company, Toungoo.

As the rains had broken, the companies were dispersed in detachments in order to maintain internal security, it being considered impossible to engage the enemy other than locally until the dry weather. All companies practised jungle

---

[1a] See later, pp. 276, 277.
[2] See Cmd. 3,900, 1930/31.

warfare and a number of flag marches were carried out in all sectors.

D/M.G. Company carried out one such march to Lamaing, fifteen miles south-east of Mandalay; and camp had just been pitched when the C.O., Major Tuely, and the District Superintendent of Police arrived with the news that rebels were reported at Bandi, some twenty-five miles to the north. The company started off at daybreak the next morning and after reaching Sedaw (fifteen miles) and stopping for the night, continued the next day but drew a blank. A week elapsed and then a platoon of C Company proceeded to Lamaing as reports of rebels in that area had again been received. The rebels were thought to be breaking southward from the Shan States, where the steps taken by the authorities had made it too hot for them. Two platoons of D/M.G. Company were ordered out to make a series of blocks along the Mandalay Canal, with one platoon of C Company on their left flank. The civil police then had a stroke of luck and arrested three men on a native bus who could give no account of themselves, and on investigation were found to be members of the major rebel Saya San's gang. One of these men consented to lead a party of military police to the rebel encampment. All posts were warned and manned, and then a party of military police, after a gruelling march of fifteen miles through jungle, rushed the rebel camp at 8 p.m. Shots were exchanged, but owing to the darkness the rebels escaped leaving behind their arms, documents and baggage. A few days later the rebels ran into a party of police operating in the hills to the north and all were rushed and captured; Saya San himself was among them, and he was later tried and executed.

The posts manned by the battalion on this occasion were part of a cordon which clearly prevented Saya San from breaking south and contributed materially to his capture. The Burma military police were to make tangible recognition of this later when they presented to the officers' mess of the battalion a handsome silver *chin-the* (the fantastic lion-dog companies from the 3/6th Rajputana Rifles. Headquarters for both sectors (right and left) was at Prome, and the whole military area was called Prome North. It was under the command of the 12th Infantry Brigade. The troops in the whole sector were the company from the Manchesters, five platoons of the Rajputana Rifles, a company from the 3/7th Dogras, and three troops of Burma mounted police. The sub-area that was held by the Manchesters differed from all others in that it was really in two valleys; the riverbed of the Nawin Chaung traversed it in an east–west direction, and a tributary stream—the Paukkaung Chaung, whose source was in the hills on the southern side of the area—traversed it also. The second point that made the sub-area rather different from the others was that there was a line of low hills on its western side. These hills were crossed by the Prome–Paukkaung road, but they were a sort of natural barrier between the Paukkaung sub-area and the areas to the west of it, which were mere divisions of the plain of the Nawin Chaung, and were separated from one another by no natural features.

The difficulties of conducting operations in the river valley can now be appreciated. The Burmese rebels had suffered so severely in the set engagements of 1930 that they were no longer inclined to risk an encounter with British troops. Fairly large areas could thus be safely allotted to single platoons and companies, but this advantage was offset by grave difficulties. Each sub-area was thronged with villages, hamlets, and farms. News that British troops were arriving, or that they were on the move, was thus carried incredibly quickly from village to village, and this made it easy for rebel gangs, which were now small, to disperse when they were threatened, to reassemble when the danger was over, and to resume their operations. The state of affairs, when the campaign began, was indeed thus described in a general instruction from headquarters at Prome.

Every village in the Nawin Chaung valley seems to have its own rebel chairman and assistant. The duty of the chairman is to give the rebels food and shelter, to lead the village rebels in

HMATTAING POST ESTABLISHED BY 12 PLATOON OF C COMPANY, SECOND MANCHESTERS, NOVEMBER 1931

THE REBEL ORGANIZATION

attacks on Government forces and to assist rebel attacks from the rear. Every village appears to be under the influence of the rebels, and nearly all have subscribed to rebel institutions. Their fear of giving information is natural, seeing that their reward is to be beheaded by the next party of rebels. When the villagers do give information (to British Government forces), their news is always late, as only old information is allowed to be given by the chairman. If information leading to a rebel's arrest is given, the informant is reported to the next rebel party by the chairman. Villagers appear to be willing to assist in the restoration of law and order but they are overawed by the rebel gangs whose punishment is always capital. Once every chairman is captured and imprisoned the situation will improve.

The intelligence that had been collected by the police, and the political agents did, however, suffice to show what had to be accomplished if British authority were to be restored in the valley. The number of raiding gangs was fairly well ascertained, and in many cases the villages and the village families to which the gang leaders were united by blood and marriage were known also. The military task was, therefore, that villages should be daily visited and searched by the troops in each sub-area, that one search should give no indication of the place that would be combed on the day following, and that, whenever the available intelligence warranted it, a specified area should be searched by a sort of combined operation in which the troops and the police collaborated. The following operation was very representative of these combined sweeps or drives.

By December 20, 1931, headquarters at Prome was satisfied that the villages along about fifteen miles of the Nawin Chaung ought to be visited and thoroughly searched. The section of the river that was thus selected was extremely tortuous, and was very thickly inhabited because the two branches of the Nawin Chaung join together in the middle part of it, and also because there are several rich loops and great bends in the traject. The operation was thus executed. Four troops of the Burma mounted police were assembled at Paukkaung, which was to the east of the area that was to be combed, and just after daylight on the morning when the drive was to begin they occupied a line about fifteen miles long that crossed the riverbed of the Nawin at right angles near a place called Cyogon. They then began an east–west drive through every village ahead of them. Simultaneously C Company of the Manchester Regiment marched to the northern end of the cordon line upon which the police assembled and moved from village to village along the northern edge of the area through which the mounted police were conducting their drive. The same was done along the villages on the southern edge by five platoons of the Rajputana Rifles.

The results of the drive are fairly representative of the peculiarities of the campaign. In one village the womenfolk of a wanted man were found and arrested. In another tattoo marks that were hitherto unknown to the intelligence officer were noticed, and, as this indicated that a new gang was forming, everybody bearing the marks were arrested. Confirmation that a new levy was being raised was found in another village near by, where a man was discovered to be the owner of an extraordinary number of charms that were supposed to protect the owners against rifle fire, detection, or capture. In another village a considerable number of magic handkerchiefs were detected and their owners arrested. Nevertheless notwithstanding that the search was so close, it was discovered that two wanted men had slipped through the cordon and got away. On another similar occasion, a gang of ten men entered a village an hour after it was searched. So great were their powers of concealment that they had, all the time, been hiding in the zone that was being combed. These special searches were repeated as often as the intelligence that had been collected warranted it. Each one resembled the one that preceded or followed it, for the objects and the method were the same. They were supplemented by orders that villages should be fenced, and by a system of police passes for harmless persons.

As has been said, Lieutenant Churchill's platoon was, all

this time, operating from Hmattaing. This place is to the south of Paukkaung, and is separated from it by a great tangle of forested hills, whose summits run roughly east and west.[4] Hmattaing itself is at the foot of the hills and has been built on the banks of a considerable river, the Wegyi, whose upper sources are deep in the hills. This river debouches into the flat alluvial plain at a small village just above Hmattaing. Lieutenant Churchill's post was therefore placed at what may be called the outer gates of a rebel citadel: for the seeds of rebellion were collected and prepared in hilly fastnesses of the upper reaches of the Wegyi, and scattered (with good hope that they would grow into a fine crop of sedition) among the villages and hamlets of the lower reaches. The district was, indeed, the very heart of a rebel area; for a man named Po Hla Gyi had made it the headquarters for his gang.

Lieutenant Churchill first searched the mountain villages of the upper Wegyi and of its tributaries. Without doubt these lonely hamlets were where Po Hla Gyi planned his operations, but no trace of the man himself could be found in them. A museum of charms was found in more than one house; but there was nothing absolutely incriminating in them, as the owners generally admitted the possession of them, and said that they were protections against illness and misfortune. Still there were signs of the gang in almost every village: an unusual number of red scarves in one place; in others, the village headmen were obviously frightened and embarrassed when the platoon entered the village, and this was always an indication that, either voluntarily or because they dared not refuse, the villagers had been harbouring rebels. It would seem, however, that some of the villagers found rebel dominion rather irksome, and would have been glad to see it ended; for in one very lonely hamlet the peasants supplied a list of the rebels with whom they were acquainted. Still, the search of the mountain villages revealed nothing and the difficulty of conducting it may be judged from the following entry in the platoon diary.

[4] See Survey of India, Sheet 85, N/10 and 14, 5,300 to 8,300.

I marched to Ngapaw [a hill village] ... great difficulty was experienced in getting across the numerous chaungs which cross this route, since they are all very steep, and the footpath is carried across them on a two-plank bridge, often with a drop of as much as forty feet into the chaung below. The country encountered on the march was dense bamboo jungle, often interspersed with teak trees. A rebel gang could hide within fifty yards of the path with the greatest of ease and would not be detected by the patrol on the path.

From the reports that were received during the early part of December, it was to be inferred that Po Hla Gyi had left the mountains and was wandering from hamlet to hamlet in the flat land between the foothills and the Prome–Rangoon railway line. The platoon was now engaged in a succession of searches that continued for two whole months. The villages where Po Hla Gyi was reported to be sleeping, or lodging, or where his wives and family were said to be hiding were all within reach of Hmattaing, and it would serve no useful purpose to enumerate the occasions upon which Lieutenant Churchill assembled his men after dark, marched through the jungle paths by night, surrounded the suspected village, and in the subsequent search of it found that Po Hla Gyi was not there. What was, perhaps, most baffling was that facts could never be collated for testing the report which had started the search. In some villages, the peasants were evasive and frightened; in others they were what Lieutenant Churchill called, "Suspiciously obliging", but whether Po Hla Gyi had or had not been there was never discovered. The platoon diary is, on this account, of extraordinary interest. Where does the truth lie? How did the man evade so many well-planned and well-executed searches? The reports that were received about Po Hla Gyi were so numerous that one must conclude that he was going from one village to another; that some of the reports were accurate, and that others were prepared by himself and deposited with the police by his own friends and agents. If his spies and informers told him that Lieutenant Churchill and his men were marching towards the village where he actually was, Po Hla Gyi moved

THE REBEL LEADER'S DEATH

on: if they informed him that Lieutenant Churchill was marching towards the village where he had reported himself to be, then he remained where he was.

Po Hla Gyi's arm was long and his vengeance implacable; and for this reason he had many enemies. It is probable also that the villagers did not wish to prolong a rebellion which had long since failed, and looked forward to a time when there would be no more military searches because there would be nobody to search for. At all events the end came unexpectedly. After a month of fruitless searching, Lieutenant Churchill was inclined to think that Po Hla Gyi had left the district: still reports that he was about, some of them quite circumstantial, continued to come in, and none could be ignored.

The road that serves Hmattaing runs nearly due south to Paungde through a succession of hamlets; for the land is here very fertile. The village of Myo Gyi, which is about seven miles to the south of Hmattaing, stands a little way off the road and is served by a track of its own. Early one morning, one of the villagers was out in the fields, bringing in his cattle to be milked and watered, when he saw three men sleeping under a tree. Po Hla Gyi and his men were not liked at Myo Gyi, the villagers were, moreover, fairly familiar with them; for the peasant left his cattle, hurried back to his village and told the headman that the three sleeping men were certainly members of the gang. The headman, who was as anxious as the others to drive the conspirators away, armed his villagers with eight guns, and set out with them. The men who had been asleep beneath the tree were now thoroughly roused and suspicious; they opened fire on the approaching villagers, who at once returned it. Two of the bandits made off; one fell wounded, and the villagers rushed on him, and slashed him to death with their dahs. It was Po Hla Gyi. A photograph taken soon after death reveals a man with a calm, rather noble countenance: whether he was a good though a misguided man, or whether he was a brutal ruffian (he may well have been either) Po

Hla Gyi was certainly endowed with all the qualities of a good conspirator.

The main purpose of the whole operation was by now (January 1932) successfully accomplished, for over forty gang leaders were in prison. By the end of the year the incessant harrying of the rebels that had been going on for over twelve months, coupled with the rebels' losses in killed and captured, had virtually put an end to the rebellion; and it was no surprise when, in February 1932, the battalion received orders to concentrate and return to India. Battalion H.Q. and A and D/M.G. Companies arrived back in Secunderabad on February 10, and B and C Companies arrived a week later.

On April 1 Lieutenant T. B. L. Churchill was appointed adjutant, vice Captain C. H. Keitley, M.B.E., and the battalion settled down again to the normal routine of an Indian garrison station. There were inspections by the District Commander, Major-General H. E. ap Rhys Price, C.B., C.M.G., D.S.O., his successor, Major-General D. Baird, and by Lieutenant-General Sir George Jefferies, the G.O.C.-in-C. of Southern Command; but the battalion's time in India was drawing to its close.

Throughout its ten-years tour in India, since the war, the battalion had had the services of an Indian platoon consisting of an Indian officer and some forty Indian other ranks of the Punjab-Mussulman sect. This platoon looked after and led the mules which were required for the transport of machine-guns and baggage on the march, and they had become quite a part of the battalion; they rejoiced with it in its successes and shared in its disappointments, and they had earned the particular affection of all ranks, from the Colonel to the recently joined recruit.

It had been a particular source of joy and pride to the battalion when Subadar Sher Bahadur Khan, I.D.S.M., the much respected and gallant commander of the Indian platoon, had earlier in the year been promoted to the rank of Subadar-Major, a rank unique amongst all the Indian

KHARTOUM

On January 9 the band and drums beat a combined Tattoo in the grounds of the Governor-General's Palace, Khartoum, during the changing of the Guard ceremony on the occasion of the visit of H.R.H. the Duke of Gloucester, who attended the ceremony. The Commanding Officer and the adjutant had the honour of breakfasting at the Palace afterwards.

The band and drums played selections at the station on the departure of the 2nd Battalion the Royal Ulster Rifles, and the arrival of the 1st Battalion the Rifle Brigade. Shortly afterwards the band and drums and sports teams travelled to Atbara to provide band programmes for the detachment and to compete at football, hockey, and cricket against the Sudan Government Railway teams.

The memory of General Gordon was still kept very green in Khartoum, and at a garden party which the Governor-General gave in the grounds of the Palace, at which a number of the officers of the regiment were present, there were also present a number of Egyptian and Sudanese officials who had served with Gordon in Khartoum during the seige. His servant, an old man, was still employed at the Palace, and his river steamer, her decks barricaded with railway sleepers, lay at her mooring on the Nile.

In April 1933, officers and men in Khartoum visited the Fairey-Napier monoplane which, piloted by Squadron-Leader Gayford and Flight-Lieutenant Nicholetts had recently created a world's record for a non-stop flight, and which was passing through Khartoum. Captain C. D. Moorhead, M.C., left the battalion to take up the post of Instructor in tactics at the School of Military Engineering at Chatham.

During the hot weather parties of troops, usually about a company strong, were taken for river picnics up the White Nile, travelling on "Flats" towed by a Nile steamer. The party generally bathed at a spot known as Gordon's Tree, and returned to Khartoum in the cool of the evening.

In June the companies were changed over. D/M.G. Company relieving C Company at Atbara, and the latter relieving A Company at Gebeit. A Company came in to headquarters at Khartoum.

A close liaison grew up in the Sudan between No. 47 (Bomber) Squadron R.A.F., based on Khartoum aerodrome, and the regiment, and the squadron organized a short five-day course which officers and other ranks attended and which included a number of flights to gain " air experience ". The squadron was equipped with Fairey-Atlas aircraft, with open cockpits. The R.A.F. also co-operated with the battalion in exercises to provide anti-aircraft practice for the battalion's A.A. section found from the drummers.

On the anniversary of the Battle of Omdurman, Mr. E. G. Sarsfield-Hall, c.m.g., the Governor of Omdurman, conducted a party of officers and other ranks over the battlefield and gave a stirring and most graphic account of the fighting on that eventful and famous day.

In October 1933, Lieutenant-Colonel E. L. Musson, D.S.O., M.C., left the battalion on leave pending retirement, and on March 5, 1933, Major R. H. R. Parminter, D.S.O., M.C., was appointed Commanding Officer and promoted Lieutenant-Colonel. About this time, too, the news was received that the battalion's next station was to be Strensall in Yorkshire, and having handed over the barracks at Khartoum, Atbara, and Gebeit to the Royal Irish Fusiliers, the battalion sailed from Port Sudan on December 13 for the United Kingdom in the trooper *Neuralia*. The 2nd Battalion the Manchester Regiment arrived at Southampton on December 27, 1933, on return from twelve years and ten months of foreign service, and the Commanding Officer and all ranks were greeted with the following telegram:

I offer to all ranks of your battalion a hearty welcome home after a tour of foreign service in which you have brought fresh credit to the regiment. I am glad to think of you all happily reunited with your families and friends and I take this opportunity of sending you my best wishes for the New Year.

GEORGE R.I., Colonel-in-Chief.

ENGLAND AGAIN

The Colonel of the Regiment, Brigadier-General W. K. Evans, C.M.G., D.S.O., went on board to welcome the battalion, as also did Colonel F. H. Dorling, D.S.O., Lieutenant-Colonel J. R. Heelis, M.C., Lieutenant-Colonel E. L. Musson, D.S.O., M.C., Lieutenant-Colonel B. G. Atkin, D.S.O., O.B.E., M.C., (Commanding 1st Battalion), and Lieutenant-Colonel R. H. R. Parminter, D.S.O., M.C.

There were two special trains alongside the quay, one to take the battalion to Strensall, and the other to take the men for transfer to the Army Reserve and for discharge to the Depot at Ashton. The battalion arrived at 8.30 p.m. and were met by Major C. S. Tuely, the second-in-command, who had made all arrangements for the comfort of the men; and they marched off by companies from the station, whence guides led them to their barrack rooms. In the following two days all those who were due to be transferred to the 1st Battalion in Jamaica were dispatched on leave, and they were followed by the remainder of the battalion except for a small detachment which remained at Strensall as a barrack party.

The accommodation at Strensall was rather mediocre. A new barracks had been planned, but only one or two of the new buildings were as yet erected, and for the most part the barracks consisted of ancient wood-and-corrugated-iron structures. The institutes, however, were excellent, and were a very pleasant change from those to which the men had been accustomed in India and the Sudan. The battalion, while living in the old barracks, watched the new ones being built, but it was their successors who were to enjoy them.

In spite of this, however, Strensall was a good station. It was close enough to York to enable the battalion to join issue with the York garrison in professional and sporting activities, and yet, being in the country and in the centre of War Department land, it was possible to make use of good training areas and an excellent range. As for amenities, there were good married quarters for both officers and other ranks, and after the year of separation in Khartoum, everyone was glad to have the families with the regiment again.

Although there was little in Strensall village to appeal to the men, and York was some distance by bus for those who merely wanted to go to a cinema, Strensall was nevertheless a popular station, since it was within easy and economical reach of Manchester for week-end leave; and from the point of view of the officers, there was some good shooting to be had in the neighbourhood and two packs to hunt with—the Middleton and the York and Ainstey.

The 1st Battalion was in Gosport when the 2nd Battalion arrived at Strensall, but was under orders for the West Indies and due to sail on January 23, 1934. The 2nd was required to turn over to the 1st no less than 229 other ranks and seven officers, and this large draft, coupled with the large number of men due for transfer to the Reserve or to be released, left the 2nd Battalion sadly depleted in numbers. Whereas in India a comany was able to furnish sixty files on a "strong as possible" parade, now in Strensall, with reduced numbers and many barrack duties to fulfil, it could seldom muster more than a dozen men on parade. The Signal Platoon which used to boast thirty trained signallers and forty under instruction, now had under thirty all told, including men transferred from rifle companies since the battalion arrived at Strensall.

Great changes took place when a battalion arrived in England from foreign service. For instance, the band had to be provided with a new set of instruments, since the "pitch" of bands in England was lower than that of bands abroad. This was a very expensive item for which the Band Fund had been carefully husbanded for the last five years in India. On the other hand, there were excellent opportunities in England for the band to recoup their expenses, since band engagements were far more numerous and well paid than was the case abroad, while the opportunities provided by civil engagements, tattoos, and dance band engagements supplied a great incentive to bandmasters and bandsmen alike. The new conditions, however, required a high standard of professional competence, and much hard work was necessary in order to qualify for the prizes available.

Similarly, the arrival in England represented a basic change for the transport section. For years now the medium of transport had been that oldest of soldiers' friends, the pack mule; but now it was to be the light draught horse. In addition, certain petrol-driven vehicles were taken over as the battalion's motor-transport, which took the place of the personnel and mules of the erstwhile Indian platoon.

B Company, under Major F. A. Levis, arrived at Southampton from Cyprus in January and rejoined the battalion, and at about the same time the personnel who had proceeded on leave after arrival at Strensall, also rejoined.

On March 13 twelve officers attended a levée at St. James's Palace, and shortly afterwards General Sir Alexander Wardrope, G.O.C.-in-C., Northern Command, inspected the battalion.

In May the Lord Mayor of Manchester, Alderman J. Binns, paid an official visit to the battalion. He was met at York and conducted to Strensall, where, after inspecting the quarter guard, he was received on the officers' mess lawn by a Guard of Honour commanded by Captain C. H. Keitley, M.B.E., After inspecting the guard, the Lord Mayor was conducted round the barracks and saw the men at dinner in the dining-hall. He then lunched with the officers in mess. In the afternoon he kicked off at a football match before leaving by train for Manchester.

The battalion settled down to individual and weapon training in barracks, and then marched to camp at Ripon for a month under canvas. While in camp the battalion attended a military church parade in Ripon cathedral at which the sermon was preached by Canon Tuckey, an old friend of the regiment, who had been with the 63rd in 1895 and also in Ladysmith. After the service Canon Tuckey and Canon Walker, also of Ripon cathedral, and whose son was killed in action whilst serving with the battalion in France in 1914, lunched with the officers in mess.

On behalf of the city of Manchester, the Lord Mayor informed the regiment that in order to mark the close ties which bound the city to its regiment, it had been decided to present a set of silver drums to each regular battalion of the regiment; and it was accordingly arranged that on the occasion of the King's visit to Manchester in July, His Majesty would receive this magnificent gift on behalf of the regiment. Thus on July 17, 1934, the battalion furnished a Guard of Honour of 100 rank and file under the command of Captain C. H. Keitley, M.B.E., in front of the Town Hall, where the eleven silver drums destined for the 2nd Battalion were piled. Lieutenant C. H. R. Hyde was the Lieutenant of the Guard, and 2nd Lieutenant J. B. R. Dereham-Reid carried the King's Colour. The sun shone brightly and Albert Square was thronged with Manchester's citizens as the King and Queen arrived and the National Anthem was played. The King then inspected the guard, of which all the men in the front rank were wearing the General Service Medal with the Burma 1931–32 clasp. On completion of the inspection, the Commanding Officer, Lieutenant-Colonel R. H. R. Parminter, D.S.O., M.C., was presented to His Majesty.

The Lord Mayor of Manchester, Alderman J. Binns, then addressed the King as follows:

> May it please your Majesty: the desire was recently expressed that there should exist between the city of Manchester and the Manchester Regiment, of which your Majesty is Colonel-in-Chief, some tangible connexion. Accordingly, as a result of public subscription, I am desirous to present to your Majesty today for acceptance on behalf of the regiment, two sets of silver drums—one for the 1st Battalion and one for the 2nd Battalion.
>
> I ought to explain that as the 1st Battalion is at the present time in the West Indies, with Your Majesty's consent, it is proposed that the set of drums for the 1st Battalion shall be presented to the battalion in the West Indies in September by Mr.

THE SILVER DRUMS

Alderman Walker, the Deputy Mayor of Manchester, who has occasion at that time to be in the West Indies.

It is hoped by the subscribers that possession of these drums, as a gift from the citizens of Manchester, will be a source of pleasure to the regiment in which the city takes great pride and interest.

The King, in reply, said:

My Lord Mayor, as Colonel-in-Chief of the Manchester Regiment, I accept with great pleasure these beautiful drums which have been given by the citizens of Manchester.

The King then handed the drums to the Commanding Officer, and remained in conversation with him for a few minutes. Lieutenant T. B. L. Churchill, the Adjutant and Drums President, then handed each drum in turn to a drummer of the 2nd Battalion. After a wait of a few minutes and on completion of an ensuing ceremony in the Town Hall, the band were again called upon to play the National Anthem, and this was appropriately the first occasion upon which these beautiful silver drums were beaten by the regiment. This terminated an historic occasion in which the King, as Colonel-in-Chief, took an active part in the affairs of the regiment, and the city of Manchester demonstrated in the most generous and tangible manner its pride and interest in the regiment.

In the middle of August the battalion again proceeded to camp, this time to Bellerby, on the Yorkshire moors, for brigade and divisional training which lasted three weeks; and immediately afterwards it took part in a four-day exercise in combined operations on the Yorkshire coast. This was the climax and termination of a strenuous year's training in which the battalion had had to learn the many new procedures and techniques which had been adopted in the home Army since the war, but which had not been observed in the Army overseas for one reason or another. The other troops in the 15th Infantry Brigade were, of course, well versed in these matters, but at the end of the training season the battalion could more than hold its own with any of them.

On March 1, 1935, Lieutenant T. B. L. Churchill vacated the appointment of adjutant and was succeeded by Lieutenant G. Frampton, and on April 7, Lieutenant-Colonel R. H. R. Parminter handed over command of the battalion to take up the appointment of Commandant of the Royal Military School of Music, Kneller Hall. He was succeeded by Lieutenant-Colonel E. B. Costin, D.S.O.

The battalion while in Strensall furnished officers, warrant officers, and N.C.O.s as instructors for the regiment's Territorial battalions during their annual training camps at Holyhead in the summer, and in addition were required to provide detachments of men as performers in the Northern Command Tattoo which was held annually at Nottingham. In 1935 and 1936 this entailed no fewer than 380 men, who presented a physical training display and a coloured lantern event.

Also during the years that the battalion was at Strensall it had to find a large number of officers and other ranks as staff instructors and duty personnel for the summer camp of the junior division of the Officers' Training Corps, which was held annually at Strensall. In view of the shortage of men in a home battalion and its many routine duties, such commitments greatly increased the difficulties of training a battalion as a fighting unit.

Battalion, brigade and divisional training all took place at Wathgill Camp in 1935 and at Waitwith in 1936. In both years the unit was under canvas for just over a month.

On January 20, 1936, King George V died at Sandringham, and the following telegram was dispatched to his private secretary:

All ranks past and present the Manchester Regiment of regular and territorial battalions and members of old comrade associations of service battalions deeply lament the passing of their beloved Colonel-in-Chief, and wish to express their most

Nous vous prions d'être nos interprétes auprès des officiers, sous-officiers et soldats de votre bataillon, pour leur exprimer combien nous apprécions le superbe envoi qu'il vous a plu de réserver a notre musée de guerre.

Veuillez croire, Monsieur le Lieutenant-Colonel, a nos sentiments très distingués.

Le Bourgmestre, Député.
Pour la Collège: le Secrétaire,
Ancien Ministre de l'instruction publique.

A Monsieur le Lieutenant-Colonel Commandant,
  le 2e bataillon The Manchester Regiment,
    Strensall Camp, Yorkshire, Angleterre.

It was while the battalion was stationed at Strensall, in the year 1936, that orders were received that the regiment was to be converted to a machine-gun battalion. This meant, of course, a fundamental change in the equipment and role of the battalion; but it also entailed an additional fundamental change as a consequence: it necessitated the total mechanization of the battalion so that it became fully mobile on its own transport.

The new establishment required the reorganization of the battalion from its existing organization of three rifle companies, one machine-gun company and Headquarter Wing, into a unit consisting of three machine-gun companies, one anti-tank company, and Headquarter Wing. This entailed the training of all personnel as machine-gunners and a large number as transport drivers, and the handing in of a large quantity of equipment and the drawing of the new equipment appropriate to a machine-gun battalion. Although the conversion would clearly involve all ranks in much hard work, the fact that the regiment had been among the four selected for this change in organization was hailed with delight by every man in the battalion and it was resolved by common and spontaneous consent that nothing should be left undone to bring about the reorganization efficiently, smoothly and expeditiously.

The first move was the institution of local courses within

A MACHINE-GUN BATTALION

the battalion to train potential instructors in the machine-gun, and these courses were arranged and staffed by the existing D/S Company—the machine-gun company. Once these company instructors were trained (and, of course, special vacancies were allotted to the battalion at the Machine-Gun School at Netheravon for the further training of N.C.O.s), every man was put through a seven-weeks course in his company on the machine-gun, and by the end of the year, machine-gun training was in full swing throughout the battalion.

Parallel with this machine-gun training, it was necessary to organize transport training for the large numbers of drivers that were required in the battalion for its mechanical transport. Once again D/S Company provided personnel who, after undergoing a special course in driving at the Army M.T. School, formed the nucleus of instructors for local courses for the other companies' potential instructors. At the same time the M.T. Section of Headquarter Wing provided a stripped chassis of a private car from local resources for instructional purposes, and soon was issued with a dual-control W.D. vehicle which was used by the M.T. staff to impart instruction in driving to classes of two months duration. These M.T. courses involved long hours which included instruction in driving in traffic, in hill-climbing and night driving as well as in convoy work and in map-reading. By January 1937, thirty-five truck drivers and twelve motor-cyclists had been trained, while a further ten drivers were under instruction; and by April there were drivers available for the fifty-one trucks, one anti-tank truck, twelve motor-cycles, two dual-control vehicles, and two light tractors which were held on the battalion's M.T. strength.

In addition to the battalion M.T. section, each company now had its M.T. section, and special brick-built garages were provided in barracks to accommodate the battalion's new vehicles. By now B Company had been nominated as the anti-tank company, and its equipment therefore included its four 2-pounder anti-tank guns and the trucks to draw them. Thus anti-tank courses had to be organized, as well as range-takers' courses, scouts' courses and even courses on the Bren gun, since this new gun was shortly to be issued throughout the Army to replace the Lewis gun.

It will be seen that 1936 and the early months of 1937 were months of unremitting toil: but by the spring the battalion was emerging from its chrysalis as a machine-gun battalion, and plans were ready for its tactical training, first by companies, and then as a battalion. Companies were dispatched in their own transport in succession to Ripon Camp for ten days of independent company training, since it was already foreseen that each company would fight independently in war; and when this was completed, the battalion proceeded to camp at Wathgill for the Machine-Gun Concentration on July 4, 1937, and this must be regarded as the completion of the battalion's conversion into a machine-gun battalion, after eighteen months of arduous and highly productive work and training.

The year 1937 also saw the second visit of a Lord Mayor of Manchester to the battalion. On March 18 Alderman J. Toole accompanied by the Town Clerk, Mr. Howell, and his secretary, Mr. Hill, arrived after a journey through deep snowdrifts between Manchester and Leeds. After inspecting a Guard of Honour commanded by Captain A. L. Alderton, the Lord Mayor visited the barracks and mechanical transport lines and then saw a demonstration of a machine-gun platoon at war strength coming into action off trucks. Later he inspected the men's dinners, and after lunching with the officers, kicked off at a football match in the afternoon.

At the Coronation of H.M. King George VI in London on May 12, the battalion was represented by three officers and fifty other ranks. Two months later the Chief of the Imperial General Staff, Field-Marshal Sir Cyril Deverell, paid a short visit to the battalion, and in August battalion and brigade training was carried out at Tow Law Camp, near Durham. At this camp the battalion transport consisted of eleven " Austin Seven " cars (allotted to officers in place of chargers), six 30-cwt. lorries, two learner vehicles, fifty-seven trucks and twenty-eight motor-cycles, all driven by battalion drivers. In the final exercise the battalion left Tow Law at 9 o'clock in the morning, and moved by a little-known and mountainous route to Catterick (in order to avoid detection from aircraft), where it arrived two hours earlier than the Directing Staff had calculated it was possible for it to arrive. This inevitably shortened the mock battle in which the battalion then engaged, with the result that the exercise was declared at an end the same evening. The battalion returned to Strensall, arriving at midnight, having covered over 100 miles with a column consisting of 112 vehicles and having only sustained one bent mudguard as damage in the course of the day.

In October a strong detachment, under the Commanding Officer, proceeded to York on the occasion of the visit of Their Majesties the King and Queen to that city, and lined the streets. In November the Colonel of the Regiment, Colonel F. H. Dorling, visited the battalion and took the salute at a march past in M.T. vehicles. He later saw a demonstration by an anti-tank gun crew and of an armoured machine-gun carrier.

The battalion had received news that it was to move to Aldershot on change of station in March 1938, and preparations were already in hand. The Lord Mayor of Manchester, Alderman J. G. Grimes, paid a visit to the battalion before it left and was accompanied by the Officers Commanding the 5th, 8th and 9th Battalions T.A. On March 10 the General Officer Commander-in-Chief, Northern Command, General Sir William Bartholomew, K.C.B., C.M.G., D.S.O., paid the battalion a farewell visit, and on the 12th the advance party left Strensall for Aldershot. On the 17th the M.T. columns left by road, and on the 18th the main body left by rail, arriving at North Camp station on the 19th and marching to Tournay Barracks. Shortly before the battalion left Strensall, Captain F. G. W. Axworthy succeeded Captain G. Frampton as adjutant.

On April 12 Their Majesties the King and Queen visited Aldershot and the battalion lined part of the route. A fortnight later, the battalion took part in a command road movement exercise. In May, the battalion went to Warminster camp to fire parts 3 and 4 of the army machine-gun course.

In June five officers and twenty other ranks from the battalion assisted the 127th Infantry Brigade in their camp at Redcar; and in August the battalion went into camp at Hackwood Park for a fortnight's higher training.

On September 17 a party of officers and other ranks visited H.M.S. *Manchester* at Portsmouth, and the Colonel of the regiment presented the ship's company with a silver bugle and two pictures of the capture of the guns at Francilly-Selency.

On November 18 Major A. W. U. Moore was appointed commanding officer of the battalion and was promoted to Lieutenant-Colonel in succession to Lieutenant-Colonel E. B. Costin, D.S.O., who was given a new appointment and promoted to the rank of Colonel. During the year 2nd Lieutenants L. G. Newton, N. K. Evans, and J. A. Gardner joined the battalion from Sandhurst, and Captain H. D. Dook retired.

1939

The year 1939 opened quietly after the alarms which had accompanied the "Munich Crisis" of three months earlier. The steadily growing rearmament programme, the defence estimates, and the continued organization of the Air Raid precautions services seemed to reassure the nation. The 2nd Battalion of the regiment was still at Aldershot, where it was attached to 2 Division of 1 Corps. Its technical designation can be described as a machine-gun battalion included as corps troops of 1 Corps, and earmarked for employment with 2 Division.

WAR IS NOT FAR OFF

General Maitland Wilson was commander of 2 Division and saw to it that training in all formations in his command was brought to a high state of proficiency. At a three-day tactical exercise without troops which he held on the Berkshire Downs near Newbury at the beginning of April he impressed the battalion officers who attended with his decisiveness and the confidence which he inspired. General Sir John Dill, the Commander-in-Chief at Aldershot, also attended, and officers listened with respect to his remarks at the conclusion of the exercise since it was generally expected that he would command the British Expeditionary Force in the event of war. It was significant that all his remarks were related to the current German tactical doctrine. In April 2nd Lieutenants J. B. H. Keitley, G. M. Williams, A. E. Holt, and K. C. L. Oliver joined the battalion from Sandhurst, and Captain T. B. L. Churchill, M.C., rejoined the battalion after a four-year secondment to the Royal Air Force.

On April 13 the King and Queen visited the troops at Aldershot and attended demonstrations of weapons on the ranges. Their visit had been kept secret until the last moment, no doubt on account of the I.R.A. activities in England which had been a feature of recent months. The battalion fired a platoon machine-gun match against the Cheshire Regiment and succeeded in winning, in spite of the fact that in the practice on the previous day they had been easily beaten. Officers regarded it as another instance of the Lancashireman's happy knack of being "all right on the night".

During this year batches of reservists arrived for training with the battalion, at first for a period of twelve days (which later lengthened to two and a half months), and the men were put through intensive courses on the machine-gun and in field training. The battalion went into camp during May at Imber, near Warminster, where Part III of the machine-gun course was fired, and the opportunity was taken to hold a movement exercise in which companies were given speeds and vehicle densities to which to conform. The technique of moving as a fully mechanized unit was something which the battalion had to learn, and much time was spent by company commanders on evolving and practising this technique. Later, each company moved to Larkhill on Salisbury Plain to fire Part IV of the machine-gun course, and in addition companies were struck off regimental routine duties in succession throughout the summer in order to enable company commanders to devote themselves to an intensive period of field training, which always ended with a scheme set and umpired by the C.O. Officers and men steadily absorbed the new lessons which had to be learnt concerning their role as a support machine-gun battalion. No longer would it be usual for the battalion to fight as a unit, but rather as four separate entities each supporting an infantry brigade, with the C.O. as co-ordinator and machine-gun adviser to the Divisional Commander. Companies had to be organized to live and feed on their own, and to be self-supporting for days on end depending on the tactical situation.

While all this technical and field training was in progress in the battalion, other aspects of training went on simultaneously. Frequent " passive air defence" schemes were held both in barracks and in the field, to practise the technique of maintaining the role of the battalion in spite of bombing and gas attack; and during this summer the battalion provided large numbers of officer and N.C.O. instructors for the 9th Territorial Battalion of the regiment which came into camp for a week at Mytchett near Aldershot, and which was in process of splitting itself into two battalions consequent on the Government's decision to "double-up" the Territorial Army.

The month of August was charged with forebodings and the wireless news was listened to by officers and men alike with grim attention. In an unreal atmosphere the battalion held its annual sports meeting and completed its cricket league fixtures. Companies consisted mainly of recruits

THE OFFICERS, SECOND BATTALION THE MANCHESTER REGIMENT ON MOBILIZATION, ALDERSHOT, SEPTEMBER 7, 1939

Back row—2/Lieutenant A. E. Holt, 2/Lieutenant J. B. H. Keitley, Lieutenant W. T. Wilkinson, 2/Lieutenant W. R. Moss, 2/Lieutenant R. Dobson, 2/Lieutenant R. K. Rose, Lieutenant G. Paulson, Lieutenant R. W. Hilton, 2/Lieutenant D. Derham-Reid, Lieutenant J. W. Ward, Lieutenant J. P. Dewar.

Middle row—2/Lieutenant J. D. M. Kirkness, Captain C. J. Abbott, Lieutenant J. M. T. Churchill, Captain G. A. Tod, Lieutenant C. K. Mott, Lieutenant J. A. C. Fitch, Lieutenant R. King-Clark, M.C., Lieutenant G. W. Ham, Captain H. D. Dook, Lieutenant G. C. Marsh.

Front row—Lieutenant H. O'Brien, Captain T. B. L. Churchill, M.C., Captain G. Frampton, Major F. A. Levis, Lieutenant-Colonel A. W. U. Moore, Major F. G. W. Axworthy, Major E. M. Hickey, Captain E. F. Woolsey, Captain K. R. F. Black.

CHAPTER VII

THE 2ND BATTALION AND THE DUNKERQUE CAMPAIGN

TWENTY-FIVE years had gone by since the first British expeditionary force had landed in France, and curiously enough, the war plan that the British Army was now operating was the exact opposite of its predecessor. In 1914 the British and French armies were to defeat the German armies on the frontier, and were then to advance into the heart of Germany: in 1939, France and England were treated as a fortress which was to be held against all German attacks, and no advance into Germany was to be attempted, until the Germans had been so weakened and demoralized by economic pressure, that an assault upon their country could be attempted.

The war plan looked backwards rather than forward: it assumed that defensive positions could be held indefinitely; and it assumed that Germany was as susceptible to economic pressure as it had been twenty-five years previously, when what was popularly called the blockade of Germany had proved to be a slow-moving but irresistible engine of war. Preparations for the war which started in September 1939 had, therefore, been of the standard pattern; for as Sir James Edmonds has said, " The end of one war is no more than the jumping off line for the mental and material preparations for the next."[1] Nevertheless, the war plan was, in some respects exceptional and peculiar. First, the military experts have never been free to criticize the plan as a plan: it had been imposed upon them by the Cabinet and by pressure of circumstances; secondly it was a plan that disregarded principles of war which military leaders of all ages and epochs have been very reluctant to set aside.

[1] *Official History*, 1918, Vol. 5, p. 585.

THE WAR PLAN

The plan was imposed upon the country's military experts because the French, who were our senior partners in a Continental campaign, would operate no other. They were as confident that a purely defensive plan could be successfully executed as they had been confident in their offensive projects twenty-five years previously: they had constructed the great fortified position called the Maginot Line because nothing had shaken their confidence in a defensive war plan, and it was quite impossible for British experts to press for another kind of plan, for neither the French nor the British Cabinet would have listened to them. Nor was the British staff in a position to urge that the defensive plan on the Continent should be accompanied by offensive action in secondary theatres. When war began, there was no secondary theatre, but quite apart from this, higher policy during the peace had kept the Army at so low a figure that the military experts were not free to follow an enterprising policy.

Nevertheless it is not too much to say that the experienced and thoughtful members of the British staff must have had misgivings, simply because the plan defied a principle that military experts have always adhered to. The generals who have practised defensive tactics and strategy successfully have been as numerous and as skilful as the great masters of offensive movement; but no general has ever willingly adopted a defensive plan which consists of waiting for an enemy to strike, and in making preparations for parrying or deadening the blow. In his memoirs, General Joffre explains impressively why this policy, which he calls *attendre le coup*, cannot be sound, and why he refused to entertain it. Similar pronouncements have been made in every age, yet in 1939 this principle was discarded.

It is, of course, known to everybody why the war plan was, in many quarters, believed to be the best that could be adopted. For four whole years (1914–1918) huge armies had been unable to break down a system of field entrenchments and improvised strong posts; and when, at long last, the German, and then the Franco-British armies loosed the deadlock and made advances of strategical significance, the change occurred only because each side began to be short of men, and because the field entrenchments that had proved to be impregnable for so long could no longer be manned with sufficient forces. General Edmonds, who has made a searching analysis of the closing battles of the campaign, has shown that defensive weapons and defensive tactics retained their old power and efficacy to the very last; that, contrary to what was popularly supposed, the appearance of the tank made but little difference; and that it did not endow offensive tactics with a new and exceptional power. Was it not, therefore plain sense to assume that a deadlock that had rested on field fortifications only could be made unbreakable if it rested upon an elaborately prepared obstacle like the Maginot Line? If the assumption was wrong then all the general staffs of Europe were in some sense deceived, for the Germans erected a Siegfried Line opposite the French Maginot.

Nevertheless the Maginot Line did not cover the whole French frontier; for from somewhere near Sedan to the sea the French were relying upon field fortifications only. Was it proper to suppose that these would prove as difficult to carry as they had been twenty-five years previously? A great technical change had certainly been introduced into all the armies of Europe during the period. They were mechanized, which meant that men and guns were henceforward carried to their destinations in mechanically propelled vehicles. This, of course, entailed a drastic revision of most of the technical manuals that were then in use, but it did not for the time being, introduce a new principle into the science of attack and defence. Also, tanks were greatly improved; they were no longer a capricious and dangerous weapon whose crews were often gassed before they reached the zone of battle. But as tanks improved, anti-tank weapons improved also, and nobody could imagine that a more efficient tank had upset the balance between offensive and defensive power. Finally, wireless and signal communications had improved during the twenty-five years of peace, and this was as much help to the defending as it was to the attacking side. Nothing that had occurred was, therefore, the equivalent to a clear unmistakable indication that defensive positions had lost any of their old strength and efficacy, and it is not surprising to find that many passages in the *Field Service Regulations* that were in circulation in 1939 were reminiscent of the orders and instructions that were being issued in 1918. Indeed, Chapter VII (Defence) of the *Field Service Regulations* of 1935 illustrates this point so clearly that it deserves to be quoted in full.

> The machine-guns, the most powerful weapon of the defence, should, whenever time permits, be considered first. They should be organized in depth . . . and should be sited so as to sweep with enfilade or indirect fire the probable lines of enemy approach, and so as to provide, as nearly as possible, a continuous belt of fire across the front of the position.

Instructions of an almost identical kind are to be found in the memoranda when the British Army was awaiting the German assault in 1918: what is most significant is that then, as in 1935, a machine-gun is stated to be the principal weapon in a defensive position.

Nevertheless, too much must not be inferred from this continuity of doctrine. Probably the staff did not consider that such mechanical inventions as had been incorporated into the weapons and equipment of the Army, during the twenty-five years of peace, justified a drastic revision of the tactical doctrines of 1918; but, as against this, every military expert in the world would agree with the German general who maintained that any system of training would do, provided that it was a system. "Because we shall all do something quite different when we go to war." Just because the staff adheres to a rather conservative traditional method of peacetime training, it by no means follows that they did not foresee great changes. The purpose of training, in peacetime, is, after all, that officers and men shall be masters of their weapons and proficient in the use of them.

One can, moreover, be a little more positive than this; it

will be shown, later, that the mechanization of the Army did, in point of fact, very much reduce the strength of fixed positions, and that when assaulted by an armoured force they did not constitute a barrier as strong, or anything like as strong, as the prepared positions of the previous war. Even if it be granted that this was not fully apparent in September 1939 is it reasonable to suppose that it was wholly unforeseen? If it was anticipated, in any quarters at all, it follows that many high-ranking officers in the British Army doubted whether it was a sound plan to man a long line of fixed positions and to wait until the enemy attacked them. In common with all the British units in France, therefore, the 2nd Battalion the Manchester Regiment was engaged in a doubtful adventure.

The battalion left its billets near Cherbourg for the forward area and reached the village of Rue du Bouteau on October 4, where it was to remain for many months. The battalion was attached to the 2nd Division, and the companies were thus distributed:

B Company was attached to 5 Infantry Brigade (7th Worcestershires, 2nd Dorsets, 1st Camerons, 5th Anti-Tank Regiment), and was at Rue du Bouteau.

C Company was attached to 6 Infantry Brigade (1st Royal Berkshires, 2nd Durham Light Infantry, 1st Royal Welch Fusiliers), and was at Rue du Bouteau.

D Company was attached to 4 Infantry Brigade (1st Royal Scots, 2nd Royal Norfolks, 1/8th Lancashire Fusiliers, 16th Field Regiment, 13th Anti-Tank Regiment), and was at Ghien.

A Company was in reserve, and was at Ghien. The Headquarters Company was at Rue du Bouteau.

Subsequently the brigade fronts were slightly altered, and the positions that were occupied by the battalion during the winter and the following spring were: B Company, Vieux Condé; C Company, Le Quenne; D Company, Bourbetin; A Company, in reserve; H.Q. Company, Rue du Bouteau.

The front on which the battalion was standing followed no

natural features; the little town of Orchies was to the left, and the rather larger town of Saint-Amand was to the right of it. The River Scarpe ran behind the front, and as the upper surface of the land is, in these parts, only a few feet above the level of the river beds, the whole countryside is intersected by thousands of drains and ditches. These dykes draw off enough water to make the fields workable and productive in the summer, but after the autumn rains have set in, the whole country becomes a quagmire. It is only rarely, however, that the drains and dykes can be made the auxiliaries of any system of field fortification, for they run in every direction.

The main roads and the railway between Saint-Amand and Orchies ran roughly parallel to the front, which was not traversed rectangularly by any large thoroughfare or waterway. A great peculiarity of the country is that the villages straggle out so much, that, in some parts, several miles of road are lined by an uninterrupted succession of cottages and small farmsteads. The villages are indeed all called *rues*, or roads, because their sites have always been natural causeways across the low waterlogged land. The country is open, as well as flat, and a man standing in any part of it can see a long way, unless the view is interrupted by a high hedge or a spinney. The system of fortification that was followed, wherever practicable, was that the villages were made into strongpoints, which were garrisoned by infantry, anti-tank guns and machine-guns. The open spaces between the villages were covered by fire zones from the strongpoints. Natural and artificial obstacles—drains, dykes, and anti-tank ditches—were covered by direct and enfilade fire from the defended areas. Roads and tracks which approached the defence line were also covered by fire from the strongpoints. The whole defence was organized in depth, but in a rather more dispersed manner than was practised later.

On the whole, it was found that a strong position could be prepared in the flat, monotonous country; but the more experienced officers considered that they were handicapped by being obliged to erect the line along the political frontier between France and Belgium, and that they could have prepared a very much stronger position if they had been free to choose their ground.

The old familiar obstacles, mud and water, announced their presence from the moment when work on the defence line was begun.

"It is only possible to dig to a depth of two feet before striking water," runs the battalion's diary for October 20. At the end of the month, the entry was: "All fields became waterlogged and in many cases large tracts were completely submerged. Where M.T. had been parked in fields, the ground immediately became cut up and a morass. Second-class roads very bad, the verges are deep in mud and water and in places impassable. Some of the roads in the forward area are very bad." To the veterans this was familiar indeed.

Hereafter there was practically nothing to record for many months, except that the roads on the front were improved by clearing the ditches, and, in places, by widening. Great progress was made, and when the exceptionally hard weather of that winter set in (late December), local comunications to the forward zone had been substantially improved. In November it was for a short time expected that the enemy would start active operations, and the divisional front was fully manned for a week. After it was ascertained that the Germans were not moving, nothing disturbed the uncanny quiet of the next five months. The thaw set in late in February; the weather was, however, very wet and the ground was waterlogged until well on into April. When at last the order was received to move forward into Belgium, an exceptionally mild and sunny spring had settled on the countryside.

It was arranged with the French army authorities that detachments from the British Army should be sent to the southern part of the front for training and experience of active warfare, and a party from D Company was dispatched

THE SAAR BATTLEFRONT

to the Saar front late in December (13, 14 and 15 Platoons, under Captain Woolsey).[2]

The company spent Christmas Day in French cattle trucks marked *hommes et chevaux*, and were billeted outside Metz. Two platoons were then moved into what the French called the *ligne de contact* near Waldweistroff, and one platoon was kept in reserve. The weather was so cold that fires had to be lit under the transport vehicles before the engines could be started up, for all lubricants were frozen hard. At night only one gun could be left in position; the other was brought into the dug-out and three tommy cookers were kept alight under the barrel. Sentries, with their feet wrapped in sacking and straw, could only be left on duty for twenty minutes and, as often as not, they were nearly insensible when they were relieved.

D Company was operating with a detachment of the Royal Norfolks and the German positions were within sight from their section of the line. Fighting patrols were sent out every night and heavy firing broke out spasmodically; but nothing that was done diverted the French and the Germans from their policy of watching and waiting. Indeed, it seemed quite extraordinary to the officers that they were forbidden to open fire unless the Brigadier's permission was first obtained; and that the electric current in Waldweistroff should come from a station that was well inside the German lines.

Captain Woolsey once saw the footmarks of men and a dog well in rear of 14 Platoon's position when he visited his posts at daybreak. On January 15, D Company detachment was relieved by a company from the Middlesex Regiment.

By January 1940, the British Expeditionary Force, of which the battalion was a part, was two army corps strong, with three divisions in each corps. It had been raised to this strength gradually; during the first months of the war, a French division (the 51st) was placed under the orders of the

[2] For full details see Gort dispatch, October 17, section 6.

British Commander-in-Chief, and was relieved as new formations came out from England. The 2nd Battalion the Manchester Regiment was in the right-hand sector of the British Expeditionary Force, which held the Franco-Belgian frontier between the Scarpe and the Lys. From the Scarpe to the little town of Toufflers, the British front ran through the flat tillage land, of which the country round the Rue du Bouteau is representative. Thereafter, the British front was in the approaches to a mining and industrial district; for the manufacturing towns of Roubaix and Tourcoing were just behind it, and the great industrial city of Lille is only a few miles from the part of the frontier where the British Army was standing.

The field fortifications, upon which the battalion was engaged, were part of a general plan that had been agreed to, before the war, by the French and British staffs. The great fortified position that is called the Maginot line did not cover the Franco-Belgian frontier: the French had, nevertheless, put up a continuous anti-tank obstacle along the entire frontier; and the general plan of defence was that this anti-tank obstacle should be supplemented by field fortifications, by additional anti-tank ditches in the forward areas, and by secondary, or reserve positions farther back.

The defences erected round the Rue du Bouteau were representative of the work that was done in the front line. The work done elsewhere was different, and consisted largely of building and emplacing concrete pill-boxes, so sighted " that they afforded protection to those weapons which formed the backbone of the fire defence through the whole depth of the position."[3] This was carried out by a specially constituted force of Royal Engineers, called X Force, and by an excavator company.

Of the whole defensive system, the Commander-in-Chief states that, by the spring of the year 1940, " the position had been developed in considerable depth." Regimental officers

---

[3] Lord Gort's dispatch, March 1941, section 12.

—was allocated to the Saar front, where it remained throughout the campaign.

In the early hours of May 10, the Germans invaded Holland, Belgium and Luxembourg, and at 06.00 hours the 2nd Division, with which the Manchesters were operating, was notified that the Dyle plan would be put into execution. The time when the advance was to begin would be notified later.

The news was a staggering surprise to the troops in the forward line, for there had been no kind of alert and leave trains were running regularly. Nevertheless, there was no hitch in the preparations for a quick move. The Colonel visited each company; maps were distributed, and all superfluous papers were destroyed. The advanced troops of the division moved off at about noon: there was some delay in transmitting the time of the zero hour to the battalion, which, however, started at about 19.00 hours and crossed the Belgian frontier soon afterwards at the little hamlet of Point Caillou.

Soon after the column entered Belgium a large twin-engined bomber flew over it, and Sergeant-Major Talbot opened fire with a Bren gun from one of the leading vehicles. The German bomber certainly came down soon afterwards, and this greatly exhilarated everybody who saw it.

The line of advance was through Ath, Enghien, and Hal; thereafter the column passed through Waterloo and the southern edge of the great forest of Soignies, and advanced into the deployment zone through Overyssche and Ottenburg. It was a fine warm night; no lights were used on vehicles, but a small red light underneath the vehicle enabled the driver behind to keep his distance. Balisage lights which had been set in place at intervals along the route on the verges of the road also assisted navigation and vehicles managed to conform to the speed laid down. Move discipline was extremely good. When the Belgians were consulted about the route they were uniformly helpful and friendly.

The distance from the starting point (Point Caillou) to the

THE POSITION ON THE DYLE

Dyle was sixty-seven miles, and companies arrived at their destinations in the early hours of May 11. A Company halted at Alsembourg, near Waterloo, B Company at Malaise, C Company at Terlaanen, and D Company at Tombeek. Battalion Headquarters established itself at the Ferme de Templiers, near Tombeek, with the Headquarters of the 13th Anti-Tank Regiment.

Company commanders at once reconnoitred their sectors of the River Dyle, and meantime those portions of companies which had become detached from their columns on the advance through the Forêt de Soignies rejoined their companies. A Company was attacked by low-flying aircraft with Belgian markings.

The River Dyle, of which the 2nd Division were to hold a sector, is not, in any sense of the word, a frontier or a boundary stream, for more than half of Belgium lies to the east of it. Nor does the river divide two different kinds of country, for it traverses the undulating districts of Belgium that lie to the east and south-east of Brussels, and then debouches into the flat country at Louvain. Some parts of the valley are a sort of cleft in the undulations; but it will always be a matter for some surprise that the Belgian staff selected this river line for their main defensive position when (as far as can be judged) a much stronger one, and one which would have made a far better junction with the French defensive system, could have been selected farther east, on the heights of the Meuse.

The town of Wavre was on the right of the portion that was allotted to the 2nd Division, and a little station on the railway between Wavre and Louvain was on the left of it. The Dyle valley is, in this part, fairly steep and wooded, and the main communication (the Wavre–Louvain line) is on its eastern side. Behind the front, the River Lasne runs roughly parallel to the Dyle through another steepish cleft: the country between the two is traversed by three fairly good roads. To the east of the front, the country is undulating, blind, densely populated, and traversed by a large number

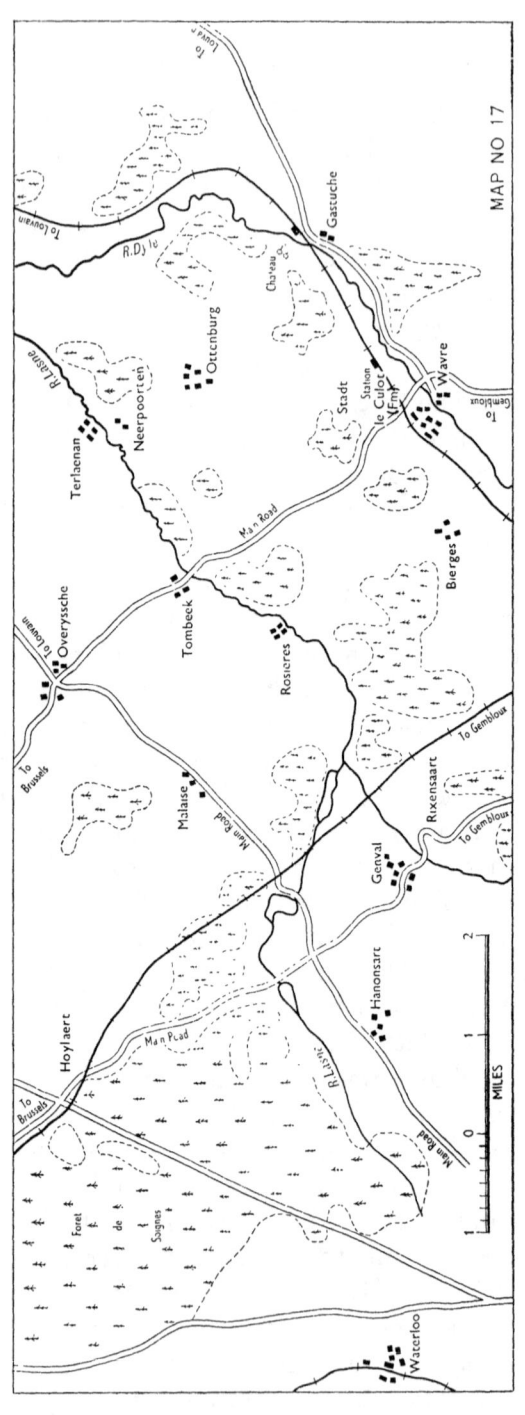

of roads which connect the towns of Namur and Liége to the capital.

The plan for occupying the 2nd Division's sector was that the Divisional Cavalry Regiment, the 4/7th Dragoon Guards, and attached troops should advance rapidly behind the 12th Lancers to the line of the River Dyle. They were to be followed by a mobile detachment under the command of Lieutenant-Colonel A. W. U. Moore, the C.O. of the 2nd Battalion the Manchester Regiment, which was to be composed of the Manchesters, the 13th Anti-Tank Regiment, and the carrier platoons of the 1/8th Battalion the Lancashire Fusiliers and the 1st Battalion the Royal Scots. Behind them would come the divisional advanced guard, the 4th Infantry Brigade, and then the main body.

The role of the mobile detachment was to support the 4/7th Dragoon Guards on to the Dyle position, and to relieve them for further advance. They were also to protect the right flank of the 2nd division. When the 4th Brigade arrived it was to take over the divisional front; the Manchesters were to remain in their positions to provide supporting fire for the brigade. When the remainder of the division arrived, the 4th Brigade was to side-step to the right to make room for the 6th Brigade on its left, and the division's line was then to run thus: On the right the 4th Brigade was to hold the town of Wavre on a position that roughly followed the Wavre–Gembloux main road, and was to make a junction with a French regiment that was to come into position above Wavre. The 6th Brigade was to link up with the 4th on the line of the Dyle at a point a little below the bridge that carries the roads from the little village of Stadt; and was to hold the line as far as the small railway station on the Wavre–Louvain line: here the 6th Brigade would meet the units of the 1st Division, which was to hold the line towards Louvain. The reconnaissance zone to the east of the front seems to have extended as far as Jodogne. The anti-tank defence line was on the heights to the west of the River Dyle.

The preliminary movement, that is, the advance of the

mobile detachment and the relief of the reconnaissance units, was completed during the afternoon of the 11th. D Company, therefore, set up its posts round Wavre and along the river line, and C Company continued the line as far as the divisional boundary. B Company was kept in divisional reserve. As the main bodies had not come up, and as the rate at which the French troops on the right were advancing was not well known, A Company was held right back, near Waterloo, to protect the right flank of the division until the French and British forces were well joined. These positions were occupied all day, and towards the evening vague reports about the German advance reached the troops in the forward areas: it was by then known that they were across the Meuse, and that some of their forward troops were advancing towards the divisional front, as they were approaching Tirlement and Perwez.

May 12. The first part of the Dyle plan was that the British front between Louvain and Wavre should be occupied by three divisions—two belonging to 1 Corps and one to 2 Corps; and it was on this day completed. The 3rd Division of 2 Corps came into line at Louvain, although on a narrower front than had been allowed for, and the 1st and 2nd Divisions occupied their positions on the Dyle. The 2nd Division, with which the Manchesters were operating, completed its advance during the early afternoon.

The 6th Brigade came in on the left, and C and A Companies (Major Frampton and Captain R. King-Clark, M.C.) were placed under its command. C Company headquarters was set up at the village of Ottenburg. A Company headquarters was farther back at Neerpoorten, the platoon posts were along the heights to the west of the river. D Company headquarters (Captain Woolsey) was set up behind Wavre in a convent on the Wavre–Overyssche road: the company was attached to the 4th Brigade, and its platoon posts covered the town from the eastern side of the river, and then followed the western bank. The 5th Brigade with which B Company (Major Hickey) was operating was placed in reserve: the

THE MANCHESTERS' POSITION

battalion headquarters was on the edge of a wood, well behind the front, and near the valley of the Lasne on the Wavre–Tombeek road.

Since the evening of the 11th and all through the day of the 12th the platoons were digging their machine-gun positions, or breaking open the pill-boxes on the river line, and installing their weapons. D Company (13, 14 and 15 Platoons), which was on the right round Wavre, disposed its guns thus: on the right, one section of 13 Platoon was dug in at a level crossing, its second section was in a dug emplacement on the side of a hill; in the centre, 14 Platoon had one section in the garden of a large house with its guns shooting through loopholes made in the wall, and the second section in a pill-box on the left; 15 Platoon (Lieutenant Chandler) had one section in a pill-box and the other on the ridge above it. The pill-boxes were, admittedly, well sited and well camouflaged: one of them was disguised as a bakery, and, what is more, disguised so well that the pretence could not be detected on a close inspection; for it was fitted with windows behind which large quantities of bread were always displayed. Nevertheless, the pill-boxes were not adapted to take machine-guns, and much work had to be done on the swinging mountings and on the embrasures before the guns could be mounted. The dug positions were made exceptionally strong by 2nd Lieutenant Holt who requisitioned some steel plates from a factory near by.

On C Company's front, 9 Platoon was placed under command of 1st Battalion the Royal Berkshire Regiment, 10 Platoon under 1st Battalion the Royal Welch Fusiliers, and 11 Platoon under 2nd Battalion the Durham Light Infantry.

The officers of the companies were busily occupied choosing and siting positions, visiting neighbouring units, and liaising with the infantry commanders. The town of Wavre was bombed on the 12th and the enemy shelled the woods and hills in the rear of the 2nd Division's lines. Our artillery was also very active.

It was in this position that the division awaited the German attack; the indications were that it would not be long delayed and that when it came it would be very severe. During the day, Louvain was severely bombed, but the German attack on this day fell most heavily upon Holland, where parachute troops established themselves firmly near the Hague and could not be dislodged.

May 13. From a fairly early hour the troops in the forward line knew that the enemy was coming up to their positions. During the morning German guns opened up on our forward posts and enemy aircraft were flying over the area that the division was holding. Later, Wavre was severely bombed, but it does not appear that D Company's posts were hit or that they suffered loss. As the Germans had not then attacked the line, the company commanders spent the day inspecting the platoon posts and improving the emplacements. It was on this day that Captain Churchill, also of D Company, saw his first wounded of the war—a French cavalry officer, shot in the elbow, who was brought in in a sidecar and passed through his position to the rear.

It is hardly possible at this date to make even a brief review of the campaign in France and Belgium, but if those facts that are established beyond all question are firmly held, the following inference can be made from them. It is doubtful whether the Dutch and the Belgians could, in any circumstances, have resisted an attack by the German armies. One thing however is quite certain, and that is that a protracted resistance by those two small countries would only have been possible if their general staffs had been allowed to disregard political boundaries and to prepare a concerted plan, in which the military forces and the natural features of both countries were used for a common purpose. The Dutch and Belgian governments had, however, never consented that this should be done because they feared to compromise themselves with the German government, and also because the two peoples are divided by great jealousies and antagonisms, and the Dutch feared that if Belgian troops ever entered their country, either as allies or as enemies, they would establish themselves in the Dutch province on the southern bank of the Schelde and would refuse to leave it.

The Germans made their greatest exertion against Holland on May 13. Nevertheless, the indications on the 2nd Divison's front were that a severe pressure might at any moment be expected; and, indeed, the Germans had at this date secured substantial advantages over the French armies to the south, about which a few words should be added.

Beyond General Blanchard's 1st French Army, the 9th Army (General Corap) held the line of the Meuse; and beyond the 9th Army, the 2nd French Army held a strongly fortified position round Sedan. On this day (May 13) the Germans had outfought some formations of both these armies, for the general state of affairs was thus reported to the French Commander-in-Chief at the close of the day: " The Belgian forces had now disappeared from our front.... To the south of Namur, the enemy had everywhere reached the river; and it was even then reported that enemy formations had crossed the river at Houx [to the north of Dinant] and at Sedan. It even appeared that this place had been abandoned."[4]

May 14. German forces reached the Dyle front during the morning; farther south, the German armies were on the Meuse line. A large part of Belgium was thus already overrun, and the province of Limburg, to the east of the 2nd Division, was in the enemy's hands. As a consequence, all the roads that led to our position were choked with refugees; the main road through Wavre was blocked, and the sideroads were no better. The officers, whose posts were literally flooded by the stream of terrified and exhausted people, did what they could to keep the human river moving; but the swarm of peasants and their families was soon augmented by masses of Belgian soldiers, who were retreating towards Brussels, and bearing with them all the tokens of half-beaten men, for they were sullen, bedraggled, and very tired. An order was,

[4] General Gamelin: *Les armées françaises de 1940*, p. 337.

indeed, received that the Belgian troops were to be stopped and regrouped, and although this was done fairly successfully in Wavre, the order was impossible to execute elsewhere, for when Captain Baker attempted it, the Belgian soldiers whom he tried to direct became so angry and threatening that he had to call upon his own men to protect him. Some Belgian officers were friendly and came into the pill-boxes to talk, but what they had to say was by no means encouraging, for they spoke of dive-bombing attacks and of artillery concentrations which no troops could withstand. The retiring Belgians were, indeed, an indication that matters were going badly: on the day before, Lord Gort had been told that the Belgian Commander-in-Chief was withdrawing the army to the Louvain–Antwerp line. This meant that Belgian resistance on the outer line had crumbled after two days' fighting: and, in point of fact, the Albert Canal had been crossed at several places, and Fort Eben Emael, the bastion of the Belgian position near Maastricht, had been stormed.

Towards the evening the enemy were right up to the Dyle: they attacked along the 6th Brigade's front, and all the platoon posts of C Company were in action. The attack was, however, not pressed, and no position was lost or compromised. After dark, the Germans attacked farther south on the 4th Brigade's front, but this appears to have been more a test or a probe than an attack proper, for it was soon over.

The greatest weight of the German advance was still on the Netherlands front, and here the Dutch were quite overpowered. The last positions in their defensive line were overrun: German armoured formations were on the outskirts of Rotterdam, and German units had joined hands with the parachute troops who had held their positions near the Hague for four days. The Dutch Commander-in-Chief, therefore, advised his government that it was fruitless to go on fighting, and was, by them, authorized to negotiate a capitulation. This collapse of the Netherlands resistance was not an immediate danger to the army on the Dyle, whose struggle on the following day. The reserve company of the Durhams, who had done the counter-attack, were relieved by a company of the Royal Welch Fusiliers, and a company of the Camerons (5th Brigade) was brought up to relieve the Welch Fusiliers. On the right of the brigade line, the Royal Scots with D Company attached to them, defended the little town of Wavre as stubbornly and as successfully as the line was held elsewhere. Their resistance must, indeed, have made a deep impression upon those who were more immediately concerned with it; for long afterwards, the diarist of the brigade (as though he feared lest all recollection of this desperate stand might be lost, and desired to record it if it were only on the typescript pages of an army form) made an entry to commemorate how valiantly the Royal Scots and the Manchesters fought on where they stood, and refused to yield a millimetre to the rising flood of assaulting Germans. The French line began on the Royal Scots' right, however, and the French troops—a division of native Algerians[6]—had not resisted so successfully, and were, in fact, so much outfought that Bierges was in German hands at the close of the afternoon. The 1st Division's right flank, indeed the flank of the whole British Army, was thus exposed, and the Commander-in-Chief, "Agreed with the commander of 1 Corps that the withdrawal of his right should take place to the River Lasne," where the corps was again to make a junction with the French left. The divisional commander transmitted the order for a retirement to the Lasne, and gave instructions that it was to begin at 22.00 hours.

Long before the order was given the inhabitants of Wavre had begun to leave the town, and our men watched the desolate stream of stricken creatures moving along the roads. Only a few remained: among them the nuns of the local convent, who refused D Company's offer of assistance and said that those who were left behind were now their charges, and that the cattle in the fields would have to be milked

---

[6] 13th Division Indigène Nord Africaine.

THE RETREAT TO THE LASNE

and tended. The unbreakable courage of these defenceless women made a deep impression on the English soldiers.

May 16. The retreat was duly executed during the night. The 6th Brigade was covered by the Royal Berkshires and by A Company, and they passed the crossroads at Ottenburg at 4 o'clock in the morning. The Durhams and a company of the Royal Welch Fusiliers had great difficulty in getting away; for after dark the Germans crept forward from the positions that they had seized, and the battalion headquarters of the Durhams was nearly encircled when the retreat began. The Welch Fusiliers were being attacked when they withdrew. C Company's posts were in the heart of what may be called the entangled zone, and 9 and 10 Platoons lost some guns before they extricated themselves.

The 4th Brigade, to which D Company was attached, were covered by the Royal Norfolks when they withdrew. Though not so severely pressed as the 6th Brigade, the forward companies were so close to the enemy that they did not get away easily; no vehicles could be sent to D Company, and the officers and men were obliged to manhandle what they could carry. The officers marched through the night festooned with belts of small-arms ammunition, and although every man was heavily loaded and carried his burden cheerfully, it was inevitable that considerable quantities of equipment were left behind. Nevertheless, every gun was extricated and brought away.

There is only one main road in the country between the two rivers (the Wavre–Brussels *grande route*) and it traverses the southern end of it. The troops were, therefore, compelled to march during the night hours along a number of winding side-roads. A large number of men lost their way in consequence, and, after daybreak, staff officers were sweeping the countryside directing stragglers to their lost units.

The retirement was, however, successfully executed, and during the forenoon the 2nd Division was re-forming on its new line. The 4th Brigade held the western bank from the village of Genval to Tombeek, the 6th Brigade continued the line to Terlaenen. The 5th Brigade was drawn back to cover the right flank (which was still exposed, as the line to which the French had retired was uncertain) and was posted on a line between Hanonsart and Genval. All the bridges on the front (Genval, Rosières, Tombeek and Terlaenen) were blown soon after daybreak, when the last troops had crossed.

The new position was not a good one; the troops were, however, allowed a short respite in which to improve it as far as they were able, for the enemy did not follow the actual withdrawal, and came up to the river during the morning. The enemy's guns opened on the 4th Brigade's posts during the day, and all forward positions were harassed by a certain amount of machine-gun fire; nevertheless the forenoon and the afternoon were fairly quiet. The men who had, for the most part, fought all one day and retired during the night following, were tired but in good spirits; for the results of the day's fighting were fairly well known, and the news was that the B.E.F. had held all its positions when the order to withdraw was issued. During the afternoon, however, while the men were strengthening their positions, an order came in that the whole division was to retire to the Dendre. This, however, was only a first instalment of what had been decided, for at 10 a.m. on that morning, Lord Gort had received an order from General Billotte, the Commander of the *groupe d'armés* in Belgium, that the Anglo-French forces were to go right back to the line of the Schelde, and were there to occupy the positions that had been allotted to them under a plan that was prepared before the decision to advance to the Dyle was taken. This was not the consequence of anything that had happened round Wavre, or upon the B.E.F. or Belgian fronts, but was because it could no longer be disguised that what had up to then been reported as a German crossing of the Meuse (Lord Gort was first informed of it on the 14th) was actually a disaster of the first order, which imperilled the Allied armies in Belgium.

For, while our troops were so stubbornly standing upon

the heights of the Dyle, the German armies had struck the blow which decided the campaign. " From the Chiers to the south of Namur, our positions had crumbled," writes General Gamelin. An officer from the Commander-in-Chief's staff, who was sent to 9th Army Headquarters, reported that everything was there in the greatest disorder, and that a horde of demoralized troops were pouring backwards. It was, indeed, at about this time that the French headquarters staff were informed that at many points the French soldiers had not fought at all, and had just left their gun pits with their hands up. The Germans had, moreover, quite easily brought a counter-attack by the $1^{\text{ère}}$ *division cuirassée* to a standstill; and by the close of the day large German forces were making a rapid westerly advance towards Maubeuge.

The briefest glance at any map of France and Belgium will show at once that this great German victory endangered all the Franco-British forces in Belgium, in that it made a huge rent in the Allied line. Precise information about the enemy's advance did not, however, come through quickly, for the 9th French Army, on which the blow had fallen, was routed after a few hours of fighting, and the Allied G.H.Q. was, in consequence, not too well supplied with reliable reports of the enemy's moves. During the afternoon of the 16th, however, it was clear that the Franco-British armies in Belgium were separated from the French armies farther south, and that, unless they were drawn back quickly, German forces might, at any moment, appear on their right flank and even behind it.

May 17. It was intended that the division should march to the canal between Hal and Brussels, and that it should be embussed after crossing it. The first movement was, therefore, carried out thus: the 5th Brigade covered the retreat; the 2nd Dorsets and the 7th Worcesters took up a position along the line of lakes of the River Argent, at the southern end of the Forêt de Soignies; the 1st Comerons drew up on the road that runs north and south through the forest, and remained in this position until the 4th and 6th Brigades passed through.

The 6th Brigade moved off first at 21.30 hours in the order: 1st Royal Berkshires, 2nd Durhams, 1st Royal Welch Fusiliers. They halted in the Forêt de Soignies for a meal, marched off again between 03.30 and 04.30 hours, and crossed the canal at Ruysbroek during the morning of May 17.

No. 11 Platoon of C Company, which had been in position on the Lasne supporting the Durham Light Infantry, withdrew with this brigade. One of its sections, under Corporal Eccles, was unable to move in daylight owing to the closeness of the enemy, and had to slip away under cover of darkness, manhandling their guns back to Overyssche where they met some carriers of the Royal Welch Fusiliers.

The 4th Brigade followed, and were covered by the 2nd Norfolks. The 5th Brigade moved off at 09.00 hours, after the last troops of the other two brigades were through the forest: they crossed the canal at Loth and Ruysbroek during the early part of the afternoon.

It is difficult at any time, and in any circumstances, to walk by night through an unknown forest, and it was only to be expected that this night march of the three brigades through the Forêt de Soignies should be very difficult. The maps were almost useless, as countless tracks and paths which were not marked upon them had been made in the forest. The brigade columns soon became mixed up, and were in varying degrees lost: the commander of the 4th Brigade was carried to the suburbs of Brussels, and subsequently spent most of the day acting as a traffic policeman. Captain Woolsey and Captain Churchill of D Company also had great difficulty in finding their way, and both they and their platoon columns became separated in the course of the night. Captain Churchill lost the company column when the driver of the vehicle in front of his fell asleep at a halt. All the following day the retirement was continued, and at 4 p.m. company headquarters was established in an *estaminet* in the

THE RIVER DENDRE

The Germans advanced over this hill and were engaged by D Company's guns from the near side of the river, May 1940. Two of D Company's M.G. posts were located in the line of trees on the left of the lower picture

village of Sarlardinge, and contact was established with 4th Brigade Headquarters.

When the canal was reached the bridges were blocked by the transport, and the retreat was impeded and made difficult by the inevitable accompaniment of refugees, for it was then known in Brussels that the Allied armies were everywhere retreating and the poorer people began to leave the town. It was, indeed, this pitiful horde of terror-stricken men and women which the officers best remember. "We just chugged along at walking pace," says Captain Woolsey, "with the poor creatures around, ahead, and behind us. It was useless to attempt to force them out of the way; for we knew that the column was twenty miles long and more."

Nevertheless, the retreat was successfully carried out, and by nightfall on May 17 the 4th and 5th Brigades halted for the night between Grammont and Geoffredinge. The 6th Brigade were not so fortunate: their transport did not meet them on the western side of the canal, and the brigade commander had no choice but to continue the retreat on foot. The brigade reached Gammerages in the early morning of the 18th; the men were then terribly exhausted; they had been in contact with the enemy for a day and a night, thereafter they had marched forty miles in twenty-seven hours.

The fortunes of the battalion during these first hours of the retreat are rather difficult to follow. The companies were much dispersed during the withdrawal through the forest; for (as the battalion diary puts it) it was often very difficult for guides and drivers to keep awake. Nevertheless the Headquarters Company and most of the battalion assembled round Grammont during the 17th. C Company, which moved with the sorely tried 6th Brigade, rested at Ogy on May 18 in reserve.

May 18. When the division thus reached the Dendre, the orders were that the river should be held between Grammont and Lessines, with the 5th Brigade on the right, the 4th on the left of the position, and the 6th in reserve. The 48th Division was to continue the line above Lessines, and the 1st

Division was to come into position below Grammont, and was to hold the town itself.

Grammont, the key to the position, was for some hours undefended, save only by a few section posts that the Royal Norfolks established on the outskirts of it; and it was not

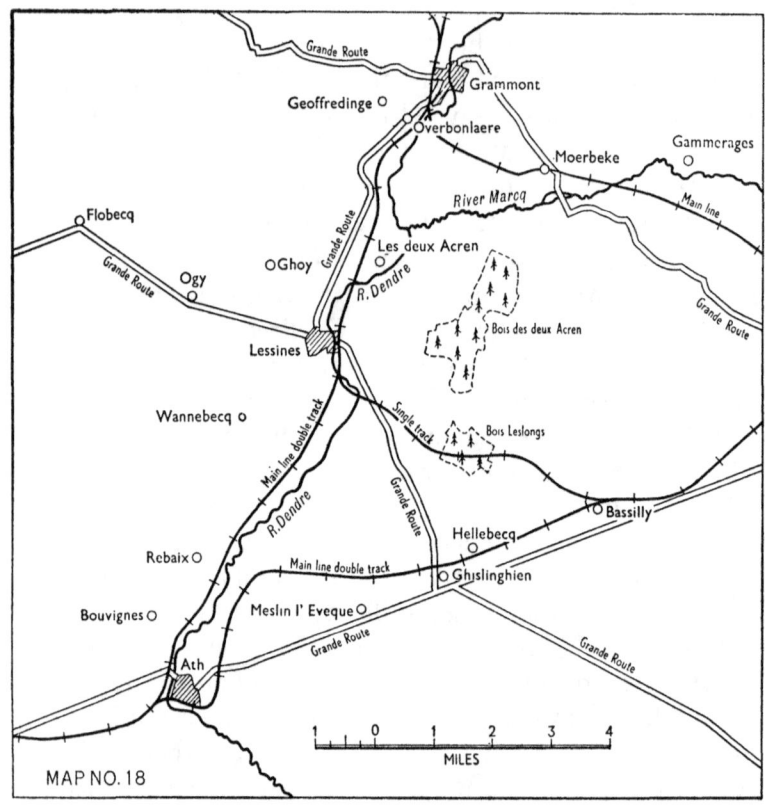

MAP NO. 18

until well on in the afternoon that troops from the 1st Division (Argyll and Sutherland Highlanders) came in and garrisoned the town.

Notwithstanding that the men were still very tired—the few hours during which they had slept since the retreat began were not enough to refresh them—they took up their new positions in great spirits, because every soldier knew at a and about fifty dead horses. The Manchesters picked up many of the wounded civilians and took them on to a civil hospital. Here Captain Churchill managed to get Captain Woolsey's wound dressed, and then took him on over the French frontier and left him with the officers' mess of a British armoured brigade. He was ultimately safely evacuated to England.

The retreat towards Tournai was, however, very arduous. Three divisions were using the same road, and one brigade of another division was embussed upon it. Renaix was packed with refugees, and the column was there halted for several hours. The 4th Brigade's diary is, indeed explicit as to the difficulties:

> Buses, which were returning to pick up the brigade, were very late, and the battalions started the withdrawal on foot. The brigade commander commandeered ten buses, the drivers of which did not know where to report, and the 1/8th Lancashire Fusiliers were taken up by them and taken as far as Renaix. The buses then returned, and, with the brigade commander as guide, picked up the 1st Battalion of the Royal Scots and carried them as far as Froidmont. Whilst embussing, the Royal Scots were spotted and heavily bombed by about fifty enemy planes, who scored no hits.

Tournai had, moreover, been severely bombed during the retreat, and it was blazing and impassable when the column approached it. The drivers of vehicles had great difficulty in keeping their eyes open owing to the ash and dust in the air.

The three brigades were, nevertheless, all grouped round Tournai by early afternoon. The 4th Brigade's headquarters was at Froidmont, south-west of the town. The 5th Brigade's position is not well recorded, and was probably between Froidmont and Tournai. The 6th Brigade H.Q. was just west of the town, near the main road to Douai.

The battalion headquarters was established at the little village of Hertain, just north of the Lille road, and the battalion commander gave orders that A and C Companies should, for the time being, be grouped together as one composite company. D Company was sent into Tournai; B Company remained with the 6th Brigade.

The British Army was now grouping on a line between Bléhairies and Audenarde; six divisions were in the forward line, and 5th Division was in G.H.Q. reserve.[9] The brigade commanders were preparing to give battle on the following

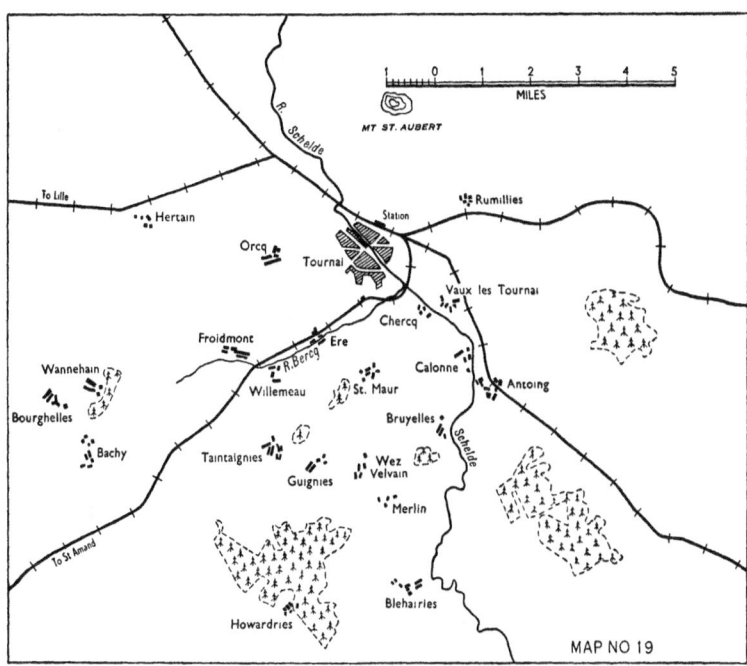

day. The men were beyond all description tired by so many moves by night, but were in good heart. The retreat had not in itself depressed them, as they were confident (the British soldier is no strategist) that it was a preliminary to some artful and well-conceived manœuvre that would put all right.

The real posture of affairs was very different; for the British Commander-in-Chief was already doubtful whether he would be able to maintain his army in France at all, and was even then considering how he could withdraw it from

[9] Lord Gort's dispatch, October 17, 1941, section 27.

the Continent. How matters then presented themselves to him can only be explained by a brief retrospect.

As we have seen, the French Commander-in-Chief decided to retreat to the Schelde on about May 15 (possibly earlier), and on the morning of the day following, his decision was communicated to Lord Gort by General Billotte. The plan then devised (which the army commanders were striving to execute on the day that we are now considering) was that the 7th French Army should be withdrawn from its position on the left of the Allied line, moved across the rear of the other Allied forces and put into the gap that the German victory on the Meuse had made to the south of the 1st French Army. The Allied line (enumerating from left to right) was then to be: Belgian army, British Expeditionary Force, French 1st Army, French 7th Army. The joining-points of the 1st and 7th Armies could, of course, only be settled when the formations of the 7th Army moved into the gap and made contact with the advancing Germans; but the French Commander-in-Chief evidently hoped, and still intended, to check the German advance on the line of the Tortille and the Canal du Nord between Péronne and Douai; and the British labour divisions that had been ordered to hold the canal between Ruyaulcourt and Arleux were, presumably, intended to act as a covering screen to the 7th Army as it moved into its new position.

On the evening of May 19, however (the date that we are now considering), it was more than doubtful whether the manœuvre that the Allied troops were executing would close the rent in the French line of battle. The French 1st Army had been pressed back to the line of the Sensee by the German armoured troops in the gap, and eight French divisions were now huddled together in the quadrilateral Maulde–Valenciennes–Arleux–Douai; to the south of them the unclosed gap still yawned; for the few units that had been so hastily thrown into it had in no sense closed it.

In the circumstances, the British Commander-in-Chief felt that his right and rear were more seriously threatened

THE DEFENCE OF THE RIGHT FLANK

than ever. General Mason-MacFarlane's force was already watching the crossings of the Scarpe between Raches and Saint-Amand. In order to strengthen it, and to give additional cover to his right and rear, Lord Gort ordered the commander of the 50th Division, which was then in G.H.Q. reserve, to send one of his brigades (the 25th) to the canal line between Carvin and La Bassée; to follow into the same area with the rest of his division, and to place himself under General Mason-MacFarlane's orders. Arras, which was now becoming the bastion of the right flank defence, was strengthened by sending the 12th Lancers into the town. The 23rd Division, which was the bulk of Petreforce, was very isolated and detached in its position along the Canal du Nord; it was therefore withdrawn to the line of the Sensee to the east of Arras.

Nevertheless, Lord Gort, even at this date, considered that his army was now finally separated from the French armies to the south of the gap. The enemy were then in Amiens, and he thus appreciated the position:

> By the evening of May 19 the situation was somewhat relieved in that the defensive flank had begun to take shape. On the other hand, the character of the operation had radically altered with the arrival of German troops in Amiens. The picture was no longer that of a line bent, or temporarily broken, but of a besieged fortress. To raise such a siege, a relieving force must be sent from the south, and to meet this force a sortie on the part of the defenders was indicated.[10]

May 19–20. When the retreat to the Schelde was finished, the 48th Division was holding the river line as a covering force, and the divisional commander intended to relieve it during the day. The 6th Brigade was to hold the river between Chercq and the southern outskirts of Tournai (which would be occupied by the 1st Division). The 4th Brigade was to hold the centre between Chercq and Calonne. The 5th Brigade was to come in on the right and defend the

[10] Dispatch, October 17, 1941, section 31.

river as far as Bruyelle, where the line was to be continued by the 48th Division.

The regrouping was, however, very difficult. Three divisions had retreated along one road, and all the consequences of a retreat were manifesting themselves. Communications between division and brigade headquarters were not good, delayed messages were contradicted by messages sent later, though more expeditiously, than the earlier ones, and there were often misunderstandings about the fronts that were to be held.

The 6th Brigade moved into positions during the afternoon of the 19th, but found that units of the 126th Brigade were already holding part of the sector. After some discussion it was decided that the units of the 126th Brigade should remain where they were: the overlapping was on the left of the front, towards Tournai. Throughout the day, troops from the 1st Division were crossing the river, and it was not until 20.00 hours that the last bridge on the brigade's sector was blown.

The brigade was now ordered to move off the river line, and to come into reserve, three miles behind the front, round Willemeau; and this was followed, soon after, by another order which, if obeyed to the letter, would have deployed the brigade along the valley of the Bercq, between Willemeau and Chercq. The brigade commander decided that the order could only refer to the anti-tank screen, and did not alter his original dispositions.

When Captain Churchill took Captain Woolsey off in his truck to find medical aid, Lieutenant Holt, who had now become second-in-command, brought D Company back through Tournai and put them into position to support the 6th Brigade in the vicinity of Froidmont. Here Captain Churchill rejoined the company, and took command of it. He discovered that the company office truck had broken down during the retreat and had been unloaded on the orders of the Company Sergeant-Major. Lance-Corporal Welsh had been posted in charge of a guard on this kit, and had been given orders to stay where they were. In an attempt to recover this N.C.O. and his guard, Captain Churchill climbed into the tank which had been retrieved on the Dendre and, taking Sergeant Graves to man the machine-guns and Sergeant Smith to drive the tank, returned to Tournai and crossed the Schelde by the last remaining bridge, where there was a party waiting to blow it. Taking the Brussels road, Captain Churchill soon came under fire of machine-guns and an anti-tank gun, so he manœuvred the tank so as to take up a position covering the approaches to the bridges, having warned the demolition party that the enemy were within 300 yards. Fifteen minutes later the tank again came under heavy fire; machine-gun bullets repeatedly hit the armour without, however, causing any harm to the occupants. The anti-tank gun now opened up again and Captain Churchill withdrew across the bridge, which was blown shortly afterwards.

It was at this time also that Private Fanning of A Company swam across the Schelde at Tournai in an attempt to rescue an officer of the Royal Welch Fusiliers who had been wounded, but when he got to him found he was dead.

The 4th Brigade did not occupy its positions until midnight of the 20th, and it then took over some of the sector that had been held by the 6th Brigade. The right (1st Royal Scots) was then at Calonne, and the left (2nd Norfolks) at the Château du Coucou (Chercq).

The enemy were approaching the Schelde during the 20th, but they were not yet in sufficient strength to harass seriously the regrouping of the 4th and 6th Brigades. As the battalions moved into their positions, the troops were occasionally exposed to intermittent mortar and machine-gun fire, but it was never severe. The 5th Brigade's movements were, however, more seriously harassed.

The brigade troops were resting round Orcq during May 19, and the orders were that they were to occupy their sector during the night, and were to complete the relief of the covering troops by 03.00 hours on the 20th. As the preliminaries to the move were being made (17.30 hours), news came in that the enemy had crossed the river at Calonne, and the brigade commander at once gave orders that the Camerons were to counter-attack and drive them out. Before this could be done, however, the brigade was ordered to move to Ere, in the valley of the little stream of Barges, and as the order was to the whole brigade, the Camerons were included in it and the counter-attack was cancelled.

The Germans had now established batteries on Mont-Saint-Aubert, below Tournai. This height overlooked the whole country round Ere, and as the place was being heavily shelled when the brigade moved into it (evening of May 20) two battalions were sent on to Froidmont. Orders now came that the brigade was to operate under orders from the 48th Division, but orders continued to be received from the 2nd Division. The river front that was allotted to the brigade was thus not occupied during this day (May 20), and at nightfall the brigade was still deployed round Froidmont, Tentaignies, and Guignes.

It would be quite impossible to trace all the consequences of the orders and counter-orders that were issued to the three brigades during this day (May 20), but the general or total consequence is clear enough; the front on the Schelde was only lightly held during the day, and the enemy's forward troops were not dislodged from the bridgehead that they had seized at Calonne.

If the divisional commander had intended (nothing can be inferred for certain, but it seems probable that he did) that the 4th and 5th Brigades should occupy the line of the Schelde from Bruyelle to Chercq, then his orders were still unexecuted by the early morning of May 21. The 4th Division was then on the Schelde between Calonne and Chercq, and the 6th Brigade was in reserve with the battalions in their battle positions between Wez Velvain and Saint-Maur. The 5th Brigade was, however, not up in the line, and the battalions were at Merlin, Tantaignies, and Guignes. Lieutenant-Colonel Moore, the commanding officer of the

ORDERS TO STAND AND FIGHT

Manchester Regiment, appears to have appreciated the original intention correctly, or to have been less baffled than the higher formations by the succession of contradictory orders, for the companies established their posts in the sectors that were originally allotted to their brigades. D Company (4th Brigade) were on the west bank near Calonne; B Company (5th Brigade) were round Bruyelle; C Company (6th Brigade) were in reserve with their posts round Merlin, and 11 Platoon under 2nd Lieutenant J. B. H. Keitley carried out a map shoot to put down harassing fire on to the main square in Tournai. A Company were in divisional reserve at Tantaignies, where the battalion headquarters was also established. The orders were to stand and fight.

Little is known of the positions occupied by the companies except that in D Company, Lieutenants Holt and Chandler put 13 and 15 Platoons in position on the edge of some woods, and that Captain Churchill stationed 14 Platoon on a sunken road between Saint-Maur and Calonne, and strengthened this position by collecting a section of B Company and three officers and about 170 men of the 1/8th Royal Warwickshire Regiment who dug in beside the machine-guns.

Like most of the rivers in the flat parts of France and Belgium, the Schelde is flanked by a wide network of drainage dykes, and, inasmuch as the border of drains and cuttings was widest on the eastern bank below Tournai, the enemy's infantry had a considerable obstacle in front of them. In the 2nd Division's sector, however, between Chercq and Bruyelle, there are fewer drainage dykes than there are in the upper and lower reaches of the river, for the Schelde here flows through country that is sufficiently raised above the river bed to supply a natural drainage. Two lines of low hills run westward from the Schelde between Tournai and Bruyelle, but, inasmuch as they run at right-angles to the river line, they do not command the crossings of the river, and are of no assistance to a defence of the west bank. The whole countryside can be overlooked from Mont-Saint-Aubert, to the north of Tournai. This commanding hill is on the right bank, and the enemy held it firmly. On the whole, it may be said that the 2nd Division's sector was not naturally as strong as the sectors to the north and south of it.

May 21. Shortly after daylight, the Germans attacked along the whole front. Owing to the confusion of the previous day, the 5th Brigade's sector was only lightly held, and it was on that sector that the enemy crossed the river at Antoing and Bruyelle. Nevertheless, the Camerons carried out the counter-attack that had been postponed on the previous day and pressed on with the greatest stubbornness until they reached the outskirts of Bruyelle. The movement was throughout supported by D Company's machine-guns. At Bruyelle the Camerons were held down by heavy and accurate artillery fire. Farther down the river, another party of Camerons reached the bridge at Antoing, and reported that the Germans were still in Calonne, but that the total numbers of the enemy on the western side of the canal was not great. It was decided during the afternoon that Calonne should be attacked during the night, and the Royal Welch Fusiliers were put under the brigade to assist in the attack.

D Company supported the attack, but their position was being heavily shelled and mortared, and casualties were rising fast; fifty officers and men of the Royal Warwickshires were killed and wounded, and four Manchesters were wounded, among them Captain Churchill, who was grazed in the thigh. The guns were sited in embrasures at the top of the bank above the sunken road, and if they had been manned continuously the crews would simply have been wiped out. Captain Churchill therefore improvised a device of wire, string, and a long pole, which enabled the crews to fire the guns from their shelters. The guns were traversed with another device: hammers were constructed of poles which were weighted with stones, and with these instruments the handles of the guns were tapped.

The Camerons did not dislodge the enemy from Calonne, which was the principal bridgehead in the sector, and the counter-attack was judged to have failed. Nevertheless, it

When the 2nd Division was ordered to leave its position on the Schelde the threat to the British right had, therefore, become an imminent and pressing danger; for the enemy were then turning northwards towards the communications that were our only exit route to the coast. The gap that needed closing was no longer an open corridor between the northern and southern armies in France and Belgium: it was a far larger one that began at the middle waters of the Schelde, and ended at the sea coast round Gravelines and Dunkerque. Moreover, if the enemy established themselves firmly in this new gap the one certain consequence was that the British Army's only avenue of escape would be closed, and that the utter destruction of the whole British Expeditionary Force would follow as a matter of course. For at this time enemy columns had reached Boulogne and were approaching Calais. Communications across the Somme were thus severed, and there was but little chance that the armoured division which had been sent to France as a reinforcement, and was then south of the Somme, would join the British forces.

The danger that the British Army might not be merely outflanked but completely encircled, had, however, been foreseen, and for several days past the British Commander-in-Chief had been collecting forces to defend the line of the rivers and canals that run through Gravelines, Saint Omer, Aire, Béthune, and La Bassée. The sector between Aire and Carvin was entrusted to Major-General Curtis, who was allotted four battalions of the 46th Division (which he himself commanded); the 25th Infantry Brigade (50th Division) and one field battery. Farther to the west and north-west, Brigadier Usher was ordered to defend the canal line to the sea, and was given the 23rd (Lines of Communications) Division with which to do so. These forces were assembling when the order to abandon the Schelde line was given, so that the canal line from Carvin to the sea was, at that time, held by a thin ribbon of about 10,000 men and a few anti-tank weapons. It was impossible even to watch all the crossings

THE SCHELDE LINE ABANDONED

with so small a force, and on May 21, German reconnaissance parties were already reported at the western end of the line.

The reinforcements that were immediately available were the units that had been put into General Mason-MacFarlane's force since its first formation on May 18. This force was, however, now inside the area into which the French 1st Army had retired, and its sector was taken over by French units.

Finally, it was decided, after consultation with the French and Belgian commands, that the rest of the Allied line should run from Maulde to Halluin, and thence north-eastwards to Courtrai and Ghent. When the French and Belgian forces had occupied their sectors in the new line, the 2nd, 28th and 44th Divisions were to be relieved and brought into G.H.Q. reserve.

The retreat from the Schelde was carried out by march route on the night of May 22. It was covered by the 4/7th Dragoon Guards, who held a line between Guignes and Froidmont until the early morning of the 23rd. During the forenoon of that day the 4th Brigade occupied positions between Bachy and Wanneheim. The 6th Brigade prolonged the line to the right as far as Mouchain. The 5th Brigade came into line round Howardries.

The battalion headquarters was established at Bonnance during the forenoon of the 23rd. During the retirement D Company, which evacuated its position at 2.45 a.m. (three-quarters of an hour after the infantry had left) picked up some wounded men of the Camerons and brought them on their trucks to company headquarters at Barges. It was then discovered that 13 Platoon had not come in and C.S.M. Talbot went to find them but reported that they were not in their former position. It was thought that they might have retired with the Lancashire Fusiliers in whose area they had been established, but when the company reached the Gort Line it was found that this was not so. Captain Churchill and Lieutenant Holt now ordered four trucks to be manned and led them back across the abandoned country. Lieutenant Holt drove, and Captain Churchill manned a bren-gun which was stuck through the windscreen. They found 13 Platoon still stubbornly manning their post, although the Germans were only a couple of hundred yards away. By good fortune the Germans did not follow the retreat closely: the returning vehicles were kept under incessant small-arms fire but the platoon was brought back safely.

Up to now, the British Army had been resisting the enemy's westward drive through Belgium. It had withdrawn, it is true, from one position to another, because the German armies were advancing so fast through northern France and Belgium, but action, when engaged, had always been against a direct advance upon the positions that were being defended. On the afternoon of this day orders came in which altered the part that the British forces were to play. The 2nd Division was to retire, after being relieved by French troops, and was to take up a position on La Bassée Canal.

The withdrawal from the Schelde and the readjustment of the Allied line had, in fact, released the 2nd, 44th and 48th Divisions, which Lord Gort was now allotting to the canal line between Gravelines and Douai. The danger was, moreover, steadily rising: Calais was invested; the 5th and 50th Divisions which, as we have seen, had been attacking on May 21, were now pressed back to Seclin with all their tanks unusable; and the Germans had actually established bridgeheads on the canal line at Aire and Saint-Omer.

When matters stood thus, the British Prime Minister had seen fit to send a message[12] to the Commander-in-Chief that the French were attacking from the south; that they had already captured Péronne, Albert and Amiens; and that it was essential that the British Army should co-operate.

The British Prime Minister is probably not to be blamed that the most important part of his message, " the capture of Péronne, Albert and Amiens," was quite untrue, and was merely a French invention. The recommendation (so worded

[12] The message was transmitted through the Secretary of State for War but was almost certainly a message from the Prime Minister. See Lord Gort's dispatch, October 17, 1941, section 38.

that it was nearly an order) that the British Army should attack from the north, while the French Army attacked from the south was, however, quite impracticable. The available reserves of the British Army (the 5th and 50th Divisions) were closely engaged by the enemy between Lens and Douai and were severely pressed. No new reserve could be collected for at least two days: when collected, it would not be ready to attack in force for at least two days more. Apart from all this, the message was sent at a moment when the enemy were massing in our rear, and when the only operation that could be considered was how to hold the canal line upon which the safety of the British Army depended.

The purpose of the moves that were now being executed was that four divisions (1st and 42nd of 1 Corps; 3rd and 4th of 2 Corps) should be on the Franco-Belgian battle-front, and that the 2nd, 44th and 48th Divisions should form 3 Corps and should hold the canal line. The 2nd Division was therefore relieved by the French 12th Division during the afternoon of May 23. The movement was to begin at 23.00 hours and the last positions were to be evacuated by 01.00 hours on the following morning.

During that afternoon it was reported that the Germans had crossed the canal and were in Saint-Venant and Calonne. The intelligence staff headquarters believed that two armoured divisions were closing in on Calais; that two more, and a motorized Schutz Staffel Division, were moving towards Saint-Omer; and that a fifth was advancing towards Béthune. The position was, therefore, as dangerous and as critical as could be imagined.

The canal that was now to be defended at all costs is a boundary between two different kinds of country. To the south and west are the undulations of Artois and Picardy: on the north-eastern side the flat Franco-Belgian plain stretches uninterruptedly to the North Sea and the mouth of the Schelde, and it was this flat monotonous plain that was to be defended.

The whole district was the theatre of the most desperate

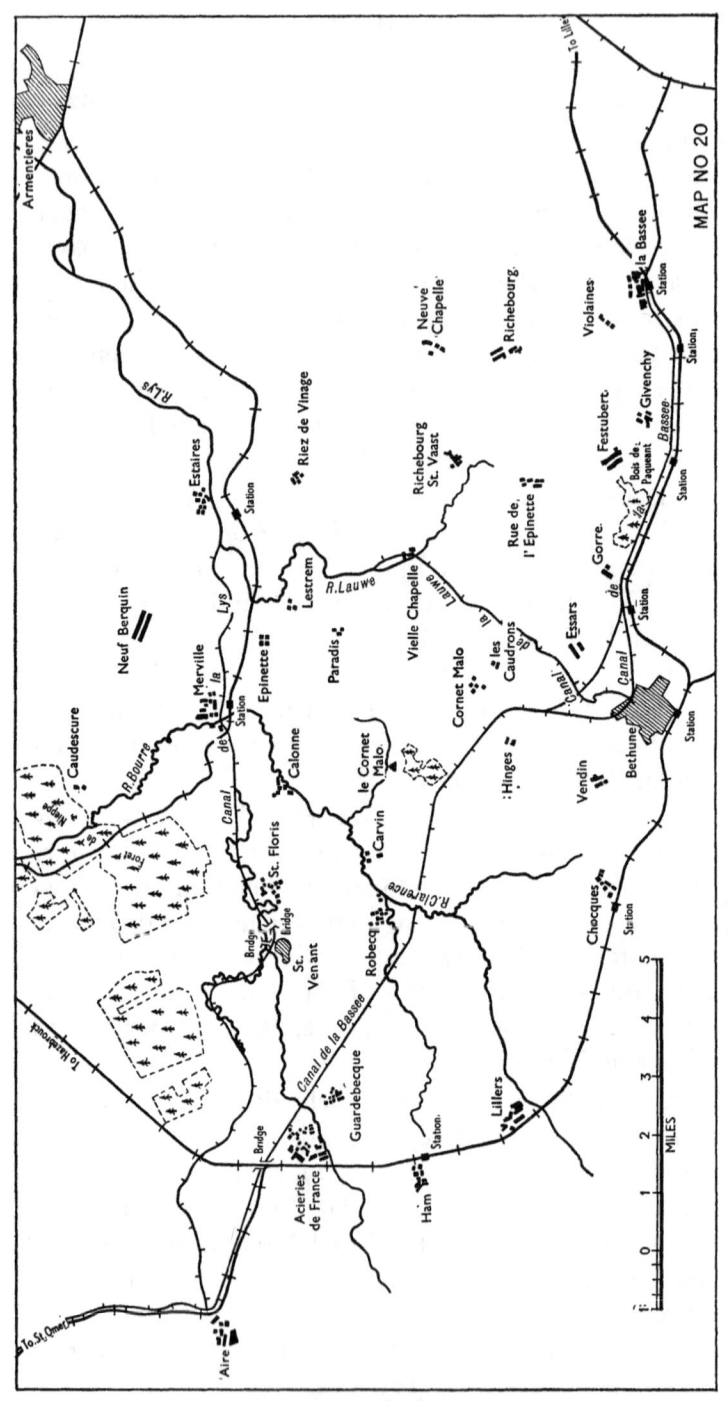

fighting during the previous war. Festubert, Neuve Chapelle, and Vieille Chapelle were then soaked with English and German blood, and it was at Givenchy that the Manchesters fought with such distinction more than twenty years ago.

The defence of this canal front was thus provided for. Major-General T. R. Eastwood was ordered to take command of the whole line. The 48th Division, with part of the 23rd Division attached to it, was responsible for the western sector of the line, between Gravelines and Saint-Omer; the 44th Division defended the line between the Forêt de Clairmarais and Aire; the 2nd Division held the line from Aire to La Bassée: the 46th Division, which had previously been the bulk or nucleus of the Polforce, continued the line as far as Raches. The three special forces, which had previously been formed for the defence of the canal, Polforce, Petreforce, and Macforce, were absorbed into the division in whose area they happened to be. A considerable part of Macforce was stationed round the Forêt de Nieppe, when the canal front was thus organized, and so became attached to the 2nd Division.

May 24–26. The three brigades were duly relieved by French troops, and they withdrew during the night of May 23. Only the 4th Brigade reached the canal line on the day following; it moved over very congested roads and reached its sector opposite Béthune during the afternoon of the 24th. The 2nd Norfolks came in on the right near the Bois de Paqueant; the 1st Battalion of the Royal Irish Fusiliers, who had been under the brigade, held the left of the sector between Gorre and Les Caudrons. The Royal Scots and the Lancashire Fusiliers were in reserve round Epinette, where the headquarters of the brigade was established.

Captain Churchill established 15 Platoon of D Company at Le Hamel with the Royal Scots, with arcs of fire covering the canal immediately opposite Béthune; company headquarters was established in a farm near Epinette. Heavy mortar fire developed during the afternoon and Major

Winchester, the second-in-command of the Royal Scots, was killed.

Early on the 25th Captain Churchill, at the request of Lieutenant-Colonel Money, C.O. of the Royal Scots, reported with his trucks at Le Hamel to transport C Company of that regiment to a position on the right flank of the brigade at Calonne, and the machine-guns of 13 Platoon of D Company were ordered to move to the same vicinity to provide support. When this was done, he reported to brigade headquarters and was requested to bring fire to bear on the high ground across the canal in the area of Hinges; and while on the way from Paradis to the Bois de Paqueant to find positions for his guns to carry out this task he ran into a burst of fire which smashed the windscreen of the truck and wounded him in the lobe of his ear. Both he and his driver, Private Isles, jumped from the vehicle and took refuge in the ditch beside the road, but later managed to recover the truck and return to company headquarters.

A little later Lieutenant Holt took some trucks and moved C Company of the Royal Scots from Calonne, where Captain Churchill had deposited them that morning, to a position just north of the Bois de Paqueant. During the move the vehicles were machine-gunned from the air and then held up by an enemy patrol with automatic weapons, but the Royal Scots debussed and killed or captured most of the patrol.

About this time an enemy anti-tank gun on the main road from Béthune began to give trouble and the 4th Brigade diary remarks that it was seen that the gun-crew was successfully put out of action by the machine-guns of the Manchester Regiment.

The 5th Brigade's withdrawal was slower because its first orders were to move to the area north of La Bassée, and it was not until the afternoon of the 24th (when brigade headquarters was at Festubert) that the brigade was ordered forward on to the canal. French formations and the 7th Queens were then holding the 5th Brigade's sector, and they were not relieved until the morning of the 26th. B Company, which was attached to the 5th Brigade, was posted round Violaines, when the brigade was finally in position. Officers were at this time all reporting that movements, great and small, were extremely difficult to carry out because so few maps were available. Very few sheets of the two large-scale maps (1:50,000 and 1:100,000) were obtainable; even the much smaller 1:250,000 was scarce.

The 6th Brigade's orders were to clear the Germans out of Calonne and Saint-Venant, to press them back over the canal, and then to defend a line running from the Lillers–Hazebrouck railway bridge as far as the right of the 4th Brigade. The move into the canal area was very difficult, as the battalions were carried along winding sideroads which the *grandes routes* crossed at right angles. It was hard to find the way, with so few maps, and whenever a main road was reached it was blocked with refugees. To add to the difficulties, the news that the enemy was in Merville came in after the brigade had started, and the route had to be changed in consequence.

During the 24th the brigade was in the Merville area. No enemy were found in Merville itself, but as the Royal Welch pressed on towards Calonne they were resisted at Saint-Floris. Both places were cleared, and by nightfall the brigade headquarters was at Calonne: the Royal Welch were at Saint-Floris, the Royal Berkshires were to the west of Merville, and the Durhams were near Calonne.

At first light on the following day the advance was continued. The Germans were forced out of Saint-Venant, and the bridge which carried the Hazebrouck road over the Canal de la Lys was repaired. Thereafter, German resistance stiffened, the battalions were held up, and they did not reach the canal line. By nightfall the brigade was occupying positions between Saint-Venant and the Bois de Paqueant. The brigade headquarters was established to the north of the Canal de la Lys, in the Forêt de Nieppe. C Company, which had accompanied the brigade in this difficult move forward, were in Saint-Venant; their headquarters were on the southern edge of the Forêt de Nieppe. The battalion headquarters, with A Company in reserve, was at Richebourg. The disorders of a long retreat were now manifesting themselves: Lieutenant Wilkinson was arrested and detained for several hours by a gunner officer who was persuaded that he was a fifth columnist, because he had asked for assistance if the Germans broke through. As everything was so uncertain, and as the enemy's position and movements were, in large measure, known only by rumour and conjecture, the battalion headquarters made preparations for resisting an attack from any quarter. The same was done at the headquarters of the brigades.

The consequence of these various movements was that on the morning of the 26th, the canal line was being held from La Bassée to the Bois de Paqueant, but that the Germans still held the crossings to the west, and were well established in the area Guardebecque, Saint-Venant, Robecq.

Such small advances as were made on this part of the front were, however, offset by a withdrawal in another part, which very much increased the danger in which the British Army then stood. For during the day it was learned that 4 Corps of the Belgian army had been driven from its positions between Menin and Desselghem on a front of over thirteen miles. The Germans had attacked with four divisions and a considerable force of tanks, and this, combined with severe pressure on the southern or canal front, declared that the enemy had assembled enough forces for a pincer movement which would finally sever the communications of the B.E.F. and leave it encircled.

> The gap between the British left and the Belgian right [writes Lord Gort], which had been threatening all day, might at any moment become impossible to close: were this to happen my last hope of reaching the coast would be gone. At this moment, it will be remembered, I had no reserves beyond a single cavalry regiment, and two divisions (5 and 50) earmarked for an attack southwards.[13]

[13] Dispatch, October 17, 1941, section 43. The attack to which Lord Gort refers was never delivered; and no attempt is here made to describe what was intended. For particulars see dispatch, section 40.

but lacked knowledge of a M.G. unit; however, we had no time to debate and accepted his command.

The enemy was now attacking from all directions except the rear and after holding them at bay, the 2nd Lieutenant decided our only chance was a quick withdrawal, but having no transport and 400 yards of sheer open country in the rear it was too late. Jerry, unable to get at close grips, had ordered their artillery up and as we were trying to get out, so we got the shells; this simply annihilated our now very depleted group and as I got up after being hit I noticed five of my platoon left; Sergeant Smith was one of these. I was dressed by one of the Norfolks as Sergeant Smith said he was going to try and get out; my leg was hit so I could not go. McKay and Hamilton refused to leave with those who could walk, saying they would carry myself and another of the platoon (Private Ogden). Sergeant Smith only got 100 yards before they all got hit and went down. I might add the 2nd Lieutenant of the Norfolks, who was already wounded, now admitted his error. He got some of his wounded and McKay assisting me, Hamilton assisting Private Ogden (who died May 29); we struggled back only to fall into an enemy group in the rear.

The 2nd Lieutenant was shot, Privates McKay and Hamilton wounded, Corporal Peel was wounded in the mouth. The Jerry, seeing the state we were in, left us and carried on his advance which no doubt had been held up considerably.

Farther east the Commander-in-Chief shortened the front that was being held by 1 and 2 Corps and made preparations for bringing them also behind the line of the Lys. His great preoccupation at this time was lest the Belgians, by being forced north-westwards, should leave so wide a gap between the British and the Belgian armies that the British would have to defend the whole of the northern side of the corridor.

May 27–31. On the 2nd Division's front the enemy were ready at first daylight, when they attacked with tanks and dive-bombers. In the 6th Brigade area the enemy passed the positions that were held by the Royal Welch and the Durhams and the battalions were cut off from their headquarters. The companies and the platoons fought on to the very end, but only a few survivors, whom Colonel Harrison collected, crossed the canal at Saint-Venant and got away. By the early afternoon, the area originally held by the brigade was completely overrun, and it was quite impossible to do what the divisional commander had first hoped—retire behind the Lys Canal and hold it—as the Germans had already turned this second canal line by penetrating into the Forêt de Nieppe. C Company, which was operating with this brigade, was cut off from battalion headquarters, and we know only that the platoons fought on with the Durhams and the Royal Welch Fusiliers and that not many came out to join the final retreat. It was during this last withdrawal that 2nd Lieutenant Keitley lost his life while striving to do something that only the bravest would attempt, for he was killed by the fire of a German tank when he was trying to extricate a section of guns which were virtually surrounded when he turned back to get them away. Ever since the battalion first went into action, this young officer had managed his platoon with the judgment of a veteran soldier; and the boy's extraordinary calmness in danger, and his skill in battle, is still remembered by those who survived the disasters of the campaign.

The 5th Brigade troops held the first attack on their sector but, soon afterwards, the enemy crossed near Gorre in some strength. The Camerons and the Dorsets still held their fronts, but their flanks were open. The Worcesters, upon whom the weight of the attack had fallen, were quite overrun, for the Camerons reported that tanks were assembling in the positions that the Worcesters had previously occupied. By the early afternoon the brigade headquarters was only keeping in touch with battalion by wireless, and as the afternoon wore on, and as each unit was passed or surrounded, even this failed. At about half-past two the Camerons sent their last message through: "Tanks closing in on H.Q. Am closing down to smash set." The message was descriptive of what was then occurring in every part of the 2nd Division's sector.

B Company shared the fortunes of the brigade. No. 7

Platoon was overrun by the enemy tanks at Gorre, and Major Hickey was captured while striving to get into touch with them. No. 6 Platoon was shelled out of its first positions early in the morning, and sent a last message later that enemy tanks were drawing in. Only a residue was left for the retreat which was finally ordered.

A fairly elaborate account has survived about what happened in the 4th Brigade's sector, and it is representative of what was everywhere occurring.

From 05.00 hours to 08.00 hours battalions reported frequently, by wireless, of the progress of the enemy's attack. Because of the A.F.V.s and tanks, company localities were soon cut off from battalion headquarters, but all continued to go on fighting. Owing to the heavy shelling, all line communications failed from this time. Lieutenant-Colonel Money reported that his battalion and the 2nd Battalion the Royal Norfolk Regiment were being repeatedly attacked from the Bois de Paqueant, while Lieutenant-Colonel Stayner reported at 07.50 hours that he was cut off from all his companies except one. . . . The order was to hold one, and at no place was any ground given whatever. . . . By 09.30 hours the situation had become hot round brigade headquarters, and there was a danger of being cut off. The brigade commander ordered the withdrawal of the brigade to behind the Béthune–Estaires Canal at Lestrem. Battalions were still in wireless touch with brigade headquarters, and were all confident, although, by this time, surrounded. . . . For the next hour, Major Ryder, commanding 2nd Battalion the Royal Norfolk Regiment, kept the brigade in touch with the situation at and around Cornet-Saint Malo. It was the same story—surrounded, every man fighting at fairly close quarters but inflicting heavy casualties on the enemy. . . . In each case they broke communication in a similar manner—surrounded by superior numbers of an enemy who were in possession of superior equipment yet each battalion was holding its own and not giving an inch.

It was at first hoped that the enemy could be checked by a counter-attack in the 5th Brigade's sector, which was to be carried out by the 25th Brigade and by some French tanks that were temporarily under the divisional general's command. This proved impossible, and, as the enemy were advancing in all parts of the sector, and as parties of them were frequently reported behind brigade headquarters, the order finally given was that the brigade was to retire behind the Lys Canal. The enemy had penetrated the Forêt de Nieppe, so that 5th Brigade was to defend the railway track between Merville and Hazebrouck.

This order was issued early in the afternoon. As it was not possible to withdraw during daylight, and as the Germans were everywhere penetrating into the rear areas—Epinette aerodrome was seen to be occupied by men and guns at 16.00 hours—the retreat was exceptionally difficult. By this time, moreover, so many units had been surrounded or overwhelmed that the brigade was composed of mere residues. Nevertheless, an attenuated force did assemble on the railway and canal line during the early morning of the 28th, when the 6th Brigade headquarters was at Caudescure. The 4th was to the north-east of Estaires, and the 5th at Neuf Berquin.

The battalion headquarters was moved to Doulieu, which was reached in pouring rain, but the battalion, like the brigades, was fast becoming a token force. It had not been in touch with C or D Companies since the struggle for La Bassée Canal began, for they had simply fought on with the battalions to which they were attached and had been submerged with them. Nevertheless, what remnants could be collected were assembled, and a last endeavour was made to use them as a coherent force. "Very early in the day," runs the battalion diary, "15 Platoon of D Company arrived at Epinette with no kit or equipment, these having been abandoned at Riez-du-Vinage.[15] Epinette was put into a state of defence by Captain Churchill who had, besides 15 Platoon, elements of L.F., R.S., R.N.R., and A. and S.H.,

[15] Sergeant-Major Talbot gives the following information about the platoon: "Many of the gun numbers remained behind and were killed whilst still firing. There were many acts of bravery, which in the heat of the battle and the confusion of the time remained unrecorded. Typical of these was Lance-Corporal Flude, the number one of his gun, who was killed with the remainder of his subsection; and Sergeant Hughes, who remained until the very last moment and escaped by a miracle."

in all about eighty men." The Brigade diary thus records what followed:

All this time, a strongpost at Epinette, the section of Captain Churchill's M.G.s, two guns of Captain Strachan's anti-tank company, and a platoon of the 1/8th Lancashire Fusiliers, with the remnants of brigade headquarters, were closely embroiled. They fought throughout the day, and, thanks to Captain Churchill's leadership, successfully managed to leave their positions and to cross the river Lys at 21.30 hours.

Headquarters of the 4th Brigade had left the village, and Captain Churchill sent all transport away with them. The 6th Brigade on the right had retired, and Epinette was isolated, with the enemy attacking from the south, west, and north. It was noticed that none of the attacks on the village were pressed home when the defenders opened up on them with their automatic weapons; and that the Germans then circled round the flanks. About three battalions of the enemy crossed the Merville aerodrome in extended order north of the village, and Captain Churchill remarks in his diary that "it was a new sensation to have one's own artillery falling behind one". At 2 p.m. four tanks attacked, but one was knocked out by Lieutenant Strachan's 25-mm. gun and the others drew off. At 6 p.m. a more determined attack got within 400 yards but was beaten off, but by 9.30 p.m. the enemy succeeded in entering the village from the west and Captain Churchill gave orders for a retirement to the Lestrem road and thence to Estaires.[16] The party found that

[16] Sergeant-Major Talbot gives the following additional information about the fighting round Estaires: "The house being used by D Company headquarters became a permanent target for the German mortar men, and what remained of the headquarters personnel took to the trench which had been prepared near by. Sufficient ammunition had been secured from an abandoned airfield nearby, where large quantities of every kind of S.A.A. were found and sent to 13 and 14 platoons. From company headquarters, the Germans could be seen occupying mortar positions about 300 yards away. These were tempting targets for the Bren gunners but orders had been given to hold fire until the Germans closed in. One mortar bomb fell close to the trench: fortunately nobody was hurt, and a German officer, who was wounded in both legs came in and surrendered. He was given first aid and was placed under guard. The enemy now moved in and the order was given to open fire on suitable targets. The crops in the fields stood high and obstructed the view from the trench: fire was therefore controlled from an attic window in the house, which overlooked the whole German position. The fire was strong enough, and well enough directed to halt the Germans until the position was abandoned."

the bridge at Lestrem had been blown, and the majority crossed the canal by a submerged iron girder, and a few swam across. Between Lestrem and Estaires Captain Churchill and Lieutenant Holt found an abandoned 25-pounder gun with limber and quod, the latter with a bullet hole through the radiator. After some trouble they got it to work, and motored it very slowly to Estaires where they handed it over to the C.R.A. who was at the bridge. "Good for the Manchesters!" he remarked as he took over the gun.

The division and its component brigades and battalions had been submerged or flooded, but never beaten; and what now remained of it would have fought as stubbornly as ever on the Lys Canal; but it was not called upon to do so. Early in the morning of the 28th all brigades were ordered to retire to Poperinghe and Watou, about eighteen miles north of the Lys, and this proved to be the preliminary to the retreat to Dunkerque.

The decision to withdraw the British Army from France, if it were possible, had indeed been taken two days previously; and while the 2nd Division was making its last stand on the canal line, while its brigades were being one by one submerged in the rising flood of German troops, 1 and 2 Corps were being moved into the Dunkerque perimeter.

For some days before the decision had been taken, the British Commander-in-Chief had been convinced that the British Army could not be maintained on the Continent; but the British Cabinet, who alone could order or sanction the withdrawal, hesitated to permit it, because they still hoped that the French armies in northern France would attack the German forces between Calais, Douai, and Valenciennes, and would re-unite the armies that the German offensive had temporarily severed into two groups. For so long as this project was entertained, indeed, for so long as responsible French ministers were stating that it was likely to achieve its purpose, it was very difficult for the British Cabinet to recall the British Army from France; and it was because the French hoped (or professed to hope) that they would make a great offensive movement from the south that the decision was delayed for so long. On May 26, however, the British Commander-in-Chief was at last freed from the servitude that high policy and Allied strategy had placed upon him; for on that day he received two telegrams, in which he was informed that the French offensive from the Somme would not be of strength sufficient to relieve the armies in the north, and that he was henceforward free to "operate towards the coast in conjunction with the French and Belgian armies".[17]

When this permission was at long last given, it was doubtful whether a bare withdrawal was any longer possible; for, nearly simultaneously, Lord Gort was informed that the Germans were again striking against the Belgians; and that the Belgian Commander-in-Chief could not undertake to keep his forces joined to the B.E.F., as the gap between the two could only be closed by a counter-attack which he could not possibly undertake. On the day following (May 27) the King of the Belgians asked for an armistice, and signed a capitulation which became effective at midnight. "I now found myself," says Lord Gort, "suddenly faced with an open gap of twenty miles between Ypres and the sea through which the enemy forces might reach the beaches." This was the position and these were the perils to which the British Army was still exposed when the brigades and the battalions of the 2nd Division were ordered to make for Dunkerque.

There is now little more to be said. The men withdrew to Dunkerque over roads where movement of any kind was at times scarcely possible.

The road in places was four abreast [runs the 4th Brigade's diary], which was made worse by many abandoned vehicles which had not been put off the road. One place was completely blocked by a string of lorries which had been bombed and caught fire. . . . Shortly afterwards, the Germans started to shell the roads and all traffic stopped. . . . The sight of the abandoned vehicles, some still with horses in the traces, some ditched, some

[17] For full text of telegrams, see Lord Gort's dispatch, section 44.

THE 2ND BATTALION'S LAST MOVE

crashed in the deep canal, the majority still blocking the approaches to the bridge, was one, once seen, which will never be forgotten.

The 2nd Division was, nevertheless, given one more order to stand and fight when, at 16.30 hours on the 29th, the divisional general was told to assemble his troops on the Bergues Canal and to defend it. It was impossible: the division was then hardly 500 men strong.[18]

The battalion's last move is thus recorded:

Battalion H.Q. forms up and marches off, led by the C.O., all transport, baggage, etc., having been abandoned. A short halt is made after about four hours' marching, and the column, now very much split up, with many stragglers, marches to Proven. ... The C.O. reports to 2 Division H.Q. at Proven and is told, in connection with 4 I.B., to collect stragglers and to push them on to Dunkerque. ... Standing in a downpour of torrential rain, the C.O. and the Commander 4 I.B. collect stragglers of their unit and put them on to any lorries that are going towards Dunkerque. One party, mostly from Battalion H.Q. and H.Q. Company, about twenty strong, left Proven for Dunkerque on various lorries, and got as far as Burges, where the transport had to be abandoned, and a march was then made to Dunkerque, about four miles as the crow flies. As marched by this party it was about ten miles, and by the time Dunkerque was approached, the party had increased to about 150—stragglers from numerous units having joined in. On the next morning this party signalled an S O S out to sea with a torch, and, by wading out to sea, and in some cases swimming, were able to get on to two Dutch cargo boats which had come in on seeing the S O S. Owing to the state of exhaustion of this party, one or two members were drowned while attempting to get near the boats in the rising tide.

The commanding officer was the last to go. He spent most of the 28th near Burges, collecting machine-guns and Brens from the streams of retiring troops in order that he might assemble a machine-gun force that would assist in the

[18] On May 28 the known strength of the 4th Brigade was hardly more than 100 men. A day later about 250 men of the 6th Brigade had been assembled. The 5th Brigade diary makes the following entry about brigade strength on May 29: "Brigade H.Q., 4 officers, 50 O.R.s; 7th Worcesters, 9 officers, 126 O.R.s; 2nd Dorsets, 7 officers, 64 O.R.s; 1st Camerons, 6 officers, 70 O.R.s".

defence of the Bergues Canal. After being joined by Captain Churchill, Major Frampton, and 2nd Lieutenant Holt, the party was about forty strong, and would have taken up a position on the canal had it not been told that a special force was being formed for the purpose. For the next two days Colonel Moore, who was now joined by Lieutenant Hewitt, 2nd Lieutenant Chandler, and C.S.M. Hibbert, combed Dunkerque and collected arms, ammunition and food for the incoming troops. The C.O.'s party of Manchesters was still thus employed when a staff officer told them to make for the Mole and to embark.

The losses were heavy and the 155 men who were missing are descriptive of the battalion's spirit: they were missing because wherever the battalion had fought, whether it was on the Dyle, the Lasne, the Schelde, or the La Bassée Canal, the officers and men had just fought on and had refused to move.

by Lieutenant-Colonel T. Brodie of the Cheshire Regiment (March 1942).

The battalion, less three companies, embarked at Birkenhead in the *Marnix van Ste Aldegonde*, a very well found Dutch vessel (April 11).

B Company embarked at Birkenhead in the *Reina del Pacifico* (April 10).

C Company embarked in the *Empress of Canada* at Glasgow (April 12).

A Company embarked at Glasgow in the *Orbita* (April 13).

The four vessels formed part of a large convoy off the coast of Scotland, and in the first days of June the battalion landed at Bombay and were sent on to the Dunkerque lines at Poona.

The battalion was inspected by Lord Wavell after its first exercise in tropical warfare (July 1942) and he congratulated Lieutenant-Colonel Brodie on its fitness and good spirit. Thereafter exercises in jungle warfare, in the crossing of tropical rivers (a far more difficult business than crossing the sluggish streams of central England), and in combined operations, succeeded one another as they had done in England. The diary leaves no doubt that the training was very thorough and very methodical: the men were even given "a demonstration of swimming with bamboo poles" (October 1942). The battalion was not, however, wholly free to prepare for battle with the Japanese invader. This, of course, was the end and purpose of every exercise that was carried out. But all was being done to a nasty jarring accompaniment of what was politely called civil disturbance. British rule in India was drawing to its close. The old system of government which had been erected on the assumption that India was a geographical expression and not a country, and that there was no such thing as an Indian nation, was fast becoming unworkable; and the British government were so convinced that a change had become a pressing necessity, that they had dispatched Sir Stafford Cripps to the country in March, with proposals for a sweeping reform. Sir Stafford's negotiations

THE CONDITION OF INDIA

failed, and he returned to England a month later. India was, in consequence, deeply disturbed, and it was probably only because a large Japanese army was assembled on the frontiers of Assam, and because the Japanese from time to time reminded every thinking Indian of the danger in which their country stood by bombing Indian harbours, that the political managers in the Indian congress refrained from embarking upon a general rebellion. But although the native Indian leaders considered that the moment had not arrived for liquidating British rule in India, the common people thought differently and riots and disturbances were reported from all parts of the country. In August, Poona was the theatre of a popular explosion. The battalion was engaged in resisting a wild mob of rioters, and for the rest of the month a company was kept at forty-five minutes' notice. The whole political background was, indeed, dark and threatening; for it was not only British rule but all constituted authority which was menaced. In October there was another effervescence, and on this occasion, it was feared that the Aga Khan's palace would be overrun and sacked. Thereafter, there was a period of uneasy calm.

In September, Lieutenant-Colonel Brodie was appointed G.S.O.1 to the 70th Division. Lieutenant-Colonel C. L. Archdale became commanding officer, and he superintended the move of the battalion to Ahmednagar in January 1943. Here, as at Poona, the demands of the civil power were heavy: 100 rifles were to be kept at two hours' notice.

In the autumn of the year 1942 the arrangements for training the Anglo-Indian army had been much perfected and special courses of instruction were given at camps where the features and configuration of the land were well adapted to a particular operation: river crossings were practised at Alandi camp; Kharakvasla was made a combined training centre; a camp at Juhu, near Bombay, was used for units that were being trained in combined operations. Later, units were sent to Belgaum, where there are dense forests, for special training in jungle warfare. As a consequence companies were continually being moved to one of these camps, after which they returned to the main camp for a short time, and were then detached again to do exercises with their brigade groups. The moves had indeed, become so frequent, that, during the month of November, B Company was successively stationed at Vizapur, Nagar, Poona, Vizapur, and Belgaum.[1] By the end of the year the battalion was permanently dispersed. A Company was with the 4th Independent Brigade Group; B with the 5th; C with the 6th; and D with the 29th Brigade of the 36th Division; and it was deemed so unlikely that it would be reassembled in one camp in any foreseeable time that each company was ordered to compile a diary of its own and to submit it to G.H.Q. 2nd Echelon. As some, but by no means all, of these company diaries have been preserved and as the battalion headquarters diary for the months of February, March, and April, has been lost, it is not possible to follow the fortunes of the battalion closely during the first months of the year 1944.

In March the call to arms was at last sounded; for on the 18th of that month the 2nd Division (Major-General J. M. L. Grover) was ordered to Dinapur in Assam.

When this order was issued, A Company was attached to the 4th Brigade (1st Royal Scots, 2nd Royal Norfolks, 1/8th Lancashire Fusiliers, 16 Field Regiment R.A., 5 Field Company R.E.) and was at Bangalore. B Company was with 5th Brigade (7th Worcestershires, 2nd Dorsets, 1st Queen's Own Cameron Highlanders, 10 Field Regiment R.A., 208 Field Company R.E.) and was at Belgaum. C Company was with 5th Brigade (1st Royal Berks, 1st Royal Welch Fusiliers, 2nd Durham Light Infantry, 99 Field Regiment R.A., 506 Field

---

[1] It would be tedious and would serve no useful purpose, to record all these moves from one camp to another, and owing to gaps in the available records it is not possible to make the record complete and exhaustive. The movements of battalion headquarters and of the headquarters company during 1943 were:

January to March .... Ahmednagar, thence to Marve.
March to May .... Marve, thence to Bhiwandi.
May to June .... Bhiwandi, Versova and Poona.
June to November .... Poona, thence to Vizapur.
November and December ...Vizapur.

THE JAPANESE ADVANCE IN BURMA

Company R.E.). The battalion heaquarters was at Vizapur, and was on its way to Belgaum.

It will be proper, at this point, to explain as briefly as possible what had occurred during the interval when the battalion was first drafted to India and the date when this order was given to it.

On December 7, 1941, the Japanese landed in Malaya; and by February 15, 1942, when Singapore fell, all the Federated Malay States were in their possession. The Japanese were thus tolerably well placed for extending their conquest northwards into Burma; for they had established such bases as they needed in Thailand and Indo-China, and the Malayan and Thai railway systems join at several points. Their advance northwards into Burma was, moreover, made easy in that there were no great natural obstacles across the route that led straight into the vital parts of the country.

The principal communications, the most fertile districts, and the great oil wells of Burma lie inside the long quadrilateral that is bounded on the west by the valleys of the Chindwin and the Irrawaddy, and on the east by the Sittang river and the mountains to the east and north of it. The rivers all run north and south and the roads and railways, being conduit pipes for the produce of the river valleys, do the same, so that any power that holds the Irrawaddy and the Sittang valleys firmly, between Mandalay and Rangoon, is certain to conquer the whole country in the course of time. Grasping this, the Japanese army commander in Thailand seized Tavoy, and then pressed northwards with all his strength. It fell to the 17th Division (Brigadier-General J. G. Smyth, v.c., m.c.) to resist the Japanese advance. One division, with a few additional formations collected into it, was, however, quite insufficient to stop an enemy who was in far greater strength, and the most that General Smyth could do was to fall back on Rangoon, where his division was to be reinforced, provided always that the Japanese advance was sufficiently delayed. General Smyth managed the retreat with great courage and ability; but as the Japanese were in such strength that they were able to work round the British flank wherever the 17th Division made a stand, they obliged the General to blow the Sittang river bridge before all the troops had crossed it: the losses during the withdrawal were, therefore, exceptionally heavy. The 17th Division did reach Rangoon, and were there reinforced by some armoured units; but the Japanese pressed on up the Sittang and the Irrawaddy valleys and blocked the northern approaches to the Irrawaddy delta. The British troops were nevertheless extricated, and retired into the Manipur district of north-eastern India, after a retreat about which we at present know very little. The Chinese troops, under General Stilwell, which had been sent into Burma at about the time when Rangoon was evacuated, were brought out by the same way. Thereafter, the Japanese advanced through the country as fast as their vehicles could carry them; and the diary of their progress runs thus:

January	12	Occupy Tarakan	}	In the Tenasserim Province, south of Rangoon
	18	„ Tavoy		
February	10	„ Martaban		
	22	Cross the Sittang River		
March	6	Establish forces on the Rangoon–Prome road		
	7	Rangoon evacuated		
	23	Occupy the Andaman Islands		
April	24	„ Taunggyi		
	29	„ Lashio		
May	3	„ Bhamo		
	8	„ Akyab		

In the first week of May 1942, therefore, the Japanese had completed their conquest of Burma; the principal roads, all the railways, the food-producing districts, and what was left of the oil wells and industrial plant (which were well devastated) were all in their hands, and it will be as well, at this point, to review the resulting position.

The Japanese did, it is true, control a continuous line of communications between Tokyo and northern Burma. The line was, nevertheless, very long; it ran over two elements—

THE JAPANESE ARE OVER-DEPLOYED

the land and the sea—and the railways only traversed a part of the land line. If, therefore, the Japanese army had made no conquest but this one, the Japanese general staff would have been burdened with a task of the first order to hold the conquest against a counter-attack. For, although considerable quantities of food were extracted from the conquered countries, every round of ammunition that was fired had to be brought from Japan itself. Burma was, indeed, only conquered so quickly because we had hardly enough forces for a token resistance.

Actually, the Japanese, either because they did not understand, or did not fear, the difficulties in which they were involving themselves, accompanied their conquest of Malaya and Burma by an immense deployment in the Southern Pacific which, for the purposes of this history (where it would be inappropriate to examine it in detail) is best presented in a table.

1941
December 17 (Borneo) Landings in the oil districts near Sandakan
22 (Philippines) Landing at Lingayen, Luzon
25 (Borneo) Occupy capital of Sarawak

1942
January 2 (Philippines) Capture Manila
10 (Borneo) Occupy Tarakan
(The Archipelago) Occupy Minahassa (Celebes)
22 (Pacific Islands) Occupy Rabaul, New Britain, and Kavieng, New Ireland

February 10 (Pacific Islands) Makassar (Celebes)
14 (Dutch East Indies) Parachute and seaborne landings near Palembang (Sumatra)
19 (Dutch East Indies) Invade Bali
20 (The Archipelago) Occupy Portuguese Timor
28 (Dutch East Indies) Invade Java at three points: Bantam, Indramayu, Rembang

March 5 (Dutch East Indies) Occupy Batavia
8 (New Guinea) Occupy Salamana and Lae
10 (Pacific Islands) Occupy Buka, Solomon Islands

April	6	(Pacific Islands) Occupy Bougainville, Solomon Islands
	12	(Borneo) Landings on Biliton (Philippines) Occupy Cebu
	16	(Philippines) Occupy Panay
May	4	(Philippines) Landings on Corregidor
July	30	(New Guinea) Occupy islands between Timor and New Guinea

If these conquests and occupations are inspected on a map; if the distances of all these places from Tokyo and Osaka are considered; if it be remembered that each new landing opened up a new supply line over zones of water so wide that they could not be secured against raiding and molestations; and if it be borne in mind that the Japanese merchant navy was not one of the first order, it is difficult to understand why the Japanese general staff ever agreed to such a dispersion and a scattering, not of their armed soldiers only, but of the warlike resources of their whole country. It may be that the ease with which they made their first conquests deceived them into believing that neither the United States nor Great Britain would ever be able to deliver a big strategic counter-attack; and certainly, if that was the Japanese calculation, then their general staff was soon shown that it was faulty; for the Japanese deployment was only just completed when the United States forces landed in the Solomons and established themselves firmly in Tulagi and Guadalcanal (August 1942). Japanese naval forces suffered considerable losses, and were driven off when the Japanese attempted to dislodge the Americans. Evidence was thus forthcoming, from the beginning, that the Japanese grip was weak at the outer end of their military tentacles, and this must be remembered by everybody who studies the campaign in Burma. Full military details of the weakness are not yet available, possibly they never will be; for the Japanese have never shown any interest in historical research, or aptitude for it. When, however, anybody studies operations against Japanese brigades or divisions at the outer ends of these immensely

THE ALLIED DEPLOYMENT

long communications, he must think of them as operations against an enemy who often lacked something, and who was not always at full fighting strength.

After the British and Chinese armies had been driven from Burma, they were distributed along the frontier in three groups: General Stilwell's Chinese divisions were round Ledo, the eastern terminus of the Bengal–Assam railway; 4 Corps of the India command was stationed round Imphal; and a third force was stationed between Chittagong and the Arakan border.[2] If inspected on a map, the communications of the Anglo-Chinese army seem better than the communications of the Japanese army in northern and north-western Burma. For the Bengal–Assam railway runs laterally behind the districts in which General Stilwell's army and 4 Corps were stationed; while the third force was supplied by the Comilla–Chittagong railway, and by the sea route to the port of Chittagong.

If it had been intended only that these three forces should defend Manipur and Assam against a further advance by the Japanese then they would have enjoyed a substantial advantage; for they would have been fighting with the Indian railway system behind them, whereas the Japanese would have been separated from the Burmese railway terminals by chains of mountains which increased in number and thickness with every advance. If, however, the military problem were con-

---

[2] The constitution of 4 Corps was:
17th Indian Division
  48 Indian Infantry Bde., 63 Indian Infantry Bde.
  Divisional troops: 21 Indian Mountain Regt., 29 Indian Mountain Regt., 129 Field Regt., 82 A.A./Anti-Tank Regt., Special Divisional Bn. (West Yorks), 4 F.F.R. Bde. Recce Bn., 7 Baluchis Bde. Recce Bn.
23rd Indian Division
  1 Indian Infantry Bde., 37 Indian Infantry Bde., 49 Indian Infantry Bde.
  Divisional troops: 28 Indian Mountain Regt., 158 Field Regt., 2 Indian Anti-Tank Regt., 28 Light A.A. Regt.
The formations in the Chittagong area were: 88 Indian Infantry Bde., 55 Indian Infantry Bde.
The formations allotted to the Arakan area were:
14th Indian Division
  47 Indian Infantry Bde., 55 Indian Infantry Bde.
  Divisional troops were: 129 Field Regt., 130 Field Regt., 23 Mountain Regt., 14 Light A.A. Regt., 9 Jat Regt.
The 77 Indian Infantry Brigade was on the Manipur Road.

sidered, whether the Bengal–Assam railway, and such roads as led into Burma from Assam, Manipur and the upper waters of the Hukaung could sustain armies advancing from India against Burma, then the matter was doubtful. General Stilwell's force was not very far from the upper waters of the Chindwin, which is one of the avenues into central Burma. Nevertheless, a range of mountains blocked the way to the Hawkaung valley, where the march down the Chindwin would begin; and a large area of mountains and very difficult country lay between the Hawkaung valley and the Burmese railheads at Myitkina and Katha.

The difficulty of advancing from the Hawkaung valley, was, however, as nothing when compared with the difficulty of advancing against Burma from Manipur; for British forces round Imphal were separated from the nearest avenue into Burma (the Chindwin valley) by a chain of lofty mountains which could only be crossed over mountain roads that are, in many places, mere tracks. Even if the approach were made through the Kabaw valley (which runs parallel to the Chindwin and serves as a second road to Central Burma) there would be the same difficulty in reaching it, and in using it as a supply route (see map 22, p. 419).

The force that was stationed between Chittagong and the upper waters of the Mayu river was better able to advance than the other two; for the mountains here run parallel to the axis of an opertion against Arakan, and a good road connects Chittagong to Akyab. This approach route, however, only enters a corner of the country—Akyab and the delta of the Kaledan. These places are not good starting points for a reconquest of Burma, from which they are separated by the natural feature that is common to the whole country—chains of mountains whose backbones run north and south and serve as a barrier against an army advancing towards Mandalay.

Finally, there was a weakness in the main supply line to the British Army from which all three forces suffered. The Bengal–Assam railway, which served the three forces, is not mander-in-Chief that some redistributions were carried out, of which a brief account should be given.

The forces on the frontier between India and the invaded territory had, hitherto, been part of one operational formation, the Eastern Army. The army was now split up into an eastern command (a static formation subordinate to the supreme India command) and into the 14th Army (Lieutenant-General W. J. Slim), whose commander directed all operations on the India–Burma frontier. In addition to the Eastern Army, however, an Indian Expeditionary Force headquarters had been formed to direct all overseas expeditions that started from India: this force was henceforward known as 23 Corps, and became, by training and composition, an ordinary army formation.

In addition more formations were trained and equipped to carry out the kind of operations that General Wingate had first planned and executed. When Lord Wavell transferred the command, the long-range penetration group (as it was then called) was composed of the 77th Brigade, which had carried out the great raid against the Japanese communications, and the 111th. It was decided to allot six brigades to the long-range penetration force, and to increase the number to eight later on; towards the end of the year, the force consisted of the 77th and 111th Indian Infantry Brigades, the 3rd West African Infantry Brigade, and the 70th British Division. When organized and trained, the battalions of each brigade were broken up into columns. Each column was an independent unit, with its own facilities for receiving supplies by air and for communicating with other units; it was armed with machine-guns and mortars; it moved on foot through the jungle, and was trained to fight as a well-equipped, fast-moving guerilla force.

By the end of 1943, the Anglo-American high command had collected sufficient forces and material for a concerted counter-attack from all three fronts. The attack upon Akyab was renewed, with larger forces and under a more comprehensive plan; simultaneously, General Stilwell advanced

OPERATION AGAINST AKYAB

across the mountains to the south of Ledo and operated against the railway between Mogaung and Myitkina; when General Stilwell was approaching the Mogaung valley, General Wingate launched an air-borne, air-maintained expedition against specially selected points in the central part of the Irrawaddy valley; and 4 Corps began to push towards the Chindwin from Imphal and Kohima.

It would be outside the purpose of this history to describe these operations in detail; but as they were the source and origin of the campaign in which the 2nd Battalion was about to be engaged, it will be necessary to review them briefly.

(i) *The second advance upon Akyab* was entrusted to 15 Indian Corps (Lieutenant-General Sir A. P. F. Christison, Bt., C.B., D.S.O., M.C.), which was composed of the 5th Indian Division (Major-General H. R. Briggs, D.S.O.), the 7th Indian Division (Major-General F. Messervy, C.B., D.S.O.), and the 81st West African Division (Major-General C. G. Woolner, C.B., M.C.). In order to thwart the manœuvre that the Japanese had so successfully executed during the previous year, Akyab was, on this occasion, approached along two of the mountain corridors that converge upon it, and the third corridor was blocked. The 5th Division took the western approach route, between the mountains and the sea, and operated against Maungdaw; the 7th Division came down the valley of the Mayu river and operated against Mutidaung and Letwedet; the 81st West African Division marched down the Kaledan river and held it against any Japanese force that might attempt to reach the rear of our communications by that route.

The opening moves were successfully executed: early in January, the 5th Division captured Maungdaw; the 7th Division advanced to a position north of Letwedet and secured the east- and west-going passes of the Mayu range in their rear; and the 81st Division established themselves in the Kaledan valley. The Japanese had, however, built a very strong system of fortifications at the southern ends of these mountain corridors, and while the 5th and 7th Divisions were hammering against them, General Sakurai, the Japanese commander, repeated the operation of the previous year. The British forces that were pressing against Maungdaw and Buthidaung were held by a frontal attack; another Japanese force advanced up a valley that runs between the Mayu river and the Kaledan (the range that separated it from the 7th Division line of operations) debouched into the Division's front and rear, and completely isolated it. (February 3–10, 1944.) The 7th Division drew back into a fortified box at a place called Sinzweya and, although the Japanese battered the place with every gun that could be ranged upon it, although they attacked it with the greatest persistence and fury, the troops of the 7th Division held the place until they were relieved. For General Slim, anticipating a powerful Japanese manœuvre to relieve the pressure upon Akyab, assembled the 26th Indian Division (Major-General C. E. N. Lomax, c.b., d.s.o., m.c.) and the 36th Indian Division (Major-General F. W. Festing, d.s.o.) near Chittagong and dispatched them to the relief of the 5th and 7th Divisions, when the Japanese were fully committed to their operation against our rear. This counter-attack to a counter-attack was very well executed; by the end of February, the 5th and 7th Divisions were not merely extricated but were again attacking the fortifications round Razabil, where the first advance had been checked; on March 10 one of the pivots of the fortified zone was stormed.

(ii) *The advance from Ledo*. All this time, General Stilwell had been advancing from the north. It had been found that the supplies of a modern army could not be carried over the track that crossed the mountains between Ledo and the Hukaung valley, and the American engineers undertook and successfully executed the tremendous task of converting it into a first-class military road. More than this, the American

ADVANCE FROM THE NORTH

pioneers and their officers undertook to build the road at such a speed that General Stilwell's advance would not be delayed.

General Stilwell's two Chinese divisions therefore started their southward march at the end of the year 1943. By the middle of January 1944 the 22nd Division was at Walawbum and the 38th at Shingbwiyang, on the southern side of the highest mountain pass. It had, however, been planned that a supplementary attack should be directed against the Japanese communications while General Stilwell was marching south; and this operation was conceived and executed in this manner. After himself inspecting a large number of aerial photographs of the Irrawaddy plain, and after studying everything that the photographic interpreters had to report about the nature and the gradients of the ground, General Wingate decided that three lonely and fairly level sites could be siezed by airborne troops and could be fortified before the Japanese could overrun them. Reinforcements were then to be carried into these fortified zones by air, and the garrisons, which would be supplied and maintained by air transport, would raid the Japanese communications between Myitkina and Indaw.

Three sites were chosen. Two of them. " Broadway " and " Chowringhee ", were in the flat land through which the Irrawaddy runs between Shwegu and Katha. " Broadway " was on the northern side, in the valley of the Kaukkwa; " Chowringhee " was to the south of the river in the great alluvial plain between the Shweli and the Irrawaddy. The third site, " Aberdeen ", was to the north-west of Indaw, in a little cup of level land in the Mangin mountains.

Before these airborne forces were sent out, however, a special force, under Brigadier B. E. Fergusson (the Queen's, the Leicesters, with detachments from the Reconnaissance Regiment, the Royal Artillery, and the Royal Corps of Signals), was to advance from Ledo and operate towards Indaw through the valleys to the east of General Stilwell's advance. At the date that we are now more particularly considering (mid-March to April 1944) these movements and operations were in the following posture:

General Stilwell's two divisions had reached the Mogaung valley. The 111th Brigade (Brigadier W. C. A. Lentaigne) and the 14th Brigade (Brigadier T. Brodie) were put down on "Aberdeen" and Brigadier Fergusson had established contact with them.³ The 77th Brigade (Brigadier J. M. Calvert) had been put down on "Broadway", but had suffered very heavy losses in equipment and stores.

At the beginning of March, therefore, the Japanese were being pressed on their northern and southern fronts, and their operations in the Arakan valleys had failed. General Mataguchi now decided to stop the Allied advance towards central Burma by a hard, rapid blow against the British centre in Manipur. Three divisions were allotted to the operation. They were (i) to seize the Allied base at Imphal, and by so doing break the British front, (ii) to cut the Bengal–Assam railway and so oblige General Stilwell to return to Ledo, (iii) to overrun the Assam airfields, and stop the air traffic between India and China.

During the first days of March the first symptoms of a Japanese advance were manifesting themselves round Imphal, where 4 Corps was watching the frontier; the 17th Indian Division (Major-General D. T. Cowan, c.b., d.s.o., m.c.) was covering Tiddim; the 20th (Major-General D. D. Gracey, c.b., m.c.) was watching the Kabaw valley; and the 23rd (Major-General Ouvry Roberts, d.s.o.) was in the Ukhrul district.

The intelligence staff at the headquarters of 11th Army Group and the 14th Army had, however, detected that a Japanese move was impending, and had also discovered that it would be directed against Kohima and Imphal. More than that, the forces that the Japanese commander would set in motion were, on the whole, accurately estimated, although the Japanese army command allotted more forces

³ Brigadier Brodie had commanded the 2nd Manchesters from March 1942 to September 1942.

to the operation against Kohima than General Slim allowed for.

The Japanese army was now committed to a move across the lines of mountains that lie between the Chindwin valley and the plains of Assam; and General Slim decided that he would allow the enemy to advance across them, and that he would bring them to battle when their communications had been so lengthened that their supply stream was weak and uncertain. It was a calculation that our generals were particularly well qualified to make, as they had been obliged to pronounce so many operations impossible because the wall of Burmese mountains lay across their advance.

General Slim therefore ordered the three divisions of 4 Corps to fall back upon Imphal and to fight the enemy to a standstill in prepared positions round the town. Imphal itself, where there was an enormous collection of administrative establishments, hospitals, labour camps, supply dumps, and engineer depots, was put into a state of defence. Over 50,000 non-combatants were brought out of the town; those that remained were allotted to the defence zones and the camp was stocked with supplies and ammunition. The 5th Division was put into 14th Army reserve and was dispatched to Imphal; the 50th Parachute Brigade was sent to the Ukhrul district to reinforce the 23rd Division.

The Japanese allotted their 33rd, 15th and 31st Divisions and 33rd Infantry Group to the operation against Imphal and Assam. The 33rd Division, which was one of the finest in the Japanese army, crossed the Chindwin between Kalewa and Sittaung with the infantry group in company and advanced on Imphal by the Kawbaw and Manipur valleys. The 15th Division crossed the Chindwin near Homalin and, after traversing the mountains of Ukhrul, established itself across the Imphal–Kohima road, and on the heights to the west of the town (see map 2). The 31st Division crossed the Chindwin somewhere to the north of Homalin and reached Kohima along the tracks that cross the mountains of the Naga country; and this at least must be said of the Japanese troops: they accomplished what only good soldiers and brave men can do by climbing two mountain ranges, 7,000 to 10,000 feet high, and by fighting as stoutly as they did upon the driblets of food and equipment that followed after them. For the Japanese supply staff could not overcome the difficulties of supplying armed men over ninety miles and more of mountain tracks; and their soldiers suffered unbelievable hardships as a consequence. The Japanese were barbarously cruel, but they had fine qualities.

The Japanese advance was costly to themselves and to us. The 17th Division, which lay across the Tiddim road, began to fall back too late, and the Japanese reached its line of retreat in strength. The 23rd Division moved south to extricate the 17th, and did so successfully; but the 17th suffered severely; for it was compelled to fight for every yard of ground during a long retreat over a mountain road which the enemy had blocked in many places. The 5th Division, on the other hand, met the Japanese 15th Division near Ukhrul and checked the Japanese advance by a fierce and prolonged resistance.

Nevertheless, the Japanese completed the first part of their operations more or less as they had designed it; for, by the last week in March, 4 Corps was isolated at Imphal and the 31st Japanese Division had surrounded the Kohima garrison and the reinforcements that had been sent to it.

In peace-time Kohima was the administrative capital of the Naga hills district. Since the war began, it had become the military centre for the Manipur road: hospitals, M.T. parks and field supply depots had been established there, which later became points of great tactical importance; for it will be shown hereafter, how the struggle raged over G.P.T. (General Purpose Transport) and F.S.D. (Field Supply Depot) ridges; and how savagely Jail Hill, the Treasury, and the District Commissioner's bungalow were attacked and defended.

As has been explained, General Slim had decided to defeat the enemy round Imphal; and although it was essential to his plan that the place should be held, it was by a timely counter-attack that he counted for a decision. The 33rd Indian Corps (Lieutenant-General Montague Stopford, C.B., D.S.O., M.C.) was therefore ordered up from Dimapur and its commander was given the task of relieving Imphal and Kohima. For General Slim was satisfied that the Japanese would never be able to maintain their army in the mountains of Manipur, if they were held at Imphal and Kohima, and if any hope of advancing farther were denied them. Part of 33 Corps was, however, shut up near Kohima; for the 161st Brigade (5th Division) which General Stopford had sent forward, was isolated and divided: one part, the 4th Battalion Royal West Kents, was in the Kohima perimeter, the remainder (the 1st Punjabis, the 4/7th Rajputs, one battalion of the Assam Regiment and one battalion of the Burma Regiment) were cut off before they reached Kohima. This force was in a bad position, for it had been encircled while it was still on the march and was simply clinging to a road and to such ground as had been hastily seized on either side of it. The Japanese guns and mortars commanded every square inch of the positions held by the Kohima garrison and by the 161st Brigade.

At Imphal the position was slightly better. The town itself is in a deep cup, for it is at the northern edge of a flat, marshy plain which is surrounded on all sides by high mountains. The garrison certainly succeeded in securing positions on the foothills of the surrounding mountains, and the air strip was throughout available for incoming supplies of food and ammunition. Also, the roads that radiated from Imphal town to the fortified perimeter were, on the whole, a better system of communications than the mountain tracks and paths upon which the besieging Japanese very largely depended. But if all these advantages were added together the sum total of them amounted to this only: that the place might be held if relief were not too long delayed.

* * * * *

This, then, was the state of affairs in Burma when the 2nd Battalion the Manchester Regiment was ordered to Dimapur. The 2nd Division, of which the 2nd Manchesters was the machine-gun battalion, was part of 33 Corps, and was being followed by the 7th Indian Division. As has been said, General Stopford's forces were to relieve Kohima, to open the Kohima–Imphal road, and to break the Japanese ring at Imphal.

The 2nd Division began to arrive in the Dimapur area during the first days of April; the companies of the battalion arrived in the following order: B Company (5, 6, 7 Platoons), attached to 5th Brigade, arrived first (April 3). C Company (9, 10, 11 Platoons) arrived in the Dimapur area on April 10, and marched forward under the command of 6th Brigade when it began its advance upon Kohima. A Company (1, 2, 3 Platoons), attached to 4th Brigade, arrived in the Dimapur area on April 15. It was moved partly by air. Battalion Headquarters, which was moved partly by sea, arrived on the 13th. The vehicles of each company arrived later. In twenty-eight days, therefore, the 2nd Division had moved from its scattered positions in the Deccan to the Assam front—a distance of 2,200 miles; nor should it be forgotten that in addition to the three brigades which have been particularly mentioned, the 149th Regiment and the 2nd Reconnaissance Regiment of the Royal Armoured Corps, the 100th Anti-Tank and A.A. Regiment R.A., and the 143rd Special Service Company were also moved, for these were the divisional troops. The move was particularly creditable to the motor transport sections of the battalion, for of the fifty-six vehicles in their charge, only four became road casualties.

The country in which the 2nd Division was about to operate was a tangle of forested hills and high mountains, which are inhabited by a race of mountaineers called the Nagas. This people had revolted from British rule during the eighteen-eighties, but later, on finding that their tribal customs were not interfered with, and that no severe taxation was imposed upon them, they became reconciled to the

FIRST CONTACT WITH THE ENEMY

was to pass the 5th near Zubza and then press on towards the beleaguered garrison near Kohima. The 4th Brigade, with the 2nd Reconnaissance Regiment attached to it, was to turn south at Jotsoma, was to move round the southern flanks of a mountain mass called the Pulebadze, and was to debouch on a line of hills called the Aradura Spur, which commanded the road between Kohima and Imphal. If these three movements were successfully executed, the Japanese would be compelled to evacuate Kohima and retire into the mountains to the east of the Imphal–Kohima road.

On April 11, as the 5th Brigade were approaching Zubza, their advanced troops (the 7th Worcestershires) came into contact with the Japanese and the first shots of the battle for the relief of Kohima were fired. The Worcestershires pressed back the Japanese screen, entered Zubza village, and occupied the high ground above it. As has been said, Zubza village overlooked the valley of the Dzutze, and is itself overlooked from the Merema ridge farther eastward. The Japanese guns on the ridge soon began shelling the Worcestershires position. The high ground to the south of the position was also held by the Japanese, and 6 and 7 Platoons of B Company (Lieutenants W. B. Wilson and A. A. Mascott) kept the Japanese under fire whenever any movement among them was detected. This was the first time that the battalion's machine-gunners had fired on an enemy since the campaign in France, nearly four years previously.

There was a pause at Zubza, during which the Brigade Commander prepared to clear the positions that blocked a further advance. Tactical headquarters was moved into the Zubza area on the 14th, and after two days of patrolling and reconnaissance, it was decided that a feature to the left of the road was the principal obstacle and that if it could be carried, the advance could be continued. The ground held by the Camerons was the nearest to this position, and on the 17th two companies of the Camerons carried the feature after an intense artillery and mortar bombardment. As the Camerons advanced, 6 Platoon supported the attack. The dust from the bombardment made it very difficult to spot the fall of the shots, and when the feature was seized it was found that the explosions had blasted away the dense jungle that covered it, and had converted what had once been a wooded spur into heath of scorched leafless trees and charred undergrowth. Severe as the bombardment had been the Japanese stubbornly resisted when the Camerons came up to them, and there was fierce fighting before the position changed hands.

The road was now cleared for a further advance, and also for the general plan to be put into operation. The direct advance on Kohima was now begun by the 6th Brigade. The 5th Brigade prepared for its advance across the Dzutze valley against the Merema Ridge, while the 4th Brigade, which was about five miles behind the head of the advance, made ready for its march round the Pulobadze massif, on the left of the Japanese position. It will be convenient to deal with the advance of the 6th Brigade first.

* * * * *

The next move forward was along two roads, called the Jotsoma and the Jotsoma Loop which separate a few miles beyond Zubza and rejoin about four miles farther on. The western junction was called "Paternoster Row" and the eastern one "Lancaster Gate."

On the 18th, the 6th Brigade made a good advance over the Jotsoma roads, and even beyond them, and during their move forward they relieved part of the beleaguered troops. For the 161st Indian Brigade, which were separated from the rest of the garrison and were cooped up near Jotsoma, were freed. The brigade was brought under the Divisional Commander, whose tactical headquarters were now moved into the forward area.

The remainder of the garrison was holding a small hill near the joining point of the Dimapur–Kohima and the Bokajan–Imphal roads. If the garrison at Kohima was to be relieved the road from the 151st Brigade's perimeter to

KOHIMA GARRISON RELIEVED

Garrison Hill had to be completely cleared; and before this could be done, two hills, which both overlooked the road, had to be carried.

These two strong points were called Picquet Hill and Terrace Hill; both were wooded, and officers standing on the Punjab Ridge could see the wooded top of the hill that the garrison was still holding behind these two summits. The road to Garrison Hill wound itself round Picquet and Terrace Hills, and became visible again behind the Picquet feature, when it clung to the slopes of the hill where the garrison were holding on.

These two features were thus the gateways to Garrison Hill, and they were fiercely contested. On the 18th, however, both were carried by the 4/7th Rajputs. While they were in British hands, the road was opened to the garrison, and some of the wounded were evacuated. The Japanese, however, realizing what it would mean to them if the two places were lost, attacked again during the night and re-established themselves on Terrace Hill. Picquet Hill remained in our hands, and on the following day (April 19) the 2nd Durham Light Infantry recaptured Terrace Hill, after very fierce fighting. No. 10 Platoon of the Manchesters, which was then in position on Picquet Hill, supported the attack. This finally cleared the road to the garrison, and the Japanese now embarked upon a last endeavour to reduce it. During the night of the 19th they attacked Garrison Hill, and almost carried it. Nevertheless the troops, though terribly exhausted, just managed to hold the position, and on the 20th the 1st Royal Berkshires and the Durham Light Infantry relieved the garrison, and its evacuation was at once begun. The beleaguered troops could not have held much longer. Major King-Clark, who was one of the first officers to enter the garrison area after it was relieved, considered that the defending troops were "on their last legs."

If this was so it was small wonder; for the garrison had been living for nearly a month on a knoll that was at all points commanded by the enemy's guns. A photograph of the place, taken after it was relieved, displays an expanse of undulating ground so blasted and scorched that the forest trees which once grew there luxuriantly were mere stumps and posts. The earth in which these wooden tusks were embedded looks like a mixture of dust and stones, where hardly a blade of grass will grow. Though outnumbered, harassed by thirst, hunger, dirt, and by what is perhaps the worst of all wants, lack of sleep, the garrison had held fast and had hardly yielded an inch of this shell-swept hill top. Twenty-four hours before the relieving troops marched in, the Japanese were still hurling themselves against strongpoints that they had failed to carry in the first assault; and the haggard and exhausted men who held them were still unbeaten.

When the troops of the 6th Division thus reached Garrison Hill, the whole road from Dimapur to the approaches to Kohima was usable by us during daylight. From their positions around Kohima the Japanese could still, however, bombard Garrison Hill, and for the next fortnight they methodically pounded it. The hill and its approaches were, indeed, the worst part of the whole battle zone. Moreover, the Japanese still held their two fortified positions ("Chester" and "Shrewsbury") on the great massif to the south of the Dimapur road, and they were strongly entrenched on a feature called Aradura Spur, on the southern edge of the battle zone. It was, indeed, to clear these positions completely that the 5th and the 4th Brigades were operating against the left and right flanks of the Japanese forces, and it will now be proper to follow their movements.

The 5th Brigade, with 6 Platoon of B Company attached, began their advance on April 26. Their starting point was the village of Zubza. The ground immediately before them fell into the Dzutze valley (which ran at right angles to their advance). Thereafter it rose to the Merema Ridge, a high, long-backed feature and, like all others, deeply wooded. The north- and south-going road between Bokajan and Imphal ran along the top of the ridge. The brigade marched by night and the rate of advance was fixed at 1,000 yards an hour. It proved, however, to be impossible to move through the jungle, even at this rate, and at daylight when the brigade halted for the daylight hours, it had not reached its first scheduled resting place. The march was begun again when night fell; not even mules could be used along the track, and many of the Naga porters who assisted on the first night's march were sent away before the second advance began. The men were thus heavily loaded. "We went on plunging into the night," wrote Lieutenant Wilson of 6 Platoon. "Had the Japanese been on the look-out for us, I am afraid we should have been in for a rough time. The golden rule of a night march—silence—was conspicuous by its absence." Nevertheless, the leading troops reached the village of Merema by daylight, and the whole brigade dug in on positions that commanded the north- and south-going road. The whole movement must have been very well concealed, for it is difficult to believe that the Japanese would have contested it so little had they known what was afoot. The first move of the 5th Brigade was now over, their next one was to operate to the right and push the Japanese from the positions that they still held to the north of the joining point of the Dimapur and Imphal roads. All this time, the 4th Brigade, with 1 Platoon of A Company attached to it, had been moving round the southern flank of the Pulobadze massif.

The details of this move are rather difficult to follow, but it seems certain that the brigade was approaching the Aradura ridge on the 28th after an extremely difficult march, for the kit, guns, tripods, and radio were all carried by the men, and the track was exceptionally difficult.

* * * * *

When the moves on the right and left flanks were thus well forward, the Divisional Commander was able to prepare for the second part of his operation—closing in his three brigades on Kohima, and thrusting the Japanese out of their last positions round the crossroads of the Dimapur and Imphal roads.

Before the operations began, the 2nd Manchesters, with the exception of two platoons that were left with the 4th and 5th Brigades, were brought under the immediate command of the division; hitherto, companies had been under brigade command. The change was made in order that all machine-gun fire plans in the forthcoming operations should be controlled from the centre. Major King-Clark was given the command of the battalion (Colonel Archdale was to remain at Galaghat); and the battalion was made responsible for the defence of Lone Tree Hill, which rises above the eastern end of the Jotsoma and Jotsoma Loop roads. The hill to which the battalion was now posted commanded the areas occupied by the divisional headquarters and by the guns of the divisional artillery; and by the units that were holding the Punjaub Ridge. It was, however, dominated by the Japanese positions on "Chester" and "Shrewsbury," which were only 100 and 400 yards away. The 2nd Recce Regiment, whom the Manchesters relieved at Lone Tree Hill, moved off to patrol the ground to the right of the 4th Brigade's flanking movement towards Aradura.

When Major King-Clark was thus ordered to concentrate his battalion on Lone Tree Hill, 1 Platoon was with the 4th Brigade; B Company headquarters and 6 Platoon were with the 5th Brigade. He therefore reconstituted his companies as follows: A Company was composed of 2, 3, and 5 Platoons, C Company of 7, 9, and 11.

A Company [writes Major King-Clark] formed an all-round, deep position in the Lone Tree Hill area, and C Company formed a box in the wooded spur between Lone Tree Hill and Punjab Ridge, with Battalion and C Company headquarters within it. These positions were heavily wired by us, and made very strong by further digging, but the threat from above was always painfully apparent, particularly as the safety of the divisional right flank depended, to a great extent, on Lone Tree Hill being held.

It would seem however, as though the Japanese on "Chester" and "Shrewsbury" were in no position to harass the British on Lone Tree Hill; they dug in deeper and deeper, mostly by night, and resisted vigorously when a Manchester patrol approached them too closely, but that was all. The Manchester companies, therefore, harassed the Japanese positions with machine-gun and mortar fire by day and night. Seeing that the Japanese were so quiet, the Rajputs were ordered to attack a spur that was below and to the east of the Japanese position at "Chester." They did so quite successfully on the night of April 29, with 9 Platoon assisting. The Japanese counter-attacked fiercely on the following night, but they were driven back. During the attack, 9 Platoon operated a pre-arranged fire plan: sixty Japanese dead were found near the Rajput's position next morning.

Meanwhile, the movements on the two flanks were being pressed with great vigour. The 5th Brigade had reached the Merema Ridge by April 28. The Japanese were holding a very strong position to the south of them, for the ridges to the east of the road rose to a summit called 5120, which commanded all the northern approaches to Kohima. It was visible from most parts of the battlefield, and conspicuous by the white huts of the Naga village of Kohima which were clustered thickly on its flanks.

The troops of the 5th Brigade advanced against these positions on May 3, when the Lancashire Fusiliers, with the platoon from B Company assisting them, attacked a feature called Bare Bottom Hill. The Japanese were found to be in greater strength than had been expected, and the attacking forces suffered severely and were withdrawn. It was found very difficult to give effective machine-gun support in this part of the battlefield, as the view was everywhere bounded by trees and jungle. On the day following, the Camerons advanced up the slopes of 5120 and nearly carried it. They were, however, held up at a point below the summit where they dug themselves in. The machine-gunners of B Company moved to the Cameron's position and helped to repulse a fierce Japanese counter-attack on the night of the 6th. Machine-gun operations were as difficult here as at Bare Bottom Hill. The 5th Brigade did not, therefore, clear point 5120 or the Naga village, and these positions dominated the entire Kohima area from the north-west, just as the Aradura spur and Pulobadze massif commanded it from the south.

On the right, the fortunes of the 4th Brigade were similar. They debouched successfully on the eastern flanks of the Pulobadze massif after a most arduous march through mountain and jungle, and, on May 5, attacked one of the spurs called G.P.T. Ridge that overlooked the south-going road from Kohima to Imphal. The Norfolks made the attack, with 1 Platoon assisting them; it was executed with great courage and spirit, but the Japanese resisted very stubbornly, and when the fighting was over, the enemy still held part of the ridge and their positions on the lower parts of the spur were untouched. The Norfolks suffered severely, but during the night they were reinforced by the 4/1st Gurkhas, who managed to creep round the north-eastern slopes of the massif from Two Tree Hill. We have no details of this move. To judge by the map, it was a remarkable achievement in what, for want of a better name, may be called jungle pilotage.

The two flank movements had not, therefore, wrested any vital position from the Japanese, but it would seem as though the enemy were uneasy at the steady pressure, for on May 7, the 2nd Recce Regiment, which was all the time patrolling on the extreme right of the Pulobadze massif, reported that the Japanese had abandoned their positions at "Chester" and "Shrewsbury." As has been explained, these positions commanded the eastern end of the Jotsoma road. "This bloodless victory," wrote Major King-Clark, "was undoubtedly of great value to the battle as a whole, as it relieved the position on the right and rear."

268th and by the 6th. The 6th Brigade, with 11 Platoon attached to it, was to move on the right, against the crest; when the crest was carried, the brigade was to support the attack of the 4th Brigade on its left. This brigade, moving out of the G.P.T. area, was to cross the Aradura nullah and carry all the posts that were to the west of the road by a frontal attack. Simultaneously, the tanks of 149th Regiment R.A.C. were to move down the Imphal Road and bombard the Japanese positions in reverse. The 5th Brigade, though not participating in the main assault, was to cover the left flank by advancing into the lower slopes of the spur, to the east of the road.

This attack was supported by a wide flanking movement by the 2nd Recce Regiment, which was ordered to go round the southern edge of the Pulobadze massif, to the south of the route that had previously been followed with such difficulty by the 4th Brigade, and to debouch on the Imphal road.

The attack was launched on May 25 and it failed. On the right, the 6th Brigade went up the slopes of the Aradura crest after the Japanese position had been heavily bombarded. They were stopped, well below the crest, by the slippery slopes and by the jungle, which was so thick that they could not find their way. On the brigade's left, the Norfolks and the Royal Scots (4th Brigade) carried two points on the Aradura Spur and 1 and 2 Platoons (Lieutenants King and Teale), who advanced with them to consolidate the positions that were gained, got their guns into position on the captured features. It was for this that Lieutenant King, who commanded 1 Platoon, was awarded the Military Cross. These gains, which were obtained by extraordinary gallantry, could not, however, be held, as the Japanese guns on the reverse slopes of the positions that were carried had not been touched by the preliminary bombardment, and put down such a concentration upon the Norfolks and the Royal Scots that they were forced to withdraw. On the left of the 4th Brigade, the 5th advanced below the Imphal road, and actually carried one of the lower knolls on the Aradura Spur, but they were obliged to go back when the Norfolks and the Royal Scots were forced out of their positions. Elsewhere, the attack failed also. The tanks of the 149th Regiment were held up by a road block. On the extreme right the 2nd Reconnaissance Regiment was held up by a small Japanese force in a tangle of jungle and unscalable slopes on the southern side of Pulobadze. Nevertheless, Colonel Bradford decided that he would make the Japanese command uneasy by remaining where he was, and dug in. The section of B Company (Lieutenant A. A. Mascett) which accompanied the Regiment carried out harassing shoots on to known Japanese positions and Japanese carrying parties. Rations and water supplies fell very low, for the Naga porters were caught by a Japanese patrol and shot down, after which all these native carriers abandoned the column and made for their villages. The men felt the low water ration severely.

On the day following the assault, the Japanese counter-attacked the 6th Brigade in the position that they had reached below the Aradura crest. The attack fell on the Royal Welch, who were leading the 6th Brigade, and they were forced to withdraw. No. 11 Platoon, which was then operating with the Royal Welch Fusiliers, fell back also. The withdrawal was done in a sousing downpour, for the monsoon had then set in, and the guns had to be wrapped in sandbags to keep the rain out. After failing to carry the Aradura crest and spur by a frontal attack, General Grover decided to make the Japanese position on the crest untenable by capturing their line of posts on the lower part of the spur, to the east of the Imphal road. This new operation must be introduced by a further description of the Aradura feature.

* * * * *

As has already been explained, the Japanese positions on the upper spur, to the west of the road, were continued along that part of the ridge that falls into the valley of a nullah by a line of posts called Dyer Hill, Little Tree Hill, Gun Spur and Garage Spur. This extension of the Aradura Spur runs north-eastward, and its north-western slopes command all that stretch of country between Aradura and Kohima, which the Japanese had abandoned when our troops seized the Kohima ridge. There are villages in the middle of this zone, and one corner of the outer-most or eastern end was by us called Assam Barracks.

General Grover's plan was that the 5th Brigade should make a wide flanking movement through the zone of the country that the Japanese had evacuated, and should attack the Aradura ridge from its extreme north-eastern end. After debouching from Assam Barracks, the Brigade was to carry Dyer Hill, and then move south-westwards towards the road through Little Tree Hill, Big Tree Hill and Garage Spur. If this last post was carried, General Grover was satisfied that the Japanese position on the high parts of the spur would be untenable.

While the 5th Brigade was thus assaulting the north-eastern end, the 6th Brigade was to keep on pressing against the highest part of the ridge. In the northern zone of the battlefield, the 7th Division were to carry point 5120 and were then to operate along an east-going track which the Japanese would need when they were forced out of their positions. This track joins the Imphal road at Kohima, to the south of point 5120, and meanders through the mountain villages to the east of the Imphal road.

This new assault succeeded. On June 4, the troops of the 5th Brigade moved off. The Camerons led the attack and 3 Platoon of the Manchesters went with them. Nos. 5 and 6 Platoons of B Company were brought up from "Chester," at the western end of the battle zone, and were stationed at the Assam Barracks, from which they could sweep the strong points against which the Camerons were advancing.

On the 5th, the Camerons attacked the outer end of the Aradura Spur, and were everywhere successful. Big Tree Hill, at the north-eastern end, fell first, and by nightfall Garage Spur, near the Imphal road, was carried.

THE JAPANESE RETREAT

The Japanese positions were now untenable, but for one day more (June 6) they resisted. The 6th Brigade were still held on the north-western slopes of the Aradura crest, while, in the north, although the 7th Division made some progress their troops did not actually carry point 5120. Still, all that day the Japanese must have been preparing to go, for on the night of June 6 they abandoned Aradura crest and point 5120, and the battle for Kohima was over and won. Matters had, indeed, been going ill with the Japanese for some time: their dead soldiers were found to be very emaciated from lack of food; their ammunition supply was spasmodic and irregular; and during the last week's of the battle our medium artillery and mortar fire had so dominated them that not a soul was ever seen to be stirring round the Japanese positions during daylight. The enemy had, moreover, lost heavily; two regiments of their 31st Division had practically melted away, and throughout the Japanese army the wounded were ill tended, for the Japanese officers were very indifferent about men who were incapacitated by wounds and sickness.

* * * * *

The pursuit of the Japanese along the Imphal road, and the relief of the Imphal garrison, were at once begun; for on the day that the Worcesters of the 5th Brigade captured the villages of Phesama and Pfechama, the 4th Brigade formed an armoured column with the 149th Regiment of the R.A.C. and pressed on down the Imphal road. The road along which the British troops were now moving had been cut along the eastern slopes of a line of mountains called the Barrail range. On the right, or western side, there is a succession of summits well over 7,000 feet high, and these are outposts to the peaks of the Barrail range itself, which are between 9,000 and 10,000 feet high. On its western side, therefore, the road is dominated by high, steep land. On the eastern side of the road, the ground falls into the beds of two parallel nullahs, the Dzula and the Chonairu Turei. To the east of this main road, however, there is a winding mountain track which joins the Imphal road at Kohima, and at Tuphema, about sixteen miles farther south. The 7th Indian Division, which had captured the northern end of this loop after the Japanese had abandoned point 5120, pressed forward along it, and, although it was a poor mountain track, through very difficult country, and although their supply services were, in Major King-Clark's words, "a skeleton," the Indian Division advanced practically as fast as the British Divisions on the main road. This quick advance was the more remarkable in that the monsoon had set in when the pursuit of the Japanese was begun, and the heavy rains made such tracks as the 7th Division followed difficult beyond all description.

The Japanese rearguards made their first stand at the village of Viswema, about fifteen miles south of Kohima. The weather was very bad, and at this point the British advance was held up for three days. The 4th Brigade was leading the advance. The Norfolks, with 1 and 3 Platoons of the Manchesters in support, established themselves on the high ground to the west of the village, and until the village was finally carried these two platoons kept it under a continuous harassing fire. At the same time, the Royal Scots, working through the lower ground to the east of the road, got a footing in one corner of the village. They were accompanied by 2 Platoon (Lieutenant Teale), and for the next three days they were under fire from the other end of the village and from the high ground above it. The attack was continued by the troops of the 5th Brigade; during the night of the 13th, the Worcestershires entered the village by the same track that the Royal Scots had followed. At dawn on the 14th, they cleared it after a very heavy preparatory bombardment. No. 5 Platoon of B Company and Nos. 1 and 3 of A Company continued to site their guns in positions from which they covered the advance of the Worcestershires by firing across (instead of along) their lines of advance.

The Japanese made their next stand at the village of Mao Songsang, which stands at the highest point on the Imphal

KOHIMA. TRENCHES ON D. I. S. RIDGE. IN THE RIGHT DISTANCE IS KOHIMA TOWN AND THE BEGINNING OF NAGA VILLAGE

AN AIR PHOTOGRAPH OF THE ROAD TO IMPHAL SOON AFTER LEAVING KOHIMA

road, where the Barrail range begins to recede from it and runs east and west. The Japanese established themselves in depth on a line of posts that commanded the road from the village of Khuzama to Mao Songsang itself. It was expected that the Japanese would hold this place tenaciously. Nevertheless, it was carried in two days by a converging movement by the Royal Berkshires, the Durham Light Infantry, and the Royal Welch, of the 6th Brigade, and by the Worcestershires, of the 5th. All three platoons of C Company, supported the attack of the Royal Berkshires against Khuzama. On June 18, the Worcestershires were pushing into the village from the west and the Royal Welch Fusiliers from the north; when the two battalions met in the village itself the Japanese had gone.

To the south of Mao Songsang, the road runs through slightly more open country. Hills still rise to the east and west of it, but they are farther back, for the steep slopes of the Barrail range no longer hug the road. The hills close in towards the village of Maram, which lies in a sort of pass or defile, and it was here that the Japanese made their last stand. The head of the British column approached the village on the 18th and found that a bridge about a mile and a half outside it had been blown. The mortar that was covering the passage was silenced by 6 Platoon, and during the night the sappers repaired the bridge. Patrols, sent out at first daylight on the following day, established that the village could best be cleared by first occupying a spur above it, to the right of the road. This was done during the morning by the Worcestershires, with all three platoons of B Company assisting. "Supporting attacks of this sort had become second nature to us," writes Major King-Clark, " and on this occasion all three platoons of B Company, controlled by line from the brigade command post, carried on firing in support of the Worcestershires to a very late stage in the attack, though the fire was directly overhead." The Japanese were forced out of the village by the early afternoon, and after our troops entered it they were presented with stirring evidence of the extent and significance of their victories. For captured documents proved that the Japanese had intended to hold the place for ten days, while their 31st Division withdrew eastwards through the mountains. The Japanese retreat from Maram was, moreover, no orderly withdrawal of a rearguard force, for they left enormous quantities of equipment and stores behind them.

The whole area was not, however, entirely cleared, for when the 4th Brigade, which was following upon the 5th, came up, the Royal Scots had to clear a spur at the eighty-second milestone, and for twenty-four hours after Maram had fallen, the Dorsetshires and the Camerons were engaging the Japanese on a spur to the south of the village. Nevertheless, the business was virtually over when our troops passed through Maram, and on June 22 the head of our column, racing southwards, met an armoured column of the 5th Indian Division which had fought its way out of Imphal to meet them. The joining point was about thirty miles south of Maram, where the road runs down the valley of a stream called the Imphal Turei, with high mountains on each side of it.

* * * * *

By holding the Japanese in the hills around Imphal the four Divisions of 4 Corps had forced a decision. When the corps was thus relieved the Japanese were beaten; the flower of their divisions lay dead in front of the positions that they had never carried; for the 23rd Division between Patel and Yaripok, the 17th Division on the western side of the Manipur, the 5th Division round Kanglatangbi, and the 20th Division round Sagelmang, had held their ground day after day and week after week. When this resistance was thus brought to a successful issue, the Japanese could no longer remain where they were; for their supply stream had been practically run dry in the wild mountain valleys behind them. All the Japanese soldiers were hungry, some were starving. Moreover, the Japanese commander had not upper valley of the Mu; to fight the British to a standstill between the lower Chindwin and the Irrawaddy; and then to rely upon the monsoon to make the tracks over which all British supplies would be carried so bad that the British Army would be compelled to go back or to starve. After engaging and defeating the British when they were thoroughly reduced by hardships and sickness, the Japanese commander hoped to collect a large force, and to overwhelm the Chinese-American army in the north.

The Japanese commander had drawn back his forces by mid-September, and thus distributed them. The 33rd Division with two battalions of the 53rd and one of the 54th Division held the valleys of the Manipur, of the Myittha, and of the Chindwin between Kalewa and Paungbyin. The 15th and 31st Divisions watched the country between Paungbyin and the Burma railway at Indaw, and blocked the valley between the Zibutaung and Mangin mountains, which is one of the northern gateways into the central plain. On the railway to the north of Katha were the 53rd Division less the battalions which were detached to the Tiddim–Chindwin area, and two independent mixed brigades, the 24th and 34th. To the east of these, and on the northern side of the great bend in the Irrawaddy between Katha and Bhamo, was the 18th Division. To the east again, the 56th and 2nd Divisions blocked the north- and south-going valley that debouches into the valley of the Irrawaddy at Myothir. These two divisions were distributed in depth: the 56th was pushed forward towards Myitkina. To the south of the quadrant that was thus held, about 30,000 lines-of-communication troops guarded the roads and the railway to Mandalay.

The 55th Division and one Regiment of the 54th were round Akyab and in the river valleys to the north of it; the rest of the 54th Division was watching the coast to the south, and arrangements were being made to bring the whole of the 54th Division on to the Akyab–Kaledan front, and to withdraw the units that were then stationed there. One regiment of the 55th Division held the western side of the Irrawaddy

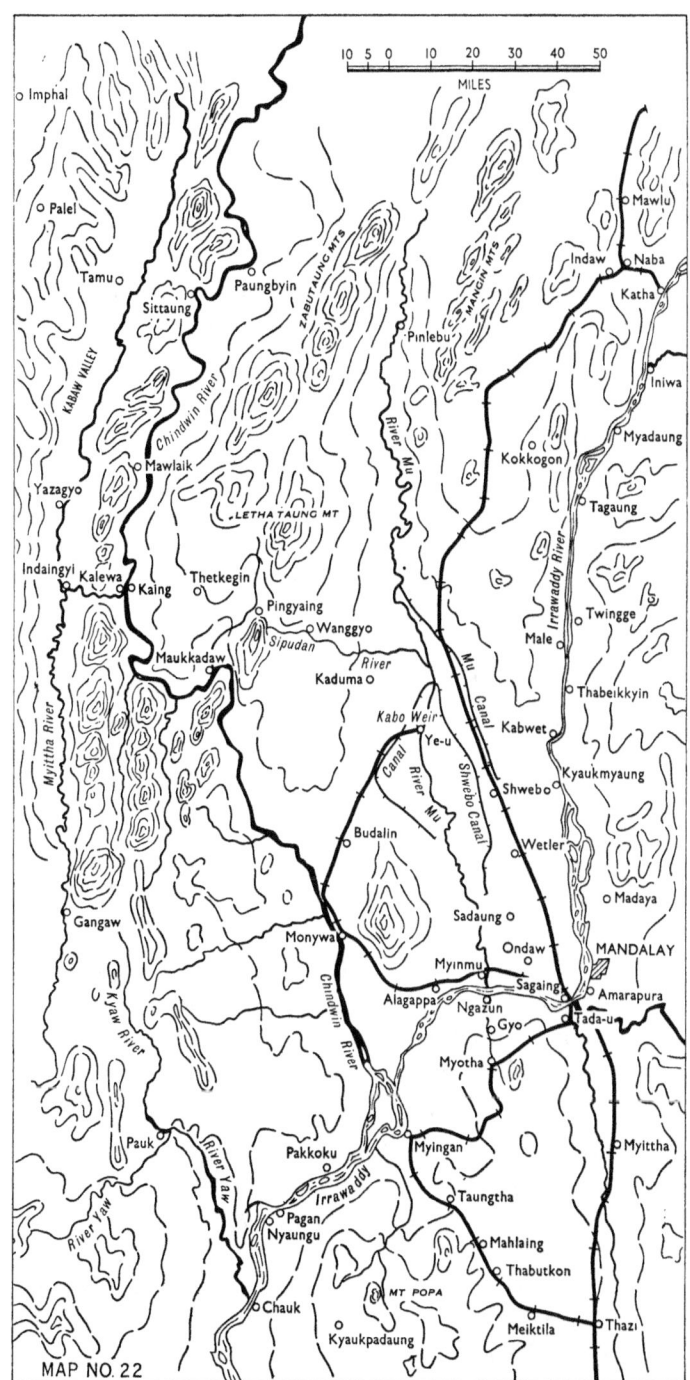

delta: the 49th Division was in the Tharawaddy area to the north of Rangoon: 20,000 lines-of-communication troops patrolled the country between Mandalay and Rangoon. The Japanese high command thus had some ten fighting divisions, two independent mixed brigades, and at least 50,000 lines-of-communication troops at their disposal. In addition they had enrolled and partially trained two divisions of Indians and seven battalions of Burmese who desired to fight against us. General Slim considered that the Japanese were shaken by their defeat, and by the sufferings consequent upon the campaign; but that all of them, including the lines-of-communication troops, would still fight stubbornly.

General Slim intended to cross the Chindwin to traverse the mountains that lie to the east of it, and to force a decision in the flat, alluvial plain between the lower waters of the Chindwin and Mandalay. Inasmuch as the Japanese commander hoped to give battle in this same area, and to bring it to a successful issue, the British troops were committed to an operation that the Japanese command may, possibly, have welcomed. Nevertheless, General Slim thus calculated the chances of victory. Provided that the Japanese were occupied and, if possible, pressed on all fronts, and provided that the special forces that had been carried by air into central Burma could continue to harass the Japanese in the middle Irrawaddy, General Slim estimated that the Japanese commander would only be able to collect five divisions, one independent mixed brigade, one tank regiment, some 40,000 lines-of-communication troops, and the Indian and Burmese levies, for the decisive battle. The 14th Army, taken as a whole, was more powerful than this, for it was composed of six and two-thirds divisions (the 2nd, 5th, 7th, 17th, 19th, 20th), the 268th Brigade, the 28th East African Brigade, and the two Tank Brigades (254th, 255th). It was, however, not possible to move the whole of this force into the Shwebo plain; and no matter what contrivances were attempted, the experts reported that only four and a half divisions could be maintained east of the Chindwin. Even this was going to be most

GENERAL SLIM'S PLAN

difficult; for those four and a half divisions would be operating 400 miles from railhead, and of that 400 miles 250 were traversed by mere earth tracks, which were no better than muddy paths after the monsoon began.

Four and two-thirds British/Indian divisions [writes General Slim] with which to attack five and a third Japanese, across a great river, and at the end of a precarious line of communications, was not the odds that I should have chosen. However, with our air supremacy, our great superiority in armour, our greater mobility in open country, and above all, the higher training and fighting value of our troops, I was prepared to risk it.[1]

That which most influenced General Slim was therefore that the troops who had outfought the enemy at Kohima and Imphal were confident that they could do it again elsewhere.

* * * * *

By way of preparation for the advance into Burma the system of command was revised. The 14th Army Commander was relieved of all responsibilities for operations in the Arakan and in the north, which were transferred to the commander of the 11th Army Group—General Giffard, and later Lieutenant-General Sir Oliver Leese. The 14th Army being thus freed of any commitment save that of bringing the enemy to battle in the Shwebo plain was now thus constituted:

    33 Corps (2nd and 20th Divisions, 268th Brigade, 254th Tank Brigade);

    4 Corps (7th and 19th Divisions, 255th Tank Brigade); and

    Special troops: 28th East African Brigade.

The 11th Army Group (later called Alfsea) reserve was composed of the 23rd Division, the 11th East African Division, and the Lushai Brigade. It was intended that these troops should be employed in central Burma in operations

[1] *The Campaign of the 14th Army 1944–1945*, p. 4.

where rapid movement would be essential. The two divisions were therefore reconstituted thus: each division, less a brigade group, was mechanized, and the brigade group was made transportable by air. It was extremely difficult to arrange this with the amount of motor transport that was allowed to the Army.

When the campaign for central Burma was thus planned, the position on the other fronts was this. The 36th Division in the north captured Myitkina in August, and both the division and the Chinese-American force were well to the south of it by November. General Stilwell had been succeeded by General Sultan and the whole force was composed of five Chinese Divisions, the 475th U.S. Infantry Regiment, and the 124 Dismounted Cavalry Regiment. In addition, the 36th Division (General Festing) had been ordered north to assist General Sultan. When General Slim put the 14th Army in motion General Festing's force had reached Mawlu. Finally a purely Chinese force under General Wei-li-Huang had reached the Salween at Kunlong and was pointing towards Lashio (see map 25, p. 483).

On November 1, 4 Corps headquarters was opened at Tamu in the Kabaw valley, and a fortnight later the forward movement began. The end immediately in view was to bring the two Corps (4 and 33) into the plain of Shwebo, and the advance was thus planned:

The 19th Division (4 Corps) was to cross the Chindwin and was to work through the defiles of the Zabutaung mountains towards Pinlebu, on the upper waters of the River Mu, it was then to operate down the Mu valley towards Shwebo, and was to effect a junction with General Festing's 36th Division. The other division of 4 Corps (the 7th) was to be kept on the western side of the Chindwin and sent forward as circumstances demanded. The Lushai Brigade and the 28th East African Brigade were also kept to the west of the Chindwin to block the valley of the Myittha, if the enemy struck at our communications by marching north through Gangaw. The whole of 33 Corps (2nd and 20th Divisions,

DIFFICULT OPERATIONS AHEAD

268th Brigade, and 254th Tank Brigade) was to cross the Chindwin on a broad front between Kalewa and Mawlaik and was to approach Shwebo through the defiles of the Letha Taung mountain (12,250 feet).

General Slim has explained the difficulties and risks of the enterprise that was thus embarked upon;[2] and indeed they can only be appreciated when professional matters—the carrying capacity of the roads, distances, air lifts, and so on —are examined. The difficulties were, however, so enormous that even a person who is not familiar with military history and administration can appreciate them by inspecting a map of Burma. If he does so, he will see a north- and south-going strip of land between Rangoon and Mandalay and Shwebo, which is bounded on the east by the Irrawaddy and is covered by a network of roads. This strip is surrounded on every side, west, north, and east, by range upon range of craggy, forested mountains which are hardly anywhere traversed by anything but paths and tracks. Our forces were, therefore, about to cross hundreds of miles of mountain wilderness, in order to meet and fight a brave and enterprising enemy who had assembled their forces in positions of their own choosing, with all the communications of Burma behind them. The enemy were certainly suffering from the shortages that were the natural consequence of operating so far from Japan. Also the war in the Pacific had taken a bad turn for them, for the Americans had repeatedly outfought the Japanese naval forces, and the Japanese were only maintaining their garrisons in the islands at a great cost, which was felt on all other fronts. Our intelligence staff was indeed collecting indications of the enemy's wants and sufferings when the march into Burma began, and occasionally they were significant. Early in December, for instance, we discovered that about 3,000 men had been drafted to the 33rd Japanese Division as replacements. Practically none of the men were in the top class for health and strength; one-third of them fell sick on the journey between Singapore and Kalewa; thereafter the

[2] *14th Army Campaign 1944–1945*, pp. 5, 6.

rate of sickness was exceptionally high as the men were very underfed. If a glimpse by the intelligence staff revealed this, one must assume that matters were not going well with the Japanese army in Burma. Nevertheless, they enjoyed great compensating advantages; and if an operation of war could be successfully prosecuted by choosing good positions and securing good communications, the Japanese would have defeated the 14th Army.

The 19th Division led the way and crossed the Chindwin on November 19. The march eastwards began on December 4 and 5. The northern brigade took a track through Wetkauk and Simlamaung; the southern brigade advanced from Paungbyin towards Wayongon and Pinlebu. The upper peaks of the Zabutaung range, which the division crossed, are between 5,000 and 7,000 feet high, and General Slim thus describes the difficulties for the advance.

> There was no road. A track built by the Japanese for the invasion of Assam meandered through precipitous, jungle-covered hills, and the division had to winch their vehicles over some of the worst slopes. Moreover the monsoon had washed away long reaches of the track and the 19th Division, with little mechanical equipment, had to cut its own road and, at times, manhandle its guns and lorries for miles. At one point the only way to get the track round a cliff was to cantilever it out on timber supports.[3]

The Japanese were only holding the passes with covering parties; but wherever they stood their ground they fought desperately. The following time-table records how the 19th Division overcame the resistance of man and of Nature. On December 12 the divisional headquarters were at Sinlamaung; on December 17 Pinlebu was carried; on December 23, the leading troops were at Kokoggon, which is on the eastern side of the Mandalay–Katha railway in the foothills of the Irrawaddy valley. Meanwhile, General Festing's division was pressing forward along the railway: on the 16th the division was debouching from Naba junction, and the

---

[3] *14th Army Campaign 1944–1945*, p. 7.

THE 2ND DIVISION'S TASK

leading troops made contact with the advanced screen of the 19th. During the next few days the two divisions joined up and pressed the advance to the south in collaboration.

The 19th Division thus fought and marched 192 miles in twenty days, and opened one of the gateways to the Shwebo plain. This great feat of arms gave a new turn to the campaign.

All this while the 11th East African Division was clearing the Chindwin valley between Paungbyin and Kalewa, and the 20th Division crossed at Mawlaik on December 3, and advanced south-eastwards through the defiles of the Letha Taung mountains towards the railway between Mandalay and Ye-U. The division advanced very rapidly, and in the first week in January they stormed the town of Budalin.

* * * * *

These were the movements on the right and left of the theatre; and it will now be proper to describe the advance of the 2nd Division with whom the second battalion was operating.

The warning order that the 2nd Division was to move to Yazagyo, in the Kabaw valley, was issued on November 5. The battalion was then at Maram, on the road between Kohima and Imphal. It had been known for some time past that General Slim intended to advance on central Burma, and the interval after Kohima was spent in thoroughly overhauling equipment and in discarding articles that would not be wanted. Weapon training was also revised as far as was possible in the circumstances.

For two years [writes General Slim] 14th Army formations had fought in jungles and amongst hills. They were now about to break out into open country, largely flat, with unobstructed views, in parts almost desertlike. Not only would the laborious tactics of the jungle have to be replaced by speed, mechanization and mobility; but commanders and troops would have to adjust their mentality to changed conditions.[4]

[4] *14th Army Campaign 1944-1945*, p. 6.

The division moved into the Kabaw valley by way of Palel. It was so insufferably dusty in the valley that the columns were enveloped in a fog of dust and grit which blotted out all but the nearest objects, and the vehicles were moved at the slowest speed. By November 27 the 2nd Division was at Yazagyo, with the 6th Brigade leading (1st Royal Berkshires, 1st Royal Welch Fusiliers, 2nd Durham Light Infantry, 16th Field Regiment R.A., 393rd Light Battery R.A., 170th Anti-Tank Battery R.A., 506th Field Company, C Company 2nd Manchesters). The enemy were still holding positions on the Tiddim road and in the Kabaw valley at the beginning of the month, and General Yamamoto, the local commander at Tiddim, even contemplated attacking us. Nevertheless, the 5th Division in the Manipur valley, and the 11th East African Division in the Kabaw so quickly overcame the enemy's parties that were there posted that, by the end of the month, it was deemed probable at headquarters that the Japanese no longer hoped to hold any bridgehead west of the Chindwin. It was, however, still thought that an advance from the Kalewa area would be stiffly contested.

By the first week in December the Kalewa area was clear, and, on December 16th the 6th Brigade crossed on the floating Bailey bridge that had been put across the river between Kalewa and Kaing. The 5th Brigade followed, with B Company attached to it. The 4th Brigade came last: it left the concentration area a week after the 6th Brigade; but when the advance was fairly started, the distance between the two was rarely more than a day's march. A Company of the Manchesters was held back on the line of communication for nine days at a post at Indainggyi where the road along the Myittha valley branched off. For reasons that will be given later this was a very important routing point. By the end of the month A Company was, however, crossing the mountains with its brigade (the 4th).

By the operation of one of those strange coincidences that occur so frequently in war, the division was advancing along one of the roads that had been used by the retreating British

why the Japanese did not destroy it; for they are not ignorant of the art of war, and they can hardly have left the weir intact out of consideration for the villagers and farmers, as they were assuredly not kind-hearted.

* * * * *

At the end of the year, therefore, the leading divisions of the 14th Army had debouched into the Shwebo plain at three points; and the 36th Division was pressing down the railway in collaboration with them. Seeing that his outer defences had crumbled, and that the British Army had crossed the mountain barrier in strength, General Kimura now decided to draw his forces behind the Irrawaddy, and to hold it strongly from Twingge in the north to Chauk in the south—the place where the River Yaw flows into the Irrawaddy. Our troops were probably so little opposed during the last part of their advance because the Japanese units in the mountains were then withdrawing. The Japanese forces were now thus distributed: the 15th Division occupied positions to the east of the Irrawaddy in the northern sector; the 53rd Division held the Mandalay area with strong bridgeheads on the western side. The 31st Division was on the right bank of the river; it occupied a strong bridgehead which rested on the natural bastion of the Sagaing hills; its left was down river near Ngazun. "This," writes General Slim, "not only gave the enemy a sally port, from which he could deliver counter-attacks on our forces as they advanced towards the river; but by occupying the only high ground on the west bank the Japanese denied us all observation over their positions and dominated ours."[5] The 33rd Division was responsible for the defence of the Irrawaddy from a position just below Ngazun to Pagan, where the 28th Army took over the defence of the river valley.

It was the decision of a wise and skilful commander, and General Slim was obliged to revise his own plan drastically.

[5] *14th Army Campaign 1944–1945*, p. 8.

The 14th Army could no longer force a battle in the Shwebo plain, for the enemy would not accept it. If, then, what was left of the original plan were adhered to without alteration, the 14th Army would be committed to a frontal attack across a great tropical river, against an enemy whose communications were far better than those of the attacking army. This was manifestly what General Kimura hoped that we should do, and General Slim was not the kind of commander who plays his enemy's game.

The British General decided to strike the decisive blow farther south. Meiktila, which is about eighty miles to the south of Mandalay, was the nodal point of the Japanese army's communications in northern Burma. It is a radiating point for the principal roads in the province, and although it is situated on the sideline to Myingan, its railway communications to Mandalay are easy through the junction of Thazi. It was here that the Japanese had accumulated enormous stocks of stores and equipment, and it was here that they had established their chief air force base. If Meiktila could be captured, the Japanese army to the north would be destroyed if it held to its positions; if, on the other hand, General Kimura withdrew his forces in time, they would be committed to a terrible retreat down the Irrawaddy valley. Indeed, after General Slim had considered the implications of a major operation against Meiktila, and had decided that it was feasible, he stated that when the place was carried, the next objective would be Rangoon.

As a preliminary, the Army was re-grouped, and the composition of its two corps was changed.

> To the 4th Corps were now allotted: the 7th Division; the 17th Division (mechanized and airborne); 255th Tank Brigade; Lushai Brigade; 28th East African Brigade.
>
> The 33rd Corps was now composed of: the 2nd Division (British); the 19th Division (Indian); the 20th Division (Indian); 254th Tank Brigade; 268th Brigade (Indian).

The 5th Indian Division (mechanized and airborne) was in army reserve.

GENERAL SLIM'S NEW PLAN

Under the new distribution, the 19th Division was therefore transferred to 4 Corps, and the 17th Division took its place. The reason was that 4 Corps—which in the original plan was on the extreme left of the advance—was to be moved down the Kabaw valley with the utmost secrecy; was to secure a bridgehead at Pakokku; and was then to strike at Meiktila, with a mechanized, armoured, and partially airborne column. The 7th Division was to be the spearhead of the thrust; behind it the 17th and 5th Divisions were to be used for exploitation. The risks were very great: three divisions and a tank brigade were to be moved for 330 miles over an earth road, which resembled the bed of a stream in wet weather, and was covered by a dense fog of dust in dry; a great river had to be crossed at the end of this terrible advance, and all the stores, ammunition, and petrol that were required for a dash against Meiktila had to be assembled on the far bank, after the bridgehead was secure. The difficulties of bringing this enormous task to a successful issue were grievously augmented when seventy-five Dakota aircraft were sent away from the 14th Army without consultation or warning.

It was, however, the very essence of the new plan that the enemy should not suspect that 4 Corps had been withdrawn from the Shwebo front; and in order that the deception should be, as far as possible, beyond detection, the 19th Division was maintained in the Shwebo section of the theatre, and all orders were transmitted to it through a dummy corps headquarters. Actually the 19th Division was placed under the commander of 33 Corps, whose duty, under the new plan, was to press on with all possible vigour, and to carry his divisions across the Irrawaddy between Mandalay and Myingyan. The great flanking movement against Meiktila could only be successful if the advance of 33 Corps were conducted so fiercely and relentlessly that the Japanese commander would remain convinced that our principal forces were engaged in it, and that it was upon this advance that General Slim depended for a decision.

Having decided that the engineers and the administrative staff of his army would accomplish what was necessary to be done upon the lines of communication, General Slim issued the preliminary orders for the operation against Meiktila on December 19: the movement was, therefore, well started when the divisions of 33 Corps debouched into the Shwebo plain, and when the leading troops of the 2nd Division reached Kabo.

* * * * *

The 2nd Division, with which the battalion was operating, was in the centre of the advance against Sagaing and Mandalay. The plain ahead is about one hundred miles long and about sixty miles wide; it is extremely flat, and is cut into two parts by the River Mu—a waterway that wriggles through the plain in a series of loops and bends, and joins the Irrawaddy near Myinmu. Two lines of hills rise from the southern part of the plain, and like every natural feature in Burma they run north and south.

The western group of hills are opposite Monywa, and are crossed by three roads which are no worse than the majority. The eastern group, called the Sagaing Hills, are a more important military feature: they are on the western bank of the Irrawaddy, opposite Mandalay; they rise very sharply to a height of over 1,300 feet, and overlook a long traject of the railway between Shwebo and Sagaing.

When Kabo weir was captured the 5th Brigade was at the little hamlet of Chaungzon, on the Kaduma–Ye-U road, and the 4th Brigade was at Kaduma. The divisional commander now ordered the 6th Brigade to reconnoitre and secure the crossings of the River Mu; the 5th and 4th were to move on Ye-U. This was, for the moment, the main thrust; there was an air-strip at Ye-U, and if it could be secured quickly airborne supplies could at once be brought in. The 2nd Recce Regiment of 2nd Division was allotted to the operation. The 5th Brigade, with B Company under command, therefore moved forward. Ye-U is built on the right bank of the River Mu, and covers one of the bridges of the waterway: the Japanese here fought far more strenuously than they had done at Kabo, but the place was surrounded and carried during the late afternoon of January 2. The whole division was now directed on Shwebo, which is the principal town in the plain.

The 4th Brigade, which had up to this time been in reserve, led the advance; and A Company, who had been doing routine duties at Indainggyi, was brought up and again placed under command. The brigade crossed the Mu on January 6, and was almost at once brought to a standstill by one of the vagaries of Nature; for within an hour, an unexpected torrent of rain turned a parched and dusty country into a vast expanse of mud and slush, wherein neither men, beasts, nor vehicles could move.

By a tremendous exertion, and thanks also to the re-appearance of the tropical sun, the brigade was on the move by January 7. The Japanese resistance was now appreciably stiffer, for a fairly strong force of aircraft bombed Ye-U during the day, and the Royal Scots, who led the brigade, were several times held up by artillery fire. No. 1 Platoon, which was attached to the leading brigade, found the locality unsuited to machine-gun fire. After a slow advance during the 7th, the brigade were opposed by a well-organized delaying party, who fought from village to village.

Time was running out, for petrol was now very short, the men were on half rations, and there was no hope of any real relief until Shwebo was captured. The decisive advance was made by the 5th Brigade, which left Ye-U soon after the 4th, and, after pushing eastwards, pressed down from the north along the line of the Shwebo canal. By January 8, the brigade was in position just north of the village of Myingatha. Here the Japanese resisted stubbornly; and the first attack was broken by a hail of grenades, mortars, and field-gun fire. No. 5 Platoon of the battalion was here engaged, and used its guns with great effect as the attacking parties streamed back. The attack was, however, at once renewed, with 5 and 7 Platoons assisting, and after a bitter struggle the village was captured. After Myingatha was carried the Japanese were not prepared to resist the advance further: for the 5th Brigade entered Shwebo on the following day. The 4th Brigade had then reached Chiba; and when the men of the 5th approached Shwebo airfield, they found that the leading troops of the 19th Division were already there. The two divisions had, indeed, been racing for Shwebo, and the honours seem even: the 5th Brigade appear to have reached the town first; the airfield, which was as important as the town, fell to the 19th Division. The place was found to be full of booby traps, and the Japanese withdrew along the line of the railway.

The Japanese air force bombed Ye-U and Shwebo after the last place had been captured, but their aiming was extremely bad, and neither airfield was made unserviceable. Airborne supplies were now assured. Also a very important document was captured in Shwebo, in which the Japanese defences in the Irrawaddy elbow were set out in detail.

When Shwebo was thus captured the 20th Division were (as we have seen) in Budalin, and were preparing for an advance on Monywa. The great flanking movement against Meiktila was starting, for the 7th Division were making their last preparations for the advance along the Kabaw valley.

* * * * *

After Shwebo fell the Divisional Commander decided to follow the Japanese into the elbow with a special force; and to rest the brigades, as far as possible, until the time had arrived for a bound forward against the Sagaing defences. The special force was called Bradforce, after its commanding officer, Lieutenant-Colonel Bradford, the commanding officer of the 2nd Recce Regiment; it was composed of the 2nd Recce Regiment, a battery of the 16th Field Regiment

THE JAPANESE DECEIVED

R.A., a platoon of the 5th Field Company R.E., and A Company of the Manchesters.

Bradforce moved south down the road and met with little opposition. On January 14 the town of Sadaung was occupied. It is a large straggling place, in the words of the battalion diarist, "A veritable death trap for a small force to defend." The place was full of spies, and it is the joining point of three important roads, which Colonel Bradford searched, though with great difficulty. Sadaung is, indeed, at the base of a rambling cluster of low hills which rise above the northern bank of the Irrawaddy; two of the roads which bifurcate from it run through fairly wide defiles; the third road goes east to the Sagaing razorback between the railway and the Irrawaddy.

Meanwhile the 19th Division had successfully started an operation that very much deceived the Japanese commander as to our real intentions. After the capture of Shwebo the division moved east and north-east towards the Irrawaddy, crossed it at Thabeikkyin and Kyaukmyaung and established bridgeheads at both places. General Katamura, the local army commander, appreciated this as an indication that the whole of 4 Corps intended to advance on Mandalay along the eastern bank of the Irrawaddy. He therefore assembled the bulk of his two divisions—the 15th and the 53rd—opposite the Kyaukmyaung bridgehead, and embarked upon a succession of desperate and unavailing attacks against it. The fighting for the defence of the 19th Division bridgehead was the fiercest and the most costly since the battles round Kohima and Imphal.

At the other side of the theatre, the Lushai brigade stormed Gangaw, and so opened the road to the Irrawaddy for the 7th Division.

When Bradforce reached Sadaung an advanced party (B Squadron, 2nd Recce Regiment, with No. 1 Platoon of A Company) moved slowly south towards Ondaw, which stands in the heart of the low hills that were then being approached. On the night of January 16 the column bivouacked at

Yinmagyin in the heart of the hills: there was still no sign of the enemy, but at daybreak Japanese field artillery opened a heavy fire upon the column from the heights above Ondaw. The enemy was now located at the exact spot that had been marked upon the captured map.

The operations of the previous month had by now established not merely how the Japanese divisions were distributed, but where the regiments and formations that composed them were placed; and when the 2nd Division was approaching the great bend in the Irrawaddy the Japanese forces between Twingge (forty miles north of Mandalay) and Pakokku were believed to be thus posted:

Round Twingge on the left bank was the 3rd Battalion of the 58th Regiment; farther south at the crossing of Thabeikkyin was a battalion of the 60th Regiment and units from the 67th Regiment. The 51st Regiment and the 2nd and 3rd Battalions of the 60th Regiment watched the river crossings between Kabwet and Kyaukmyaung. To the south of this place, the units belonged to the 55th Division, and between it and Sagaing the 119th, 151st, 53rd Recce and 128th Regiments were on the left bank; while the 2nd and 3rd Battalions of the 58th Regiment and the 2nd and 3rd Battalions of the 138th Regiment were on the right bank. By thus distributing his forces, the Japanese army commander hoped to hold our advance against Sagaing, and to operate against the rear of Bradforce and the 268th Brigade if an opportunity offered.

Below Sagaing the Japanese had withdrawn all their forces to the left bank save only at Ywathitgyi, where some units of the 124th Regiment held a small bridgehead on the north side of the river. The 31st Division held the river line between Sagaing and Myinmu: the 124th Regiment and the 2nd Battalion of the 154th Regiment (which had been lent by the 54th Division) were between Sagaing and Ywathitgyi. The 33rd Division held the river below Myinmu and Pakokku with the 213th and 214th Regiments. The 31st and 33rd Mountain Artillery Regiments, a battery of the 21st for the Japanese repeatedly infiltrated into the positions that the Scots were occupying outside the village, but they were confronted by a fighting spirit and an obstinacy that was equal to their own, and at about half-past five on the evening of February 2 the Royal Scots were masters of the village.

February 4. The machine-gun company was at once directed to assist the Lancashire Fusiliers in their attack on Kyaukse, which was cleared on February 4. The machine-gun fire from the Ondaw heights was exceptionally effective, and the fight for the village was considered by the battalion to be the occasion when the machine-gunners had their finest opportunity for assisting the infantry.

February 6. The attack on Saye was not so successful, as the enemy's guns on the heights to the east of it commanded every inch of the Norfolks' approach line. No. 1 Platoon, which was there operating, lost a gun while under fire. Saye thus remained in Japanese hands for the time being; but with Sadaung, Ondaw, Kyaukse, and Ywathitgyi thus in our hands, and with the left flank of the advance well covered, the approach to the northern bank to the Irrawaddy was opened. Before describing the next moves of the division it will, however, be proper to make a brief review of what was occurring in other parts of the theatre.

On January 22, when the 4th Brigade was preparing its attack upon Ondaw, the 20th Division stormed Monywa after a desperate resistance, and pressed on to the Irrawaddy. Advanced troops of the division actually reached Myinmu, on the northern bank, on the day when Monywa was taken. At the end of the month the division was reconnoitring the crossings of the river and was sending out patrols to the southern bank, which, in General Slim's words, " maintained a reign of terror and thuggery among the Japanese posts." Further west, the 7th Division had passed through Pauk, and the 17th Division was assembling in the Gangaw valley behind the 7th. In the north, the 19th Division was still successfully drawing off the Japanese forces on the eastern bank. The 62nd Brigade was enlarging its bridgehead at

THE IRRAWADDY IS REACHED

Kyaukmyaung; two battalions of the 92nd Brigade held the crossing at Thabeitkyin. The headquarters of the division were on the right bank near Kyaukmyaung. General Katamura's forces were still furiously and fruitlessly battering the bridgeheads. The 268th and 254th Brigades were drawn back round Shwebo. The Corps headquarters was near Sadaung.

* * * * *

Throughout these operations the River Mu had been the boundary between the 2nd and 20th Divisions' zones of operations and it remained so after the Irrawaddy was reached. The river front allotted to the division is about twenty-five miles long, and the river is in most parts about three-quarters of a mile broad. The southern side is hillier than the northern, for the last foothills of a north- and south-going ridge fall into the valley round Ngazun. This place is the principal town on that section of the southern bank and is the key to that part of the waterway, for the main road through the hills to the south, and the river road to Tada-U and Mandalay go through it. There is an island just opposite the town which is sometimes part of the southern bank and is sometimes separated from it. At the date with which we are now concerned, Ngazun island was a real island with a fast-flowing stream between it and the mainland. Patches of very high dense grass cover the extreme edges of both banks.

February 7. The planning for the crossings of the Irrawaddy and the selecting of the best positions for them was left to the commanders of the corps and divisions, and on February 7 the preliminary instructions were given to the formations of the 2nd Division. The 5th Brigade was to secure the crossing and to open the bridgehead by advancing into the hills on the south bank along the course of a stream that joins the Irrawaddy at Ngazun. The 6th Brigade was to cross after the 4th, and was to enlarge the bridgehead to the eastward while the 5th Brigade was advancing to the south. While the crossing was thus being made, the 4th Brigade and the 2nd Recce Regiment were to come under corps command, and were to cover the eastern flank of the 5th and 6th Brigades during the crossing and the first build-up; thereafter, the force was to be reduced, slowly, and sent into the bridgehead. Bradforce was to watch the exits of the Sagaing hills to the east of the railway between Saye and Tangyi. The communications to the north were to be patrolled by the 268th Brigade.

When these orders were received the 6th Brigade had been brought up from the Shwebo area and was on the river at Ywathitgyi; the 5th Brigade was to the west at Maungdaung. The 4th Brigade was at Ondaw, preparing to renew the attack on Saye. The Manchesters were now commanded by Lieutenant-Colonel R. King-Clark, M.C., for Lieutenant-Colonel Archdale had been posted to the 20th Division as second-in-command of a brigade. B Company was allotted to the 5th Brigade, and when later the Royal Welch Fusiliers were lent to the brigade, so that the first crossing should be carried out by four battalions, No. 9 Platoon was allotted to the Royal Welch Fusiliers. No. 10 Platoon was attached to the Durhams (6th Brigade); A Company remained with the 4th Brigade; B Company with the 5th.

February 12. While the 5th and 6th Brigades were preparing to cross, two extremely important moves were completed farther west. After the 20th Division stormed Monywa the road to the Irrawaddy was opened to them, and on February 12 the division crossed it at Allagappa, about ten miles west of the Mu. The river is about 1,500 yards wide at the point of crossing, which was chosen on the boundary line between the 31st and 33rd Japanese Divisons. By dawn on the 13th the leading brigade was well established on the southern bank, and by nightfall on the following day the bridgehead was six miles wide and two deep.

February 13. On the day following the first crossings of the 20th Division, the 7th Division crossed at Nyaungu, about fifteen miles below Pakokku. In General Slim's words, " The crossing was an outstanding example of how such an

PREPARING TO CROSS

operation should be done."[6] It was, indeed, exceptionally difficult, as the landing places were mere clefts in high, cliffy banks, the approaches to them were open, and the outboard motors of the crossing craft often failed. By good fortune the Japanese army commander regarded the crossing as a diversion, and only second-rate units disputed it. Behind the 7th Division were the 17th, less an airborne brigade and the 255th Tank Brigade which were brought down to Pauk. Three divisions were now across the Irrawaddy and the great flanking movement was well forward. Also the Japanese command were still misinterpreting whatever indications of our real intentions they were then collecting; for General Katamura continued to batter the 19th Division at the northern end of the theatre, and was, as far as we could tell, convinced that it was here where the real danger lay and that it was in this part of the theatre that we should strike our heaviest blows.

The commander of the 2nd Division was now pressing on hard with his preparations for crossing. The divisional headquarters was established at Maungdaung. A two-way track was completed along the east bank of the River Mu, and was continued along the northern side of the Irrawaddy as far as Myinze. The assembly area was chosen between Letpantha, Myinze and Legyi, and the divisional artillery was concentrated at Myinze.

February 7–8. The river front was, at first, very quiet, but on the night of February 7 the Worcestershires were severely attacked at Dawete by a party of Japanese who crossed the river after dark. The fighting went on all night; neither side realized the strength of the other; and towards morning the Japanese re-crossed the river, as the Worcestershires, who were then beginning to get the upper hand, threatened to cut them off. This was rather disturbing, as it was to be supposed that the Japanese reported that strong forces were assembling on the northern bank. Strangely enough the Japanese did

[6] *14th Army Campaign 1944–1945*, p. 16.

not renew their patrols; our preparations continued undisturbed, and, as far as we could tell, undetected. For the time being the greatest need was boat drill.

On February 14 a party of the 5th Brigade, led by Flight-Lieutenant Avery, made a careful and skilful reconnaissance of the opposite bank. The party crossed in an assault craft which was manned by fourteen officers and men, and found a beach that was very suitable for assault troops: it was about 150 yards long and was protected from fire from the upper parts of the bank by an extremely steep cliff, which was, however, low enough to be scalable. The party left the northern bank at 19.40 hours and returned two hours later without being molested by the enemy. The reconnaissance was repeated on the following night, and on their return the party reported that the opposite bank was in places very badly wired (so badly, in fact, that no troops were likely to be stopped by the obstruction) and that the landing area was very thinly held. The reconnaissance was not once interfered with, and no sounds came from the country beyond the patrol area.

On February 17 a party from the Durham Light Infantry crossed farther east and reconnoitred the approaches to Letpanzin. The party ascertained that the village was held fairly strongly, and returned without loss.

February 21. Four days later the Royal Berkshires sent a party on to the island opposite the village of Shepyishinkyun. The men spent some time there—for it was certainly not occupied—and they neither saw nor heard an enemy on the southern bank. By this time everything was ready, and it was decided that the crossing should be made on the night of February 24.

While these last preparations were being made the Norfolks attacked and carried Saye. Two days later (February 22), the Lancashire Fusiliers cleared the enemy out of Pegado, which was an outpost of the Sagaing defences. The capture of these two points very much strengthened the eastern flank of the division.

A BRIDGEHEAD SECURED

On the extreme right of the theatre of operations the flanking movement continued with mechanical precision; for on the day when Pegado was captured, the 17th Division and the 255th Brigade were brought across the Irrawaddy, and were concentrated in the 7th Division's bridgehead round Nyaungu. The bridgehead was now being rapidly enlarged; for, as the 17th Division came into it, an armoured column advanced against Hnawdwin and captured it. Hnawdwin is on the road to Taungtha, and is fifteen miles outside the first bridgehead perimeter. Simultaneously, or nearly so, another armoured force struck at Kyaukpadaung on the Meiktila road.

* * * * *

As has been explained, the divisional plan was that the 5th Brigade, brought up to four battalions by the loan of the Royal Welch Fusiliers, should make the first crossing, and that the 6th Brigade should follow. The first landings were to be made a little to the west of Ngazun. At 21.30 on February 24 the first flights of the Worcestershires and the Camerons were waterborne, and at 22.20 the Royal Welch Fusiliers, with No. 9 Platoon, landed at Ngazun island unopposed, and took up a position from which the western approaches to the village were well covered. Twenty minutes later, good and bad news was received at the brigade headquarters. The Camerons were across, but the Worcestershires had been severely enfiladed from two machine-gun posts near Ywathit; a large number of their boats were sunk and, what was perhaps worse, many other boats were so leaky that they had sunk without being fired on at all. A small party did, it is true, secure a footing on the southern side, but as they were isolated and without hope of being reinforced they returned. The Worcestershires lost heavily, and by midnight the survivors were streaming back to the northern bank. Shortly after this, however, the Royal Welch Fusiliers reported that they had secured a bridgehead opposite their first landing-place on Ngazun island.

As has been said, the Camerons were over. Many of their boats had proved to be almost unusable, but, by a singular piece of good fortune, the Japanese did not seriously dispute the crossing, and by midnight the Camerons were holding a two-company bridgehead about four miles west of Ngazun. A tremendous effort was now made to enlarge what had been won and to repair what had gone awry. The remainder of the Camerons, with No. 7 Platoon of the Manchesters, followed hard upon the first companies, and between one and two in the morning brigade headquarters reported to the division that the greater part of the battalion was on the southern bank.

Meanwhile, as soon as the report of the check to the Worcestershires was received, orders were given that no more crossings were to be made from the Worcestershires' starting point (Dawete), and that all craft and formations there assembling were to be sent to the Camerons' starting point (Myittha). The 2nd Dorsetshires and the 16th Field Regiment R.A. were the first units to be affected by the diversion, and were ordered to reinforce the Camerons as soon as boats were available. During the night the Worcestershires were re-formed.

An exact diary of the movements across the river cannot be drawn up from the documents that have survived, but the general succession of events during the two difficult days that followed upon the first crossings is well established and can be set out in order.

February 25. It was at first difficult to get the boats back from the southern bank (not one had returned by 01.00 hours), and this made the early hours difficult and critical, for although the Camerons had secured a foothold on the southern bank, their position was in the last degree dangerous. They were just clinging to the slopes of a high bank, and their bridgehead was nowhere more than twenty yards deep. They had, moreover, lost severely during the crossing from the fire of an L.M.G. which was cunningly concealed in the high grass of the southern bank, and

EXTENDING THE FOOTHOLD

which enfiladed the whole passage. This machine-gun was operated by a single, dauntless Japanese soldier, whom neither the infantry nor the artillery on the northern bank could dislodge. This brave man remained at his post until his last round was gone (his foxhole was subsequently found and was knee-deep in spent cartridges), and for as long as he remained there, all daylight crossings into the bridgehead that was still so precariously held were endangered.

It would appear, indeed, that a steady flow of reinforcements was not assured until the early part of the forenoon; for it was only at 10.00 hours that all the Camerons were across, and it was not until 15.30 hours that the 2nd Dorsets were coming into the bridgehead area. Had the Japanese been able to attack the Camerons during the forenoon the issue would have been very finely balanced; they did not do so, and merely shelled the Camerons' area.

Some time during the afternoon the Camerons and the Dorsetshires received orders to extend the foothold to the east and west. We have no details of the fighting that followed, and know only that it was well done; for just before midnight, companies of the two battalions were on the western edge of Ngazun village. The most critical and dangerous hours appear, therefore, to have been between midnight and the early afternoon.

February 26. At 09.15 hours the first flight of tanks crossed on rafts, and during the early hours and the first part of the forenoon the Worcestershires were taken over and were formed up for the attack on Ngazun, which was timed to take place during the afternoon. The movements across the river were indeed now thoroughly in order, for a considerable force of artillery assisted the attack when it was delivered. Just after noon the commander of the division arrived at his battle post in the bridgehead area to the west of Ngazun village. At 13.15 hours Ngazun village was attacked from the air, and the bombing continued for twenty-five minutes. When it was finished the Worcestershires, the Dorsetshires, and the Camerons were at their starting point. Nos. 5, 7, and 9 Platoons of the Manchesters were engaged in the assault: the two first were with the Camerons and Worcestershires; No. 9 Platoon was still on Ngazun island in positions that commanded most of the village. At 14.10 hours the artillery bombardment began, and at 14.30 hours the Dorsetshires and the Worcestershires were right through the village; its capture was the decisive action of the crossing.

The 6th Brigade had now moved into the disembarkation area, their first units (companies from the 1st Royal Berkshires and the 2nd Durham Light Infantry) were on the southern bank soon after Ngazun was carried; Nos. 9 and 10 Platoons of the battalion came with them. Matters were indeed deemed to be in so good a posture that the 4th Brigade were now ordered to leave their positions round Saye and Pegado to the 268th Brigade and to come into the bridgehead. No. 2 Platoon was, however, left behind at Saye to operate with the 268th Brigade. The forces at this point were often engaged in stubborn fighting, for the Japanese army command still clung to a plan for counter-attacking along the northern bank of the Irrawaddy. The platoon were much admired and respected by the Nepal State troops of the brigade.

The first units began to arrive in the assembly area during the afternoon. When darkness settled in, therefore, Ngazun (which, as has been explained, was the key to the southern bank) was in our hands, the tactical headquarters of the 5th and 6th Brigades, and most of the two brigades themselves, were on the southern bank, and the 4th Brigade was preparing to cross.

February 27. As has been said, the Yazawin chaung makes a cleft in the hills to the south of Ngazun, and as the Japanese could have launched a dangerous counter-attack against the bridgehead from the railway town of Myotha, at the upper end of the valley, it was of great importance to enlarge the bridgehead into the first foothills. The riverside village of Nyaunggyin was chosen as the first point of attack, and the 6th Brigade was ordered to carry it. The village is on beginning to press back the enemy forces that had exhausted themselves by so many fruitless attacks against the bridgehead perimeter, and on February 25 the division had cleared both banks of the Irrawaddy as far as Singu ferry. The Japanese had always been sensitive to a threat from this quarter, and the news that General Katamura's troops were no longer holding the 19th Division may well have aggravated the difficulties and uncertainties that were then besetting the Japanese high command.

On February 28, however—the day when the 2nd Division completed the crossing and when the Divisional Commander inspected the headquarters of the three brigades on the southern bank—General Slim's great stroke was delivered with stunning violence and geometric precision. For on that day a strong armoured force from the 17th Division reached Meiktila and surrounded it. As at Taungtha the local commandant could only assemble administrative units and "infantry companies improvised from odds and ends"[7] for the defence of the place, and its capture was only a matter of time. On the following day, however, the airborne brigade of the 17th Division was flown into Thabutkon, on the Myingan–Meiktila railway, and sent on to Meiktila. The attacking force was now overwhelmingly stronger than the garrison and the town was completely in our hands by March 4 after three days of bitter fighting.

In the first days of March, therefore, more than two British divisions were established in the very heart of the Japanese communications, and in the very centre of their administrative area, for practically every Japanese unit and formation between Yenangyaung, Mandalay, and the corridor to the north of it, depended in some degree upon the Meiktila depots. General Slim thus describes the consequences.

The plan to concentrate resources against the 33rd Corps was abandoned. The reinforcing formations moving towards the

[7] *14th Army Campaign 1944–1945*, p. 21.

JAPANESE COMMANDERS LOSING CONTROL

Mandalay area were either put into reverse or directed on Meiktila. Even some of the troops already fighting that corps were pulled out of the fight and turned against the new danger. ... The sudden changes, the bombing of his headquarters, which we were increasingly able to locate, and the depredations of our roving armoured columns began to affect the enemy's communications and control. From now onwards his commanders began gradually to lose control of their formations and of the battle.[8]

The Irrawaddy was thus crossed, at a time when this confusion and these contradictory purposes were thoroughly infecting the Japanese army command, and the operations that were undertaken after the division had crossed the river were executed while the Japanese were making their principal exertion in another part of the theatre, Meiktila. This is probably the explanation of why both operations were often stubbornly contested by local units, but never by an organized, concerted resistance.

* * * * *

During the first week in March the 2nd Division was consolidating and preparing for a fresh advance, and on March 7 contact was made with the 20th Division when a Ghurka patrol entered the bridgehead perimeter. It well illustrates how difficult the whole country was, that for the week previous the two divisions had been groping for one another without success. On one occasion patrols from each division were in the same village without making contact. Orders were, however, now received that the whole division was to advance eastwards against Ava and Tada-U, the two southern outposts of Mandalay.

Ngazun and the mouth of the Yazawin chaung which were the starting points of the last advance are about twenty miles from Ava, where the railway bridge across the Irrawaddy reaches the southern bank. A north- and south-going ridge lies between the Yazawin chaung and Ava and comes

[8] *14th Army Campaign 1944–1945*, p. 22.

right down to the river bank at Kyauktalon. The ridge is about seven miles thick; its eastern flank falls into the flat alluvial plain to the west of Tada-U.

The 5th Brigade led the advance, and struck against the road that runs into the hills, the 2nd Recce Regiment formed a right flank screen. On their right rear the 6th Brigade advanced by way of Tamabin; to the right of them again the 4th Brigade struck south-eastwards towards the upper part of the Kyauktalon road.

On March 10 the Worcestershires (5th Brigade) attacked and carried the heights above Kyauktalon with the whole of B Company assisting. To the machine-gunners of the battalion the action was as gratifying as any that they had been engaged in since the Irrawaddy was first reached, for the fire plan and the communications worked without a hitch, and the machine-gun fire contributed substantially to the success of the day. It was after this action that the men of B Company acquired a piece of booty that had never before been captured during the campaign—a Japanese 81-mm. mortar in perfect condition, with the sights undamaged and a stock of ammunition beside it.

The Kyauktalon heights were the key to the southern bank as far as Tada-U and Ava, and after they were thus carried, Japanese resistance became spasmodic and disconcerted. To the right of the 2nd Division the same was happening, for on the day when Kyauktalon was captured parties from the 20th Division reached the Yazawin chaung at Gyo. Two days later the division were in Myotha—an important road and railway town that lies in the heart of the hills to the south of Ngazun.

If the Japanese resistance was becoming weaker it was small wonder, for just when the 2nd and 20th Divisions were beginning their advance to the east, the 19th struck a heavy blow further north. Being convinced that the long and fruitless battering against his bridgeheads had exhausted General Katamura's force, General Rees decided that the moment had arrived for a forward move. When executed it was a

THE MACHINE-GUNNERS DISAPPOINTED

leap or a rush rather than a move, for on March 10 the division reached Mandalay Hill, which overlooks the city from the north-east; while, on the day following, another party occupied Maymyo after traversing the high mountain defiles to the north-east of Mandalay. To the Japanese these two advances were a disaster of the first order; their elaborate defences on the left bank round Madaya were overrun, and their railway link to their force at Lashio was severed. Nor could the Japanese commanders round Mandalay have entertained any hope that the lost points would be recovered, for every available reinforcement was then being drawn into the struggle for Meiktila.

To the machine-gunners of the battalion the advance to the east was fatiguing; cheering in that the evidences that the enemy were outfought and beaten accumulated during each day's advance; but, from a purely professional standpoint, disappointing. "The eastward move of the division continued unabated," writes the battalion diarist. "Practically every day villages were captured by some unit, and almost invariably a platoon of the 2nd Manchesters was in position to assist, though frequently their assistance was not required." The advance had, indeed, become a matter of clearing pockets, for the Japanese did at least strive to delay the advance, and their small scattered parties, combined with their mines, inflicted considerable loss.

The town of Ava which stands at the confluence of the Myittinge and the Irrawaddy is, as it were, the southern gateway to Mandalay city, it is surrounded by an old earthwork called Ava Fort, and on March 17 the Camerons (5th Brigade) captured the fort, secured the crossing of the Myittinge river, and advanced to the southern end of the great railway bridge from Sagaing. "No. 7 Platoon kept up with them with great energy," says the diary, "carrying their gun kit for more than three days on end." When Ava Fort was captured Nos. 6 and 7 Platoons brought their guns into action. "As usual, however, their energy and zeal were largely unrewarded, for there were no decent targets." The officers and men of the battalion were now very tired, for they had been engaged in long marches, and had been obliged to carry their gun kit on nearly all occasions. Even in the temperate English climate this is recognized to be the most exhausting thing that machine-gunners can be ordered to do.

At this date (March 17), the 19th Division had cleared Mandalay, and the Japanese were streaming southwards along the Mandalay–Myittha railway, and the Mandalay–Kyaukse road. They were thus retiring across the fronts of the 4th, 5th, and 6th Brigades, whose last advances turned the retreat into a rout. For by March 20, the 4th and 6th Brigades had secured the line of the Myittinge and the railway round Paleik; while farther south, the 20th Division was approaching Kyaukse. The battalion's luck changed for the better during these last actions of the Mandalay campaign, for the whole of A Company assisted the Norfolks to clear Myobyingyi, and the officers of the brigade very freely acknowledged that the company's performance was impressive testimony to what a massed Vickers company could effect. A massed shoot is, moreover, the most difficult firing operation that machine-gunners can be called upon to perform; it is very seldom ordered, for the guns are controlled by a ground observer after the range and elevation have been calculated.

C Company were privileged to carry out the last mass shoot of the campaign. A party of Japanese had established themselves on an island in one of the great bends of the Myittinge river above Paleik. These men held their post with a courage and skill that should be remembered with honour. They were only thirty strong, but they had provided themselves with two heavy guns, an anti-aircraft gun and a sprinkling of automatic weapons. With this equipment, and thanks also to a marsh which surrounded their island, these brave men successfully resisted two full battalion attacks in which all C Company assisted with mass shoots, two dozen air strikes, and concentrated artillery and mortar fire. "Every available device was used," says the battalion diarist; "machine-guns, light and heavy cannon, rockets, fire bombs, small bombs and big bombs"; but the island was never carried nor were its defenders ever captured. They slipped away under cover of darkness after holding out for six entire days.

On March 23 the officers and men became aware that the battle for Mandalay was over. "On the 22nd there had been sporadic encounters on at least three places on the divisional front. On the 23rd there were no Japs anywhere. The battle was over, Mandalay was ours." When the struggle for Mandalay and the middle Irrawaddy was thus over, the 5th Brigade was in the southern suburbs of Mandalay and was in contact with the 19th Division; the 4th and 6th Brigades were rather huddled together in the Myittinge–Paleik area. The 20th Division were to the west of Kyaukse and were confronted by a far stiffer resistance than was being felt in the Myittinge area, which the Japanese had by then abandoned. This belated retirement—for the Japanese commander would have been wiser if he had ordered it earlier—was a consequence of what was happening farther south, of which a brief review should now be given.

When Meiktila was first captured, the Japanese Commander-in-Chief declined to regard a general withdrawal as inevitable and made a great exertion for its recovery. To do so, he assembled the 18th Division (less one regiment), which was drawn in from the northern front; one regiment of the 53rd Division was brought up from the reserve round Mandalay, and one regiment of the 33rd Division was pulled back from Pakokku. These formations attacked the town from the north, while the 49th Division, less one regiment, which had travelled all the way from Pegu in a fortnight, assaulted it from the south. Miscellaneous army units, medium artillery formations, and what was left of a tank regiment were thrown in. Simultaneously General Yamamoto was ordered to press north from Yenangyaung along both banks of the Irrawaddy, to recover the river crossings and to isolate our forces between Meiktila and the river.

The first counter-attacks against Meiktila were successful enough to be extremely dangerous, for the Japanese formations worked round to the west of the town and so isolated it that the tail of the 17th Division, the 255th Tank Brigade, and some 5,000 soft vehicles could not get in. Thereafter the Japanese made a tremendous effort to recover the airstrip which lies about two miles outside the town. The most stubborn, desperate struggle followed, and the issue was in doubt for several days.

The airborne brigade of the 5th Division was flown in on March 17. The Japanese were then getting dangerously near the airstrip, which was under artillery fire; nevertheless the American air commandos, who were bringing in the brigade, completed every sortie, although their machines were being destroyed on the ground after landing. Soon afterwards the Japanese captured the airfield. A small airstrip inside the town was still left, but it was only usable by light aircraft. All landings ceased, and supplies for the 17th Division had to be dropped, which entailed a heavy reduction in the daily deliveries. Replacements for casualties and reinforcements ceased to come in at all. Nevertheless, the struggle for the airstrip continued without respite.

Outside the town the 255th Brigade and the tail of the 7th Division pressed hard against the Japanese who were blocking Meiktila from the west, and during the last days of the month the struggle turned definitely in our favour; for on that day, the 255th Brigade captured a dominating hill to the west of the town, and the main airstrip was again in our hands. The hard fighting was still not over, for the Japanese guns still swept the airstrip; but the Japanese counterstroke had then spent its force.

Farther west General Yamamoto's advance against the bridgehead failed also; after a brief success against the 28th East African Brigade his troops were pressed back by the 7th Division on the left bank, and by the end of the month

THE JAPANESE ARMY IS BROKEN

his counter-attack had been brought to a standstill. It was at about this time that a Japanese staff officer noticed with sorrow that General Yamamoto, who, to give him his due, was a stout-hearted Japanese warrior, was lamentably impressed by the prowess of the British Army.

What was perhaps equally important was that while the struggle for Meiktila was fiercest, the 7th Division captured the river town of Myingyan. The town stands at the joining point of the Chindwin and the Irrawaddy and is the re-starting point for all traffic from the Kalewa area. "Its capture caused a sigh of relief from the administrative staff of the Army," writes General Slim, "and wharf construction and repair of railway bridges began feverishly almost under fire."[9]

At the end of the month of March, therefore, when it fell to General Slim to decide what operations should follow upon the capture of Mandalay, the whole course of the Irrawaddy from Katha to Chauk and the debouching points of the Chindwin and the Kabaw valleys were in our hands. The Japanese army was split into two rather huddled groups. Yamamoto still stood round Yenangyaung with the 153rd Regiment (49th Division), part of the 112th Regiment, the 72nd Independent Mixed Brigade, and the 54th Divisional Infantry Group. Drawn out along the railway between Myittha and the Thazi were fragments of the 33rd, the 53rd, the 18th, and the 49th Divisions; in the mountains to the east of the railway were parts of the 31st Division (the 2nd Division's opponent at the crossing of the Irrawaddy), and of the 15th Division. None of these divisions was any longer in fighting shape, and their recovery, though still possible if they were given time, was made difficult by their terrible losses in equipment, guns and stores. Still, if the Japanese had their difficulties we had ours, for the monsoon was then fast approaching.

* * * * *

[9] *14th Army Campaign 1944–1945*, p. 24.

General Slim had never swerved from his determination to capture Rangoon and to recover all Burma before the monsoon began, and even on March 18, when the struggle for Meiktila was still in the balance, he issued a preliminary instruction in which the advance on Rangoon was outlined.

At the beginning of April the monsoon was only seven weeks away, and the 14th Army was thus grouped: the three divisions of 33 Corps were pushing the scattered fragments of the 15th Japanese army into the foothills to the east of the Mandalay–Thazi road; the 5th and 17th Divisions and the 255th Tank Brigade were round Meiktila; the 7th Division was astride the Irrawaddy round Chauk.

The natural, indeed the only, approach routes to Rangoon were the Irrawaddy valley and the roads and railway to the north of Rangoon. The Army was obviously compelled to advance along both axes; and the road and railway route was chosen as the line of the principal advance. For it was found upon examination that the operation against Rangoon could only be brought to a successful issue by a force of about two and a half divisions, moving at a steady rate of about twelve miles a day. This could only be done by a mechanized force with a tolerable road beneath its vehicles.

Of the two corps available, the 4th Corps was the most suitably constituted for the advance along the railway line, and it was, moreover, concentrated fifty miles to the south of 33 Corps. In order, therefore, to redistribute the divisions of the Army in their new zones of operation, General Slim ordered what was then called the "Union Jack manœuvre", whereby the 2nd and 20th Divisions were moved from the north-eastern to the south-eastern part of the theatre in the Irrawaddy valley, while the 5th Division was brought from the river to the railway zone, where it was to participate in the advance south. The 7th Division remained in the valley and was transferred to the command of 33 Corps.

It was, however, deemed quite impossible to maintain all seven divisions of the Army between Mandalay and Rangoon after the monsoon began, and the 2nd and 36th were

CHAPTER X

D COMPANY, 2ND BATTALION: 1942—1945

IT will have been noticed that D Company has not once been mentioned in this long account of the 2nd Battalion's operations in Burma and the explanation (which will presumably have been suspected) is that the company was detached to the 29th Brigade in the early part of 1943. Thereafter the theatres in which D Company operated were separated from the places where the remainder of the battalion was fighting by hundreds of miles of mountain, paddy field, and jungle.

The 29th Brigade (1st Royal Scots Fusiliers, 2nd Royal Welch Fusiliers, 2nd East Lancashires and 2nd South Lancashires) had just returned from service in Madagascar when D Company was attached to it. During the year 1943, the 36th Division (Major-General F. Festing, D.S.O.) was formed out of the 29th and 72nd Brigades (6th South Wales Borderers, 9th Royal Sussex, 10th Gloucesters), and D Company, which was the only machine-gun unit in the area, came under divisional command.

As has been explained, the 36th Division was moved into the Arakan in the early part of 1944, and it there contributed to the severe fighting in the mountains north of Akyab. Because some records have been destroyed, others mislaid, and, more particularly, because only one copy (which is now so jealously guarded in London that it is virtually inaccesible), had been taken of many more, it is not possible to follow the fortunes of D Company in the Arakan from its own records. The Commanding Officer, Major Denis Bean, has, however, kept a memorial of the campaign, and of the part that his company played in it; and, as it is the only

IN THE ARAKAN

coherent account that at present exists it will be best to quote it *verbatim*.

Shortly after Christmas 1943, orders were received for 36th Division to take part in the thrust that was to be made by 15 Corps down the Mayu peninsula in the Arakan with the object of recapturing Akyab. 36th Division's role was to make a landing in the Akyab area to coincide with an advance by land from the north.

D Company moved with the remainder of the Division by rail from Poona to Calcutta, and, after two days, from there by sea to Chittagong, where they arrived on February 18, 1944. By this time the Japanese had made their counter-thrust during which they recaptured the Ngakeindauk pass across the Mayu range, cut off and surrounded the 7th Indian Division in the Kalapanzin valley and effectively disorganized the 15 Corps' advance southwards. Any attack from the sea to Akyab was clearly impossible, and 36th Division was committed on the land to help to restore the situation. D Company were placed under the command of 29th Brigade, and, moving by rail to Dohazari and thence by road to Bawli Bazaar, went into their first positions on the outskirts of that village. There they stayed a few days while the 29th Brigade took over various hilltop positions on the Mayu ridge from troops of 5th Indian Division and, by the end of February, D Company was distributed over the brigade area. The Japanese thrust had, by now, largely failed, the Ngakeindauk pass had been opened by the 26th Indian Division, and 7th Division had been relieved. Groups of enemy were still at large and were being gradually rounded up, or were escaping in small parties to the south. In fact, a rough front had been established which stretched from Maungdaw (now in British hands) across the Mayu range to the Kalapanzin valley where Buthidaung was still occupied by the enemy.

From then until the breaking of the monsoon in June, 36th Division were occupied in driving the enemy from one hilltop position to another, in capturing two tunnels through which the road from Maungdaw to Buthidaung runs, and later in occupying the Sinzweya defended area at the eastern end of the Ngakeindauk pass.

First contact, as far as D Company were concerned, was when a force of about 100 Japanese filtered through the forward positions and attacked 29th Brigade Headquarters on the night March 5/6.

Sergeant-Major Bailey gives the following account of this attack upon Brigade Headquarters:

The brigade had gone into laager in a deep depression which was surrounded on all sides by high forested hills. The company headquarters was just beside the brigade laager, and a path ran between the two. It was a fine night; the moon was up, but it was not possible to distinguish objects clearly as the shadows were very deep and dark. During the dark hours the Japanese were approaching our position along tracks that the wild animals had made for themselves in the jungle, but it was only about half-an-hour after midnight that we knew that the enemy were about, for grenades then began to fall in the company headquarters. We all stood to, but nothing happened for some time; then suddenly, the Japanese were firing on us from every direction. We all returned the fire as best we could, but as no Japanese could be seen we could only fire at the flashes. It was, moreover, impossible to fire into the path along which the Japanese were approaching as we should then have been shooting into the brigade laager. The firing continued until about half an hour before daybreak, and we knew that brigade headquarters was as severely engaged as we were from the sounds that came from their laager. Suddenly the firing died down, and in a few minutes everything was quiet; the Japanese were then making off. Their object in attacking the laager had been to get to the guns and disable them. They did get into the main gun position, where they killed several gunners; but the guns were so well concealed that the Japanese never found them and did no damage.

Major Bean adds, rather laconically, that D Company learned some very valuable lessons from this attack.

Later [he continues], D Company machine-guns supported every attack made by the 29th and 77th Brigades. The points at which D Company were particularly engaged were Hill 731, where they supported the Royal Welch Fusiliers; features 1301, where they supported the South Lancashires; and the Western Tunnel, where they were operating with the South Wales Borderers.

The chief feature of operations in the Arakan was the difficulty of the country, which consisted of open paddy fields in the valleys, and of very steep, vegetated hills. The latter were

D COMPANY WITHDRAWN

completely waterless until the breaking of the monsoon, and every drop had to be carried up very steep paths by mules.

The weather grew progressively hotter as the year advanced, and was at its worst in May with the thermometer near the hundred mark: the rising dampness of the approaching monsoon made matters worse.

At this point the 2nd South Lancashires left 29th Brigade to join the 5th Division.

By April, the Japanese offensive across the Chindwin was in full swing: 5th Indian Division had been with drawn from 15 Corps and flown to that front, and consequently, all hopes of capturing Akyab before the monsoon had to be abandoned. Operations of 15 Corps were limited to the recapture of Buthidaung and commanding positions along the road between there and Maungdaw. In parenthesis it should be added that the monsoon exerts great influence over the strategy of operations in the Arakan where 200 inches fall in four months.

Early in June 1944, 36th Division was withdrawn from the Arakan and was sent to Shillong in the Assam hills: D Company went with the division, and its service in the Arakan was over. General Festing was now ordered to place his division at the disposal of the American General Stilwell. It will, at this point, be necessary to make a brief retrospect of the operations upon which General Stilwell was engaged.

As has already been explained, General Stilwell was serving in Burma when the Japanese armies invaded the country; he evaded the pursuing Japanese and reached Assam at the head of a very small force through the mountain passes to the west of Homalin. Thereafter he established his headquarters at Ledo, where he trained an army that was predominantly Chinese though stiffened by a nucleus of American regulars. Also, and this proved of almost decisive importance later, General Stilwell and his staff organized a regular air supply service between Ledo and Yunnan, notwithstanding that the eastern chain of the Himalayas ran right across the route.

Now, although General stilwell's operations were always co-ordinated to those of the 14th Army farther west, the principal task that was allotted to his army was distinct: it was to re-enter northern Burma, and to re-open the road communications with China which had been severed by the Japanese invasion. The main China road ran from Mandalay to Lashio, where it bent to the north and reached the Chinese frontier at Mu-se in the Mao valley; thereafter it passed through Lungling and Paoshan. Properly speaking, therefore, the Burma road could only be re-opened when Mandalay was recovered; but there was an alternative. For Mu-se can be reached by a road from Bhamo on the Upper Irrawaddy; and Kyaukme, an important point on the Lashio–Mandalay road, is joined to Katha by a winding side-road that runs through Mabein, Myitson, Mong Mit, and Mogok. To sum up, therefore, if engineers and equipment were available to improve bad roads (and the Americans never lacked either), communications with China could be fully restored if the Irrawaddy valley between Twinnge and Bhamo, and the Shweli valley between Inywa and Mong Mit, were occupied, and if a Chinese force could capture Lashio and join hands with the army on the Irrawaddy and Shweli waterways. A Chinese army was allotted to this duty: it was advancing from the triangle Tengchung–Lungling–Paoshan, and was commanded by General Wei-li-Huang. The 36th Division and all its units and formations were now ordered to contribute to this project.

Ledo, where General Stilwell's army began its march south, is about 180 miles from the valley of the Upper Irrawaddy at Myitkina. A range of high mountains, called the Paktai bum, bars the way south, and when these are crossed through a high pass that is about forty-five miles long, the way forward still goes through the defiles of mountainous country for many miles. There is this slight alleviation, that after the Paktai bum is crossed the valleys between the mountain chains run roughly north and south, but as the roads down these valleys are mere jungle tracks, as all the impediments of a tropical forest and of a tropical jungle abound on either side of the track and across it, and as

GENERAL STILWELL'S OPERATIONS

marshes and swamps obliterate it frequently, the alleviation is not great.

General Stilwell determined to move against Myitkina by this route, and the American engineers undertook to turn the track along which the army advanced into a usable supply road, thirty feet wide and bordered by a clearing, so that the surface of the road should dry as quickly as possible after wet weather. The rate of General Stilwell's advance and the rate at which the road was completed behind him were about equal. Roads have been built over steeper gradients than the slopes of the Paktai bum, and across even more difficult country than the velleys between Shingbwiyang and Myitkina; but only a very great industrial country could deploy the stupendous quantities of equipment that were required for completing such a project, at such a speed. Nor should it be forgotten that as soon as a section of the road was completed, the supplies and ammunition of an army in the field were carried over it, and that maintaining the road was in consequence a heavy burden.

Three Chinese divisions and two American infantry regiments were under General Stilwell's immediate command, and he started his march south in December 1943; his route ran through Shinburiyang, Walaw bum, Shadazup and Kamaing. A north- and south-going mountain chain—the Kumon bum—lies to the eastward of this line of march, and the valley of the Mali runs at the foot of its eastern flanks. As the Japanese had used these parallel valleys with such good effect in the Arakan, General Stilwell passed a special force of Gurkhas and Kachin levies into the Mali valley. His immediate left was protected by a force under General Merrill, which marched along tracks and footpaths of the western slopes of the Kumon bum; the right and rear of the American army were protected by Brigadier Lentaigne's 111th Brigade, which was part of the airborne and air-supplied forces that had established themselves in the fortified camps of "Broadway", "Aberdeen", "Blackpool", and Chowringhee.

The natural obstacles to General Stilwell's advance were great; but it does not appear that the Japanese were holding the country to the north of Myitkina with forces strong enough to resist the American army. Shangbwiyang, which stands at the southern entrance to the pass over the Paktai bum, was occupied early in January; and on March 19 the Chinese and American troops reached the Mogaung valley at Shadazup. At present we do not know a great deal about General Stilwell's operation, save only that the Japanese resisted stiffly after Shadazup was passed; Kamaing was reached on May 17, and as the American troops closed in on it, General Merrill reported that he had crossed the Kumon bum by a difficult and little-known defile, and had reached Myitkina. The air strip was captured; but a Japanese garrison of about 1,500 men had fortified the approaches to the town and were preparing a desperate resistance.

When General Festing's Division was placed under General Stilwell's command the Chinese and American forces had, therefore, reached the upper waters of the Irrawaddy and were forcing the Japanese out of the lower reaches of its tributary, the Mogaung. In the western part of the Burma theatre the Japanese advance against Assam was at full flood: Kohima was isolated, the Japanese were closing in upon Imphal, and as our measures for holding and defeating them were only just set in motion, the issue was still doubtful. It was for this reason that General Stilwell was accepting a great hazard when he ordered the march to the south to be continued; for if the operations in Assam had turned out ill, very large forces would have been dispatched against him, and he would have been compelled to undertake a terrible retreat up the Mogaung valley, and thence to the defiles of the Paktai bum, with the Japanese swarming on his flanks and rear.

Owing to the loss and disappearance of so many documents and diaries, it is, unfortunately, not possible to trace the movements of the 36th Division during the months of May, June and July; but it is quite clear that General Festing

ADVANCE ALONG THE RAILWAY

was ready to begin his southerly advance in the first days of August, for during the first week of that month the two brigades were flown from Ledo to Myitkina airfield.[1] While they were being flown in, Myitkina was stormed. (See map 25, p. 483.) The Japanese garrison had resisted for seventy-eight days with a courage and tenacity that did them honour, for they were outnumbered, outgunned, and battered by air forces that bombed their positions without let or hindrance; and every officer and private in the garrison must have known that he would never be relieved. General Festing's orders were to advance southward along the railway that runs between Myitkina and Mandalay, and during the interval between when he was first ordered to join General Stilwell and the date when he was ready to execute his orders and to march south, our position in the whole theatre had considerably improved. First, Myitkina was a place of great value: before the war its airfield had been a station on the air route between India and China, and now that it was again in our hands supply planes to China were no longer forced to

---

[1] Major McEachran has, however, supplied the following information:

36 Division had remained in Arakan until June 5, but little of importance had happened because of the major events in the area of Kohima. The period at Shillong, from June 5 to the end of July, was spent in re-equipping and training for this new operation. 72 Brigade were flown in to Myitkina by July 27, and 28 Brigade by July 31; D Company was flown in by August 1. It required six sorties to fly the Company in, each aircraft taking 17 men, 900 lb. of stores, and 200 lb. of rations. No vehicles were, of course, taken. The Company were to have em-planed on July 31, but this was delayed because of bad weather. All the Company's heavy equipment, including the Vickers guns, had been taken to Dinjan for packing and subsequent air-drop after the Company arrived in the forward area. Actual em-planing arrangements were very smooth as H.Q. 36 Division had a staff on the air-strip and serials were called forward from the Transit Camp as aircraft became available. Take-off was at 08.00 hours for the first serial and by 11.00 hours the whole Company had been landed at Myitkina. The flight itself was uneventful, as all there was to see was miles of jungle relieved only occasionally by rivers and open patches of paddy. The reception arrangements at Myitkina were primitive, mainly because of the chaotic conditions in the town, but by courtesy of some U.S. troops, tea and food was procured for the Company. The Company spent that night in some discomfort on railway flats in the rain. The next day, August 2, D Company moved by train in two parts to join 72 Brigade in the area of Mogaung. Arrangements for the air-drop worked well, and heavy stores were dropped and recovered on August 3, not without some trouble from Chinese troops who thought that machine-gun spares were good to eat. The actual advance of 36 Division began on August 4.

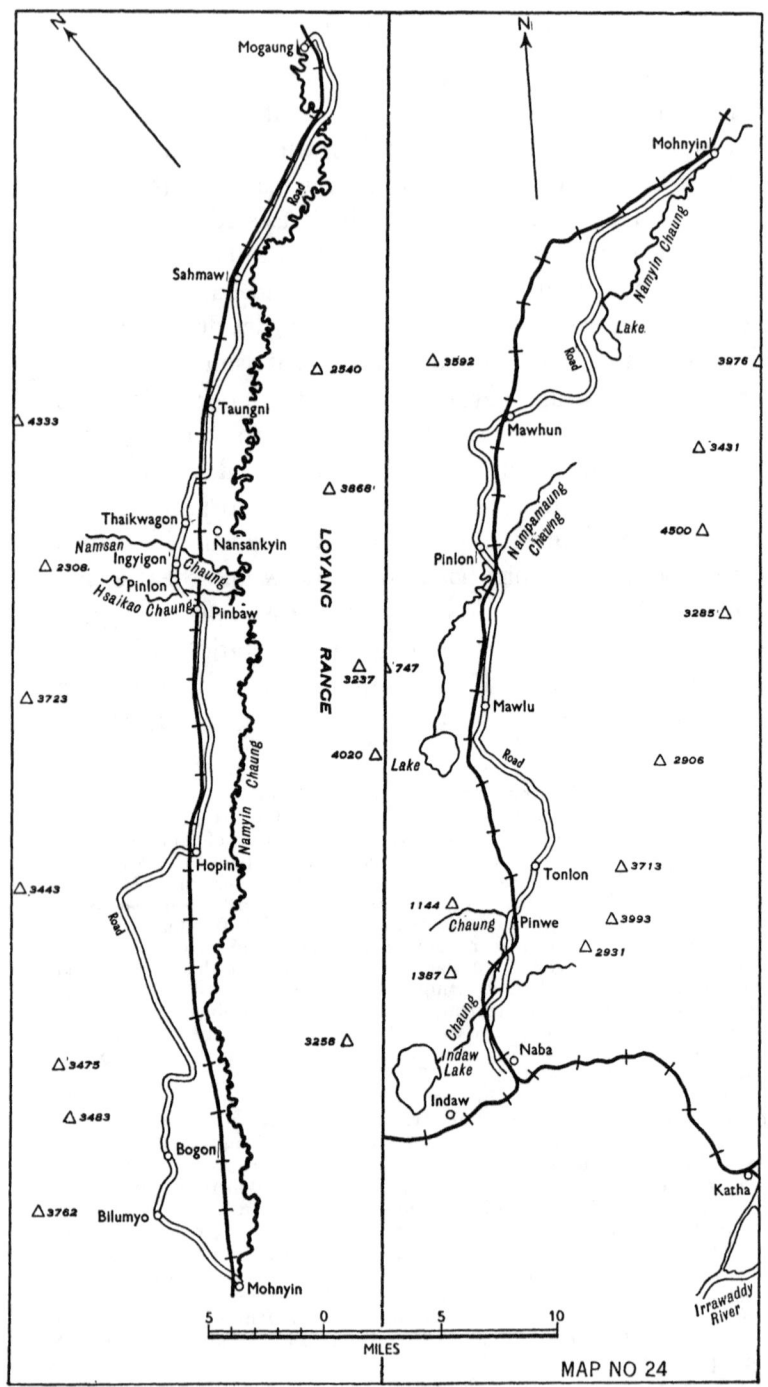

area for the attack was near the village of Thaikwagon, about ten miles down the line; the intervening country was traversed by a road along which no rapid movement was possible, and by what the brigade diary calls "a three-stage, jeep-operated railway track." Nevertheless, the preliminary movement was completed by nightfall on the 24th, and the attack was duly begun at dawn on the following morning.

The plan was to turn and break down the left of the Japanese position, which rested on the village of Ingyigon and the foothills to the west of it, and to press the centre of their line while this decisive manœuvre was being executed; the first part of the programme was entrusted to the East Lancashires and the Royal Scots Fusiliers; the second to the Welch Fusiliers.

It rained during the night (August 25/26) and as far as could be foreseen the day promised to be cloudy. This was much welcomed as experience had shown that casualties from heat-strokes were heavy when an operation was carried out in the full heat of the sun. At 01.00 hours two companies of the East Lancashires left their billets for a starting line in the hills to the west of Thaikwagon, and another company advanced against the Japanese position at a bridge on the main road between Thaikwagon and Ingyigon.

By 06.00 hours both these groups had made good progress: for the two companies were then on their objective—an enemy outpost in the foothills—while the third company had driven the Japanese from the road bridge and had captured it, though only by a narrow margin. The machine-gunners were here operating with the leading parties of the East Lancashires. Captain Baker and Captain McEachran crossed the bridge with their men without meeting any opposition; but when they were between fifty and a hundred yards beyond it, heavy firing broke out in their rear, and they saw that the Japanese had closed in on the bridge and that they themselves were cut off. Captain Baker states that they lay very low until things got better. By good fortune the following parties from the East Lancashires drove the

ONE OF D COMPANY'S GUNS IN ACTION DURING THE ATTACK ON INGYIGON, AUGUST 26, 1944

[Pte. H. Bowers, the No. 1 in this picture, was later killed in action and posthumously mentioned in dispatches for gallant conduct]

THE ADVANCE CONTINUED

Japanese off the road bridge after engaging them for about twenty minutes, and then secured it. In the centre and on the left the Scots Fusiliers entered the village of Nansankyin (which stands to the east of the railway), while another party from the same battalion made contact with the East Lancashires at the road bridge. As the East Lancashires on the right had advanced so fast, it was now decided that they should pass on towards Ingyigon without waiting for the left bank of the Namsan chaung to be cleared, as had originally been intended. Shortly after noon the East Lancashires were in the village of Ingyigon and were clearing the enemy out of the jungle-covered hills to the west of it.

The road to Pinbaw turns south after clearing Ingyigon, passes through another village called Pinlon, and then enters Pinbaw by a road bridge across the stream that flows past the northern and north-eastern sides of the settlement. The last Japanese position ran along this stream—the Hsaikao chaung—and Pinlon village was an outpost to it.

It was now decided to clear Pinlon before nightfall and the Royal Welch Fusiliers were ordered to do it.

The Welshmen passed through the East Lancashires at Ingyigon and started their attack just before four o'clock in the afternoon, after a severe bombardment by the artillery. There was a fierce struggle in the village, but at about six o'clock the place was cleared and the forward company occupied some high ground to the south of the settlement. The Welch Fusiliers now dug in for the night; the Japanese retired to their last position on the Hsaikao chaung, and all through the night they were calling out "Come and get us" for our forward pickets were quite close to them.

August 27. The ground between the two chaungs, over which the troops had been fighting all day was, for the most part, paddy fields and very boggy meadows. After Pinlon, a belt of jungle covers the ground to the north of Pinbaw, and the Hsaikao chaung meanders through it.

The road bridge outside Pinbaw appeared to be the chief buttress of the Japanese position, and at about 06.00 hours a company of the Royal Welch Fusiliers attacked it. The Welshmen pressed back an outpost of about twenty Japanese, but, soon afterwards, they came under a heavy fire from two machine-guns and a grenade discharger, and withdrew to the forward positions, where they asked for help from the gunners. After putting down a heavy concentration, the gunners ceased fire at 11.10 hours and the Welch Fusiliers again went forward and cleared the bridge. It seemed, indeed, that the way to Pinbaw was now open, but this was not so, for when the forward company pushed on through the jungle between the bridge and Pinbaw, the Japanese rallied and drove them back. Our troops were, therefore, ordered to dig in for the night, and it was arranged that the Royal Welch Fusiliers should make a quick, short advance on the following day; that the East Lancashires should pass through them and should then push on into Pinbaw. While this was being done, the Royal Scots Fusiliers were to probe the Japanese positions on the railway and to the east of it.

Shortly after noon the Royal Welch went forward, and it was soon clear that the Japanese were withdrawing, for there was no resistance. Soon after the advance began the Royal Scots reported that they had reconnoitred the enemy's position on their front and that the Japanese had left the place. The second attack by the East Lancashires was, therefore, not necessary, and during the afternoon our troops entered the village. They were in very good heart, for they knew that the Japanese had withdrawn because they had been outfought, and it was to be assumed that the enemy knew it also. It was some time before the Japanese again made a stand, and the division entered Hopin on September 8. A halt was called here, and Captain McEachran took the opportunity of overhauling the company's equipment and preparing for the next advance.[2] Additional equipment and armament

[2] At this time a number of officers and men of the camp of D Company were suffering from the climate. One of these was Major Bean, who was away from the Company for several weeks suffering from jungle sores.

were, indeed, beginning to be brought in along General Stilwell's Ledo road: a few more vehicles were available, while a battery of 3.7-inch howitzers and a 25-pounder had been salvaged from the Chindit base at "Broadway". During the halt at Hopin, important news came in from the Chinese army on the Salween; for, on September 21, General Wei-li-Huang's force stormed Tengchung, which is the road junction for the two routes to Bhamo. The northern and less frequented one runs along the gorges of the Nemti and the Tayingho; the southern one goes through the mountain city of Lungling and thence to the valley of the Nam Mu. On October 15 the division again moved on; the information that had then been collected and, as far as possible, verified was that the Japanese were likely to make another stand at Mohnyin, about seventeen miles farther on; and that, as a preparation, they had occupied the village of Bilumyo, which lies to the north-west of Mohnyin and blocks the main road to it.

The 29th Brigade led the advance, and D Company was attached to it. A Platoon operated with the Royal Welch Fusiliers, B Platoon with the East Lancashires, and C Platoon with the Royal Scots Fusiliers. The weather was cooler, and the rains were nearly over; the ground was still, however, waterlogged. The Brigade was, moreover, ordered to approach Mohnyin by night marches, and this proved very trying, for the road was still in the worst possible state, and the chaungs that traversed it so frequently were only to be crossed by makeshift bridges upon which the mules would never venture. The beasts had, therefore, to be led down a slippery, scrub-covered bank to the nearest ford, where they had to be persuaded or forced to wade the river; after this they had to be brought back to the road up another bank, which was generally as steep and as slippery as the first one. All this would have been slow and difficult in broad daylight: it was barely possible in darkness.

The plan for carrying Mohnyin was that the Royal Welch Fusiliers with A Platoon and the East Lancashires with B

Platoon were to assemble on either side of the village of Bogon and were to attack the Japanese outposts at Bilumyo, which was about two and a half miles to the south-west of the assembly area. After Bilumyo was carried Mohnyin was to be turned from the west while the Royal Scots advanced straight against it along the railway. The plan was duly executed; but the Japanese resisted so little that they were probably under orders to observe the British advance only. Bilumyo was captured on October 18, and Mohnyin was entered two days later. General Festing ordered the advance to be continued without pause or respite.

Up to Mohnyin, the division had been advancing along a cultivated valley; thereafter the face of the country changed, for the village fields ceased and the enormous trees of the Burma teak forests covered the land. The road and the railway track were, henceforward, mere forest clearings; moreover, the road left the railway at Mohnyin, and rejoined it about fifteen miles farther on at Mawlian.

The principal advance was made along the road while a company from the Royal Scots Fusiliers moved along the railway at about the same pace as the main column. The Japanese were still in no condition to resist; strong positions which they had abandoned were frequently found; occasionally a mine exploded; occasionally also, mortars and machine-guns opened on the head of the column, and in the approach to Mawhun the Scots Fusiliers and C Platoon deployed against what appeared to be a well-held position and made arrangements for shooting the enemy out on the following morning. On this, and on many similar occasions subsequently, however, the Japanese were only prepared to make what the battalion diarist calls a tip-and-run opposition, and the division moved slowly forward more impeded by Nature than by man. On October 28 Mawhun was occupied, and preparations were made for the move to Mawlu.

The Brigade advanced along the road and railway, and certainly the enemy checked our advance for several hours from some positions that they had prepared to the south of

THE MACHINE-GUNNERS' DIFFICULTIES

Pinlon, about six miles to the north of Mawlu. For it was here that the Royal Welch and a machine-gun section under Captain Baker were held up by severe fire from machine-guns, heavy and light, while the East Lancashires and another machine-gun section were brought to a stand on the road near by. This was the stiffest opposition since Mohnyin was captured, but it proved to be the resistance of a withdrawing rearguard, and Mawlu was entered on November 1. The company were now finding it difficult to use their Vickers machine-guns effectively in the forest through which the division was advancing. Enemy positions and our own troops were alike invisible at quite short distances, and as the Japanese knew from which direction our troops were approaching, and when to expect them, this gave their machine-gunners the advantage. The severe burst of fire that was directed against Captain Baker's men when they were advancing along the railway practically wiped out a gun team. As against this, when a bunker position could be located, sustained and rapid machine-gun fire, at the short ranges that the teak forest imposed, proved very effective.

The division remained round Mawlu for eight days, and its condition was appreciably improved by reinforcements and additional supplies, and of the general state of affairs Major Bean writes thus:

> Rations continued to be excellent, the cigarette supply was adequate and the mail supply, both out and in, was functioning smoothly. Casualties were evacuated by light planes from forward air strips, although it was not always possible to find clearings of sufficient size. This resulted in casualties having to undergo considerable discomfort in being moved, either by bearer party or jeep ambulance, for considerable distances over bad roads. Despite all this, however, the work of the field ambulances was speedy and efficient, and, in the circumstances, evacuation was to hospitals at Myitkina and farther north into Assam.[3]

[3] Major McEachran has supplied the following additional details:
For the first six weeks of the operation, D Company, together with the rest of the division, had existed on American "K" rations, the monotony of which was infrequently relieved by air-drops of "bully" and dehydrated

Meanwhile, the Chinese on the Salween front had broken down another gateway into eastern Burma, for General Wei-li-Huang was now across the main road to Bhamo, at Lungling. Also, the moment when the British would burst in from the Chindwin front was approaching, as 4 Corps headquarters was opened at Imphal, and preparations for the advance on Pinlebu were being pushed on.

The march south began again on November 9. The 72nd Brigade was ordered to lead the advance, and Major Bean allotted A Platoon to the 6th South Wales Borderers and C Platoon to the 9th Royal Sussex. B Platoon was attached to the Royal Scots Fusiliers, who remained in the Mawlu area, which the 29th Brigade were to make into a firm base for the time being. When the advance began the weather was much better, for the days were fine and the nights cool. The tracks were drying up, and digging-in was fairly easy; the company was now well practised in making itself invisible whenever and wherever a halt was called for the night. About a dozen mules were allotted to each platoon; guns and ammunition were, however, manhandled whenever contact was expected; a jeep and a trailer were allotted to the headquarters section of the company.

The section of the railway that the Japanese had abandoned was not absolutely essential to any operation upon which they were then engaged. When our troops marched out of Mawlu, however, they were threatening positions that no enemy would yield without a struggle. For Katha is a tolerably well-equipped river port on the Irrawaddy, and Naba is the railway junction through which the land-borne

---

potatoes. After six weeks, however, the rations steadily became more human, and fresh bread, vegetables, etc., became available. It was not until October that the first regular supplies of " Compo " pack began to arrive, but from this date onwards the rations maintained a very high standard, considering that every single item was air-dropped. Fresh meat was rarely available as supplies depended upon the finding of stray bullocks which were either locally purchased or impounded. There was generally an adequate canteen supply service situated thirty to forty miles in the rear, from which the necessities of life (and some luxuries) could be bought. It was necessary, of course, for stores to be bought in bulk and brought forward by Company H.Q. for re-sale to platoons.

that they were only two miles beyond their starting point by the late afternoon. In the valley the bitter struggle between our troops and the enemy continued with varying fortune. The 9th Royal Sussex certainly fought themselves clear of the enemy who had surrounded them on the previous day and moved into Tonlon, but the Japanese infiltrated a party between the brigade headquarters and the South Wales Borderers; and when the Brigade Commander tried to reach the Borderers (Captain McEachran was accompanying him) they ran into an ambush and only extricated themselves after twenty minutes of hard fighting.

November 16. Difficulties continued to beset the 10th Gloucesters, for the mountain flank along which they were striving to move forward was so steep that they made no progress at all; parties were sent forward to find the east- and west-going track into Pinwe, which the battalion was striving to reach, and as the mules were virtually useless in such country most of them were sent back. B Platoon were thenceforward carrying their guns, although a few mules were kept for the reserve ammunition. In the valley the Japanese reached the main road at a point about a mile to the south of Tonlon, and thus drove a wedge between the Royal Sussex at Tonlon, and the South Wales Borderers, who were now isolated.

November 17. The Royal Sussex moved out of Tonlon and attacked the road block that the Japanese had established between them and the South Wales Borderers, but they could not drive the enemy from it and were themselves beaten back. When this attack was repulsed the position of the South Wales Borderers was critical, for they had only enough food and ammunition for another day's fighting. The chances that the flanking move in the mountain would oblige the enemy to abandon his positions on the railway and along the chaung were now very doubtful. After making every possible exertion, the 10th Gloucesters reached a spur from which Pinwe might be attacked on the following day, but the move along the mountainsides had been so slow, that it was to be assumed that the Japanese were well apprised of the threat, and had made whatever preparations were necessary for meeting it. The plan for the following day was, therefore, that the Japanese road block should be attacked from both sides, by the 9th Royal Sussex working southwards from Tonlon, and by the South Wales Borderers, who were to break out of their perimeter to join them.

November 18. The two battalions started their attack upon the road block soon after eight o'clock, and after some hours of desperate fighting the Japanese were forced off the road. Nevertheless they established themselves fifty yards away from it, and from this position they endeavoured to keep the road under fire and to make it impassable. Captain McEachran of D Company now took command of a supply column and conducted it into the position held by the South Wales Borderers in defiance of the Japanese fire. Most of the column reached the South Wales Borderers safely, but our positions and those of the Japanese were so interlocked that the leading van passed right through the Borderers into the Japanese lines. The van was, of necessity, abandoned, but as soon as the Borderers were certain where it was they attacked, reached the van and burned all the stores in it. The attack was, indeed, so fiercely pressed that the Japanese were forced out of some positions that they had held from the beginning of the struggle. The relief to the South Wales Borderers was only just in time; for when Captain McEachran reached A Platoon, he found that they had only one belt of ammunition per gun. A few minutes after Captain Baker received the extra ammunition for his platoon, he was wounded and evacuated.

Nevertheless, the deadlock on the chaung and the railway track was still unresolved, and the flanking movement from the mountains was, on this day, brought to nothing. After overcoming all the obstacles that precipices and a tropical forest had placed along the line of their advance, the 10th Gloucesters debouched from the hills and reached a point which they believed to be within two hundred yards of the railway track, but which, in point of fact, was a great deal farther away from it. Here they were brought to a standstill in front of well-prepared and well-concealed positions. After exerting what pressure they could, and failing to make any impression at all upon the Japanese on their front, the Gloucesters broke off and retired to their assembly position in the hills, and were ordered to come right back into Tonlon on the next day.

November 19–21. The Japanese were still barring the way, and every attempt to dislodge them had failed, and the day was spent in regrouping the battalion. The South Wales Borderers were taken out of the forward position that they had held hitherto and were brought into Tonlon. The Royal Sussex sent two companies on to that part of the main road where the Japanese had previously established the road block that separated the two battalions, and the Royal Scots relieved the Royal Sussex on the railway. The 10th Gloucesters came into Tonlon and were laagered just to the south of the village; they were warned that they would deliver the next attack against the Japanese positions on the chaung. The next two days were spent patrolling, resting, and preparing.

November 22–23. The Gloucesters, with A Platoon attached to them, passed through the Royal Sussex position and attacked the Japanese with great spirit after a carefully directed bombardment. They reached the chaung and crossed it, but were brought to a standstill on the farther bank. A Platoon took up a position on their left flank, and the Royal Sussex moved forward to support them; but the deadlock was as rigid as ever at the end of the day's fighting, and on the day following, the patrols from the Gloucesters and the Royal Sussex revealed a strong and well-sited network of positions on either side of the road. A party of the Japanese infiltrated between the Gloucesters and the Royal Sussex and were dealt with, though not easily; and all through the day Japanese snipers in the trees galled the Gloucesters and their patrols.

November 24. The Royal Sussex with B Platoon attacked

through the small bridgehead that the Gloucesters had established on the 22nd, and after advancing a little way found that they were held up and isolated from the Gloucesters behind them, as the Japanese had worked round their flanks. The Royal Sussex prepared a defended perimeter, and, according to the Battalion diarist, they were "reasonably unmolested during the night."

General Festing now decided to relieve the 72nd Brigade in the forward area and to renew the attacks upon the Japanese positions, which were now known to extend from a position 300 yards east of the road to the railway and beyond it; by November 26 the relief was completed. The 9th Royal Sussex were extricated and were brought back into reserve. The position to which they had advanced was not reoccupied, and the 1st Royal Scots Fusiliers relieved the Gloucesters in the bridgehead over the chaung. The 2nd East Lancashires came into position behind the Royal Scots.

D Company was not relieved and remained in the forward area. A and B Sections came under the Royal Scots: C Section was attached to the Royal Welch Fusiliers, who were assembled across the railway line a little distance behind the forward battalion. D Company was now three officers and ninety-four men strong, and A Section was brought up to platoon strength.

When these reliefs were completed the Royal Scots Fusiliers patrol in the forward area discovered, in quick succession, that the Japanese had evacuated their bunkers, and that they had withdrawn from Pinwe. The Royal Welch Fusiliers and the Royal Scots Fusiliers occupied the railway station of the village during the 30th.

Why the Japanese decided to withdraw is not known, for they had successfully repulsed every attack that had been launched against them, and, as it had proved impossible to use our greater numbers for a flanking movement, there was every likelihood that the enemy would have resisted the 29th Brigade as successfully as they had resisted the 72nd. Possibly they had suffered more severely than we know from our batterings. Possibly, also, the pressure of General Wei-li-Huang's army on the Salween front and the opening moves of our army on the Chindwin front were obliging the Japanese command to call in their detachments and to re-group; for by this time it must have been apparent at Japanese headquarters that we were massing against them in the western part of the theatre. The 19th Division had crossed the Chindwin between Paungbyin and Wetkauk, and was advancing at a great pace towards Sinlamaung and Pinlebu, and some information about the great movements in the Kawbaw valley must have been reaching the Japanese high command.

Nevertheless, it must be accounted a fine feat of arms that this Japanese detachment in Pinwe should have held its positions on the chaung for seventeen whole days and should have defied our efforts to expel it. Let it be granted that the narrow, deeply forested valley where the Japanese made their stand conferred great advantages on the defending side, as it obliged the attackers to deploy on a narrow front that could not be enlarged; but even when this is admitted, it has to be admitted also that only very good soldiers would have clung as tenaciously to their positions as the Japanese did.

The patrols that were at once sent forward after Pinwe was occupied reported that the enemy were in full retreat, and the three towns that were covered from Pinwe—Indaw, Naba Junction, and Katha—were entered without incident (December 7–12).

The whole area had been fought over by the Chindits some months previously, and the state of the two towns was an indication that things were going ill with the Japanese. Both places were wrecked, and were beyond all description filthy; and although the Japanese had occupied them for months, unburied and decaying corpses still lay in the streets and alleys, and the stench of putrefaction was insufferable. At Katha, Major Bean disinfected what remained of the town by turning it into a crematorium, and by setting it alight with phosphorous bombs. It was at Katha, moreover, that

CONTACT WITH THE GHURKAS

the men were astounded to see what appeared, at first sight, to be Japanese soldiers lying prostrate or sitting propped up against a wall; and to find, upon approaching, that these figures were complete sets of uniforms which no longer covered a human being. The ants had consumed all: flesh, sinews, hair and bones; and when the posture of some of these empty uniforms was studied, it seemed as though the ants had begun to devour their occupants before they were dead. As this dreadful squalor had been allowed to accumulate, it was to be inferred that the Japanese had grown listless and indifferent.

While the Division was halted between Indaw and Katha it was reinforced by 26th Indian Brigade (2nd Buffs, 1/1st Ghurkas, 1/19th Hyderabads, 2/8th Punjabis), and General Festing was ordered to leave the railway corridor and to operate to the east of the Irrawaddy towards the country where General Wei-li-Huang's army was expected to debouch. The 72nd and 26th Brigades and the Divisional Headquarters were to cross at Katha and were then to advance along the eastern bank of the Shweli river towards Mabein and Myitson. The 29th Brigade, with D Company attached, was to descend the Irrawaddy as far as Tigyaing, was to cross it at that place, and then, after clearing the eastern bank of the Irrawaddy as far as Twinnge, was to operate eastwards towards Mong Mit.

Just before the advance to Tigyaing began, patrols from the Royal Scots Fusiliers made contact with the 1/6th Ghurkas of the 19th Division near Indaw, and it encouraged the officers and men to see this outward and visible sign of the force that was closing in upon the heart of the Japanese position farther south. This, moreover, did not stand alone, for the 20th Division was now across the Chindwin at Mawleik, and the 11th East African Division had secured the crossing at Kalewa. These particulars about the irruption from the west were, of necessity, concealed from the troops of the 36th Division, for all the moves on the Chindwin front were covered by as dense a fog of secrecy as could be spread. The Japanese generals can, however, have entertained no doubts that a period of trial was approaching.

The 9th Royal Sussex of the 72nd Brigade crossed the Irrawaddy at Katha on December 14, and were the first British troops to make a foothold on the eastern bank of the great river. Two days later the 2nd Division, with the other three companies of the Manchesters, began to cross the Chindwin at Kalewa: the advance against Central Burma was now an accomplished fact; for in addition to this closing in from the north and west, General Wei-li-Huang was pressing on from Lungling, and had reached Namhkan.

The 29th Brigade began their advance against Tigyaing on December 17. It lasted a week and was uneventful: a few very poor mines were discovered and exploded, but the Japanese commander was now drawing in all his outlying detachments, and this part of the Irrawaddy valley was virtually abandoned. The 29th Brigade entered Tigyaing on December 23, and it was at Tigyaing that Christmas Day was celebrated with scrupulous regard to tradition. Live geese, ducks, chickens, pigs, and Christmas puddings, were dropped from Dakotas. The Christmas dinner was served to the men by the officers and sergeants in obedience to the ancient custom of the British services that on this occasion the first shall be last and the last first. D Company spent the day in a Burmese house that overlooked the river, and the dinner was followed by a concert. These European and Christian celebrations were a strange intrusion of the West upon the East, for Tigyaing is little but an assembly of Budhist temples.

The Japanese did not oppose the crossing of the 29th Brigade; had they done so the passage would have been difficult, for only one large raft with two outboard motors and a smaller raft on native canoes could be secured for the heavy equipment; it was upon these that the guns of an entire field regiment of artillery, the 100 vehicles of an Indian G.P.T. company, all the brigade motor transport, and the field ambulance were carried across. Nevertheless, the entire

CPL. MOUNTAIN OF D COMPANY (WHO WAS WOUNDED SHORTLY AFTERWARDS) POINTING OUT HIS DEFENSIVE POSITION TO MAJ.-GENERAL FESTING, THE DIVISIONAL COMMANDER, NEAR HOPIN

Left to right—Ptes. Walls, Shattock, Whitehead, and Newton, Cpl. Mountain and General Festing

was then at the little hamlet of Pathin, to the north of the road. "This is the first time," wrote the company's diarist, "that the whole company has been on one perimeter since the operation began."

D Company was now attached to the 26th Indian Brigade, and as it is probable that its war diary and the documents that are supplementary to the war diary, have been put with the records of the Indian Brigade, it is not possible to follow the fortunes of the company closely beyond this point. Japanese resistance in this part of Burma was, however, at an end. The brigade was not opposed in the defiles between Mong Mit and Mogok, where a well-equipped, well-prepared enemy could have blocked the advance almost indefinitely, for the track just clung to the mountain flanks, and was for many miles so narrow that a single transport vehicle occupied its entire breadth. At Kyaukme the brigade joined hands with the American forces that were advancing along the road from Lashio, and thereafter the move southward was little but an ordinary march from town to town and from village to village. D Company was flown out to Calcutta from the air strip at Maymyo. By this time the Japanese position was fast becoming desperate, and the enemy commander-in-chief no longer had any troops to spare for operations in the northern part of the theatre. Meiktila, the vital organ of the Japanese position in Burma, was in our hands; the 19th Division had cleared the eastern bank of the Irrawaddy as far as Mandalay Hill; the 2nd Division was on the south bank and was advancing fast towards the southern communications of the Mandalay garrison.

CHAPTER XI

by BRIGADIER T. B. L. CHURCHILL, C.B.E., M.C.

PART 1

THE 1ST AND 2ND BATTALIONS FROM 1945 UNTIL AMALGAMATION IN 1948

THE 1ST BATTALION

THE 1st Battalion ended the war at Hamburg, where they were employed in accepting the surrender of many thousands of members of the German armed forces and disarming them, and it was in this town that they celebrated V.E. Day. Not long afterwards, however, they were moved to Schleswig-Holstein, where they were engaged in disarming the German army which was moving south from Denmark, and sending it on to collecting areas in the peninsulas on the west coast, where arrangements had to be made to feed and accommodate the personnel.

The next move was to Essen, where the battalion relieved a U.S. Parachute Regiment; but their stay in this heavily bombed and destroyed town was of short duration, for by November 1945 they were at Seesen on the verge of the Hartz mountains, and had left the 53rd Division, with which they had fought so long, and had joined the 5th Division.

Seesen lies to the south-east of Hanover in lovely country with opportunities for duck, deer and pig shooting, and the battalion enjoyed its first five months during which it was concentrated in the town. A stable of fifteen horses was established with German grooms, eight of the horses having been hacked some 200 miles from Essen when the battalion moved.

In March 1946, Lieutenant-Colonel E. F. Woolsey, D.S.O., succeeded Lieutenant-Colonel H. B. D. Crozier, D.S.O., as Commanding Officer, and the latter took up an appointment as an instructor at the School of Infantry at Warminster. About the same time the battalion was split up into company detachments in the countryside, Battalion Headquarters being established at Schloss Soder, fifteen miles south-east of Hildesheim. The companies were dispersed over a wide area, A Company being at Bavenstedt, B Company at Bad Salzdetfurth, C Company at Hildesheim, and D Company at Peine, near Brunswick. The companies were engaged in finding guards on dumps and stores and in patrolling the area. A Company was responsible for guarding a salt-mine which had been filled with ammunition of every description. The company billets were for the most part good. B Company at Bad Salzdetfurth was established in a particularly attractive village in the Hartz mountains, and although the men of all companies were on duty for long hours, they were well content with their station.

In the summer of 1946 the battalion moved yet again, but this time they were to remain in their new station for eighteen months. Battalion Headquarters, Headquarter Company, and D Company moved to an aerodrome just outside the town of Goslar where they were accommodated in excellent German air force barracks. A Company went to Braunlage and B Company to Bad Satcha, both pretty German spas in the Hartz mountains, enjoying unlimited facilities for skiing and skating in winter, though liable to be cut off from time to time by heavy falls of snow. C Company was sent to the School of Infantry at Warminster as the machine-gun demonstration company, and a platoon of mortars from D Company went with them. It will thus be seen that the battalion was widely scattered, and the Commanding Officer found it difficult to visit all companies frequently, especially in winter.

If the battalion's last station was considered a good one by the men, this new one was voted even better. It was indeed much coveted as a station by troops in the British Army of the Rhine, since the localities had been untouched by the war, the scenery was beautiful, and the climate healthy. The countryside consisted of pine forests, mountain streams, waterfalls, and upland meadows, and the views were magnificent. The training that could be carried out was restricted owing to the heavy duties that had to be performed, and consequently it was concentrated on specialists such as signallers, M.T. drivers and potential N.C.O.s.

The duties performed by the battalion at this time included the patrolling of the whole area by day and by night to discover whether crimes had been committed, and, if so, to ensure by contact with Burgomasters and other officials that investigations were proceeding; the checking of black market activities, especially by "snap" checks of vehicles at night; the guarding of dumps and stores, though this duty was slowly being taken over by allied police under Military Government control; and finally, the patrolling of seventy kilometres of frontier between the British and the Russian zones, and the checking up on reports of illegal frontier crossings. As most of the frontier was covered with thick pine-forest, it was inevitable that a good deal of illegal traffic proceeded.

In June 1946 Lieutenant-Colonel C. L. Archdale succeeded Lieutenant-Colonel E. F. Woolsey, D.S.O., as Commanding Officer of the battalion, and this change in command constituted the return to the peacetime system of substantive command.

It was also in the summer of 1946 that "Operation Union" was put into effect, under which the wives of officers and men were brought out from England to join their husbands in Germany, and this added to the attractions of an already attractive station, especially since life in England at this time was still cold and cheerless as a result of the war.

The administration and training of the battalion at this time presented certain problems. A large number of men, and this, of course, included N.C.O.s, were being released to civil life every month, and the continual turn-over of full-rank instructors made the maintenance of continuity very difficult. Reinforcements arriving were all infantry-trained, and so had to be instructed in machine-gun duties.

In September the battalion was visited by Lieutenant-General Sir Richard McCreary, the Commander-in-Chief, and in the following month by Lieutenant-General G. I. Thomas, the Corps Commander. At this time, too, the Bishop of London paid a visit to the troops and preached at a number of services.

In the winter of 1946–47 the officers and men were encouraged to take up skiing, and battalion and company centres were opened to give instruction under German ski instructors. The companies in the Hartz mountains were particularly well situated for this form of exercise. In early 1947 C Company returned from Warminster, and they brought with them the Colours and the Officers' and Sergeants' Mess silver. In the early spring a Lumber Group was formed from a company from each of the four battalions in the district, with the object of providing timber for export to the United Kingdom to assist the building trade. The machine-gun companies went to camp in turn during the spring.

In December 1947 the battalion was recalled to England, and on its arrival it was greeted with a telegram from Her Majesty the Queen:

To the Officer Commanding.
I extend my warm greetings to you and to all ranks of the 1st Battalion on your return to this country.
The battalion has had a fine record in action overseas. I hope each one of you will now enjoy a happy reunion with his family and friends at home, and I wish you all a happy Christmas.
ELIZABETH R., Colonel-in-Chief.

Battalion Headquarters, Headquarter Company, and A and B Companies were now stationed at Maghull, and C and D Companies at Formby, both these places being near

Liverpool. It was here that orders were received that the battalion was to return once more to the infantry role, and consequently all its energies were taken up in reconverting its officers and other ranks. Many were dispatched on courses, a number of battalion cadres were formed, and many stores had to be handed in and a new issue, appropriate to an infantry battalion, drawn.

It seems inevitable that as soon as a major war ends the machine-gun units which have been built up and trained in the war must be done away with, perhaps for reasons of economy or perhaps because the gun itself is regarded as being obsolete. Certainly it is true that a machine-gun battalion is less adaptable to garrison duties or those of imperial policing than an infantry battalion, and so might be accounted less economical in a peacetime army (though he would be a bold man who predicted that the present peace would last for twenty-one years, as did the last one). As to the obsolescence of the gun, it is perhaps difficult for the designers and small arms enthusiasts of the atom age to accept the fact that a gun basically designed half a century ago still retains its pre-eminence on the modern battlefield. Time will show if its usefulness is ended; but perhaps the men of the regiment who fought in World War II may be allowed to record their scepticism of this proposition, for not only do they know the capabilities of the gun and the requirements of fire support better than most, but they have seen the same gun abolished and then brought back so often before.

In May 1948 the War Office issued instructions that the amalgamation of the 1st and 2nd Battalions of the Manchester Regiment was to take place immediately, and in consequence the title of the 1st Battalion was changed to " 1st Battalion the Manchester Regiment (63rd/96th) ".

The 2nd Battalion

In April 1945 the 2nd Battalion was flown out of Burma to Calcutta, where it was earmarked for a seaborne operation against Rangoon, but these plans were never put into practice because the Imperial Japanese Army, having been fought to a standstill, surrendered. With the end of the war came orders for the battalion to move to Secunderabad, Deccan (where it had served before from 1930 to 1932), but its stay this time was to be a short one. In a matter of weeks it was moved again, this time to Poona, and in October Lieutenant-Colonel B. F. G. Blood of the Royal Northumberland Fusiliers succeeded Lieutenant-Colonel R. King-Clark, M.C., as Commanding Officer.

The release of men to civil life seriously reduced the numbers of the battalion during its period of service in Poona, and indeed during the remainder of its time in India its strength was seldom to exceed 400 rank and file. It received a large draft in November 1945, but these men were all from infantry regiments and had to be trained as machine-gunners. The problem of maintaining sufficient N.C.O.s as instructors was a real one, for no sooner had a corporal been trained sufficiently to impart instruction than it was time for him to be held in readiness for embarkation for release.

In January 1946 the battalion took part in a searchlight tattoo on Poona racecourse, and shortly afterwards it took its part in the Victory Parade. In March, however, orders were received for another move.

The battalion's new station was a camp on the banks of Lake Kharakvasla, and the whole battalion regarded it as an improvement on their quarters in Poona. During its stay, however, its numbers became very reduced, and it was difficult to perform essential duties and at the same time achieve any real training. However, only two months later it was ordered to move to Arkonam, sixty miles west of Madras, and the battalion entrained on May 10. It now had a new Commanding Officer, for Lieutenant-Colonel J. H. Orgill had arrived to take over command from Lieutenant-Colonel Blood on May 2, as the substantive C.O.

At Arkonam the battalion took over an Air Trooping

SERVICE IN INDIA

Transit Camp which offered quite good accommodation and was equipped with two cinemas. There were, however, a number of Internal Defence commitments to be undertaken in the new station, and it was difficult to carry out these tasks owing to the battalion's organization as a machine-gun battalion and the reduced number of men with the unit.

Just over one month later the sorely tried 2nd Battalion found itself faced with yet another move, the sixth in fourteen months. The Headquarters and B Company were next stationed in Fort St. George, Madras, while A and C Companies moved to Saidapet, six miles outside Madras. Owing to the climate, the companies changed their locations in rotation, spending one month in the town and two months at Saidapet. On the whole the men preferred the amenities of Madras to their last station at Arkonam, for the battalion was, as always, composed of more than 90 per cent of townsmen, and they felt less isolated.

In December the Colours arrived in India, having been sent out from the depot, and to mark their arrival a parade was held at which the Commander of the Madras Area took the salute. Internal Defence duties continued to be required and, in addition, machine-gun training was carried on so far as the numbers in the battalion permitted. In November Lieutenant-General Sir Arthur Smith, the General Officer Commanding-in-Chief Southern Command, visited the battalion, and in January 1947 inspections were carried out by Field-Marshal Sir Claud Auchinleck, the Commander-in-Chief, and by General Sir Richard O'Connor, the Adjutant-General to the Forces, who was paying a visit to India.

In January 1947 orders were received that the battalion was to reconvert to an infantry battalion, and while this process was slowly proceeding intimation arrived that another move was pending: in May, the unit was to move to Bangalore to join the 72nd British Brigade Group. In due course the move was completed, but no sooner was it over than order and counter-order followed each other in quick succession, first ordering that the battalion was to be put into "suspended animation" in June, and then conveying a cancellation but leaving the veiled impression that suspension was nevertheless well within the realms of possibility. It was while the battalion was in this unsettled state that it was announced that India was to be granted her independence on August 15th, and that British troops were therefore to leave India before that date. By this time the battalion was so low in numbers that two companies had been disbanded, and the remaining weeks in India were spent in packing up equipment, handing in stores, closing accounts, and preparing for the final audit before leaving.

The battalion left Bangalore on September 24 and moved to Kalyan Transit Camp near Bombay; and it sailed from Bombay on October 9, 1947, in the troopship *Franconia*. It was almost sixty-five years to the day since the 2nd Battalion first landed at Bombay from H.M.S. *Euphrates* and the steamship *Adjutant* on October 30 and November 3, 1882.

The *Franconia* reached Liverpool on October 30, 1947, and the Colonel of the Regiment, Major-General C. D. Moorhead, C.B., D.S.O., M.C., went on board by launch to welcome the battalion and to read to them the following telegram:

> Please convey to the officers and men of the 2nd Battalion the Manchester Regiment my warm greetings on their return home. I wish them all a pleasant leave and a happy reunion with their families and I look forward to meeting them at a regimental gathering in the future.
>
> ELIZABETH R., Colonel-in-Chief.

The men disembarked on the following day and proceeded to Fort Crosby, near Liverpool, where they were housed in a wartime camp; and it was here that the definite news, not by now altogether unexpected, was received that, owing to a further reduction in the number of infantry battalions which would be required in the future order of battle, the 2nd Battalion of the Manchester Regiment was one of many which would shortly be placed in "token cadre form" and kept in being at regimental depots.

were on their way to receive the signal honour of being inspected by the King, who last December became Colonel-in-Chief of the Regiment.

It is many years since such a parade was held before the King at the Palace on his express invitation. This was the first military ceremony that the King has attended since his illness.

The 140 officers and non-commissioned officers who were there with the regimental band heard from the King's lips memorable praise of the "noble record of service and sacrifice" of the Manchesters in the wars. Well might Colonel Freyberg, the famous V.C., speak in his reply of the "peculiar pride" which the regiment felt today.

Early this bright spring morning the contingent paraded at the Wellington Barracks for their short march across the great open space in front of the Palace. The officers and non-commissioned officers of the 1st Battalion had come up on Tuesday from their station at Shorncliffe and were joined at the barracks by the representatives of the depot and territorial battalions from Lancashire.

As a matter of military history the presence of the officers and non-commissioned officers of the territorial battalions with the service battalions of a regiment on such a parade was a remarkable, perhaps an unprecedented, thing. The King in his speech expressed especial pleasure at their inclusion.

When, at about 10.30, the Manchesters marched across to the Palace there was already a big muster of sightseers. Among them were some scores of old comrades who had come up with the rest of the regiment from Manchester. Owing to practical difficulties it had been found impossible to include ex-servicemen in the parade, but they were there outside the railings and on the steps of the Victoria Memorial to cheer the men in khaki as they went by.

At the head of the contingent was Colonel Freyberg, commanding the 1st Battalion and, in the absence of General Lawrence, in charge of the parade. Medals won in the Great War glittered on the tunics of all the men in the parade: most of them wore three; one or two wore the Victoria Cross.

So, all spick and span, with the band in front, the drum sergeant-major proudly flourishing his staff, and with the drummers twirling their sticks in the air, the detachment went smartly along. The scarlet sashes of the non-commissioned officers made a jolly show of colour against the khaki. London has grown unaccustomed since the war to the sight of soldiers

H.M. KING GEORGE V, COLONEL-IN-CHIEF OF THE MANCHESTER REGIMENT, ADDRESSING THE REPRESENTATIVE DETACHMENT OF THE REGIMENT IN THE GROUNDS OF BUCKINGHAM PALACE, MAY 16, 1930

HOW THE MANCHESTERS PARADED

in khaki and this spectacle revived many memories in the crowd that watched or ran alongside the Manchesters until they turned into the Palace courtyard and disappeared from view beyond the screen of buildings that hides the gardens from the street. The ceremony in the grounds was private, and the eye of the public was represented only by the camera.

The parade took place in front of the garden façade of the Palace, which, with its golden-coloured stone, its low windows, and picturesque diversity, has the look of a great country house planted down in the heart of London. This part of Buckingham Palace is invisible from outside and is only seen when the King holds a garden party.

The Manchesters paraded in three long ranks immediately below the terrace, Colonel Freyberg standing in front. Behind them stretched the immense lawn with its background of woodland, and far in the distance the roofs of the West End mansions. The King, who wore the khaki service uniform of a Field-Marshal, walked out of the bow window and stood on the top of the steps leading to the gardens. The Queen accompanied him, and as this was a private affair only those in attendance on the King and Queen were present.

The band of the regiment played the National Anthem. There was an impressive salute. Then the Colonel-in-Chief passed slowly along the ranks of non-commissioned and warrant officers, and spoke to many of them, asking questions about their war service and so on. It was remarked with pleasure that he was looking very well, and throughout the parade took the liveliest interest in all that happened.

THE KING'S SPEECH

Returning to the terrace the King addressed the regiment as follows:

"The Manchester Regiment has a glorious history. Though scarcely half a century has elapsed since this title was conferred upon it, the present two battalions existed as the 63rd and 96th Regiments of Foot, having been raised respectively in 1756 and early in the nineteenth century.

"The 63rd Regiment was raised at the outbreak of the Seven Years War, and three years later took part in the capture of Guadaloupe. The regimental badge of the fleur-de-lys is a relic of that engagement. Again, in the Crimea, it rendered distinguished service, losing at Inkerman one-third of its strength, the bearers of the Queen's and Regimental Colours being killed by the side of the Commanding Officer. In 1801 the 96th Regiment of Foot fought in the Battle of Alexandria, and in the Peninsular War from 1808 to 1811. After 1881 the Regiment, under its title the Manchester Regiment, served in the Egyptian War and in South Africa, including the defence of Ladysmith, where two Victoria Crosses were gained.

"In 1908, when the Territorial Force was established, these battalions were joined to the regiment, the traditions of which they have inherited and worthily maintained, and I am glad that detachments from these battalions are present here today.

"During the Great War the regiment expanded to forty-two battalions. Twenty-seven proceeded overseas and fought in all theatres of war—in France and Belgium, Italy and Salonika, Gallipoli and Egypt, Palestine and Mesopotamia—gaining seventy battle honours. More than fourteen thousand officers, non-commissioned officers, and men were killed during those terrible years. Twice that number were either wounded or missing. Eleven Victoria Crosses were gained by the regiment. It is indeed a noble record of service and sacrifice, in keeping with the finest traditions of the British Army.

"I am proud to have become Colonel-in-Chief of so distinguished a regiment and it gives me great pleasure to see this representative parade under the command of Colonel Freyberg, the gallant commander of our first battalion."

THE COMMANDING OFFICER'S REPLY

Lieutenant-Colonel B. C. Freyberg, V.C., C.M.G., D.S.O., LL.D., replying on behalf of the regiment, in the absence of General Sir Herbert A. Lawrence, G.C.B., D.C.L., LL.D., Colonel of the Regiment, said:

"Your Majesty,—The regiment has endeavoured loyally and faithfully to serve the sovereign during seven reigns.

"Our record of past service, which your Majesty has been graciously pleased to recall, will serve as an inspiration to us on whom the future of the regiment depends. The confidence which your Majesty has placed in us will have a far-reaching effect. By becoming our Colonel-in-Chief, your Majesty has conferred an honour upon the whole regiment, a personal mark of royal favour which the regiment will cherish for all time. It is with peculiar pride that we stand here today. It will help us not only now but in the years to come in the execution of any task which in the course of our duty may fall on us."

THE CITY OF MANCHESTER'S PRESENT

After the speeches Colonel Freyberg called for three cheers for the King and the men swung their hats into the air as they cheered.

The Colonel afterwards introduced the officers to the King, who shook hands with each of them. The proceedings became less formal when the King and Queen were photographed on the terrace in the group of officers. The King was informed that a copy of this picture would be sent to the 2nd Battalion in India. This battalion was represented by officers home on leave.

The Manchesters then marched out into the road and across the few hundred yards to the barracks, well pleased with their meeting with their Colonel-in-Chief. The parade was attended by sixty officers, eighty warrant and non-commissioned officers, and the band of the regiment. Besides representatives of the 1st and 2nd Battalions there were present members of the 5th (Wigan), 6/7th (Hulme, Manchester), 8th (Ardwick, Manchester), 9th (Ashton-under-Lyne), and 10th (Oldham) battalions of the Territorial Army.

On May 10, 1932, General The Hon. Sir Herbert Lawrence reached the age for retirement and was succeeded as Colonel of the Regiment by Brigadier-General Wilfrid K. Evans, C.M.G., D.S.O. The new Colonel was commissioned to the regiment in 1900 and saw active service in South Africa from 1900 to 1902, and in France from 1914 to 1918, being awarded the D.S.O. and bar, being mentioned in dispatches eight times, and receiving the C.M.G. He commanded a brigade from 1917 until the end of the war, and, in 1924 was given command of the 1st Battalion. He retired in 1925 owing to ill-health.

The Lord Mayor of Manchester intimated to the regiment in 1934 that in order to mark the close ties which bound the city to its regiment it had been decided to present a set of silver drums to each regular battalion of the regiment. In due course arrangements were made for His Majesty the King to receive this magnificent gift on behalf of the regiment during his visit to the city on July 17, 1934. An account of this ceremony will be found in Chapter VI, and an account of the presentation of the 1st Battalion's drums by the Deputy Mayor of Manchester in the West Indies is recorded in Chapter I.

Brigadier-General Evans died on July 18, 1934, and he was succeeded as Colonel of the regiment by Colonel Francis H. Dorling, D.S.O. The new Colonel was the son of Colonel F. Dorling who had served in the regiment from 1869 to 1879, and was himself commissioned as a Second-Lieutenant in the regiment in 1897. He commanded the 1st Battalion from 1920 to 1924.

In July 1935 a start was made to set up a regimental museum, and on May 9, 1936, the Colonel of the regiment performed the opening ceremony at the Depot at Ashton-under-Lyne.

In December 1935 War Office letter 20/Inf./2472/A(502) dated December 18 was received stating that the regular battalions of the Manchester Regiment had been selected, together with those of twelve other infantry regiments, for conversion to machine-gun battalions and conversion accordingly proceeded in 1936 and 1937.

His Majesty King George V, Colonel-in-Chief of the regiment, died at Sandringham on January 20, 1936, and the news was received with heartfelt sorrow throughout the regiment. The Colonel of the regiment and a representative detachment attended the funeral in London on January 28.

Plans for the establishment of a Regimental Chapel had been going forward since 1934, when the project was first mentioned by the Colonel of the Regiment to the Dean of Manchester. On February 12, 1936, the matter was officially initiated at a meeting held at the Headquarters of the 6/7th Battalion at which it was announced that the Earl of Derby had agreed to the dedication of the Derby Chapel in Manchester Cathedral for the use of the Manchester Regiment as a Regimental Chapel. An executive committee under the chairmanship of Colonel T. Blatherwick, C.B., D.S.O., T.D., D.L., was appointed and in due course appeals were issued; as subscriptions were forthcoming, work was

THE REGIMENTAL CHAPEL, MANCHESTER CATHEDRAL, 1937

Very considerable extensions were now necessary at the depot, and a large outside camp was constructed. While it was being erected two companies were accommodated in the Withington district of Manchester at Ladybarn and Moseley Road Schools. Whittakers Mill, about half a mile from Ladysmith Barracks, which for some years had been disused, was requisitioned and largely converted for the training of signallers, range-takers and personnel to maintain and drive mechanical transport.

After the evacuation from Dunkerque some hundreds of officers and men from many different units and in every sort of condition were received at the depot and accommodated, reclothed and dispatched to their various destinations. At this time also the Home Guard was being formed and the depot was used for training and for the accommodation of mobile reserves and columns which were held in readiness for immediate action.

In July 1940 Lieutenant-Colonel E. L. Musson left the depot on promotion to command a Sub-Area and was relieved by Lieutenant-Colonel F. A. Levis, who had been second-in-command of the 2nd Battalion during the retreat to Dunkerque. In the autumn of the same year the band of the 2nd Battalion was re-formed under Bandmaster F. L. Statham, L.R.A.M., A.R.C.M., and the bandsmen who had served in France with the battalion in various capacities were recalled to the band.

In December 1940 Manchester was heavily bombed and on the night of December 22 the Regimental Chapel was hit and much of the roof and walls destroyed. Fortunately the various stands of Colours, the altar furniture, and the parchment books from the Shrine had been removed to a place of safety forty-eight hours earlier, but, even so, much furniture was reduced to splinters.[2] During this blitz on Manchester the depot provided men for work and rescue parties, as

---

[2] The Chapel has been rebuilt again since the war, and is now restored to its former glory as the Regimental Chapel.

COLONEL FRANCIS H. DORLING, D.S.O., COLONEL OF THE REGIMENT, 1934–47

indeed it did again in the summer of 1941 when Liverpool was heavily attacked.

The training system for machine-gun regiments was reorganized in August 1941 and No. 24 Machine-Gun Training Centre was opened at The Dale, Chester, to train men for all four machine-gun regiments. The Royal Northumberland Fusiliers, the Cheshire Regiment, the Middlesex Regiment, and the Manchester Regiment each found one company at The Dale, and it was in this company that men were trained for their respective regiments. When this arrangement came into being, Ladysmith Barracks ceased to be used for the training of men for the Manchester Regiment. A depot party under Major H. R. C. Green, however, remained in the barracks and became responsible not only for regimental property already stored there but also for regimental societies, records, funds, and for the band of the regiment which remained attached to the depot for administration and all duties. A R.E.M.E. Training Unit moved into the spare accommodation and the organization for training here described remained unaltered for the remainder of the war.

In July 1946 the Council of the city of Manchester unanimously passed a resolution placing on record their high appreciation of the achievements and glorious traditions of the Manchester Regiment and conferring on the regiment the privilege of marching through the city with Colours flying, drums beating, and with bayonets fixed. At the same time arrangements were made for the ceremony of the Honouring of the Regiment which was fixed for October 19, 1946, at which ceremony an illuminated scroll was to be handed over to the regiment, and the regiment would be invited to exercise for the first time its new privilege.

On the appointed day the troops taking part in the ceremony assembled on the war-damaged site in Piccadilly, Manchester, at 2.30 in the afternoon. A Guard of Honour of one hundred rank and file, commanded by Major C. H. R. Hyde, was found by No. 24 Machine-Gun Training Centre, and Captain N. K. Evans and Lieutenant J. B. H. Barrett carried the Colours. The other officers of the Guard were Captain L. W. Sully, M.C., and Lieutenant L. B. Hyde. C Company of the 1st Battalion, which was doing duty as machine-gun demonstration company at the School of Infantry, was also present with Captains J. L. L. Perez (in command), A. Greening, and R. K. Salt, and Lieutenants L. Baldwin and G. G. Guest. A detachment of officers and men who were in England on leave from the 2nd Battalion included Major J. Morrell, Lieutenants J. Burke, W. G. S. Bullock, and acting-R.S.M. T. Williams. The band of the 2nd Battalion headed the parade and sixty members from each of the 1st, 2nd, 3rd, 4th, 5th, 6th, and 7th Cadet Battalions, and some 650 members of the Old Comrades Associations of the regular, territorial, and service battalions completed the parade.

The troops marched off at 3.0 p.m. and proceeded by Market Street and Cross Street to Albert Square. The silver drums of the 2nd Battalion were piled below the dais in front of the Town Hall, and the Lord Mayor and the Colonel of the Regiment were received with a general salute. The Lord Mayor then inspected the Guard, and Lord Derby, who, owing to indisposition was in his car at the side of the dais, at the invitation of the Lord Mayor, made an impromptu speech into a microphone which was held for him. Speaking as a Freeman of Manchester, he welcomed the regiment as brethren. Lord Derby's words were warmly applauded, and the Town Clerk, Mr. Philip Dingle, then read the resolution of the City Council.

When this was completed the Lord Mayor addressed the regiment, and in the course of his speech he said:

By presenting to the regiment today a parchment bearing a resolution of the Manchester City Council, which places on record for all time their high appreciation of the glorious achievements of the regiment, there is symbolized the great respect and deep admiration that the citizens of Manchester have long had for the Manchester Regiment. . . . I am sure that the full import of this ceremony will be appreciated, and that henceforth we shall all feel—the Manchester Regiment no less than the civic authorities—that the regiment is, in a sense, an integral part of the city's corporate life. I hope that in future we shall see the Manchester Regiment taking an appropriate part in our civic and public ceremonies. In other words, that it will not be necessary to have world wars from time to time to make both the regiment and the civic authorities conscious of each other's existence and, indeed, interdependence.

I now hand to you, sir, on behalf of the Corporation of Manchester, this parchment, a token of the ties existing between the Manchester Regiment and the Manchester Corporation. It is the sincere belief of the citizen that the Manchester Regiment will ever stand ready and strong to serve our King, our Country and the Commonwealth. To all who serve in the Regiment, we, the citizens, express our greetings and good wishes.

The Lord Mayor then presented the resolution, elaborately illuminated and framed in a walnut case, to Colonel Dorling, and photographic reproductions, also framed in walnut, were presented to representatives of the 1st, 2nd, 5th, 8th, 9th, and Service Battalions. The Colonel of the Regiment then replied to the Lord Mayor in an appropriate speech which concluded:

In accepting the gift of the scrolls with their exquisite workmanship, I want you to know that they will be treasured amongst the proudest possessions of the battalions, and I wish, on behalf of all ranks of the Manchester Regiment, past and present, to express our very sincere thanks and appreciation of this very high honour which the city has seen fit to accord us. I hope, my Lord Mayor, that you will also convey our gratitude and thanks to your Council and to all others concerned.

The parade then marched off, the Guard with Colours flying, bayonets fixed and drums beating, round Albert Square and past the Lord Mayor.

In 1946 a new system of grouping of infantry regiments on a territorial basis was introduced to replace the Cardwell system which no longer was able to meet the post-war commitments of the Army. Under the new system the Manchester Regiment became grouped with the King's Own

Royal Regiment, the King's Regiment, the Lancashire Fusiliers, the East Lancashire Regiment, the Border Regiment, the South Lancashire Regiment, and the Loyal Regiment in the Lancastrian Brigade, and a Lancastrian Brigade Training Battalion was established at Hadrian's Camp, Carlisle, to carry out the basic training of recruits for all the regiments in the Lancastrian Brigade. Each regiment was, however, required to carry out the primary training, lasting six weeks, of its recruits, and to this end Primary Training Centres were set up by each regiment which were established together with the regimental depot, the latter becoming known as the headquarters of the regiment.

The 63rd Primary Training Centre (as the Manchester Regiment's P.T.C. was called) was established at Dunham Park, Altrincham, Cheshire, and accordingly the regimental depot had to move from Ashton-under-Lyne, where it had been established since 1881, to Altrincham to join up with the 63rd P.T.C. This move was accomplished in November 1946 and the first intake of recruits was received on December 5. Lieutenant-Colonel P. W. Buchan was appointed Commanding Officer of the 63rd P.T.C., while Major H. R. C. Green remained in command of the Regimental Depot.

On May 11, 1947, Colonel F. H. Dorling retired from the Colonelcy of the regiment, having reached the age of retirement. With his name will always be coupled the setting up of the Regimental Chapel, the founding of the Regimental Museum, and the initiation of the writing of the history of the regiment since 1922. He strove tirelessly to strengthen the bonds between the regiment and the city and between the regular and the Territorial battalions; and his services to the regiment will always be remembered with gratitude.

Colonel Dorling was succeeded as Colonel of the Regiment by Major-General Charles Dawson Moorhead, c.b., d.s.o., m.c., who was commissioned to the regiment in 1915. He was adjutant of the 1st Battalion from 1920 to 1922, and

HER MAJESTY THE QUEEN, COLONEL-IN-CHIEF OF THE REGIMENT, STEPS DOWN FROM THE DAIS TO INSPECT THE PARADE, ALTRINCHAM, JUNE 1, 1948, FOLLOWED BY MAJOR-GENERAL E. B. COSTIN, D.S.O., COLONEL OF THE REGIMENT

some, I hope, may be in the ranks of the Territorial Battalions of the regiment which, I am very glad to see, have sent detachments here today.

They and the Cadet Battalions can make a contribution to the regiment of a value which I cannot exaggerate, and no one can do a greater service to his old regiment than by offering to one or other of these bodies his experience and his example.

I look forward to see so many Old Comrades of all battalions on parade. I trust they will long retain their association with the regiment in which they served, and whose proud history they have helped to write.

Since the war there has been much reorganization, but I am pleased to learn that our 2nd Battalion, the old 96th Foot, is not to be disbanded. Instead it has been amalgamated with the 1st Battalion, retaining the old regimental numbers of 63rd and 96th. Thus the name and traditions of both battalions are kept alive, and welded together into a new unity and strength. You, of the 1st Battalion will shortly be returning to Germany for another tour of duty.

Do not forget that your country, and its way of living, will be judged by your bearing; and by setting an example of tolerance, discipline, and good manners you will maintain the honoured tradition that a British soldier is an ambassador for peace. I wish you all every good fortune.

Lastly, I have been asked to present this silver Centrepiece to the city of Manchester, a gift from the officers of the regiment. We remember with pleasure the presentation of the Scroll of Honour in 1946, and the two sets of silver drums in 1934. By encouraging its sons to go forward to serve in the regiment, the city is playing its part, and the regiment in return gives them back, in most cases fitter physically, mentally, and morally, to take their place as worthy citizens.

It is our hope, my Lord Mayor, that this Centrepiece may be placed in the Town Hall, there to remind all who see it of the close and valued link which binds the city to the regiment which proudly bears its name.

Her Majesty then presented the Centrepiece to the Lord Mayor, who replied in a short speech expressing the gratitude of the city for "this splendid and beautiful gift, the value of which has been so greatly enhanced by its presentation by Your Majesty as Colonel-in-Chief of the regiment".

HER MAJESTY TAKING THE SALUTE AT THE MARCH PAST, JUNE 1, 1948

INSPECTING THE OLD COMRADES

THE INSPECTION FINISHED

Three cheers were then given for the Queen, followed by a Royal Salute, and the troops marched off parade.

After many more presentations had been made, the Queen walked through the Families' and Old Comrades' enclosures, speaking to a large number of people. She then drove to the Officers' Mess where, after further presentations, she took tea with the officers and their guests. The Queen was later photographed with serving regular and Territorial Army officers. This ended Her Majesty the Colonel-in-Chief's most memorable visit to the regiment, and she drove away by car at 5.30 in the evening.

APPENDIX I

TABLES SHOWING THE NUMBERS OF OFFICERS AND OTHER RANKS OF THE 1ST AND 2ND BATTALIONS OF THE MANCHESTER REGIMENT WHO WERE KILLED OR DIED DURING WORLD WAR II WHILST SERVING WITH THESE BATTALIONS

TABLE 1
Battle Casualties, 1st and 2nd Battalions

Batta-lion	Period	Campaign	Killed	
			Officers	Other Ranks
2nd	May–June 1940	Dunkerque	2/Lieut. J. B. H. Keitley	61
1st	February 1942	Singapore*	Major W. J. Douglass Lieut. D. M. Howe Lieut. D. W. Low Lieut.(QM.) T. Quinn, M.M.	56
2nd	April 1944–May 1945	Burma	—	38
1st	June 1944–May 1945	N.W. Europe	Major G. L. Northcote Lieut. K. L. Oliver Lieut. J. Bromley-Davenport	44
1st and 2nd		Total ...	8	199

* Figures include 1 Officer and 21 Other Ranks killed in action at sea on board H.M.S. *Dragonfly*, February 14, 1942.

526

Table 2

Officers and Other Ranks of 1st Battalion who died in Japanese captivity

Locality	Officers	Other ranks
Singapore P.O.W. Camps	—	26
Thailand P.O.W. Camps	Major G. D. Cooper	62
Japanese Transports	—	50
F and H Forces	Lieut. G. H. Isherwood	222
P.O.W. Camps other than above	—	16
Total ...	2	376

Table 3

Officers and Other Ranks of 1st and 2nd Battalions who were killed in action or died during World War II (including figures in Tables 1 and 2 above)

Battalion	Officers	Other ranks
1st	9	504
2nd	1	122
Total ...	10	626

APPENDIX II
HONOURS AND AWARDS
WORLD WAR II

The names of all officers and other ranks who gained honours and awards while serving with the 1st or 2nd Battalions are included in this list together with the names of those *regular* (and supplementary reserve) officers, and other ranks *serving on regular engagements*, of the Manchester Regiment who gained honours and awards whilst serving on the Staff or with other units

THE MOST HONOURABLE ORDER OF THE BATH
Companion

Rank		Number	Date of Award	Unit	Theatre
A/Maj.-Gen.	Moorhead, C. D., D.S.O., M.C.	13555	14.10.43	Staff	M.E.

THE MOST DISTINGUISHED ORDER OF THE BRITISH EMPIRE
Companions

Colonel	Parminter, R. H. R., D.S.O., M.C.		20.12.40	Staff	B.E.F.
T/Brig.	Clowes, N., D.S.O., M.C.	49673	18.2.43	Staff	M.E.
Brig.	Torrance, K. S., M.C.		12.9.46	Staff	Malaya

Officers

Lieut.-Col.	Holmes, E. B., M.C.	5904	12.9.46	1st	Malaya
T/Lieut.-Col.	Truss, R. C. B.	68592	6.6.46		Burma

Members

Capt.	Abbott, C. J. F., M.C.	21162	11.7.40		B.E.F.
T/Capt.	Potter, W. R.	78905	9.9.42		M.E.
Lieut.(Q.M.)	O'Brien, H.		43	2nd	India
Capt.(QM.)	Maloney, F.	216847	21.6.45		N.W.E.
T/Major	Spanton, E. J. C.	56578	28.6.45	Staff	Burma
T/Major	Marsh, L.	180685	11.10.45	1st	N.W.E.
T/Major	Eckersley, B.	98879	17.1.46	2nd	Burma
Capt.	Gutteridge, W. F.	121942	6.6.46	2nd	Burma
W.O.1	Greenwood, H.	3523756	6.6.46	2nd	Burma

The Manchester Regiment

British Empire Medal

Rank		Number	Date of Award	Unit	Theatre
Sgt.	Carney, J.	3524990	14.2.47	1st	Malaya

The Distinguished Service Order

Bar to D.S.O.

T/Lieut.-Col.	Churchill, J. M. T., D.S.O., M.C.	34657	20.7.44	Cmdo.	Yugoslavia

D.S.O.

B/Lieut.-Col.	Moorhead, C. D., M.C.	13555	11.7.40	Staff	B.E.F.
Lieut.-Col.	Brittorous, F., M.C.	12475	20.8.40		B.E.F.
T/Lieut.-Col.	Churchill, J. M. T., M.C.	34657	13.1.44	Cmdo.	Italy
Lieut.-Col.	Venour, W. A.	32188	22.3.45	Dorset	N.W.E.
T/Lieut.-Col.	Woolsey, E. F.	38349	24.1.46	1st	N.W.E.
T/Lieut.-Col.	Crozier, H. B. D.	115944	24.1.46	1st	N.W.E.

The Military Cross

T/Capt.	Churchill, J. M. T.	34657	20.12.40	2nd	B.E.F.
Lieut.	King, W. E.	180684	22.3.45	2nd	Burma
Lieut.	Muskett, H. T.	180691	29.6.45	2nd	Burma
T/Capt.	Pleass, D. S.	130190	2.8.45	1st	N.W.E.
T/Capt.	Baker, B. W. R.	121524	3.9.45	2nd	Burma
T/Major	Tod, G. A.	45003	11.10.45	1st	N.W.E.
Lieut.	Sully, L. W.	107522	13.12.45	1st	Malaya
T/Major	Blackburn, C. J.	121940	17.1.46	2nd	Burma
T/Major	Bean, D. G. L.	113533	6.6.46	2nd	Burma

The Distinguished Conduct Medal

Sgt.	Bebbington, W. Y.	3525822	27.8.40	2nd	B.E.F.

The Military Medal

Bar to M.M.

Sgt.	Abbott, E. F. G., M.M.	6844135	2.8.45	1st	N.W.E.

M.M.

A/Sgt.	Graney, A.	3526729	27.8.40	1/9	B.E.F.
Pte.	Thorne, R. L.	3531066	22.7.43	2nd	Burma
Sgt.	Rogers, D.	3859709	21.12.44	1st	N.W.E.
Sgt.	Bardsley, J. W. H.	3533532	1.3.45	1st	N.W.E.
A/Sgt.	Sullivan, J. S.	3530301	1.3.45	1st	N.W.E.
L/Cpl.	Kelly, D.	3530571	28.6.45	2nd	Burma
Sgt.	Kenyon, N.	3532797	20.9.45	2nd	Burma

THE MANCHESTER REGIMENT

Rank		Number	Date of Award	Unit	Theatre
Sgt.	Walters, B.	3909793	11.10.45	7th	N.W.E.
Pte.	Woodward, J.	3527662	13.12.45	1st	Malaya
A/Sgt.	Leeson, R.	3533443	24.1.46	1st	N.W.E.

Mentions in Dispatches

Officers

Rank		Number	Date of Award	Unit	Theatre
Lieut.-Col.	Moore, A. W. U.	5739	20.12.40	2nd	B.E.F.
Major	Webb, C. F.	23018	20.12.40		B.E.F.
Capt.	Archdale, C. L.	31252	20.12.40		B.E.F.
Capt.	Holt, A. E.	85678	20.12.40		B.E.F.
A/Capt.	Ham, G. W.	53772	20.12.40		B.E.F.
A/Capt.	Dent, H. D.	63623	11.2.41	Staff	M.E.
B/Lieut.-Col.	Moorhead, C. D., D.S.O., M.C.	13555	29.4.41	Staff	B.E.F.
A/Brig.	Clowes, N., D.S.O., M.C.	49673	30.12.41	Staff	M.E.
T/Major	Almond, W. E.	41567	16.9.43		N. Africa
Capt.	Liddiard, A. J.	60245	11.11.43		N. Africa
A/Maj.-Gen.	Clowes, N., C.B.E., D.S.O., M.C.	49673	6.4.44	Staff	M.E.
T/Lieut.-Col.	Black, K. R. F.	34443	6.4.44	R.A.F. Regt.	M.E.
T/Capt.	Clutterbuck, R. G.	95515	22.3.45	1st	N.W.E.
Lieut.	Brown, R. W.	304985	22.3.45	1st	N.W.E.
T/Major	Spanton, E. J. C.	56578	5.4.45	Staff	Burma
Lieut.	Muskett, H. T.	108691	5.4.45	2nd	Burma
T/Major	Simpson, C. A.	67731	10.5.41	1st	N.W.E.
T/Capt.	Marsh, L.	180685	10.5.45	1st	N.W.E.
Lieut.	Royals, J. W.	273246	10.5.45	1st	N.W.E.
T/Major	Eckersley, B. S.	98879	19.7.45	2nd	Burma
T/Capt.	Hewitt, A.	67695	19.7.45	2nd	Burma
T/Major	Walker, C. B.	98965	9.8.45	1st	N.W.E.
T/Capt.	Batterbury, P. C.	109559	9.8.45	1st	N.W.E.
T/Capt.	Clutterbuck, R. G.	95515	9.8.45	1st	N.W.E.
T/Major	Dent, H. D.	93623	27.9.45		Burma
T/Capt.	Simpson, A. J. F.	115942	8.11.45	1st	N.W.E.
Lieut.	Moore, S. W.	321843	8.11.45	1st	N.W.E.
Lieut.	Pears, C.	311252	8.11.45	1st	N.W.E.
T/Major	Redfern, G. H.	74322	29.11.45		Italy
T/Major	Eckersley, B. S.	98879	10.1.46	2nd	Burma
T/Capt.	Harrison, E.	262491	4.4.46	1st	N.W.E.
T/Capt.	Paynter, J.	156717	4.4.46	1st	N.W.E.
T/Capt.	Waddington, J. E. W.	149500	4.4.46	1st	N.W.E.
T/Capt.	Weaver, J. R.	255805	4.4.46	1st	N.W.E.

APPENDIX IV

SUCCESSION OF COMMANDING OFFICERS SINCE 1922

1st Battalion

Lieutenant-Colonel F. H. Dorling, D.S.O.	September 1, 1920
Lieutenant-Colonel and Brevet-Colonel W. K. Evans, C.M.G., D.S.O.	August 25, 1924
Lieutenant-Colonel C. C. Stapleton	February 3, 1925
Lieutenant-Colonel B. C. Freyberg, V.C., C.M.G., D.S.O.	February 3, 1929
Lieutenant-Colonel L. C. Bostock, O.B.E., M.C.	March 6, 1931
Lieutenant-Colonel B. G. Atkin, D.S.O., O.B.E., M.C.	March 6, 1933
Lieutenant-Colonel N. Clowes, D.S.O., M.C.	March 6, 1937
Lieutenant-Colonel E. B. Holmes, M.C.	June 30, 1939
*Lieutenant-Colonel J. H. Orgill	June 3, 1942
*Lieutenant-Colonel H. S. Hoseason	August 9, 1942
*Lieutenant-Colonel C. H. P. Harington, M.C. (Cheshire Regiment)	April 12, 1944
*Lieutenant-Colonel P. H. Earle (Royal Northumberland Fusiliers)	September 14, 1944
*Lieutenant-Colonel H. B. D. Crozier	December 8, 1944
*Lieutenant-Colonel E. F. Woolsey	March 4, 1946
Lieutenant-Colonel C. L. Archdale	June 30, 1946

2nd Battalion

Lieutenant-Colonel W. B. Eddowes	November 5, 1921
Lieutenant-Colonel J. R. H. Heelis, M.C.	November 5, 1925
Lieutenant-Colonel E. L. Musson, D.S.O., M.C.	November 5, 1929

THE MANCHESTER REGIMENT

Lieutenant-Colonel R. H. R. Parminter, D.S.O., M.C.	March 5, 1933
Lieutenant-Colonel E. B. Costin, D.S.O. .	April 7, 1935
Lieutenant-Colonel A. W. U. Moore .	November 18, 1938
*Lieutenant-Colonel F. G. W. Axworthy	October 12, 1940
*Lieutenant-Colonel T. Brodie (Cheshire Regiment)	March 23, 1942
*Lieutenant-Colonel C. L. Archdale .	September 17, 1942
*Lieutenant-Colonel R. King-Clark, M.C.	February 2, 1945
*Lieutenant-Colonel B. F. G. Blood (Royal Northumberland Fusiliers) .	October 23, 1945
Lieutenant-Colonel J. H. Orgill . . .	May 10, 1945

* Non-substantive appointments

APPENDIX V

THE COLOURS

THE following paragraphs list what is known of the various stands of Colours that have been presented to the regiment, and where those stands now are (1953).

63RD REGIMENT

1st Stand 1765

The first stand of Colours recorded as issued to the 63rd Regiment was presented in Dublin in 1765. These Colours were carried during the American War of Independence and in Jamaica, and were not renewed until the regiment returned to England in 1784. There present whereabouts is unknown.

2nd Stand, 1784

The second stand was issued in Bury St. Edmunds in 1784 and was carried in action in Holland, the Windward Islands, Honduras, and The Helder. There is no information as to when this stand was retired but it appears likely that it was in the early years of the nineteenth century since a sketch of the new colours issued to the regiment includes the red cross of St. Patrick which was only added to Colours after the union of Great Britain and Ireland in 1801. The present whereabouts of this stand is unknown.

3rd Stand, c. 1803

The third stand was issued in the early years of the nineteenth century and probably in Ireland. The Colours were carried at Walcheran and in the West Indies, and were retired in 1826. Their present whereabouts is unknown.

4th Stand, 1826

The fourth stand was issued, probably at Windsor, in 1826,

and was carried in Portugal, India, and Australia. The King's Colour was carried at the ceremony of the founding of Perth, Australia. Milne says in his book *Standards and Colours of the Army*, page 201, "The last mention of painted Colours in the Inspection Returns is in 1838. The 63rd Regiment in Madras is stated to have Colours painted, the number also in figures not Roman letters. These painted Colours of the 63rd were issued in 1826 and retired in 1842, being probably the last used by an infantry regiment, though painted Colours were in use by the Brigade of Guards for many years after that date." The whereabouts of this stand is unknown.

5th Stand, 1842

The fifth stand was presented on September 20, 1842, by Brigadier-General Joseph Logan, commanding Tenasserim Province, Burma, and consecrated by the Bishop of Calcutta, Dr. Daniel Wilson. These appear to have been the first consecrated Colours to be carried by the 63rd. The Regimental Colour is laid up in Manchester Cathedral, and the centre of the Queen's Colour is framed in the Officers' Mess of the Depot.

6th Stand, 1854

The sixth stand was presented on May 10, 1854, on the Nine Acres, Phoenix Park, Dublin, by Mrs. Swyny, wife of the Commanding Officer, who had been deputed by Major-General Kenah, C.B., to perform the ceremony in his absence. These Colours were carried in the Crimean War and are the most famous Colours in the regiment. At the battle of Inkerman Lieutenant-Colonel Swyny was killed as he rode near the Colours that his wife had presented only five months before, as also was Ensign Clutterbuck, who carried the Regimental Colour. Lieutenant Twysden who carried the Queen's Colour was mortally wounded and died four days later.

When Lieutenant Twysden was mortally wounded and Ensign Clutterbuck killed, the Colours were seized by

Sergeant Roberts and Colour-Sergeant Brophy who defended them although both of these non-commissioned officers were severely wounded. Major Slack records that the Colours "were ordered back to the Windmill to await there the return of the regiment, as so many officers and men were killed, wounded and scattered about. On our return to camp we took the Colours with us". "Such," says Milne, "was the last appearance of British Colours in an European pitched battle; the rest of the campaign being siege work, it is doubtful if Colours were brought out again."

These Colours were, however, carried in action again, for F. H. D. Vieth of the 63rd in his book *Recollection of the Crimean Campaign*, in describing the landing at Cherson Bay in the expedition against Odessa in 1855, says: "An exciting race was run between the boats filled with men of the different regiments, each striving to touch land first. Three containing my regiment and the 17th led the van and every nerve was strained as the sand beach got nearer. I was the subaltern that day carrying the Queen's Colour, Lacy, my chum, having the Regimental one. Scarcely had the boats touched, when, grasping the staff, I jumped into the water and wading ashore drove the end of the staff into the sand, letting the Colour float on the breeze. It has been said that a boat of the 17th Regiment landed first, but the fact remains that the Queen's Colour of the 63rd Regiment was the first flag on the soil of Russia proper."

This stand continued to be carried until 1872. About a quarter of each of the Queen's and Regimental Colours are encased under glass and preserved in the Regimental Museum. Ensign Clutterbuck's sword and scabbard is attached to the case. In addition, there are two circular carved wooden frames containing respectively the centre of the Queen's Colour and a Crown from the Regimental Colour, which hang in the Officers' Mess of the Depot.[1]

---

[1] Certain other portions of these Colours which were stained with the blood of the officers who were killed carrying them were destroyed in a fire at Tipperary many years ago.

7th Stand, 1872

The seventh stand was presented by Mrs. Bowles, the wife of the Commanding Officer, on February 12, 1872, at Hazaribagh, India, and consecrated by the Bishop of Calcutta, Dr. Robert Milman. These Colours are still on charge to the 1st Battalion the Manchester Regiment but were lodged at the Depot in 1951, when the battalion proceeded to Malaya, owing to their age and frailty. The Colours of the 2nd Battalion, now amalgamated with the 1st, were taken instead (January, 1953).

96TH REGIMENT

There survive records of the colours of only two of the regiments which were numbered 96 prior to 1824.

The Colours of the British Musqueteers, which was raised in 1779 and disbanded in 1783, were presented to the 96th Regiment (later the 2nd Battalion the Manchester Regiment) in 1879 by Colonel J. J. Whyte, who had inherited them from his grand-uncle, General Whyte, who had been in command of the British Musqueteers when they were disbanded. For many years these Colours were kept in the Officers' Mess of the 2nd Battalion, but since the amalgamation of the two battalions in 1948 they have been loaned to the Regimental Museum.

In 1798, after the capture of Minorca, Colonel John Stuart raised what was then called the "Minorca Regiment" from Swiss prisoners of war found in the island. It fought with distinction at the battle of Alexandria and later became known as the "Queen's German Regiment". It was at the battle of Alexandria that Private Anthony Lutz captured the "Invincible Standard" from the French, and this standard was deposited at the Royal Hospital, Chelsea, in 1811. On September 28, 1947, however, this Colour was handed over to Major-General C. D. Moorhead, C.B., D.S.O., M.C., the Colonel of the Regiment, at a special parade at the Royal Hospital and it is now preserved in the Regimental Museum.

Little silk remains visible on this standard now, but originally when it was captured the following battle-honours surrounding a bugle could be discerned: Le Passage de la Scrivia; Le Passage du Tagliamento; Le Passage de l'Isonzo; La Prise de Graz; Le Pont de Lodi.

In 1812 as a mark of royal approbation for its distinguished services this regiment was restyled "Queen's Own" and its facings were changed to blue. It also received a change of Colours, and its old Colours, under which it had fought at Alexandria in 1801 and in the Peninsula from 1808 to 1811, were presented to Lieutenant-General Sir John Stuart who had been its Commanding Officer at Alexandria. These old Colours came into the possession of the 2nd Battalion the Manchester Regiment and were preserved in the Officers' Mess until the amalgamation of the 1st and 2nd Battalions in 1948, when they were loaned to the Regimental Museum.

1st Stand, 1824

The first Colours to be carried by the 96th Regiment (which later became the 2nd Battalion the Manchester Regiment) were issued without ceremony in Manchester in 1824 soon after it was raised. These Colours were not consecrated until June 26, 1825, when, in Halifax, Nova Scotia, by order of Major-General Sir Howard Douglas, the ceremony was performed and the Colours were handed to the regiment by Lady Lumly. These Colours were carried until 1861 and are now laid up in Manchester Cathedral.

2nd Stand, 1861

The second stand to be issued to the 96th was presented on May 8, 1861, by Major-General H. Shirley, C.B., at the Curragh, Ireland. They were carried until 1886, and are now laid up in Manchester Cathedral.

3rd Stand, 1886

The third stand of Colours was presented on January 21, 1886, at Delhi, by General Sir Frederick Roberts, V.C.,

Commander-in-Chief in India, and consecrated by the Rev. J. Adams, v.c., Chaplain to the Forces. These Colours were carried until 1911 and are now laid up in the Church of St. Michael and All Angels, the parish church of Ashton-under-Lyne. They were the first universal Regimental Colours to be presented to the regiment.

4th Stand, 1911

The fourth stand was presented on July 7, 1911, at Dublin by His Majesty King George V. These Colours were carried by the 2nd Battalion the Manchester Regiment until the amalgamation of the 1st and 2nd Battalions in 1948, and are now carried by the 1st Battalion 63/96 (January 1953).

3RD AND 4TH BATTALIONS THE MANCHESTER REGIMENT

The 3rd Battalion was presented with Colours on May 24, 1902, by Field-Marshal Lord Roberts, v.c., these Colours being consecrated by Bishop Taylor Smith, Chaplain-General to the Forces. The 4th Battalion was presented with Colours on July 31, 1903, by H.R.H. Field-Marshal the Duke of Connaught.

On the disbandment of these Battalions in 1906 their Colours were placed in the Town Hall, Manchester, but were later removed and are now in Manchester Cathedral (January 1953).

APPENDIX VI

REGIMENTAL MARCHES

"THE origin of Regimental Marches is one of the mistiest aspects of military research, but it is also one to which considerable attention has been given. The adoption of a tune by a regiment in the past was done purely at the instigation of the regiment itself and received no mention in General Orders. This suggests that the best source of information today is the regiment itself."[1]

Unfortunately no records appear to have been kept by either the 63rd or 96th, so that information has to be collected from outside sources. A great deal of valuable information has been obtained in this way, from which the following histories have been compiled.

"The Young May Moon"

The air of this tune has been identified by Mr. Kennedy, Director of the English Folk Dance and Song Society, as an old Irish dance tune. The composer's name is not known as the origin of these "folk" tunes can rarely be defined.

According to Dr. Farmer, who has a most comprehensive record, this tune appeared under many names before it was known as "Young May Moon": e.g. Swallow's MS. (before 1800) calls it an "Irish Air"; Gow's *Repository* (3rd Book, 1806) calls it "Dandy O"; while Davie's *Caledonian Repository* (1820 et seq.) calls it "Honest Harry"; and according to Mr. Harry Mortimer it appeared in the opera *Robin Hood* as "My name is little Harry O", after which it becomes in turn "The Dandy O", "Pat and Kate", and "The Irish Wedding".

The tune, however, first became popularized in England

---

[1] Extract from a letter from the Assistant Librarian, Royal United Services Institution.

APPENDIX VII

THE JESH INCIDENT
March 1938

by Major Claude Webb, f.r.g.s.

THE following narrative was kindly communicated by Major Webb. The incident is referred to in the battalion diaries, but Major Webb's account contains details that are not to be found in any other source, and it has, on that account, been decided to print it without alteration.

In 1938 the 1st Battalion the Manchester Regiment was stationed in Northern Palestine during the Arab rebellion against the Jews and suffered a few casualties in consequence. The Battalion disposition was as follows:

Bn. H.Q., B and D Companies at Tiberias.
A Company at Acre.
C Company at Safad.

Each Company was a self-contained unit and could operate as an independent striking force to deal with Arab bandits who continually attacked the Jews in their villages and towns, and during road movements.

Ambush warfare was the Arab bandits favourite pastime. The country over which the battalion had to operate suited the ambush tactics of the Arab raiders, and it was policy to get off the road and into billets before dark.

The Syrian Arab would cross the frontier road and over the River Jordan and would infiltrate into the hillside villages and create a state of merry hell until they were driven out by the battalion. Many raids took place and

THE JESH INCIDENT

various incidents were very unpleasant; they were short and sharp.

As the disposition of the battalion covered a large area of hill country in Northern Palestine the companies were organized into mobile columns. The motor vehicles allotted for the task were sometimes hired civilian transport and liable to break down at a most inconvenient time and place. The composition of each company column was unique inasmuch as each had a matter of ten Cyprian donkeys as pack animals to carry the machine-guns and wireless equipment, etc., to enable the troops to operate across country and off the beaten track. These animals had to be lifted and carried in a motor vehicle. They enabled the machine-gunner to take on the Arab bandit in most unlikely places much to the surprise of the "bad men" hiding in the mountain villages and low-lying wadis and caves.

It was during one of these battalion operations that the unfortunate "Jesh incident" occurred. Fortunately C Company knew Jesh and its neighbouring villages and hamlets very well as the village of Jesh came into C Company's area near Safad, and the troops had carried out daylight reconnaissance patrols and so could if called up operate by night in their area. This fact proved very important during the "Jesh incident".

The 16th Infantry Brigade with headquarters at Haifa had news of a large force of Arab bandits scattered in the hills and caves in Northern Palestine and decided to drive the whole area with R.A.F. support and kill or capture all the Arab bandits located.

The 1st Battalion the Manchester Regiment carried out a drive northwards, all companies co-operating, and maintained contact by wireless. C Company was under command of Major C. F. Webb, with Lieutenant James Deirham-Reid as second-in-command. The company was ordered to occupy a hill village just south of the new frontier road which follows closely the Syrian frontier. A lot of the cutthroat Arab bandits came across the frontier, carried out their raids, and nipped back across the road into Syria and became neutral and peaceful landworkers and it would all happen in a few seconds.

C Company was thus placed five miles away on the western flank of the battalion during the drive northwards to the frontier road. The village occupied by C Company was a hill village well off the beaten track and the pack animals had a hard time. The company cleared the village of all the "bad men", and had settled down to tea when the wireless operator received a message from Battalion Headquarters ordering C Company to close on Battalion Headquarters in the village of Sa-Sa and the company to billet the night in the village of Jesh, which was only about 1,000 yards east of the village of Sa-Sa. C Company closed and returned to the frontier road to receive the motor transport which was to carry the company to Jesh.

It was sunset before the motor vehicles arrived with Captain and Adjutant Bill Usher to pick up C Company. This was successfully carried out, and the column arrived at Battalion Headquarters after dark.

The battalion drive halted for the night at Sa-Sa on the general line of the new frontier road, A Company being allotted an Arab village about 1,000 yards along the track east of the village of Jesh. This track also served Jesh and it was a very soft track and very muddy and unfit to take a motor column. To lighten the column the pack animals were ordered to be unloaded and proceed along the track to Jesh by walk march with an escort under the command of Lieutenant Deirham-Reid. The remainder of C Company motor column were ordered to press on along the track and occupy the village of Jesh for the night. The motor vehicles had lights on as it was dark and the track was very difficult to negotiate. The track dipped into a nullah with a horseshoe bend in it and came up on the far side at a steep incline; the country each side of the track was scattered with rough boulder-stones and a small olive grove. On topping the nullah the track entered open country through the small

THE JESH INCIDENT

olive grove which ended at the foot of the hill village of Jesh.

On the C Company column front along the track was a pile of A Company's kit piled on the right side of the track with a machine-gun escort, the escort was encircled by Arab bandits and a first-class ambush battle was in progress. C Company column immediately got stuck in the track mud and immediately went into action. The O.C. C Company could see the flashes of the Arab bandits' rifle fire coming from the cover of the large boulder-stones which formed a semi-circle from near Sa-Sa to Jesh. (See sketch.)

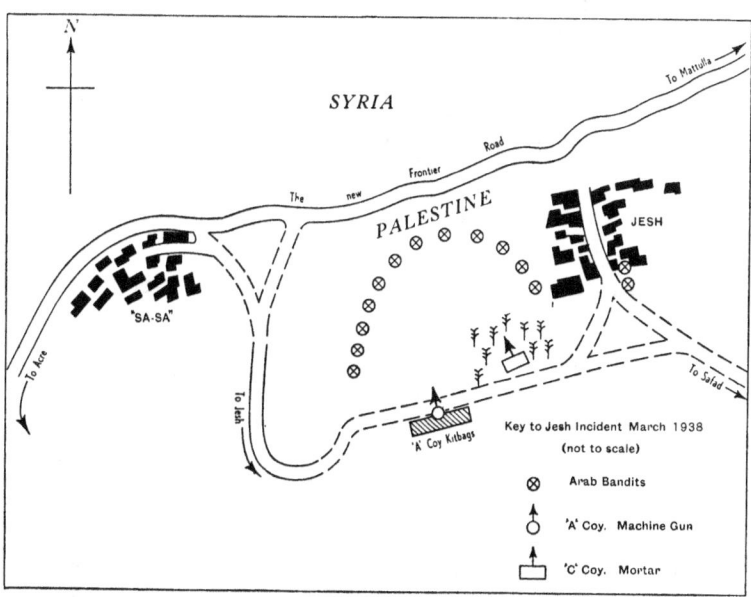

A Company machine-gun fire could not dislodge the bandits from the boulder-stones and O.C. C Company made a quick mental appreciation and ordered his mortar section into action in the olive grove. The fire of the mortar had to be very carefully directed to prevent firing upon Lieutenant James Deirham-Reid and his pack animals, estimated at the time to be negotiating the nullah on the track, and also from preventing overs reaching Battalion Headquarters in the village of Sa-Sa on the left arc of mortar fire. Also care had to be taken from blowing up the women and children in the village of Jesh on the right arc of the mortar fire. The O.C. Company knew this spot of country very well and was able to direct the mortar fire successfully and within about half an hour the mortar section silenced all the bandits' fire and the Arab raiders retired in great haste into the village of Jesh. But unfortunately before the bandits could be driven off Private Fiery, one of A Company's machine-gun escort on the pile of kitbags, had been killed and another man of A Company had been shot in the back but his life was saved by the fact that this man had his pack on and inside his pack had his tin plate, which stopped the bullet penetrating his spine. The R.A.M.C. medical orderly attached to C Company attended the casualties on the track and found that the bullet that killed Private Fiery of A Company had entered Private Fiery's right armpit and come out through his left armpit. The medical orderly tried hard to save Private Fiery, but without avail.

Captain Charles Archdale, O.C. A Company, arrived on the scene with C.S.M. Smith, and O.C. C Company reported the sad news of the fate of Private Fiery who belonged to A Company. Firing by this time had ceased and A Company collected their kitbags unmolested. But C Company had still to occupy the village of Jesh, in which the Arab bandits had taken cover. C Company pressed on on foot with fixed bayonets and on arrival were fired on at point-blank range; but fortunately for C Company not a man was hit. C Company's advanced guard immediately returned the fire and the bandits dashed off into the darkness and with a "hop-step-and-a-jump" crossed the new frontier road into Syria and became peaceful Syrian landworkers, taking their Pai dogs with them.

C Company had no further trouble and settled down to a quiet night. Guards were posted on the highest buildings and issued with Mills hand grenades, and the Arabs of Jesh behaved themselves.

INDEX

FIRST BATTALION 1922–1945

ADELAIDE RIFLES, affiliated Australian regiment, 44
Aller, River, crossing of, 245
Antwerp, Battalion H.Q. in, 166
Ardennes, The, 205
Arnhem, 170 ff
Arromanches, arrival off, 111
Austria, annexation of, 35

BAGHDAD, crisis in, 21
Bermuda, see West Indies
Bisley, 8, 11 ff
Bocholt, capture of, 239
Burma–Thailand railway, Chung Kai affair, 101 ff
— —, forced work on, 90 ff, 97

CAEN, capture of, 114
—, operations against, 127
Captivity, in Japanese hands, 79 ff
"Changi University," establishment of, 83
Channel Islands, duties in, 1 ff, 6
Cholera, 91
Colchester, training at, 11
Cyprus, detachment duties in, 22

DUBLIN, duties in, 5
Dunkerque, 44
—, arrival in, 19
—, duties in, 19, 21
—, en route for, 18
—, sport in, 22

FALAISE, capture of, 159
Far East, situation in 1939, 37
Fifty-third Division, front of, 121
— —, training exercises with, 107 ff
— —, withdrawal from the Ardennes, 209

First Battalion, reconstitution of, from Sixth, 104
Formosa, prison camp on, 95

GERMANY, advance into, 211 ff
Goch, capture of, 225
Gosport, 12
Grimblemont, attack on, 209

HAMBURG, entry into, 253
Heinsberg, 213
Honshu, prison camps on, 93

IRELAND, 4, 5

JAMAICA, see West Indies
Japanese barbarities to prisoners, 98 ff
— forces, increasing strength of, 50
— landings in Malaya, 53
— mainland, prison camps on, 93 ff
— prison camps, conditions in, 81 ff
Japanese–English relations, 1939, 37

KANBURI, prison camp at, 96
Khartoum, return from, 14

LARKHILL CAMP, 10
Lebanese frontier, military posts established on, 29
Lommel, Battalion H.Q. in, 171

MACHINE-GUN BATTALION, reorganization as, 35
Manchester, bombing of, 44
Meuse salient, the, 191
Middle East, situation in 1935, 18
Munich crisis, 34

Nijmegen bridgehead, 179
Normandy, embarkation for, 110
—, fighting in, 121 ff
—, invasion of, 109
—, plan of campaign in, 125 ff

Odon bridgeheads, 131 ff
Organization, repeated changes in, 109
Orne, crossing of, 155

Palestine, casualties in, 33 ff
—, departure from, 34
—, duties in, 24 ff
—, mobile columns organized in, 27
—, ration convoy attacked, 30
—, threatened general strike, 21
Prison camps, Japanese, administration of, 87
— — —, conditions in, 81

Regimental colours, sent to Australia for safe keeping, 44
— Chapel, destruction of, 44
Reichswald forest, 214 ff
Rethem, 247
Reunion at Southampton 1935, 18
Rhine, the, crossing of, 235
Rhine Army, duties with, 7 ff
— —, return from, 9
— —, sporting successes with, 7 ff

Sanctions, 19, 35
s'Hertogenbosch captured, 185
Shorncliffe, return to, 9
Silver Bugles, presentation of, 35
— Drums, presentation by Deputy Lord Mayor in Jamaica, 15

Singapore, arrival in, 35
—, beach defences of, 52 f
—, defensive plan of, 39 f
—, departure for, from Suez, 35
—, departure of specialist party from, 104
— island, withdrawal to, 54
—, mobilization of foreign service battalion, 43
— reservoirs, defence of, 65
—, seige of, 61 ff
—, situation in on fall of France, 46
—, surrender of, 77
Sinn Fein, campaign against, 4
Southampton, reunion en route from West Indies to Egypt, 18
Syrian frontier, military posts established on, 29

Tactics, Battle, review of, 113 ff
"Tegart's Wall", 29
Transjordan frontier, military posts established on, 29

Unveiling 1st Battn. Window, St. George's Church, Moascar, 23

VE day, 253

War with Germany, outbreak of, 36
Weeze, capture of, 229
Western desert, duties in, 20
West Indies, arrival in, 14
— —, departure from, 17
— —, duties and training in, 17
— —, sport in, 17
— —, visit of H.R.H. the Duke of Gloucester to, 16

SECOND BATTALION 1922–1945

"Aberdeen", 389
Ahmednagar, transfer to, 375
Akyab, operations against, 387

Aldershot, arrival at, 297
—, training at, 298 ff
Arakan, 465 ff

INDEX

Arakan, operation in, 383
Armament, reorganization of Battalion's, 265, 294

BATTLE TACTICS, review of, 304 ff
Bellerby, 291
Beverley, training at, 372
"Broadway", 389
Burma, training difficulties in, 257
—, rebellion in, 269 ff
Burmese rebels, operations against, 271 ff

CALCUTTA, return to, 463, 496
Chanbattia, 255
Cherbourg, arrival at, 303
"Chowringhee", 389
Colour, trooping the, 257, 268
Connaught, T.R.H. the Prince and Princess Arthur of, 257
Cyprus, 283

DECLARATION OF WAR, 302
Dendre River, retreat to, 333
Dunkerque campaign, the, 304 ff
—, condition of Battalion after, 371
—, withdrawal from, 367 ff
Dyle, River, 316 ff
Dyle, River, retreat from, 328

FORTIFICATIONS, field, 312

GEBEIT, 283
Ghurkas, contact with, 491
Gnatong, Sikkim, 255

IMPHAL, operations against, 411 ff
India, closure of British rule, 374
—, disturbances in, 375
Indian platoon, attached to Regiment, 282
Invasion by Germans, expected, 372
Irrawaddy, advance to, 439 ff
—, crossing of, 449
— villages, unrest in, 262
—, voyage up, 262

JALAP LA PASS, 255

Japanese advance in Burma, 377 ff
Jubbulpore, 255
—, Durbar, 256
—, training in, 256

KATHA, 482 ff
Kabaw valley, 434
Khartoum, conditions at, 284
—, departure from for U.K., 286
King George V, inspection by, 290
— — —, death of, 292
King George VI, coronation of, 296
— — —, visit of to Aldershot, 302
Kohima, 392 ff
Kotwali, disturbances in, 256

LA BASSÉE CANAL, 352 ff
Ledo, 468
Lasne, River, retreat to, 328
Lord Mayor, visit to Strensall, 289
— —, visits to Battalion, 296, 297

MALAYA, Japanese landings in, 377
Maymyo, 496
—, arrival at, 263
—, transfer to, 261
Mandalay, battle for, 417 ff
—, capture of, 457
Mechanization, military thought in 1927 turning towards, 260
Mianpur, 268
Mobilization, 301
—, for service in Burma, 268
Mohnyin, advance to, 479
Mons, souvenir of battalion sent to, 293
Mount Popa, 461
Munich crisis, 298

Po HLA GYI, rebel leader, 279 ff
Poona, arrival at, 374
Port Blair, departure for, 256
Prome, 273

553

RANGOON, amenities of, 258
—, departure for, 256
—, sporting successes, 259 f
Ripon, 289
Russia, invasion of, 373

SAAR BATTLEFRONT, 311
Schelde, abandoned, 351
—, retreat to, 336 ff
Secunderabad, conditions in, 266
—, departure from, 283
Silver drums, presentation by the Lord Mayor, 290
Strensall camp, 287 ff

Syriam, 258

THEBAW, PALACE OF KING, 263
Trimulgherry, arrival at, 265
Tropical service, preparations for, 374

U.S. LANDING IN SOLOMONS, 380

VICEROY OF INDIA, visit of, to Burma, 264
—, visit to Hyderabad State, 266

YE-THA-LAUK-KON CAMP, 263

FIRST AND SECOND BATTALIONS 1945–1948

ASSOCIATED REGIMENTS, 515

BANGALORE, 503

CENTREPIECE, presentation by Regiment to City of Manchester, 524

DUNHAM PARK, 505

ESSEN, 497

FACINGS, changed from white to deep green, 514
First and Second Battalions, amalgamation of, 501, 505

GERMANY, post-war duties in, 498

HAMBURG, 497

INFANTRY BATTALION, conversion into, 501, 503

JESH INCIDENT, THE, 546

KING GEORGE V, death of, 512
—, inspection by, 507

MADRAS, 503

POONA, 502
Privilege conferred on Regiment, 517

QUEEN ELIZABETH, Colonel-in-Chief, 521
—, inspection by, 505, 522
—, presentation of regimental brooch to, 521

RECALL TO ENGLAND, 500, 504
Regimental Chapel, dedication of, 513
—, destruction of 516
Regimental Museum, setting up of, 512

SECUNDERABAD, 502
Seesen, 497
Silver Drums, presentation of by City of Manchester, 511

WUFFERTAL, arrival at, 505